T0304664

Crisis Communication

Crises come in many shapes and sizes, including media blunders, social media activism, extortion, product tampering, security issues, natural disasters, accidents, and negligence – just to name a few. For organizations, crises are pervasive, challenging, and catastrophic, as well as opportunities for organizations to thrive and emerge stronger.

Despite the proliferation of research and books related to crisis communication, the voice that is often lost is that of the stakeholder. Yet, as both a public relations and management function, stakeholders are central to the success and failure of organizations responding to and managing crises in a cross-platform and global environment. This core textbook provides a comprehensive and research-driven introduction to crisis communication, critical factors influencing crisis response, and what we know about predicting stakeholder responses to crises. Incorporated into each chapter are global case studies, ethical challenges, and practitioner considerations. Online resources include an extensive set of multimedia materials ranging from podcast mini-lectures to in-class exercises, and simulation-based activities for skills development (https://audralawson.com/resources/crisis-communi cation-managing-stakeholder-relationships/).

Demonstrating the connection between theory, decision-making, and strategy development in a crisis context, this is a vital text for advanced undergraduate and postgraduate students of Communications, Public Relations, Marketing, and Strategic Management.

Audra Diers-Lawson is a Senior Lecturer at Leeds Beckett University, United Kingdom. She serves as chair of the Crisis Communication Division of the European Communication Research and Education Association (ECREA) and sits on several journal editorial boards with recent publications on topics like consumer trust, intercultural crisis communication, crisis atonement, whistleblowing, and stakeholder anger at organizations in crisis.

Crisis Communication

Managing Stakeholder Relationships

Audra Diers-Lawson

Routledge
Taylor & Francis Group

LONDON AND NEW YORK

First published 2020
by Routledge
2 Park Square, Milton Park, Abingdon, Oxon OX14 4RN

and by Routledge
52 Vanderbilt Avenue, New York, NY 10017

Routledge is an imprint of the Taylor & Francis Group, an informa business

British Library Cataloguing-in-Publication Data
A catalogue record for this book is available from the British Library

Library of Congress Cataloging-in-Publication Data
Names: Diers-Lawson, Audra, 1975– author.
Title: Crisis communication : managing stakeholder relationships /
    Audra Diers-Lawson.
Description: Abingdon, Oxon ; New York, NY : Routledge, 2020. | Includes
    bibliographical references and index.
Identifiers: LCCN 2019024200 (print) | LCCN 2019024201 (ebook) |
    ISBN 9781138346253 (hardback) | ISBN 9781138346246 (paperback) |
    ISBN 9780429437380 (ebook)
Subjects: LCSH: Communication in crisis management. | Public relations—
    Management.
Classification: LCC HD49.3 .D44 2020 (print) | LCC HD49.3 (ebook) |
    DDC 659.2—dc23
LC record available at https://lccn.loc.gov/2019024200
LC ebook record available at https://lccn.loc.gov/2019024201

ISBN: 978-1-138-34625-3 (hbk)
ISBN: 978-1-138-34624-6 (pbk)
ISBN: 978-0-429-43738-0 (ebk)

Typeset in Sabon
by Apex CoVantage, LLC

Visit the eResources: www.routledge.com/9781138346246

Contents

List of figures   xv
List of tables   xvii
List of practitioner perspectives and case studies   xix
List of contributors   xxi

Part 1   Crisis communication and the stakeholder relationship
         management perspective   1

1   Introducing crisis communication as a field of practice   3
    Defining crisis, crisis communication in a 21st century context   3
    Growth and change within the field of crisis communication   5
        The past and the present in crisis communication   7
            How has crisis communication changed with time?   12
            *Crisis communication's present: An interdisciplinary
                field of study   15*
            *What are the practical implications of the past and present
                in crisis communication for students and scholars?   18*
        The five critical factors to understand crisis communication   19
            Issue factors   20
            Organizational factors   20
            Stakeholder factors   21
            Crisis response factors   21
            Outcome factors   22
    References   23

2   Situating crisis communication within the fields of public
     relations and management   27
     Risk management   28
     Crisis management   34
        Crisis management challenges   34
        Factors influencing crisis management   35
     Crisis communication   36
     In review . . .   37
     References   38

3   The stakeholder relationship management perspective on
     crisis communication   41
     Stakeholder relationships   41
        Complexity within organizational environments   42
        Advocacy and stakeholder perceptions   44
     Stakeholder relationship management model   45
        The relationship between the organization and issues   46
        The relationship between the stakeholder and issues   47
        The relationship between organizations and stakeholders   48
     In review . . .   49
     References   50

Part 2   Issue factors: Evaluating stakeholders, risks, and crisis types   57

4   The importance of managing complex and changing
     organizational environments   59
     Issues, expectancy violation, issues management, and stewardship   59
        Issues and expectance violations   60
        Issues management and stewardship   61
     The issues management process   64
        Scanning   65
        Monitoring   67
        Decision-making   68
        Evaluation   73
     In review . . .   74
     References   75

5   From friends to frenemies: Mapping an organization's stakeholders   79
     Mapping a dynamic stakeholder environment   80
        Stakeholder power   81

Stakeholder legitimacy   83
Relational history   84
Relational valence   85
Urgency   86
Classifying stakeholders once they are mapped   87
Strategic stakeholders   89
Desirable stakeholders   89
Moral stakeholders   89
Dangerous stakeholders   90
In review . . .   90
References   91

6   **Playing the blame game to classify types**   93
Blame and crisis severity   94
Typology of crisis types   95
Transgressions   95
Events   98
Reputational crises   102
Disasters   104
In review . . .   107
References   109

Part 3   **Internal stakeholders and organizational factors: Evaluating
the organization's crisis capacity**   113

7   **Defining crisis capacity in a modern environment**   115
Crisis management and crisis response   116
Organizational capacity for crisis response   120
Effective crisis management is inextricably linked with
communication   120
Crisis capacity defined   122
Organizations, industries, and crisis capacity   123
In review . . .   124
References   125

8   **Building crisis capacity from the inside out**   129
*Organizational culture, social responsibility, and crisis
capacity*   130
Organizational culture   130
Social responsibility   132

*Building crisis capacity with employees as internal
    stakeholders   135*
    Hard and soft skills needed to build crisis capacity   136
    Simulation's role in crisis capacity building   137
In review . . .   142
References   143

9   **The leadership challenge for organizations in crisis**   149
    Leadership and management are different constructs   149
    Core crisis leadership roles   150
        Psychological and emotional role   151
            Why does the psychological and emotional role matter?   151
            *Behaviors to enact the psychological and emotional role of crisis
                leadership   152*
        Functional role   154
            What are the qualities of functional leadership during crises?   154
        Public relations role   157
    In review . . .   158
    References   159

Part 4   Stakeholder factors: Shifting from the inside out   163

10   **The missing link of stakeholder attitudes to understand
    crisis communication**   165
    Persuasion's contribution to understanding stakeholder attitudes   165
        Theory of planned behavior   167
        Elaboration likelihood model   168
        Health belief model   169
        Extended parallel process model   170
    Emotion's contribution to understanding stakeholder attitudes   170
        Factors influencing strong emotional reactions to crises   171
    Culture's contribution to understanding stakeholder attitudes   172
    In review . . .   174
    References   175

11   **Issue-related attitudes influencing stakeholder reactions to crises**   181
    Situational crisis communication theory, crisis severity, and blame   181
        Crisis severity   182
        Blame attribution   182

Competence, commitment, and clear association 183
What makes stakeholders particularly angry during crises, and how do
we know? 184
In review . . . 185
References 186

12   Organization-related attitudes influencing stakeholder
reactions to crises   191
The stakeholder relationship model as a recursive process 191
Understanding stakeholder evaluations of organizations in crisis 192
Legitimacy and stakeholder evaluations of organizations 193
Building blocks of the stakeholder relationship with organizations 194
Reputation 194
Trustworthiness 196
Value congruence 197
Perceived knowledge 198
Identification 198
In review . . . 199
References 200

Part 5   Message factors: Crisis response that focuses on
stakeholder needs   205

13   The realities of crisis response in multi-platform,
multi-actor environments   207
Communities and co-creation of crisis response 208
Brand communities 208
Virtual communities and the co-creation of crisis response 209
*Adversarial stakeholder relationships and counter
branding 212*
Counter branding, risk, issues management, crisis,
and complex environments 213
*Counter branding to change stakeholder relationships with
organizations 214*
Activism and counter branding 215
Whistleblowing and counter branding 216
In review . . . 217
References 218

14   One size seldom fits all: A taxonomy of crisis response tactics   223
      Taxonomy of crisis response tactics   224
          Brief summary of the categories   224
          Common patterns of crisis response   230
          Ethical apology in crisis response   231
      In review . . .   234
      References   234
          Table references   236

15   Comparing theories of crisis response   239
      Theory-informed practice improves performance   240
          What is theory?   241
          What are the theoretical options in risk and crisis
              communication?   243
              Risk and crisis theories   243
              Communication theories   246
              Theories from complementary fields of study   248
      Developing theory-informed crisis response   249
          Using theory to build crisis capacity   249
          Using theory to choose crisis response strategies   251
      In review . . .   252
      References   253

16   Strategically planning crisis response messages   255
      Crisis planning as a tailored campaign   255
          Internal obstacles to good crisis planning   257
          Have confidence that crisis planning works   258
      Creating an effective crisis plan   261
          Step 1: Risk summary   261
          Step 2: Contingency planning for crisis   263
              Part 1: Understanding <insert crisis type name> crises   264
              Part 2: Activating the crisis team   265
              Part 3: Trigger points   265
              Part 4: Situational assessment   266
              Part 5: Stakeholder assessment   266
              Part 6: Action recommendations   267
              Part 7: Crisis response strategy   268
              Part 8: Message samples for each of the potential strategies   270
      In review . . .   271
      References   271

Part 6   Shaping crisis outcomes: What do crises mean for organizations?   273

**17   Agenda setting: The intersection of multi-actor environments
and media engagement during crises**   275
*The importance of information consumption and
    the media   276*
Brief introduction to agenda setting   278
    The most susceptible to agenda setting effects   279
In review . . .   281
References   282

**18   Learning their lessons? Crisis outcomes and crisis-driven
organizational change**   285
An overview of crisis outcomes   285
    Possible crisis consequences   286
Crises: Driving or inhibiting the conditions for change?   289
Learning in crisis and organizational change   290
In review . . .   292
References   293

19   Measuring behavioral outcomes to crises   297
Yes, research is practical and necessary   297
    Developing research methods knowledge   299
What should we measure or evaluate?   300
In review . . .   305
References   306
    SRM measurement tool references   307

Index   309

Figures

1.1	Dominant themes in the field of crisis communication	6
1.2	Growth of the field of crisis communication over time	7
1.3	Crisis communication in medicine and health	15
1.4	Crisis communication in STEM fields	16
1.5	Crisis communication in management and business	16
1.6	Crisis communication in social sciences and the humanities	17
1.7	Crisis communication in communication and language	17
1.8	Crisis communication in applied industry journals	18
2.1	Risk management	30
2.2	Crisis strategy overview	37
3.1	Examples of stakeholders that organizations may have	43
3.2	The stakeholder relationship management model	45
4.1	Adaptation of Meng's (1992) issues management process	62
4.2	Issues management process overview	65
5.1	A sample of stakeholder complexity	80
5.2	Beginning the stakeholder mapping process	81
5.3	Power in the stakeholder mapping process	82
5.4	Legitimacy in the stakeholder mapping process	83
5.5	Relational history in the stakeholder mapping process	84
5.6	Relational valence in the stakeholder mapping process	85
5.7	Urgency in the stakeholder mapping process	87
5.8	Stakeholder classifications in the stakeholder mapping process	88
6.1	Continuum of crisis type based on reasonable blame attribution	108
7.1	Jet2 passenger experience timeline	118
8.1	Trice and Beyer's (1993) conceptualization of the forms of organizational culture	131

8.2	Pathway to improving CSR's impact on crisis response capacity	135
8.3	Traits needed by PR practitioners	138
8.4	Skills needed by PR practitioners	139
9.1	Summary of the critical concerns in management versus leadership	150
10.1	The stakeholder relationship management model	166
10.2	Summary of Ajzen's (2005) theory of planned behavior	167
10.3	Summary of Petty and Cacioppo's (1986) elaboration likelihood model	168
10.4	Summary of health belief model	169
10.5	Summary of Witte's (1992; 1996; 2000) extended parallel process model	170
12.1	Thinking about the SRM as a recursive process	192
13.1	Continuum of stakeholder relationships with organizations	208
14.1	Model of ethical apology	233
15.1	Risk and crisis theories applied in crisis communication research	244
15.2	Communication-related theories applied in crisis communication research	247
15.3	Theories from complementary disciplines applied in crisis communication research	250
16.1	The crisis planning process	256
16.2	Issues management process overview	262
17.1	False missile alert sent across Hawaii's Emergency Alert and Commercial Mobile Alert System at 8:07 a.m. on January 13, 2018	276
18.1	Summary of Antonacopoulou and Sheaffer's (2014) learning in crisis model	291
19.1	Full stakeholder relationship model	301

Tables

1.1   Keywords and concepts studied in crisis communication
       articles 1953–2015   8
2.1   Factors influencing perceptions of risk   29
4.1   Recommended information to capture for risk registers   69
5.1   Routine stakeholder mapping with a spreadsheet or database   88
6.1   Transgression types, definitions, and examples   96
6.2   Event types, definitions, and examples   99
6.3   Reputational crisis types, definitions, and examples   103
6.4   Disaster crisis types, definitions, and examples   105
8.1   Simulation benefits adapted from Avramenko (2012)   140
14.1   Taxonomy of crisis response tactics potentially used
       by organizations   225
16.1   Issue severity summary   263
16.2   Issue response (pre-crisis) recommendations   263
16.3   Key responsibilities table example   265
16.4   Tangible problems underlying the triggers, causes, and examples   266
16.5   Key stakeholders, relationship to the issue, and relationship to
       organization   267
16.6   Action recommendations, urgency, roles, and resources   268
19.1   Stakeholder relationship model measurement tool   302

Practitioner perspectives and case studies

2.1 Ben Duncan: Practitioner perspective – How crisis communication evolved from being "corporate PR" to a life-saving intervention 31

4.1 Audra Diers-Lawson: Case study – Contrasting two approaches to issues management 63

6.1 Kjell Bratass: Practitioner perspective – Victims across borders 106

7.1 Audra Diers-Lawson: Case Study – "They don't care about you people at all"; when crisis management works but communication fails 116

8.1 Doug Ashwell: Case study – Questioning Fonterra's authenticity 133

13.1 Kjell Bratass: Practitioner perspective – Victim communities of support and advocacy 211

16.1 Robert Minton-Taylor: Practitioner's perspective – The tobacco industry's big PR lie 259

17.1 Tess Morimoto: Citizen perspective – It just takes 40 minutes to decide to sign up for Twitter 277

18.1 Cheng Zeng: Case study – When an online search leads you to the devil: The role of Chinese search engine Baidu in Wei's death 288

19.1 Ben Duncan: Practitioner perspective – How do we know what works? 298

Contributors

Doug Ashwell, Ph.D., Palmerston, New Zealand. Associate Head of the School of Communication, Journalism, and Marketing at Massey University, New Zealand

Kjell Bratass, Oslo, Norway. Senior Communications Advisor, author of *Crisis Communications – Case Studies and Lessons Learned* (Routledge, 2018).

Ben Duncan, Edinburgh, Scotland. Risk Communication Consultant to WHO Health Emergencies Programme, Alarmed Not Alerted Enterprises, Ltd.

Robert Minton-Taylor, Leeds, England. Member Chartered Institute for Public Relations and Public Relations and Communications Association, Senior Lecturer Leeds Beckett University (retired).

Tess Morimoto, Honolulu, Hawaii, United States. County of Maui Lānaʻi Police operations employee.

Cheng Zeng, Fargo, North Dakota, United States. Assistant Professor at North Dakota State University.

PART 1

Crisis communication and the stakeholder relationship management perspective

What do media blunders, social media activism, extortion, product tampering, security issues, natural disasters, accidents, and negligence all have in common? They are crises. For organizations, they can be ever-present, challenging, catastrophic, and even opportunities for organizations to thrive and emerge stronger.

The first research on crisis communication was published in the early 1950s and since then the field has grown steadily. However, since 2010 there has been an explosion of theory development, international engagement, methodological diversity, and topic diversity reflecting the growing multinational and multi-platform environment in which organizations and people interact.

Despite the proliferation of research, collections of articles, and books related to crisis communication, the voice that is often lost is the stakeholder's voice. As both a public relations and management function, stakeholders are central to the success and failure of organizations responding to and managing crises in a cross-platform global environment.

In Part 1 of this textbook, I will begin by exploring what crisis communication is from the stakeholder relationship management perspective. In Chapter 1 I will focus on the evolution of crisis communication as a field of study and practice. Chapter 2 will situate crisis communication within public relations and management. Finally, Chapter 3 will provide the stakeholder relationship management perspective that will ground the rest of the book.

1 Introducing crisis communication as a field of practice

Learning objectives

By the end of this chapter, the reader should:

- Understand the evolution of the field of crisis communication from the 1950s to present
- Be introduced to the five critical factors driving knowledge and research in crisis communication
- Reflect on the state of crisis communication's research and practice

Defining crisis, crisis communication in a 21st century context

From the first study of crises and crisis communication in the mid-20th century to the turn of the century, crises were generally thought of as a "low probability, high-impact event that threatens the viability of the organization and is characterized by ambiguity of cause, effect, and means of resolution, as well as by a belief that decisions must be made quickly" (Pearson & Clair, 1998, p. 60). This definition of crisis was supported by a small body of research that had emerged throughout the previous 40 years.

However, while both practitioners and academics recognized that crises are challenging because they are often ill-structured and complex (Mitroff, Alpaslan, & Green, 2004), they had also witnessed a growing and diverse number of crises like the 1989 Exxon Valdez oil spill in Alaska, the Iran–Contra Affair of the mid-to-late

1980s, the American Red Cross tainted-blood scandal in the early 1990s, Enron's accounting scandal of 2001, and the 9/11 terrorist attacks of 2001. As a result of the risks posed by modern crises in an information-rich world, the research interest in crisis management and crisis communication began to grow substantially.

These new experiences with crisis demonstrated that crises can affect all types of organizations. The causes of the crises can range from circumstances entirely out of an organization's control to careless mistakes of individuals within an organization, to systematic breakdowns or inefficiencies (Argenti, 2002; King, 2002; Pearson & Clair, 1998; Reilly, 1987). With the growth of interest in crises, crisis management, and crisis communication, how we define a crisis has also evolved. Instead of thinking of crises and low-probability and high impact events with ambiguous causes and outcomes, we should be thinking of crises differently.

Defining a Crisis

A crisis is typically defined as an untimely but predictable event that has actual or potential consequences for stakeholders' interests as well as the reputation of the organization. . . .

That means a crisis can harm stakeholders and damage the organization's relationship with them. . . .

Respond well and survive the crisis; respond poorly and suffer the death of the organization's reputation and perhaps itself.

(Heath and Millar, 2004 p. 2)

Heath and Millar's (2004) definition of crisis provides us with a few important characteristics of crises that seem to be consistent across different types of crisis, in different parts of the world, and with different levels of blame and severity. **First, crises are inherently public in nature** (Moore, 2004); therefore, to understand crisis management, we ought to understand the nature of crisis communication. In fact, what should be clear in Heath and Millar's definition of crisis (2004) is that strategic planning around crisis risk ought to be an inherent part of doing business in the 21st century. **Second, while crises happen to or because of an organization, organizations do not exist in isolation.** Crises affect people – people within the organization, its community, country, and region(s) in which an organization operates. This means that crisis management and crisis communication should always be focused on the people and groups with an interest in the organization and its activities – that is, its stakeholders (Freeman, 1999). **Third, the core stake at risk in a crisis is the relationship between an organization and its stakeholder(s).** If this relationship fails, then the outcomes of that failure can range from reputational damage to the failure of the organization and/or its mission. Likewise, if the relationship is strengthened, then an organization can prosper despite the crisis – or perhaps even because of the crisis.

This definition of a crisis also suggests there are two parts to crisis response. The first is the material crisis response – that is, solving the problem that triggered the crisis. The material crisis response can include mitigating the effects of the crisis, recovery of control of the situation, fact finding, and or damage control. Part 1 focuses on crisis communication. Crisis communication involves three equally important elements.

- **Stakeholder relationship management:** Managing, building, or re-building stakeholder relationships
- **Narrating the crisis:** Media engagement and direct stakeholder engagement across different platforms of communication – from face-to-face to social media
- **Communication strategy development and implementation:** A campaign-based approach using measurable objectives, good intelligence, and continual evaluation of the effectiveness of the approach

However, if we ask this question – What is crisis communication? – differently, the question is more challenging to answer because there are many concepts and factors that influence the stakeholder relationship management process, being able to effectively narrative a crisis, and development and implementing crisis strategy. Figure 1.1 provides us with a collection of the most important key words and concepts connected to the global study of crisis communication for the last 60–70 years. Thus, answering the question of what crisis communication is, is challenging. This is what I will explore throughout this textbook.

It is from this point that I move forward in Chapter 1 to explore the field, its evolution, and ultimately the five critical factors that influence crisis communication and ground this textbook.

Growth and change within the field of crisis communication

The past 60–70 years has seen the field of crisis communication emerge as a cross-disciplinary field of study and begin to coalesce into a distinctive field within the last decade. There are noteworthy figures who have meaningfully contributed to the intellectual growth of the field and the emergence of a genuinely global community of scholars and scholar practitioners including William Benoit, Glenn Cameron, Timothy Coombs, Sherry Halliday, Robert Heath, Finn Frandsen, Yan Jin, Winnie Johansen, Brian Reber, Andreas Schwarz, Matthew Seeger, Tim Sellnow, and Deanna Sellnow, to

Figure 1.1 Dominant themes in the field of crisis communication

name some of the most influential. Yet the growth in the number of studies published in crisis communication in the last ten years (see Figure 1.2) suggests that we are beginning to see a diverse group of voices and perspectives emerging in the field. This section will not only highlight the developments in the field of crisis communication but also identify the key areas of practice and differences in approach within them.

In addition to the growth and emergence of crisis communication as a field of practice in public relations (PR) and an area of academic study in communication, within the last several years there has also been an interest in reflecting on the field. In academic contexts, this navel gazing usually involves meta-analyses of the research available on the subject of interest – essentially, collecting all of the research available within certain parameters and then reviewing it to identify the core themes that emerge. While it is as nerdy as it seems, it does serve an important function. Think

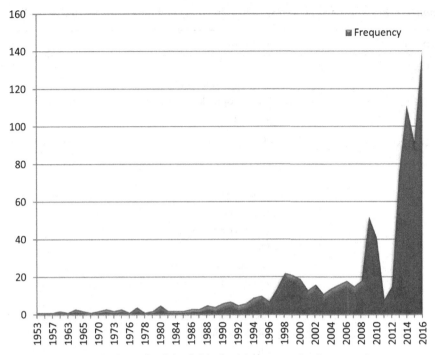

Figure 1.2 Growth of the field of crisis communication over time

of this as an academic stock check to identify what we have done, what we have not done, and so prescribe what we should be doing in the near future to improve the field. There have been three such analyses of crisis communication in recent years. One tracked trends in PR scholarship (Kim, Choi, Reber, & Kim, 2014), one examined crisis communication's interdisciplinary approach (Ha & Boynton, 2014), and one analyzed all available research connected to crisis communication across academic journals (Diers-Lawson, 2017a, 2017b).

My interest in downloading, reading, and categorizing every journal article that I could find using the search term 'crisis communication' (really, this seemed like a brilliant idea at the time) emerged out of a frustration in seeing the field defined in terms of just a few journals and a few authors, when I knew that the research that I was finding in journals and book chapters, presentations from academics and practitioners at specialist conferences, and fields of practice related to crisis communication was so much broader.

The past and the present in crisis communication

For scholars, practitioners, and students just beginning to explore the field of crisis communication, Table 1.1 provides a concise summary of what we study in crisis

Table 1.1 Keywords and concepts studied[1] in crisis communication articles 1953–2015

Concept categories	Concepts	N	%
Crisis type	Transgressions	87	**12.6**
	Organizational events		
	Events outside control		
	Reputational		
Crisis context	Accidents	253	**36.7**
	Activism		
	Advertising		
	Celebrity		
	Corruption		
	Counter branding		
	Disease		
	Emergency response		
	Environmental		
	Financial		
	Food/food quality		
	Globalization		
	Health		
	High-reliability organization		
	International relations		
	Multinational corporation		
	Natural disaster		
	News/breaking news		
	Nuclear disaster		
	Politics		
	Pop culture		
	Product harm crisis		
	Public safety		
	Scandals		
	Terrorism		
	Urban crisis		
	War/Cold War		
Industry/organization type	Agricultural	163	**23.6**
	Airline		
	Automobile		
	Defense (national)		
	Finance		
	Food manufacturing		
	Fortune 500		

(Continued)

Concept categories	Concepts	N	%
	Hospitality		
	Journalism		
	Marketing		
	Mining		
	Nonprofit/charity		
	Oil/energy		
	Pharmaceuticals		
	Police/law enforcement		
	PR		
	Public sector/government		
	Retail		
	Schools/universities		
	Small Business		
	Social movement organizations		
	Sports		
	Technology		
	Tourism/travel		
	Unions		
Crisis response/message assessment	Accounts	240	34.8
	Ambiguity		
	Apology		
	Argumentation		
	Crisis spokesperson		
	Dialogic communication		
	Diplomacy		
	Discourse		
	Forgiveness/atonement		
	Message effectiveness		
	Message involvement		
	Persuasion		
	Renewal		
	Response strategies		
	Rhetoric		
	Strategic communication		
	Symbols/metaphors		
	Third-person effect		
	Timing		
	Visual communication		
Relational factors	Relationship management	41	5.9
	User-generated content		

(Continued)

Table 1.1 (Continued)

Concept categories	Concepts	N	%
Media analysis	Agenda setting Media Media effects Media coverage Television	68	9.9
Crisis management	Audits Crisis management Decision-making Knowledge management Media relations	162	23.5
Crisis planning	Contingency planning Crisis plans/planning Documentation	41	5.9
Internal crisis management	Human relations Internal PR/employee relations Team/teamwork	32	4.6
Leadership		58	8.4
Interorganizational relationships	Boundary Spanning Strategic Alliances	15	2.2
Issue management	Issue Management SWOT Analysis	26	3.8
Crisis training and education	Pedagogy Simulations Training	14	2.0
Crisis assessment	Blame attribution Conflict Sensemaking Severity Urgency	60	8.7
Organizational assessments	Charisma Commitment Credibility Crisis history Halo effect Image	220	31.9

(Continued)

Concept categories	Concepts	N	%
	Impression management		
	Legitimacy		
	Organizational behavior		
	Organizational change		
	Organizational culture		
	Organizational identity		
	Power		
	Trustworthiness		
	Values/value congruence		
Attitudinal assessments	Attitudes	52	7.5
	Efficacy (self and response)		
	Self-protective behavior		
	Susceptibility		
	Uncertainty		
Crisis outcomes	Community development	94	13.6
	Crisis outcomes		
	Crowdsourcing		
	Customer loyalty		
	Negative publicity		
	Organizational learning		
	Public opinion		
	Sponsorship		
	Sustainabililty		
	Trauma		
	Word-of-mouth		
Culture and cultural Analysis	Cross-cultural comparison	70	10.1
	Culture		
	Cultural change		
	Individualist/collectivist		
	Power distance		
Emotion	Emotion	39	5.7
	Humor		
Information management	Information clarity	46	6.7
	Information consumption		
	Information expectations		
	Information sharing		
Demographics	Gender	16	2.3
	Race/ethnicity		

(Continued)

Table 1.1 (Continued)

Concept categories	Concepts	N	%
Risk	Risk Risk communication Risk management Risk perception	52	7.5
Social media	Big data/analytics Blogs Digital convergence Engagement Facebook Internet Online community Social Media Technology Twitter	126	18.3
Stakeholders (external)		106	15.4
Meta-analysis, methods	Best practices Meta-analysis Paradigm influence, philosophy Research methods	18	2.6
Corporate social responsibility		27	3.9
Ethics		29	4.2
Networks		11	1.6

[1]Multiple concepts and keywords possible for each article

communication and how commonly the concept categories appear in published academic journal articles on crisis communication.

How has crisis communication changed with time?

Table 1.1 provides us with a snapshot of everything that is or has been crisis communication. However, it is worth understanding how the field has changed over time. There are a number of ways that the field has changed across the last seven decades.

First, the field is increasingly data driven

The first wave of crisis communication research focused on questions of what crisis communication is, how it fits within the communication and management domains, as well as what 'best practices' in crisis communication are. These are important pieces, but they are inherently not empirical – they are meant for reflection and conceptual growth or development. The second wave of crisis communication focused on the organization and its crisis response emphasizing applied research and case studies that provided the groundwork for much of the theoretical developments of the late 1990s.

As the field has been able to better define itself and to understand the nature of crisis response from the organization's perspective, the third wave has emerged: research focused on the stakeholder. Here, the core questions focus on stakeholder reactions to crises, crisis response, and how that can affect the organization. Yet, some researchers argue that the third wave is unlikely to have a significant impact on practice because "historically, many practitioners have not made routine use of academic research on crisis communication that is and has long been available" (Lehmberg & Hicks, 2018, p. 358).

However, I would argue that the third wave has emerged, in part, because practitioners have challenged academic researchers to develop more conceptual models for practical application. For example, in 2016 at the International Crisis and Risk Communication conference in Orlando, Florida, practitioners asked an academic panel why we did not have better conceptual models to help them design and implement better response strategies. We, as academics, did not have a great answer to that question because the third wave of research has only just begun.

The importance of data-driven research matches the changing reality in the broader field of PR. We see evidence of this in the *Global Communications Report* produced in collaboration between the British-based Holmes Report and the USC-Annenberg Center for Public Relations as well as agency-based research from global PR firms like Weber Shandwick and Edelman Intelligence, we can draw three conclusions about the modern realities of PR. First, research improves strategy. Second research demonstrates the return on investment (ROI) in communication. Third, it facilitates informed decision-making.

Second, conceptual interests in crisis communication have changed

In recent years, we have seen less of a focus on crisis management, internal crisis management, and crisis planning evidenced in the research. In part, this is probably attributable to the emergence of the third wave of crisis research and a move away from non-data driven 'best practices' pieces.

However, the field's lack of focus on internal crisis management is potentially problematic. In a talk in 2014 at the University of Manchester, Brian Gilvary – BP's chief financial officer throughout the 2010 Gulf of Mexico crisis – indicated that the hardest part of managing the financial side of the crisis was the emotional labor of his employees as they watched the events unfold and were experiencing the crisis. Yet, we see little new research emerging focusing on the employee experience of a crisis.

That said, we are seeing an increasing amount of research connected to the influence of the type of crisis, overall situation, industry, social media, and emotion in crisis communication, suggesting that there is a growing trend to humanize crises – shifting away from an organizational-centric view and understanding of crisis to one that is more stakeholder centered.

Third, crisis communication is increasingly global

When we talk about crisis communication, the voices that we have heard have been disproportionately American, with about 60% of all empirical journal articles in crisis communication published since 1953 researching from a US point of view. Let me put this into perspective: 417 of 690 articles focus on the United States. This is an inconvenient truth in crisis communication. Additionally, 126 articles focus on Europe as a region, with most research in Europe focused on the United Kingdom, the Netherlands, Denmark, and Sweden. Further, 71 articles focus on Asia, with the majority of these representing a Chinese viewpoint; while 21 articles represent Australasia, with most focusing on Australia. Finally, we find the least-covered regions – the Middle East, South and Central America – with six articles each, and only eight focusing on the entire continent of Africa. This is the embarrassing reality: We know very little about crises, crisis management, and crisis communication across much of the world – especially the developing world.

If the field considers voice and experience somewhat more broadly, the West's (i.e., North America and Europe) voice is dominant, with 83% of all articles articulating the Western voice. Though this is a weakness in the field at present, the positive side is that this has been significantly changing with a decrease in US-centric research, an increasing focus on Europe, an increasing focus on China, and overall a more global approach to crisis research. It is also important to note that this is not a grand conspiracy; rather, it is a reflection of the access to organizations, news, and information about crises by the academics who research crises. As our field grows and changes, research is also becoming more diverse. Not only that, but as we are increasingly global, we will be able to get more views from practitioners and researchers representing voices from across the world.

Crisis communication's present: An interdisciplinary field of study

Certainly, the field of crisis communication will continue to develop and change with time. In as much as it is useful to have a broad overview of crisis communication, it is also useful to understand the influence that different fields have on research and practice connected to crisis communication. This influences the present as much as questions of culture, changing technologies, and stakeholders do. Not surprisingly, much of the focus for crisis communication is connected to management and business, communication and language, and the social sciences and humanities. However, research in crisis communication is applied across most fields of practice.

Though there are commonalties that emerge when we ask *what themes related to crisis communication influence each of these fields*, we also find that what crisis communication is will differ depending on the industry or context in which it is being applied.

In **medicine and health,** representing about 3% of the research and application in crisis communication, we are more likely to see research emerging from Australasia focusing on the crisis context, and risk assessment. However, we are less likely to see a US focus, discussion of the particular industry, interest in crisis responses, or organizational assessments (see Figure 1.3)

In the fields of **science, engineering, and technology,** representing about 6% of the research and application in crisis communication, we are more likely to see research emerging from the Netherlands focusing on crisis management, training and education, crisis outcomes, information management, risk, and social media. However, we

Figure 1.3 Crisis communication in medicine and health

are less likely to see a focus on crisis response, media analysis, or assessments of the organizations in crisis (see Figure 1.4)

In **management and business**, representing 30% of the research and application of crisis communication, we are more likely to see research addressing relational factors that influence crises, crisis management, crisis planning, organizational assessment, stakeholder analysis, corporate social responsibility (CSR), and ethics. Yet, we are also significantly less likely to see research from Africa or about crisis context or research taking culture into account, information management, risk, or social media (see Figure 1.5).

Figure 1.4 Crisis communication in STEM fields

Figure 1.5 Crisis communication in management and business

In **social science and the humanities,** representing 31% of the research and application of crisis communication, we are significantly more likely to an American-centric focus, an interest in crisis responses, and emotion. But, we are significantly less likely to see research from European scholars, with a focus on crisis management, or on crisis outcomes (see Figure 1.6).

Figure 1.6 Crisis communication in social sciences and the humanities

In **communication and language,** representing 26% of the research and application of crisis communication, we are likewise significantly more likely to see an US-centric focus, an interest in crisis type, crisis response, media analysis, and emotion. We are also significantly less likely to see European-centered research or focus on crisis management, crisis planning, internal crisis management, leadership, training/education, crisis outcomes, and risk (see Figure 1.7).

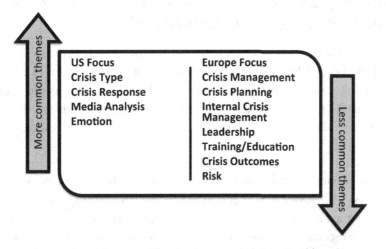

Figure 1.7 Crisis communication in communication and language

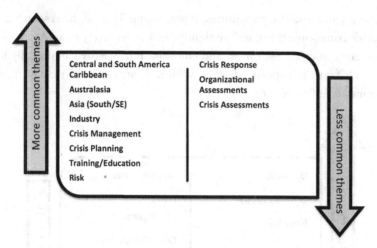

Figure 1.8 Crisis communication in applied industry journals

Finally, in **applied industry perspectives**, representing about 4% of the research and application of crisis communication, we are significantly more likely to see geographically diverse research with more representation of Central and South America, the Caribbean, Australasia, and Asia. We are also significantly more likely to see direct discussions of the implications of crises on industry, crisis management, crisis planning, training/education, and risk. However, we are significantly less likely to see research and application directed towards crisis response, organizational assessments, and assessments of crises themselves (see Figure 1.8).

What are the practical implications of the past and present in crisis communication for students and scholars?

So, we should ask the practical question, aside from a tour through the past and present of the field: What does it matter if we understand how crisis communication is evolving as a field of study or is presently practiced? I would argue there are three benefits to understanding the history and application of crisis communication that center on the overlapping benefit of theory and research-informed practice.

1   **If we want to understand what crisis communication is, we must be reading across disciplines.** This advice is as useful to academics who already research crisis communication as it is to the newcomer to the specialty. While different disciplines may have practical reasons for their focus, when we read and cite research within

a single field only, we are more likely to have a limited and siloed view of the field. That is, there is a greater risk of dogmatic attitudes about crisis communication emerging, limited application of our understanding of crisis globally, and limitations to make the connections between industries and work contexts that emerge as issues, politics, and conditions dictate.

2 **Reading broadly across domains of practice connected to crisis communication better prepares us to understand the opportunities and limitations within fields of study and practice.** For example, if we read research and practice from the field of communication only, we would be significantly less likely to develop an understanding of the training and education needs for crisis practitioners and would be less prepared to apply crisis theory and recommendations in a global context. Likewise, if our only exposure to crisis communication is in medicine and health, we have a weaker understanding of the role that crisis response messages play in public attitudes towards health risk. Bottom line: To be good academics or practitioners, we need to be well-read.

3 **Reading across disciplines positions us better to identify opportunities for improving research and practice within our own fields.** In as much as we can be limited when we fail to read across different domains of research connected to crisis communication, being well-read in the field can allow us to more critically reflect on the state of research or practice and innovate in our own areas. For example, health campaigns have long been addressing problems of attitude, resistance to messaging, and the impacts of global pandemics to local epidemics. We can learn much about disaster response by understanding how health communicators have addressed difficult topics with diverse audiences from around the world. That is, all areas of practice connected to issues management, risk, and crisis communication can learn from each other. So, it is not important to read across the domains only to avoid dogmatism, but also to innovate and improve issues and crisis response in all industries and contexts.

The five critical factors to understand crisis communication

This brief journey to define crisis communication, explore the field's development, its strengths, its shortcomings, and the differences within current areas of practice and research in this first chapter provides a template for the approach to this book. The rest of the book is organized around the five critical factors that drive our understanding, research, and practice in crisis communication: issue or risk, organizational, stakeholders, message, and outcomes (Diers-Lawson, 2017b).

Issue factors

Heath (1998, 2004) has argued that crises emerge when issues management fails. He describes issues management as a process that helps organizations to detect and mitigate risks related to trends or changes in an organization's sociopolitical environment; in short, Heath defines it as anticipatory strategic management (2002). More importantly, he also describes issues management as a stakeholder-centered process that emphasizes an organization's obligations as stewards of those affected by the work the organization does. This suggests that when we talk about what it means to manage issues and risk factors, we are also talking about creating socially responsible organizations – those that stakeholders believe actually care about the impact the organization has on their employees, communities, and world (Kim & Lee, 2015; Lacey, Kennett-Hensel, & Manolis, 2014; Sohn & Lariscy, 2014; Vanhamme & Grobben, 2009). Yet, even in a modern context being 'socially responsible' may even represent a risk or issue to be managed (Coombs & Holladay, 2015). Issue and risk management is never easy – it would not be interesting if it were.

Part 2 of this text focuses on understanding the issue factors by exploring the importance of managing complex and ever-changing organizational environments. In Chapter 4 I not only discuss the challenge of these environments, but also discuss a model for approaching issues management to systematically evaluate an organization's risk. Part 2 also focuses on the complicated relationships that organizations have with different stakeholders and introduces a tool that allows practitioners to map their organization's stakeholders to help better understand issues and risks in the context of stakeholder interests. Finally, in Part 2 I will explore the risk that different types of crises pose for organizations by highlighting the two critical factors that predict stakeholder reactions to crises: Blame and severity.

Organizational factors

When we explore issue factors, one of the points that emerges is that to understand crisis communication, we must simultaneously look outside and inside the organization to better understand the situation and an organization's ability to respond to it. This suggests that it is essential to understand some of the organizational factors that contribute to crises and organizations' ability to manage them. Two broad theories help to frame the core organizational considerations in crisis communication. First, Loosemore's (1999) theory of crisis management suggest that the emergence of crises also causes a ripple effect of problems emerging within organizations. Crises can prompt power struggles bubbling to the surface and also highlight inadequacies in leadership and management communication. Second, Stacks's (2004) multidimensional model of PR argues that crisis management is primarily a matter of marshaling internal resources to effectively manage public perceptions of the crisis.

Taken together, these theories highlight the importance of an inside-out approach to crisis communication. In short, we have to ask what internal factors are likely to facilitate both issues and risk management as well as crisis response. Part 3, therefore, evaluates an organization's capacity to respond to crises by highlighting critical factors like industry, crisis history, and (in Chapter 7) the challenges of crisis management. Part 3 also asks us to not only consider an organization's employees as critical stakeholders in a crisis but also reflect on the influence that an organization's culture and values has on approaches to crisis management (in Chapter 8). Finally, in Part 3, Chapter 9 explores the leadership challenge in crisis and the different types of roles that leaders are expected to play.

Stakeholder factors

The first two factors emphasize the situation and context in which crises develop and are managed. However, the biggest 'x-factor' in crises is how stakeholders will react to the issues, the crisis, and the organization. In the study of crisis communication, stakeholder factors remain one of the most challenging and under-studied factors influencing crises; yet, in practice they are probably the most important. More attention is typically paid to the response strategies that organizations use rather than evaluating stakeholder evaluations and the social psychological factors influencing those evaluations (Oles, 2010; Piotrowski & Guyette, 2010; Weber, Erickson, & Stone, 2011). However, in recent years important research and application has begun to take form in better understanding stakeholder emotion in crises (McDonald, Sparks, & Glendon, 2010), culture (Falkheimer & Heide, 2006), national identity (Rovisco, 2010), and the interrelationships between stakeholders, organizations, and the issues that affect them both (Diers-Lawson, 2017c; Diers, 2012).

As the book then focuses more directly on the stakeholders affected by crises, Part 4 explores the factors affecting stakeholder attitudes in Chapter 10, issue-related attitudes that influence stakeholder reactions to crisis in Chapter 11, and organization-related attitudes that also influence stakeholder reactions in Chapter 12.

Crisis response factors

Each of the previous factors are essential in understanding crisis communication, but the fourth factor highlights what we know about crisis response messages. Crisis response tactics or strategies have been studied for more than 20 years, with several taxonomies emerging including Benoit's (1997) summary of image repair tactics,

Coombs (2007) discussion of tactics used in situational crisis communication theory, Mohamed, Gardner, and Paolillo's (1999) taxonomy of organizational impression management tactics, and Diers and Tomaino's (2010) categorization of crisis response tactics. The result of these works was the identification of more than 40 distinctive response tactics that could be used in a nearly infinite number of combinations in order to respond to a crisis.

As these response tactics emerged, so have different theories of crisis response, including foundational crisis communication theories such as Benoit's (1997) image repair theory and Coombs's (2007) situational crisis communication theory, in addition to more than 80 theories that have been developed and applied to better understanding and predicting successful crisis response over the last seven decades. As such, Part 5 will explore the message factors associated with crisis communication by focusing on crisis response addressing stakeholder needs, first addressing the realities of crisis response in multi-platform, multi-actor environments in Chapter 13. Then, I will explore the taxonomies of crisis response in Chapter 14. I will compare the theories related to crisis response in Chapter 15. Part 5 will also focus on the application of theory to message design in Chapter 16 focusing on strategically planning crisis response messages.

Outcome factors

The final part of our tour of crisis communication will come in Part 6 – the exploration of the critical outcomes of crises. Here I will answer the question, what do crises really mean for organizations? Crises can mean disaster and doom, but more often than not they do not spell the end of an organization. Instead, they can represent meaningful opportunities for organizations to learn and reflect on their practices not only to meet stakeholder expectations but also to minimize the likelihood of the recurrence of crises in the future (Antonacopoulou & Sheaffer, 2014; Blackman & Ritchie, 2008; Huzey, Betts, & Vicari, 2014). The theme of organizational learning is explored in Chapter 18.

Certainly, internal reflection about crises and change after crisis is important; however, most organizations are more concerned with anticipating and mitigating negative outcomes associated with stakeholder behavioral intention during and after crises. How stakeholders are likely to react and act in response to a crisis is at the forefront of most practitioners' minds. Therefore, understanding the impact of a crisis on an organization's brand community (Dawar & Lei, 2009), consumer purchase intention (Yum & Jeong, 2014), or the effects of word-of-mouth and social media engagement on stakeholder attitudes throughout a crisis (Canhoto et al., 2015) are all essential to understanding the outcomes of a crisis. These themes are explored throughout Part 6.

Review your understanding

By the end of this chapter, you should be able to understand and explain the following.

- Crisis
- Three characteristics of crisis
- Three elements of crisis communication
- Crisis communication
- Key themes in crisis communication
- Three ways that the study and practice of crisis communication has changed over time
- Differences in the key themes in research and practice in crisis communication in:
  - Medicine and health
  - Science engineering, and technology
  - Management and business
  - Social science and the humanities
  - Communication and language
  - Applied industry perspectives
- Three benefits to understanding the history and crisis communication across different domains of practice and research
- The five critical factors to understanding crisis communication

References

Antonacopoulou, E. P., & Sheaffer, Z. (2014). Learning in crisis rethinking the relationship between organizational learning and crisis management. *Journal of Management Inquiry*, 23(1), 5–21. doi:10.1177/1056492612472730

Argenti, P. (2002). Crisis communication: Lessons from 9/11. *Harvard Business Review*, 80(12), 103–109.

Benoit, W. L. (1997). Image repair discourse and crisis communication. *Public Relations Review*, 23(2), 177–187.

Blackman, D., & Ritchie, B. W. (2008). Tourism crisis management and organizational learning: The role of reflection in developing effective DMO crisis strategies. *Journal of Travel & Tourism Marketing*, 23(2–4), 45–57.

Canhoto, A. I., vom Lehn, D., Kerrigan, F., Yalkin, C., Braun, M., & Steinmetz, N. (2015). Fall and redemption: Monitoring and engaging in social media conversations during a crisis. *Cogent Business & Management*, 2(1), 1084978. doi:10.1080/23311975.2015.1084978

Coombs, T., & Holladay, S. (2015). CSR as crisis risk: Expanding how we conceptualize the relationship. *Corporate Communications: An International Journal*, 20(2), 144–162. doi:10.1108/CCIJ-10-2013-0078

Coombs, W. T. (2007). Protecting organization reputation during a crisis: The development and application of situational crisis communication theory. *Corporate Reputation Review*, 10(3), 163–176.

Dawar, N., & Lei, J. (2009). Brand crises: The roles of brand familiarity and crisis relevance in determining the impact on brand evaluations. *Journal of Business Research*, 62, 509–516. doi:10.1016/j.jbusres.2008.02.001

Diers, A. R. (2012). Reconstructing stakeholder relationships using 'corporate social responsibility' as a response strategy to cases of corporate irresponsibility: The case of the 2010 BP spill in the Gulf of Mexico. In R. Tench, W. Sun, & B. Jones (Eds.), *Corporate social irresponsibility: A challenging concept* (Vol. 4, pp. 177–206). Bingley, UK: Emerald.

Diers, A. R., & Tomaino, K. (2010). Comparing strawberries and quandongs: A cross-national analysis of crisis response strategies. *Observatorio*, 4(2), 21–57.

Diers-Lawson, A. (2017a). Crisis communication. In *Oxford research encyclopedia of communication*. Oxford University Press. Retrieved from http://communication.oxfordre. com/view/10.1093/acrefore/9780190228613.001.0001/acrefore-9780190228613-e-397. doi:10.1093/acrefore/9780190228613.013.397

Diers-Lawson, A. (2017b). A state of emergency in crisis communication an intercultural crisis communication research agenda. *Journal of Intercultural Communication Research*, 46(1), 1–54.

Diers-Lawson, A. (2017c). Will they like us when they're angry? Antecedents and indicators of strong emotional reactions to crises among stakeholders. In S. M. Croucher, B. Lewandowska-Tomaszczyk, & P. Wilson (Eds.), *Conflict, mediated message, and group dynamics* (pp. 81–136). Lanham, MD: Lexington Books.

Falkheimer, J., & Heide, M. (2006). Multicultural crisis communication: Toward a social constructionist perspective. *Journal of Contingencies & Crisis Management*, 14(4), 180–189.

Freeman, R. E. (1999). Divergent stakeholder theory. *Academy of Management Review*, 24(2), 233–239.

Ha, J. H., & Boynton, L. (2014). Has crisis communication been studied using an interdisciplinary approach? A 20-year content analysis of communication journals. *International Journal of Strategic Communication*, 8(1), 29–44. doi:10.1080/1553118X.2013.850694

Heath, R. L. (1998). Dealing with the complete crisis – The crisis management shell structure. *Safety Science*, 30, 139–150.

Heath, R. L. (2002). Issues management: Its past, present, and future. *Journal of Public Affairs*, 2(2), 209–214.

Heath, R. L. (2004). Crisis preparation: Planning for the inevitable. In D. P. Millar & R. L. Heath (Eds.), *Responding to crisis: A rhetorical approach to crisis communication* (pp. 33–35). Mahwah, NJ: Lawrence Erlbaum Associates.

Heath, R. L., & Millar, D. P. (2004). A rhetorical approach to crisis communication: Management, communication processes, and strategic responses. In D. P. Millar & R. L. Heath (Eds.), *Responding to crisis: A rhetorical approach to crisis communication* (pp. 1–18). Mahwah, NJ: Lawrence Erlbaum Associates.

Huzey, D., Betts, S. C., & Vicari, V. (2014). Learning the hard way vs. vicarious learning: Post crisis learning for small business. *Journal of Management and Marketing Research*, 15, 1.

Kim, J. T., & Lee, W.-H. (2015). Dynamical model for gamification of learning (DMGL). *Multimedia Tools and Applications*, 74(19), 8483–8493.

Kim, S.-Y., Choi, M.-I., Reber, B. H., & Kim, D. (2014). Tracking public relations scholarship trends: Using semantic network analysis on PR Journals from 1975 to 2011. *Public Relations Review*, 40(1), 116–118. doi:10.1016/j.pubrev.2013.11.017

King, G. I. (2002). Crisis management and team effectiveness: A closer examination. *Journal of Business Ethics*, 41, 235–249.

Lacey, R., Kennett-Hensel, P. A., & Manolis, C. (2014). Is corporate social responsibility a motivator or hygiene factor? Insights into its bivalent nature. *Journal of the Academy of Marketing Science*, 42(3). doi:10.1007/s11747-014-0390-9

Lehmberg, D., & Hicks, J. (2018). A 'glocalization' approach to the internationalizing of crisis communication. *Business Horizons*, 61(3), 357–366.

Loosemore, M. (1999). A grounded theory of construction crisis management. *Construction Management and Economics*, 17, 9–19.

McDonald, L. M., Sparks, B., & Glendon, A. I. (2010). Stakeholder reactions to company crisis communication and causes. *Public Relations Review*, 36(3), 263–271.

Mitroff, I., Alpaslan, M. C., & Green, S. E. (2004). Crises as ill-structured messes. *International Studies Review*, 6(1), 165–182.

Mohamed, A. A., Gardner, W. L., & Paolillo, J. G. P. (1999). A taxonomy of organizational impression management tactics. *Advances in Competitiveness Research*, 7(1), 108–128.

Moore, S. (2004). Disaster's future: The prospects for corporate crisis management and communication. *Business Horizons*, 47(1), 29–36.

Oles, D. L. (2010). Deny, delay, apologize: The Oprah Winfrey image-defense playbook. *Northwest Journal of Communication*, 39(1), 37–63.

Pearson, C. M., & Clair, J. A. (1998). Reframing crisis management. *Academy of Management Review*, 23(1), 58–76.

Piotrowski, C., & Guyette, R. W. (2010). Toyota recall crisis: Public attitudes on leadership and ethics. *Organizational Development Journal*, 28(2), 89–97.

Reilly, A. (1987). Are organisations ready for a crisis? *Columbia Journal of World Business*, 79–87.

Rovisco, M. (2010). One Europe or several Europes? The cultural logic of narratives of Europe views from France and Britain. *Social Science Information*, 49(2), 241–266. doi:10.1177/0539018409359844

Sohn, Y., & Lariscy, R. W. (2014). Understanding reputational crisis: Definition, properties, and consequences. *Journal of Public Relations Research*, 26(1), 23–43. doi:10.1080/1062 726X.2013.795865

Stacks, D. W. (2004). Crisis management: Toward a multidimension model of public relations. In D. P. Millar & R. L. Heath (Eds.), *Responding to crisis: A rhetorical approach to crisis communication* (pp. 37–49). Mahwah, NJ: Lawrence Erlbaum Associates.

Vanhamme, J., & Grobben, B. (2009). "Too good to be true!". The effectiveness of CSR history in countering negative publicity. *Journal of Business Ethics*, 85(2), 273–283.

Weber, M., Erickson, S. L., & Stone, M. (2011). Corporate reputation management: Citibank's use of image restoration strategies during the U.S. banking crisis. *Journal of Organizational Culture, Communication and Conflict*, 15(2), 35–55. doi:2439571401

Yum, J.-Y., & Jeong, S.-H. (2014). Examining the public's responses to crisis communication from the perspective of three models of attribution. *Journal of Business and Technical Communication*, 29(2), 159–183. doi:10.1177/1050651914560570

2 | Situating crisis communication within the fields of public relations and management

Learning objectives

By the end of this chapter, the reader should:

- Understand what crises, crisis and risk management, and crisis communication are in an applied context
- Differentiate between the public relations and management functions within crisis and risk management

In Chapter 1 I discussed what crises were and began to differentiate between crisis management and crisis communication, so I should begin to deepen the understanding of what crisis communication is in an applied context. A **crisis** can address can address anything from a customer service crisis played out on social media to major disease outbreaks around the world. There are three characteristics that all crises share:

- They are inherently public
- Organizations trying to manage crises do not exist in isolation; rather, there are complex relationships that influences the choices organizations make
- The core stake at risk in a crisis is the relationship between an organization and its stakeholder(s)

I will discuss the different types of crises and their implications for organizations in depth in Chapter 6, but if I assume that while there are a lot of different types of crises, they all share these three characteristics, then I can focus on understanding the process connecting risk management through crisis response. By focusing on the process, it should become clear that communication and management are both necessary and complementary but have different responsibilities throughout the process. This means that responding to crises is both a public relations and a management function.

Risk management

In Chapter 1, I made the point that one of the key shifts in our understanding of crises in the last couple of decades was that they should not be considered surprises. In fact, Heath and Millar (2004) argue that crises should not be viewed as unpredictable, just untimely. This means that modern crisis management and communication is as much about risk management as it is about responding to crises once they emerge.

Risk is often a difficult concept for social or behavioral scientists to unpack because much of what we have to manage is peoples' perception of risk rather than the probability that a crisis will happen (Freundberg, 1988). For example, an engineer can calculate the probability that a bridge will fail or an infectious disease expert can calculate the spread of disease based on population density and a number of other factors; however, risk management is not about the material risk but about the reduction of the risk and communication of information about the risk.

One of the challenges in this process is that technical information has to be translated – and public decisions about risk are not always rational (Freundberg, 1988). In exploring reactions to the impact of disease, epidemics, and bioterrorism, Covello, Peters, Wojtecki, and Hyde (2001) identified 15 factors that influenced peoples' perception of risk (see Table 2.1). Though the 15 factors are all very different, what is consistent is that the unknown, uncontrollable, or nebulous make people less willing to accept the credibility of threats; however, at the same time once people judge risks to be 'real,' those factors that made people resistant to accepting them as credible also mean that they are perceived as greater threats. Put simply, people often bury their heads in the sand, pretend that the risk is not real until it is unavoidable – and then they may overestimate the negative effects it could have.

In Comfort's (2007) review of Hurricane Katrina – an American example of very poor risk and crisis management – she summarizes a four-step process for risk management that complements much of the relevant research connected to crisis communication and management (see Figure 2.1).

Risk detection is a natural first step in the process. Before an organization can plan to minimize the risks that it or its stakeholders could experience, those risks must be known (Comfort, 2007; Dilenschneider & Hyde, 1985; Hayes & Patton, 2001, p. 621; R. Heath, 1998a; Kash & Darling, 1998; Ritchie, 2004; Stacks, 2004). From there, in the second step the risk has to be **evaluated** in as objective and effective way

Table 2.1 Factors influencing perceptions of risk[1]

Risk perception factor	Findings
Voluntariness	People are less likely to accept a risk as a credible threat if it is involuntary; they view involuntary risk as greater once they believe that it could affect them.
Controllability	When people believe they no have control in a situation, they are less likely to accept a risk as a credible threat; but once they accept it, they believe that it is greater if they cannot control the situation.
Familiarity	If people are unfamiliar with a risk, they are less likely to accept it as credible; but once they accept it, they believe it is a greater threat than if it previously had been known.
Equity	People are less likely to believe that risks are credible when they are perceived as being unevenly distributed than when everyone is equally at risk.
Benefits	People are more likely to accept the credibility of risk if the benefits of taking the risk are clear; however, they are also likely to perceive the risk as less severe if the benefits are unclear or questionable.
Understanding	If people do not understand the risk, the risk is viewed as less credible but also carries a higher evaluation of threat than risks that are perceived as being understood.
Uncertainty	People are less likely to accept risks where the outcomes are highly uncertain; however, they are more likely to view those risks as more severe once accepted.
Dread	If a risk evokes fear or anxiety in people, it is less readily accepted as a credible risk but judged to be a greater threat.
Trust in institutions	If people do not trust organizations, they are less likely to accept the risks associated with them – and those risks are more likely to create more threat than risks associated with trustworthy or credible organizations.
Reversibility	People are less likely to accept the credibility of risks that are viewed as irreversible, but more likely to perceive greater threats from those whose effects are reversible.
Personal stake	If people believe they could be directly and personally affected, they are less likely to accept the risk as credible; however, once they accept the risk, they feel a greater level of threat.

(Continued)

Table 2.1 (Continued)

Risk perception factor	Findings
Ethics and morals	When people perceive risks as being ethical or moral problems, they are less likely to view the risk as credible but perceive it to present a greater threat.
Human vs. natural	People are less likely to accept risks as credible threats when they are caused by people; however, they view them as bigger risks than natural disasters.
Victim identity	When people can identify with specific real or potential victims of risks, they are less likely to accept the credibility of threat – but they are more likely to view the threats as more severe than if they connect risks with 'nameless and faceless' people in general.
Catastrophic potential	People are less likely to accept the credibility of a threat when it can produce fatalities, injuries, or illness; however, once they accept it, they perceive it as a greater risk than threats whose impact may be either scattered or minimal.

[1]Adapted from Covello et al.'s (2001) risk perception model

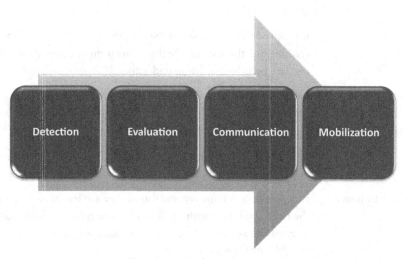

Figure 2.1 Risk management

as possible so that a straightforward judgment of the likelihood and severity of the risk can be made (Comfort, 2007; Dilenschneider & Hyde, 1985; Freundberg, 1988; Massey & Larsen, 2006).

The third step is the **communication of risk** (Comfort, 2007). However, as Freundberg (1988) pointed out, this step is challenging because technical information does not always translate directly. Furthermore, peoples' perceptions of risks are affected by a number of factors (Covello et al., 2001). Nevertheless, communicating risk is vital to ensure that relevant stakeholders – such as members of the organization, regulators, the media, and those directly affected – can appropriately understand the situation and are prepared to deal with it (Johansson & Härenstam, 2013; Ley et al., 2014). Thus, the communication of risk focuses on exchanging knowledge that is essential to managing the risk.

In the fourth and final step, sharing information allows for the **organization and mobilization of a collective response** to reduce risk and respond to danger (Comfort, 2007; Dilenschneider, 1985; Heath, 1998b). The mobilization of collective response includes communication-related tasks like issue management, managing stakeholder relationships, developing communication plans and protocols, and staff development (Hayes & Patton, 2001; Heath, 1998a; Heath & Millar, 2004; Johansson & Härenstam, 2013; Kash & Darling, 1998; Perry, Taylor, & Doerfel, 2003; Reilly, 2008). It also includes management related tasks like developing teams and decision-making systems to facilitate the process (Hayes & Patton, 2001; Horton, 1988; Jindal, Laveena, & Aggarwal, 2015; Nunamaker, Weber, & Chen, 1989).

A starting point in understanding what crisis communication does in the real world is to think of it as an integral part of helping organizations manage risk. This means that the role for crisis communication is not just about management or public relations; it has evolved from being 'corporate PR' to a part of life-saving interventions across industries. In Box 2.1 Ben Duncan, a practitioner who has worked with the World Health Organization to manage the communications response to epidemics around the world, explains that what we do in risk and crisis communication is more than just protecting an organization's reputation; we have the potential to make a strong positive impact on the world around us.

Box 2.1 Practitioner perspective: How crisis communication evolved from being "corporate PR" to a life-saving intervention

By Ben Duncan

How the health sector thinks about and uses crisis communication has undergone a profound shift over the past two decades.

I became an EU media officer dealing with health and food safety in 2002. This was just at the tail end of the European Union's 'Mad Cow disease' crisis. Bovine spongiform encephalopathy (BSE), to give 'Mad Cow' its scientific name, emerged in British cattle herds in the late 1980s. UK government ministers spent nearly a decade proclaiming that BSE posed no threat to human health and that "British beef is safe." When new evidence forced the UK health minister to announce a 'probable' link between BSE and a deadly human brain disease (variant-CJD), it provoked a crisis. It evolved into a wider EU crisis in subsequent years when BSE reached cattle herds in other EU member states, and then when cases of variant-CJD were seen in some of these countries. Crisis communication strategy in the health sector at that time centered primarily on issues of corporate reputation: How to repair the reputational damage done by 'Mad Cow' and how to prevent such damage in the future.

The SARS outbreak of 2003 introduced a subtle but far-reaching shift in what crisis communication meant for the health sector. SARS was a form of acute pneumonia cause by a new, and seemingly highly infectious, virus. It was identified in an outbreak in Hong Kong in February and March 2003. SARS then spread rapidly across Southeast Asia and to North America, causing an outbreak in Toronto, Canada. Between March and June 2003, when the outbreak was finally contained, SARS was a significant health sector crisis. It emerged during this time that the outbreak had probably started in Guangdong Province, China, as early as November 2002. The reluctance of the Chinese health authorities to communicate openly and transparently about the outbreak was bad crisis communication in that it damaged their reputation. More than this, though, the lack of communication about SARS had allowed it to spread unchecked. If health workers and the public don't know about a disease, they can't take steps to stop it spreading.

Over the subsequent five years, I did a lot of work with EU countries and the World Health Organization (WHO) on influenza pandemic preparedness. The emergence of a new, highly infectious, and potentially deadly form of influenza would be a significant health crisis. However, those of us working on preparedness soon realized that enabling people to protect themselves from the virus, rather than just protect corporate reputations, needed to be our key focus. In the opening stages of an influenza pandemic, when there is no vaccine available against the new virus and it's not yet known whether antiviral drugs will work, communication is one of the few interventions available to health authorities. Communication must be part of the crisis response, rather than an add-on.

From the 2000s onwards, risk and crisis communication experts in the health sector pushed to be equal members of the crisis management team. Positioning crisis communication as a health intervention, of course, supported our claim to be professionals on a par with epidemiologists and lab experts in the response team. But we also passionately believed that bad crisis communication in a health emergency could cost lives.

The truth of this belief was soon tragically illustrated. In the early months of 2014 an outbreak of Ebola virus emerged in Guinea, West Africa, and spread to two neighboring countries: Sierra Leone and Liberia. The outbreak response team strategy was to identify people who were already ill with Ebola, identify everyone they had been in contact with since developing symptoms, and then isolate them all. This would break the chain of infection and stop the outbreak. The team issued a set of science-based key messages: "Ebola kills," "There is no treatment for Ebola," and "If you or a family member has Ebola symptoms come to the Isolation Centre." These proved to be counterproductive. People with Ebola-like symptoms thought. "If I am going to die, I would rather die at home with my family than in an Isolation Centre." The affected communities therefore hid their sick and refused to cooperate with the outbreak response teams. The outbreak continued to accelerate and became the largest-ever Ebola epidemic, with over 11,000 lives lost.

Crisis/risk communication was one among many things that went wrong in the West African Ebola epidemic. However, WHO took the need to integrate communication into emergency response as one of its lessons learned (Report of the Review Committee on the Role of the International Health Regulations, 2005) In 2017 this was codified in WHO's internal *Emergency Response Framework* (2017) and its guideline to EU member states on risk communication (WHO, 2018a).

More than just codifying this approach, WHO is also putting it into practice. For example, there was a sizable communication component to WHO's response to an outbreak of Pneumonic Plague in Madagascar in 2017. A risk communication expert and a medical anthropologist were among the first international experts WHO sent to support the Madagascan Ministry of Health (personal communication of the author), and training materials in Malagasy were developed for local health workers to help them recognise and safely treat people with Plague. Then when a large Ebola outbreak flared up in Equateur Province, Democratic Republic of Congo in 2018, WHO, UNICEF, and their partners ran a sophisticated communication campaign to support the outbreak response. This included studying the beliefs and practices of affected communities, engaging with communities via trusted intermediaries and identifying at-risk minority groups such as pygmy populations (WHO, 2018b).

Crisis management

If we think of crisis management as the material part of crisis response, then it is clear that it is intertwined with risk management and crisis communication. Jindal, Laveena, and Aggarwal (2015) define crisis management as a **process allowing organizations to deal with major problems that pose a threat to the organization and/or its stakeholders.** For organizations, crisis management is a learned behavior that focuses on mitigation and control of the internal and external dynamics of the crisis itself; yet it is not like being a mechanic that finds a problem in the car and fixes it – it is still about managing people and their decisions.

After watching organizations manage crises in the construction industry – an industry that is particularly crisis prone – Loosemore's theory of crisis management (1999) identifies both challenges posed by crises as well as factors influence the effectiveness of crisis management.

Crisis management challenges

Loosemore's theory of crisis management argues that crises produce four management challenges. First, **power struggles are likely to emerge during crises.** These can occur within the organization as it tries to manage the situation across different departments or groups. However, they can also emerge externally between organizations in the same industry as well as between organizations trying to coordinate to respond to the risk and for a host of reasons from who is responsible to who will get credit for action.

Second, **communication is connected to 'efficiency,'** which can create a crisis management challenge. Loosemore argues that one of the critical challenges in a crisis is ensuring that the right people have the right information at the right time. There is a suggestion that communication during crises serves a functional purpose that is not always conducive to managing positive relationships – that is, people can often tread over feelings, position, and responsibility in order to get the problem solved. While this may serve a short-term benefit, it can be problematic for long-term relationship management both within the organization and between organizations.

Third, **crises tend to encourage conflict.** In this case we are talking about conflicts within an organization or group of partners working to solve a problem. Sources of conflict can range from task to relationship, to process (Jehn, 1997) but what Loosemore (1999) found was that during crises, the sources of conflict were amplified by the emotional intensity of the situation. Naturally, this creates a challenge for crisis management because in order to manage the crisis, the conflict also has to be managed. For this reason, we can also think of crises as an inside-out problem: Everything has to be working within an organization and between partners in order for an external crisis to be effectively managed. This is one of the reasons that Part 3 of the book directly examines improving an organization's capacity to respond to crises.

Fourth, **crises discourage collective responsibility.** In short, we like to blame someone and really would prefer it is not us. Loosemore found that most people have at least a minor predisposition to minimizing the perception that they are at fault in a crisis. Averting blame is often a combination of manifestations of our own guilt, not wanting to 'get in trouble,' and wanting to know where the finger of blame is pointed. Yet, this is problematic for crisis management because a lot of times people are more worried about blame than solving the problem.

Factors influencing crisis management

Notice that the problems of crisis management are less about solving the material problem and more about being able to focus teams on solving the material problem. This is because the reality of crisis management and overall risk management is that poor responses to crises often create secondary crises (Grebe, 2013) that also have to be managed. As such, what Loosemore (1999) identifies as the critical factors influencing effective crisis management are all human management factors.

First, **social adjustment** is necessary for crisis management. This means that competing interests have to be balanced to successfully manage a crisis; organizations have to create the conditions for change to be managed within the organization and its relationships with critical internal and external stakeholders. The core assumption is that crises cause change and everyone has to get used to it. When crisis management is effective, it facilitates the change process (Carroll & Hatakenaka, 2001; Mehta & Xavier, 2012).

Second, **managing behavioral instability** is a vital part of crisis management. Crises have a destabilizing effect on anyone affected. Loosemore (1999) observed that crises often create behavioral instability by creating the conditions that desensitize people to the needs of others. In short, crises tend to evoke strong emotions that cause people to focus on their own interests but also can affect how they view the organization(s) managing the crisis (Diers-Lawson, 2017; Edwards, Lawrence, & Ashkanasy, 2016; Heide & Simonsson, 2015; Jin, 2010).

Third, Loosemore (1999) found that **managing social structures** in order to better disseminate information is a vital crisis management function. The social structures of organizations and communities help to influence reactions to crises by determining, in part, the effective and timely flow of information to interested and important stakeholders. In a modern context, this means that crisis management must also use effective platforms of communication with different stakeholders no matter whether those are face-to-face, on social media, or through more traditional internal and external channels.

Fourth, effective crisis management means that organizations can take advantage of **diametric opportunities**. Though a combination of what is happening outside and inside the organization as well as the nature of the crisis itself, crises can create environments that can be both constructive and destructive to organizations. In a destructive context, a crisis can draw an organization into a self-perpetuating cycle of escalation prolonging the crisis and wasting resources. However, crises also provide opportunities for organizations and their stakeholders to improve their cohesion, harmony, and efficiency. This can also become self-perpetuating, which minimizes the crisis.

Loosemore's theory of crisis management (1999) has been cited in a lot of crisis research and practitioner work in the last couple of decades because it identifies the important human qualities of crises that both enable and complicate crisis management In short, effective crisis management is about learning from past experiences, adapting to situations, and evaluating actions and behaviors in order to more effectively mitigate or minimize the risks causing the crises (Gilbert & Lauren, 1980; Heath, 1998b; Taneja, Pryor, Sewell, & Recuero, 2014).

Crisis communication

Naturally, crisis management is inherently intertwined with crisis communication in managing risk, even if the people managing the crises or communicating with critical stakeholders are different. Effective crisis management and communication rely heavily on teams, group decision-making, staff development, simulation, and constant evaluation (Hayes & Patton, 2001; Ritchie, 2004; Taneja et al., 2014).

Nonetheless, our focus in communication is also distinctive from crisis management because crisis communication focuses on stakeholder relationship management, narrating the crisis, and the development and implementation of communication strategy for crises. I will address stakeholder relationships in Chapter 3 and Part 4, and I will focus on narrating the crisis and crisis strategy in Part 5. However, it is important to think about the development and implementation of crisis strategy – or the public relations function in crisis communication – as a campaign. What we do in crisis communication broadly follows the same form and function as any other strategic communication campaign but with a crisis plan and crisis response at the heart of the campaign's purpose. Figure 2.2 summarizes this campaign structure and will be something that I will come back to later in the book.

Figure 2.2 Crisis strategy overview

In review . . .

In the end, in this chapter I have focused on the connection between crises, risk management, crisis management, and crisis communication. I have explored the differences between crisis management and crisis communication. Finally, I have begun to explore what crisis communication means in a modern context – that it is not only about image and reputation but can also be about saving lives.

Review your understanding

By the end of this chapter, you should be able to understand and explain the following:

- Three characteristics of crisis
- What risk and risk management are
- Factors affecting perceptions of risk
- The process connected to risk management
- What crisis management is

- Loosemore's theory of crisis management:
  - The four management challenges posed by crises
  - The four factors influencing successful crisis management
- The differences between crisis management and crisis communication

References

Carroll, J. S., & Hatakenaka, S. (2001). Driving organizational change in the midst of crisis. *Mt. Sloan Management Review* (Spring), 70–79.

Comfort, L. K. (2007). Crisis management in hindsight: Cognition, communication, coordination, and control. *Public Administration Review*, 67(S1), 189–197.

Covello, V. T., Peters, R. G., Wojtecki, J. G., & Hyde, R. C. (2001). Risk communication, the West Nile virus epidemic, and bioterrorism: Responding to the communication challenges posed by the intentional or unintentional release of a pathogen in an urban setting. *Journal of Urban Health*, 78(2), 382–391.

Diers-Lawson, A. (2017). Will they like us when they're angry? Antecedents and indicators of strong emotional reactions to crises among stakeholders. In S. M. Croucher, B. Lewandowska-Tomaszczyk, & P. Wilson (Eds.), *Conflict, mediated message, and group dynamics* (pp. 81–136). Lanham, MD: Lexington Books.

Dilenschneider, R. L., & Hyde, R. C. (1985). Crisis communications: Planning for the unplanned. *Business Horizons*, 35–38.

Edwards, M. S., Lawrence, S. A., & Ashkanasy, N. M. (2016). How perceptions and emotions shaped employee silence in the case of "Dr. Death" at Bundaberg hospital. In N. M. Ashkanasy & C. E. J. Hartel (Eds.), *Emotions and organizational governance* (pp. 341–379). Bingley, UK: Emerald Group Publishing Limited.

Freundberg, W. R. (1988). Perceived risk, real risk: Social science and the art of probabilistic risk assessment. *Science*, 242, 44–49.

Gilbert, A. N., & Lauren, P. G. (1980). Crisis management: An assessment and critique. *Journal of Conflict Resolution*, 24(4), 641–664.

Grebe, S. K. (2013). Things can get worse: How mismanagement of a crisis response strategy can cause a secondary or double crisis: The example of the AWB corporate scandal. *Corporate Communications: An International Journal*, 18(1), 70–86. doi:10.1108/13563281311294137

Hayes, D., & Patton, M. (2001). Proactive crisis-management strategies and the archaeological heritage. *International Journal of Heritage Studies*, 7(1), 37–58.

Heath, R. L. (1998a). Dealing with the complete crisis – The crisis management shell structure. *Safety Science*, 30(1), 139–150.

Heath, R. L. (1998b). Looking for answers: Suggestions for improving how we evaluate crisis management. *Safety Science*, 30(1), 151–163.

Heath, R. L., & Millar, D. P. (2004). A rhetorical approach to crisis communication: Management, communication processes, and strategic responses. In D. P. Millar & R. L. Heath (Eds.), *Responding to crisis: A rhetorical approach to crisis communication* (pp. 1–18). Mahwah, NJ: Lawrence Erlbaum Associates.

Heide, M., & Simonsson, C. (2015). Struggling with internal crisis communication: A balancing act between paradoxical tensions. *Public Relations Inquiry*, 4(2), 223–255. doi:10.1177/2046147X15570108

Horton, T. R. (1988). Crisis management. *Management Review*, 77(9), 5–8.

Jehn, K. A. (1997). A qualitative analysis of conflict types and dimensions in organizational groups. *Administrative Science Quarterly*, 530–557.

Jin, Y. (2010). Making sense sensibly in crisis communication: How publics' crisis appraisals influence their negative emotions, coping strategy preferences, and crisis response acceptance. *Communication Research*, 37(4), 522–552. doi:10.1177/0093650210368256

Jindal, S., Laveena, L., & Aggarwal, A. (2015). A comparative study of crisis management-Toyota v/s General Motors. *Scholedge International Journal of Management & Development*, 2(6), 1–12.

Johansson, A., & Härenstam, M. (2013). Knowledge communication: A key to successful crisis management. *Biosecurity and Bioterrorism: Biodefense Strategy, Practice, and Science*, 11(S1), S260–S263. doi:10.1089/bsp.2013.0052

Kash, T. J., & Darling, J. R. (1998). Crisis management: Prevention, diagnosis and intervention. *Leadership & Organization Development Journal*, 19(4), 179–186.

Ley, B., Ludwig, T., Pipek, V., Randall, D., Reuter, C., & Wiedenhoefer, T. (2014). Information and expertise sharing in inter-organizational crisis management. *Computer Supported Cooperative Work (CSCW)*, 23(4–6), 347–387.

Loosemore, M. (1999). A grounded theory of construction crisis management. *Construction Management and Economics*, 17, 9–19.

Massey, J. E., & Larsen, J. (2006). Crisis management in real time: How to successfully plan for and respond to a crisis. *Journal of Promotion Management*, 12(3/4), 63–97. doi:10.1300/J057v12n0306

Mehta, A., & Xavier, R. (2012). Tracking the defining moments in crisis process and practice. *Public Relations Review*, 38, 376–382. doi:10.1016/j.pubrev.2011.12.009

Nunamaker, J. F., Weber, E. S., & Chen, M. (1989). Organizational crisis management systems: Planning for intelligent action. *Journal of Management Information Systems*, 5(4), 7–31.

Perry, D. C., Taylor, M., & Doerfel, M. L. (2003). Internet-based communication in crisis management. *Management Communication Quarterly*, 17(2), 206–232.

Reilly, A. H. (2008). The role of human resource development competencies in facilitating effective crisis communication. *Advances in Developing Human Resources*, 10(3), 331–351.

Report of the Review Committee on the Role of the International Health Regulations (2005) in the Ebola Outbreak and Response. Retrieved from http://apps.who.int/gb/ebwha/pdf_files/WHA69/A69_21-en.pdf?ua=1

Ritchie, B. W. (2004). Chaos, crises and disasters: A strategic approach to crisis management in the tourism industry. *Tourism Management, 25*(6), 669–683.

Stacks, D. W. (2004). Crisis management: Toward a multidimension model of public relations. In D. P. Millar & R. L. Heath (Eds.), *Responding to crisis: A rhetorical approach to crisis communication* (pp. 37–49). Mahwah, NJ: Lawrence Erlbaum Associates.

Taneja, S., Pryor, M. G., Sewell, S., & Recuero, A. M. (2014). Strategic crisis management: A basis for renewal and crisis prevention. *Journal of Management Policy and Practice, 15*(1), 78.

WHO. (2017). *Emergency response framework* (2nd ed.). Geneva: WHO. Retrieved from www.who.int/hac/about/erf/en/

WHO. (2018a). *Communication risk in public health emergencies*. Geneva: WHO. Retrieved from www.who.int/risk-communication/guidance/en/

WHO. (2018b). *Risk communication and community engagement considerations: Ebola response in Democratic Republic of the Congo*. Geneva: WHO. Retrieved from www.who.int/risk-communication/guidance/considerations-ebola-drc/en/

3 | The stakeholder relationship management perspective on crisis communication

Learning objectives

By the end of this chapter, the reader should:

- Be able to integrate the relationship metaphor into public relations (PR) and crisis communication
- Recognize and understand the foundations of the stakeholder relationship management model

Identify and evaluate the implications of the model for crisis communication

In the previous two chapters, I have defined crisis communication and reviewed a contemporary understanding of the field that reveals the five critical factors to understanding crisis communication: issue, organizational, stakeholder, response, and outcome. Likewise, as we define crisis communication as a field that represents the convergence of risk and crisis management, then we necessarily have to place the stakeholder at the heart of the field.

In this chapter, I introduce the central assumption for this text: It is the relationship(s) between organizations and all of their internal and external stakeholders that drive not only PR but also crisis communication.

Stakeholder relationships

In the organizational context, **stakeholders** are those groups and/or people who can affect or be affected by an organization (Freeman, 1994). Much of the foundational work in stakeholder theory in organizational communication (Connolly, Conlon, & Deutsch, 1980; Frooman, 1999; Henriques & Sadorsky, 1999; Mitchell, Agle, & Wood, 1997; Rowley, 1997) identifies the **dimensions of interorganizational relationships** as characterized by five factors.

1. The **relational valence,** or positive to negative affect between an organization and the stakeholder (Atkins & Lowe, 1994)

2. The **history of interaction** between organizations and particular stakeholders that allows for structures and rituals of interaction to emerge (Harris, 1994; Jennings, Artz, Gillin, & Christodouloy, 2000; Scott & Lane, 2000; Trice & Beyer, 1993)

3. An organization's assessment of a stakeholder group's **legitimacy** – that is, its recognizeability, reputation, and/or expertise relevant to the organization's core work (Haley, 1996; Suchman, 1995)

4. The **power** that a stakeholder has to influence the organization or its success (Heath, 1994; Mitchell et al., 1997)

5. The **urgency** of a stakeholder's interest in the organization, that is extent to which a stakeholder's interest or influence is time sensitive or critical to the organization (Connolly et al., 1980; Mitchell et al., 1997; Scott & Lane, 2000)

Thus, while discussing stakeholder relationships is the heart of most PR work, it is also important that we not conflate relationships between organizations and stakeholders with interpersonal relationships because, as these dimensions point out, there are differences between stakeholder and interpersonal relationships (Coombs & S. J. Holladay, 2015)

Complexity within organizational environments

As if it was not complex enough for organizations to manage relationships with particular stakeholders, organizations are also subject to a lot of pressures because they serve multiple groups at any given time (Connolly et al., 1980; Frooman, 1999). These stakeholders range vastly and can include groups like employees, customers or clients, regulators, competitors, and the like (see Figure 3.1 for examples).

But even these interactions between organizations and stakeholders do not happen in isolation, rather in a web of relationships (Rowley, 1997). In fact, Fombrun (1982) suggests that we should think of an organization's environment as a series of overlapping networks that help to explain why organizations act, do not act, and even how they perform. Furthermore, Heath (1994) argues that what an organization is and does is really just an outcome of all managing all of the interests of the stakeholders

Figure 3.1 Examples of stakeholders that organizations may have

it values. The role and purpose of communication is to help an organization and its stakeholders enact and manage their relationship (Heath, 1994).

In a modern organizational context, we must also consider the different levels at which organizations operate. Organizations have internal, local, national, and often even international stakeholders. Even where we might see overlapping types of stakeholders at different levels, that does not mean they are the same groups; they may even have competing interests. For example, a company like Amazon doing business globally must manage its corporate relationships with multiple governments, vendors, and contractors – all while trying to maintain a consistent brand identity and offering.

This is why academics and practitioners argue that in order for organizations to keep up with the digital age, they must be mindful of their relationship management practices across all platforms of engagement (Briones, Kuch, Liu, & Jin, 2011; McCorkindale, DiStaso, & Sisco, 2013; van der Merwe, Pitt, & Abratt, 2005; Vorvoreanu, 2009). One example of the changes in relationship management in the broader field of PR is that stakeholders demand more direct or two-way engagement and more visual engagement with organizations (Tench, Verčič, Zerfass, Moreno, & Verhoeven, 2017).

Advocacy and stakeholder perceptions

In an era when stakeholders not only are demanding different forms of engagement but also crises are increasingly common, stakeholder expectations of organizations are changing as well. For example, as new generations (e.g., Generation Y) are gaining voice as young adults and workers, their expectations of organizations – including social responsibility, transparency, and ethical decision-making – are fundamentally influencing PR practice (Curtin, Gallicano, & Matthews, 2011).

These changes mean that organizations have to change the ways they relate to and communicate with different stakeholder groups in competitive message environments. For example, instead of an organization just positioning itself as having a desirable product or service, it feels increasingly pressured to have more socially responsible value propositions – it cannot just sell a good product, it also has to do good – all in an environment where its competitors and critics might be talking about the organization relative to their own interests. Haley (1996) was interested in understanding how consumers reacted to such advocacy in the context of advertising. In particular, he was interested in how stakeholders reacted to different types of cause-related advertising messages. In his work, Haley identified three perceptions that affect how compelling an organization's promotional messages.

1 **The perception of the organization and self.** He argued that a central component of consumers' understanding of advocacy messages from organizations was based in their perception of the relationship between the organization and the consumer. On the whole, if the organization was recognizable and likeable, it was more likely to be persuasive. For example, Ben & Jerry's Ice Cream is generally viewed positively by consumers for a host of reasons from product quality to the organization's identity.

2 **Perception of organization and issue.** Next, Haley argued that how consumers understand the relationship between the advocacy issue and the organization would influence their acceptance of the advocacy message. For example, one of the key issues that Ben & Jerry's advocates about is climate change. Whether the company is successful in advocating about climate change would depend on whether

consumers perceived a direct relationship between Ben & Jerry's core business – producing ice cream – and climate change; whether the company was knowledgeable enough about climate change to offer credible arguments whether it genuinely cared about the environment; and whether it wanted to do good with its advocacy related to climate change.

3 **Perception of the issue and self.** Finally, in order for advocacy advertising to be effective, Haley argued that consumers also had to have a measure of investment in the issue. So with our example of Ben & Jerry's, in order for the company to be persuasive, ice cream consumers would have to find the issue of climate change important to themselves, to society, and believe that positively affecting climate change was possible.

Stakeholder relationship management model

In the PR context, Haley's (1996) discussion of the relative success of advocacy advertising makes a lot of sense. I like to think of his discussion of the three perceptions as the 'love triangle' that PR practitioners have to negotiate when they are trying to build, maintain, or repair relationships with stakeholders. Yet, unlike interpersonal relationships, stakeholder relationships are necessarily based on perceived vested interests – that is, the organization and/or the stakeholder want something relatively tangible from the other and, as Heath (2002) argues, the relationship should be mutually beneficial. For me this provides something concrete and measurable that can be tested in order to diagnose, manage, and improve relationships. In fact, much of my research in the last several years (Diers-Lawson, 2017; Diers, 2012) has focused on identifying different factors influencing each of these relationships. Figure 3.2 summarizes the stakeholder relationship management model.

The stakeholder relationship model (SRM) provides us a way to organize previous findings that establish that stakeholder characteristics, public pressure from interested

Figure 3.2 The stakeholder relationship management model

stakeholders, and engagement are all likely to influence stakeholder evaluations and behavioral intentions towards organizations. The model aligns with previous research establishing that consumer attitudes (Claes, Rust, & Dekimpe, 2010), public pressure from interested stakeholders in the face of crises (Piotrowski & Guyette, 2010; Uccello, 2009), and engagement with stakeholders (Hong, Yang, & Rim, 2010) are all likely to influence consumer evaluations and behavioral intentions towards organizations. Previous applications of the model to analysis of post-crisis communication have demonstrated its effectiveness in identifying factors influencing consumer evaluations of the firm, such as an organization's reputation, consumer knowledge of the organization, perceptions of the organization's concern regarding the crisis, and consumers' interest regarding the crisis (Diers, 2012).

It is important to note that the SRM focuses on the stakeholder's perspective and trying to understand that perspective. The reason is simple: It is in an organization's interests to plan its communication activities around its stakeholders, so beginning with a good understanding of the stakeholder perspective will help organizations inside and outside of crises to better understand the communication needs of their stakeholders.

Additionally, I need to note what I mean by **issues** in the context of the model. This distinction in the stakeholder perspective on issues is important in Part 2 when discussing issues management because what stakeholders care about is discussed there. For a stakeholder, issues can represent anything from the products or services that the organization offers. But they can also represent topics that stakeholders care about, like health care or the environment. What is critical for the model, however, is that stakeholders believe there is a direct and clear connection between the issue and the organization. Think about issues like the baggage that comes with the relationship between organizations and their stakeholders.

If we can imagine that issues represent risks or even opportunities for organizations, then we can focus on the connections between issues, organizations, and stakeholders as what constitutes stakeholders' relationship with an organization. Stakeholders' judgments about organizations are not only about whether they like the organization's products, services, policies, customer service and so on, but also about how stakeholders evaluate the organization's performance relative to issues and topics that also matter to the stakeholders.

The relationship between the organization and issues

Let us take a closer look at each of the types of judgments that stakeholders make about organizations and whether they want a good relationship with an organization by starting with the relationship between the organization and issues. Stakeholders make judgments about organizations, and their connection to the issues they care about are based on a number of factors. While research is still identifying all of the factors, four have emerged across a large body of research (from multiple authors, books, and journal articles) in the last 10–15 years.

Blame or responsibility attribution emerges from the research on attribution theory (Weiner, 1985, 2006); this is an evaluation of the degree to which stakeholders believe that an organization has control over a particular issue. The more responsibility that a stakeholder attributes to the organization, the more likely they are to ascribe more definitive expectations on the organization with regards to the issue. Blame attribution is one of the most important predictors of stakeholder attitudes about an organization after a crisis and is a core concept in situational crisis communication theory (Coombs, 2007; Coombs & Holladay, 2004; Jeong, 2008; Schwarz, 2008) – however, it is also applied in other related crisis communication research connecting to other factors like corporate social responsibility, crisis history, and ethics (Kim, 2013; Ping, Ishaq, & Li, 2015).

Competence asks whether stakeholders judge that the organization has the capacity to successfully address the issue (de Fatima Oliveira, 2013; Hyvärinen & Vos, 2015; Sohn & Lariscy, 2014).

Positive intention, concern, and commitment all represent value judgments from stakeholders about their belief that the organization is authentically interested in the issue (Huang, 2008). Positive intention is often connected with hygiene-motivation theory (Lacey, Kennett-Hensel, & Manolis, 2014), which suggests that if a stakeholder believes that an organization's intentions are positive when it comes to social responsibility, then it benefits the organization's reputation. However, if stakeholders believe the organization's interest in an issue is inauthentic, then it does not matter how good the organization's behaviors, it is unlikely to positively influence the organization's reputation.

Finally, **clear association** also matters. If stakeholders believe there is a logical connection between an issue and the organization's core business or mission, then the organization's interest in the issue is more compelling to the stakeholder and can thus change the stakeholder's judgement about the organization, particularly after a crisis emerges (Claeys & Cauberghe, 2015; Coombs & S. Holladay, 2015; De Bruycker & Walgrave, 2014; Kernisky, 1997; Knight & Greenberg, 2002).

The relationship between the stakeholder and issues

From a risk or crisis management perspective, the more intensely that stakeholders feel connected to issues, the more likely those issues are going to trigger the stakeholders to act. Yet, in crisis communication research, this relationship is one that is only beginning to emerge as an important predictor. There are clear indications of several vital factors that influence stakeholder evaluations of issues.

First, **emotional involvement** with issues is vital to understand. At their heart, crises are incredibly emotional for organizations and stakeholders alike, with a lot of emotionally charged communication but with a dearth of research examining the implications of emotional reactions for organizations (van der Meer & Verhoeven, 2014). Fortunately, there is an increasing recognition that emotional reactions affect the outcomes of crises. Some of the most vital research connecting stakeholder emotion and issues has emerged from Jin and her research partners over the last several years. For example, Jin, Liu, Anagondahalli, and Austin's (2014) research to develop the social-mediated crisis communication model (SMCC) provides instrumental insight into understanding the measures of emotions and types of emotional reactions to crises.

Moreover, stakeholders' **prior experience with issues** and **issue-specific attitudes** should also be understood. For example, Ki and Brown's (2013) findings suggest that response to the crisis itself may not affect attributions of blame nor relational quality outcomes; however, what makes the biggest difference is the quality of the relationship between organizations and stakeholders before the crisis begins. That suggests that crisis communication begins long before a crisis emerges. Of course, crises will often damage stakeholder satisfaction and trust, but if the relationship was strong to begin with, then it will often survive most crises.

Focusing on the formation of attitudes is consistent with most approaches in persuasion research, where theories such as the health belief model or social cognitive theory emphasize the importance of understanding the implications of constructs like **perceived susceptibility, severity, beliefs, demographics, and perceived efficacy** as key predictors of reactions to stimuli and situations (Rosenstock, Strecher, & Becker, 1988). Similarly, theories like the theory or reasoned action or theory of planned behavior assume that people typically behave sensibly and that our intentions to act (or not) are directly related to our **existing attitudes, social norms, and perceived situational control** (Aizen, 2005). In fact, these findings do align with some important research that has been done analyzing emotions in crisis communication. This research find that, for example, stakeholder perceptions of their own control over situations and **uncertainty perceptions** affect not only emotional reactions to crises but also attitudes and actions towards the organizations in crisis (Jin et al., 2014; McDonald & Cokley, 2013; Mou & Lin, 2014).

The relationship between organizations and stakeholders

Finally, we consider the relationship between the organization and the stakeholder. Stakeholder attitudes towards organizations, especially those in crisis, has been studied the most in crisis communication (Diers, 2012). Often treated as outcomes of a crisis, these judgments have been assessed across multiple fields of study, from communication and marketing to industry-specific studies in such different areas like health care and tourism. If researchers and practitioners want to understand this relationship, they should be directly analyzing factors like an organization's **reputation** (Benoit, 1995; Carroll, 2009, p.709). There is considerable work in PR, and crisis communication more directly, that explores topics like the influence of a favorable pre-crisis reputation in protecting an organization's reputation during and after a crisis (Claeys & Cauberghe, 2015), the role of the media and other external groups in influencing an organization's reputation during crises (Einwiller, Carroll, & Korn, 2010), and the growing influence of social media on an organization's reputation in the context of crises (Brown & Billings, 2013; Ott & Theunissen, 2015; Utz, Schultz, & Glocka, 2013), to name just a few ways that reputation influences the stakeholder evaluations of organizations.

However, there are a number of other factors that influence the relationship, such as stakeholders' **perceived knowledge** of the organization: This not only changes under different circumstances, but also is influenced by stakeholder perceptions of crises (Diers, 2012). For example, in studying attitudes about BP a year after the 2010 spill in the Gulf of Mexico, I found that if a crisis made stakeholders feel like they had less knowledge about an organization, the stakeholders were more likely to evaluate the organization negatively. Evaluations of stakeholder attitudes towards organizations also tend to invoke more personal feelings about organizations, like stakeholder assessments of whether an organization is fundamentally **trustworthy** (Freberg & Palenchar, 2013), whether stakeholders believe the organization in crisis has **values that are congruent** to their own (Koerber, 2014), whether they feel the relationship itself is **satisfactory** (Ki & Brown, 2013), or even whether the stakeholders feel **loyalty** to the organization in crisis (Helm & Tolsdorf, 2013).

In review . . .

Taken together, the judgments that stakeholders make about organizations and issues should be viewed as an interplay in stakeholder identities, attitudes towards the organization in crisis, and issues that matter to them, as well as their evaluation of the organization's connection to the issue affected by the organization's work. The connections between these three parts of our love triangle can help to explain why organizations are more or less successful when managing situations and crises. The best example of these differences might be the case of the 2010 BP oil spill in the Gulf of Mexico. While many analysts, media outlets, government agencies, and the public more broadly panned BP for being socially irresponsible in its management of the crisis, the reality was a bit different. After analyzing every press release, tweet, and

Facebook post that BP made during the five-month crisis, my research found that BP's response strategy was socially responsible; they worked very hard to communicate a strong focus on the people and environment affected by the spill. However, the negative media framing, BP's crisis history, and the way their messages were communicated made the 'right' message strategy much less effective that when the messaging strategy is more closely examined BP's response strategy emphasized social responsibility and worked to communicate a strong connection with people affected by the crisis (Diers-Lawson & Pang, 2016; Diers & Donohue, 2013). The case demonstrates that if we can understand the interplay between stakeholder evaluations of the organization, the organization's connection to the issue, and the stakeholder's own connection to the issue, then we can more easily understand their reactions to crises.

Review your understanding

By the end of this chapter, you should be able to understand and explain the following:

- What a stakeholder is
- The five factors that influence interorganizational relationships
- The complexity in modern global environments for stakeholder relationship management
- Haley's work on advocacy advertising
- The SRM:

  - The relationship between the organization and issues and the factors influencing it
  - The relationship between stakeholders and issues and the factors influencing them
  - The relationship between the organization and stakeholders, and the factors influencing it

References

Aizen, I. (2005). *Explaining intentions and behavior: Attitudes, personality, and behavior* (Vol. 2). Berkshire, England: McGraw-Hill Education.

Atkins, M., & Lowe, J. (1994). Stakeholders and the strategy formation process in small and medium enterprises. *International Small Business Journal, 12*(3), 12–25.

Benoit, W. L. (1995). Sears' repair of its auto service image: Image restoration discourse in the corporate sector. *Communication Studies, 46*(1–2), 89–105.

Briones, R. L., Kuch, B., Liu, B. F., & Jin, Y. (2011). Keeping up with the digital age: How the American Red Cross uses social media to build relationships. *Public Relations Review, 37*(1), 37–43.

Brown, N. A., & Billings, A. C. (2013). Sports fans as crisis communicators on social media websites. *Public Relations Review, 39*(1), 74–81.

Carroll, C. (2009). Defying a reputational crisis – Cadbury's salmonella scare: Why are customers willing to forgive and forget? *Corporate Reputation Review, 12*(1), 64–82.

Claes, F., Rust, R. T., & Dekimpe, M. G. (2010). The effect of consumer satisfaction on consumer spending growth. *Journal of Marketing Research, 47*(1), 28–35. doi:10.1509/jmkr.47.1.28

Claeys, A.-S., & Cauberghe, V. (2015). The role of a favorable pre-crisis reputation in protecting organizations during crises. *Public Relations Review, 41*(1), 64–71. doi:10.1016/j.pubrev.2014.10.013

Connolly, T., Conlon, E. J., & Deutsch, S. J. (1980). Organizational effectiveness: A multiple-constituency approach. *Academy of Management Journal, 5*(2), 211–217.

Coombs, T., & Holladay, S. (2015). CSR as crisis risk: Expanding how we conceptualize the relationship. *Corporate Communications: An International Journal, 20*(2), 144–162. doi:10.1108/CCIJ-10-2013-0078

Coombs, W. T. (2007). Attribution theory as a guide for post-crisis communication research. *Public Relations Review, 33*(2), 135–139.

Coombs, W. T., & Holladay, S. J. (2004). Reasoned action in crisis communication: An attribution theory-based approach to crisis management. In D. P. Millar & R. L. Heath (Eds.), *Responding to crisis: A rhetorical approach to crisis communication* (pp. 95–115). Mahwah, NJ: Lawrence Erlbaum Associates.

Coombs, W. T., & Holladay, S. J. (2015). Public relations' "relationship identity" in research: Enlightenment or illusion. *Public Relations Review, 41*(5), 689–695. doi:10.1016/j.pubrev.2013.12.008

Curtin, P. A., Gallicano, T., & Matthews, K. (2011). Millennials' approaches to ethical decision making: A survey of young public relations agency employees. *Public Relations Journal, 5*(2), 1–22.

De Bruycker, I., & Walgrave, S. (2014). How a new issue becomes an owned issue. Media coverage and the financial crisis in Belgium (2008–2009). *International Journal of Public Opinion Research, 26*(1), 86–97.

de Fatima Oliveira, M. (2013). Multicultural environments and their challenges to crisis communication. *International Journal of Business Communication, 50*(3), 253–277. doi:10.1177/0021943613487070

Diers, A. R. (2012). Reconstructing stakeholder relationships using 'corporate social responsibility' as a response strategy to cases of corporate irresponsibility: The case of the 2010

BP spill in the Gulf of Mexico. In R. Tench, W. Sun, & B. Jones (Eds.), *Corporate social irresponsibility: A challenging concept* (Vol. 4, pp. 177–206). Bingley, UK: Emerald.

Diers, A. R., & Donohue, J. (2013). Synchronizing crisis responses after a transgression: An analysis of BP's enacted crisis response to the Deepwater Horizon crisis in 2010. *Journal of Communication Management, 17*(3), 252–269.

Diers-Lawson, A. (2017). Will they like us when they're angry? Antecedents and indicators of strong emotional reactions to crises among stakeholders. In S. M. Croucher, B. Lewandowska-Tomaszczyk, & P. Wilson (Eds.), *Conflict, mediated message, and group dynamics* (pp. 81–136). Lanham, MD: Lexington Books.

Diers-Lawson, A., & Pang, A. (2016). Did BP atone for its transgressions? Expanding theory on 'ethical apology' in crisis communication. *Journal of Contingencies and Crisis Management, 24*(3), 148–161.

Einwiller, S. A., Carroll, C. E., & Korn, K. (2010). Under what conditions do the news influence corporate reputation? The roles of media dependency and need for orientation. *Corporate Reputation Review, 12*(4), 299–315.

Fombrun, C. J. (1982). Strategies for network research in organizations. *Academy of Management Review, 7*, 280–291.

Freberg, K., & Palenchar, M. J. (2013). Convergence of digital negotiation and risk challenges: Strategic implications of social media for risk and crisis communications. In H. S. N. Al-Deen & J. A. Hendricks (Eds.), *Social media and strategic communications* (pp. 83–100). London: Palgrave Macmillan.

Freeman, R. E. (1994). *Ethical theory and business.* Englewood Cliffs, NJ: Prentice Hall.

Frooman, J. (1999). Stakeholder influence strategies. *Academy of Management Journal, 24*(2), 191–205.

Haley, E. (1996). Exploring the construct of organization as source: Consumers' understandings of organizational sponsorship of advocacy advertising. *Journal of Advertising, 25*, 19–36.

Harris, S. G. (1994). Organizational cultures and individual sensemaking: A schema-based perspective. *Organizational Science, 5*, 309–321.

Heath, R. L. (1994). *Management of corporate communication: From interpersonal contacts to external affairs.* Hillsdale, NJ: Lawrence Erlbaum Associates.

Heath, R. L. (2002). Issues management: Its past, present, and future. *Journal of Public Affairs, 2*(2), 209–214.

Helm, S., & Tolsdorf, J. (2013). How does corporate reputation affect customer loyalty in a corporate crisis? *Journal of Contingencies and Crisis Management, 21*(3), 144–152. doi:10.1111/1468-5973.12020

Henriques, I., & Sadorsky, P. (1999). The relationship between environmental commitment and managerial perceptions of stakeholder importance. *Academy of Management Journal, 42*(1), 87–99.

Hong, S., Yang, S., & Rim, H. (2010). The influence of corporate social responsibility and customer – Company identification on publics' dialogic communication intentions. *Public Relations Review, 36*(2), 196–198. doi:10.1016/j.pubrev.2009.10.005

Huang, Y. (2008). Trust and relational commitment in corporate crises: The effects of crisis communicative strategy and form of crisis response. *Journal of Public Relations Research, 20*, 297–327.

Hyvärinen, J., & Vos, M. (2015). Developing a conceptual framework for investigating communication supporting community resilience. *Societies, 5*(3), 583–597. doi:10.3390/soc5030583

Jennings, D. F., Artz, K., Gillin, L. M., & Christodouloy, C. (2000). Determinants of trust in global strategic alliances: Amrad and the Australian biomedial industry. *Competitiveness Review, 10*(1), 25–44.

Jeong, S. (2008). *Attributions in crisis communication: A test of attribution model and situational crisis communication theory.* Paper presented at the National Communication Association, San Diego, CA.

Jin, Y., Liu, B. F., Anagondahalli, D., & Austin, L. (2014). Scale development for measuring publics' emotions in organizational crises. *Public Relations Review, 40*(3), 509–518. doi:10.1016/j.pubrev.2014.04.007

Kernisky, D. A. (1997). Proactive crisis management and ethical discourse: Dow Chemical's issues management bulletins 1979–1990. *Journal of Business Ethics, 16*(8), 843–853.

Ki, E.-J., & Brown, K. A. (2013). The effects of crisis response strategies on relationship quality outcomes. *Journal of Business Communication, 50*(4), 403–420. doi:10.1177/00219436 13497056

Kim, S. (2013). Corporate ability or virtue? Relative effectiveness of prior corporate associations in times of crisis. *International Journal of Strategic Communication, 7*(4), 241–256. doi:10.1080/1553118X.2013.824886

Knight, G., & Greenberg, J. (2002). Promotionalism and subpolitics: Nike and its labor critics. *Management Communication Quarterly, 15*(4), 541–570.

Koerber, D. (2014). Crisis communication response and political communities: The unusual case of Toronto mayor Rob Ford. *Canadian Journal of Communication, 39*(3).

Lacey, R., Kennett-Hensel, P. A., & Manolis, C. (2014). Is corporate social responsibility a motivator or hygiene factor? Insights into its bivalent nature. *Journal of the Academy of Marketing Science, 42*(3). doi:10.1007/s11747-014-0390-9

McCorkindale, T., DiStaso, M. W., & Sisco, H. F. (2013). How millennials are engaging and building relationships with organizations on Facebook. *Journal of Social Media in Society, 2*(1).

McDonald, L. M., & Cokley, J. (2013). Prepare for anger, look for love: A ready reckoner for crisis scenario planners. *PRism, 10*(1), 1–11.

Mitchell, R. K., Agle, B. R., & Wood, D. J. (1997). Toward a theory of stakeholder identification and salience: Defining the principle of who and what really counts. *Academy of Management Review*, 22(4), 852–886.

Mou, Y., & Lin, C. A. (2014). Communicating food safety via the social media: The role of knowledge and emotions on risk perception and prevention. *Science Communication*, 36(5), 593–616. doi:10.1177/1075547014549480

Ott, L., & Theunissen, P. (2015). Reputations at risk: Engagement during social media crises. *Public Relations Review*, 41(1), 97–102. doi:10.1016/j.pubrev.2014.10.015

Ping, Q., Ishaq, M., & Li, C. (2015). Product harm crisis, attribution of blame and decision making: An insight from the past. *Journal of Applied Environmental and Biological Sciences*, 5(5), 35–44.

Piotrowski, C., & Guyette, R. W. (2010). Toyota recall crisis: Public attitudes on leadership and ethics. *Organizational Development Journal*, 28(2), 89–97.

Rosenstock, I. M., Strecher, V. J., & Becker, M. H. (1988). Social learning theory and the health belief model. *Health Education and Behavior*, 15(2), 175–183. doi:10.1177/1090198 18801500203

Rowley, T. J. (1997). Moving beyond dyadic ties: A network theory of stakeholder influences. *Academy of Management Review*, 22(4), 887–910.

Schwarz, A. (2008). Covariation-based causal attributions during organizational crises: Suggestions for extending Situational Crisis Communication Theory (SCCT). *International Journal of Strategic Communication*, 2(1), 31–53.

Scott, S. G., & Lane, V. R. (2000). A stakeholder approach to organizational identity. *Academy of Management Review*, 25(1), 43–65.

Sohn, Y., & Lariscy, R. W. (2014). Understanding reputational crisis: Definition, properties, and consequences. *Journal of Public Relations Research*, 26(1), 23–43. doi:10.1080/1062 726X.2013.795865

Suchman, M. C. (1995). Managing legitimacy: Strategic and institutional approach. *Academy of Management Review*, 20(3), 571–610.

Tench, R., Verčič, D., Zerfass, A., Moreno, Á., & Verhoeven, P. (2017). *Communication excellence: How to develop, manage and lead exceptional communications*. Cham, Switzerland: Springer.

Trice, H. M., & Beyer, J. M. (1993). *The cultures of work organizations*. Upper Saddle River, NJ: Prentice Hall.

Uccello, C. (2009). Social interest and social responsibility in contemporary corporate environments. *Journal of Individual Psychology*, 65(4), 412–419.

Utz, S., Schultz, F., & Glocka, S. (2013). Crisis communication online: How medium, crisis type and emotions affected public reactions in the Fukushima Daiichi nuclear disaster. *Public Relations Review*, 39(1), 40–46.

van der Meer, T. G., & Verhoeven, J. W. (2014). Emotional crisis communication. *Public Relations Review*, 40(3), 526–536. doi:10.1016/j.pubrev.2014.03.004

van der Merwe, R., Pitt, L. F., & Abratt, R. (2005). Stakeholder strength: PR survival strategies in the internet age. *Public Relations Quarterly*, *50*(1), 39–48.

Vorvoreanu, M. (2009). Perceptions of corporations on Facebook: An analysis of Facebook social norms. *Journal of New Communications Research*, *4*(1), 67–86.

Weiner, B. (1985). An attributional theory of achievement motivation and emotion. *Psychological Review*, *92*(4), 548.

Weiner, B. (2006). *Social motivation, justice, and the moral emotions: An attributional approach*. Mahwah, NJ: Lawrence Erlbaum Associates.

PART 2

Issue factors: Evaluating stakeholders, risks, and crisis types

In Part 1 of this textbook, I laid out the core concepts and approaches to our exploration of crisis communication by examining the history and development of the field, differentiated crisis communication and crisis management situating crisis communication within the field of public relations (PR), and introduced the central theoretical perspective for the text – the stakeholder relationship model. However, more than that, I explored crisis communication as a concept that goes beyond PR by exploring its function in saving lives.

In Part 2 I will introduce a number of practical tools and the research behind them to help organizations more effectively manage the issues that create risk and crisis for them. By the end of this chapter, readers should be ready to help an organization make strategic recommendations to mitigate risk and potentially avoid crises.

The importance of managing complex and changing organizational environments

Learning objectives

By the end of this chapter, the reader should:

- Understand the scope and nature of issues management within a public relations (PR) and crisis context as risk management
- Analyze the complexity of issues management in changeable organizational environments
- Determine realistic issues management process goals
- Apply the issues management process

Issues, expectancy violation, issues management, and stewardship

In the introduction of the stakeholder relationship model (SRM) in Part 1, I argued that organizations ought to view their behaviors and business practices through the eyes of their stakeholders because their stakeholders determine whether the organization is sustainable. Additionally, within the context of the SRM, issues could represent anything from the products or services that the organization offers to those topics related to an organization's business in which a stakeholder is interested. In short, issues represent risks or opportunities for organizations because they are often the glue that connects organizations and different stakeholders.

Issues and expectance violations

In the context of issues management, when we talk about **issues,** we are talking about a more technical or precise concept. In this context, an issue should be thought of as a controversial gap between an organization's behavior and its stakeholders' expectations. The resolution of these differences can lead to important consequences for organizations (Heath, 2002, 2004; Heath & Gay, 1997). While the resolution of an issue might lead to positive outcomes for an organization, the issue is always a risk.

It is also important to note that there are a lot of risks that organizations face that do not emerge as issues organizations must manage. There are two necessary conditions before we can classify a risk as an issue:

- There is an expectancy violation
- There is the potential for controversy as a result of the expectancy violation

Given that issues management focuses on expectancy violation, we should briefly talk about expectancy violation theory (EVT). Though Burgoon (1993) discusses EVT in an interpersonal context, the core principles are applicable in an organizational context. EVT focuses on the expectations that people build up for others' behavior in particular situations and what can happen when the actual behaviors fall short of their expectations. Burgoon argues there are two types of expectancies: **predictive expectancies,** which define communication and interactions happening within a particular environment or context; and **prescriptive expectances,** which focus on appropriate behaviors displayed within an existing environment. For example, when we go out to a sit-down restaurant, we know what is likely to happen: we are seated and given menus; someone will take our drink and food orders, then deliver the food; and then we pay the bill. As a result, we normally communicate with the wait staff in a predictable manner.

However, when we travel to different countries, there can be different norms associated with the food-ordering ritual. As travelers, we can violate both these situational (predictive) and behavioral (prescriptive) expectances. Burgoon (1993) talks about these differences in terms of three factors that drive peoples' expectations. First are the **interactant characteristics,** including age, sex, and other personality traits. Second are the **relationship characteristics,** including the nature of the relationship between the person – and, in our case, the organization. Third are the **environmental characteristics,** including cultural influences as well as social situations.

If these seem somewhat familiar, it is because they align with the SRM, which I discussed in Chapter 3. When we start with the assumption that stakeholders have expectations of organizations that are connected to their personal interests, their connection to an organization, and the larger organizational environment, then it is easier to think about the risks inherent for organizations in violating different stakeholders' expectations of the organization. When we ask "What is an issue?" in the context of issues management, we begin with the assumption that the organization has violated an expectation.

From there, we should think about two additional components associated with issues. First, we should expect that stakeholders and organizations might differ in their perspectives and interests connected to an issue. Though we discuss the complexities of environments, stakeholders, and the implications of different points of view throughout this text, suffice it to say that while organizations and stakeholders might be concerned about the same issue, their perspectives are rarely the same. As such, organizations need to be able to understand the different perspectives on issues and the likely risk to the organization of these contestable points of difference if they are to help manage the issue (Breakwell, 2000; Freberg & Palenchar, 2013; Ginzel, Kramer, & Sutton, 1993; Scott & Lane, 2000; Slovic, 1987).

Second, we should think of managing issues as distinctive from conducting a Strengths, Weaknesses, Opportunities, and Threats (SWOT) analysis because in this context, there is always inherent risk associated with emergent issues. A SWOT analysis is a general discussion of an organization's strengths, weaknesses, opportunities, and threats and is a vital part to ensuring that an organization is prepared for crises (Coombs, 2014); however, it is distinctive from issues management because issues management focuses on the weaknesses that could develop into crises.

Issues management and stewardship

If issues management is distinctive from SWOT analysis, then how should we think about it? When we adopt a stakeholder-centered view of organizations and crisis communication, then we also need to think about issues management as a process that is more than just managing an organization's risks, but also as a process that manages the relationships between organizations and their stakeholders. Heath's (2002) perspective on issues management is stakeholder centered in that he argues that it is stewardship for building, maintaining, and repairing relationships with stakeholders and stake seekers. He argues that successful issues management:

- Enhances an organization's ability to plan and manage its activities
- Enhances an organization's ability to behave in ethical and socially responsible ways, as a part of routine business
- Enhances an organization's ability to monitor its environment
- Enhances the organization's ability to develop strategic dialogue to manage relationships more effectively

However, for issues management to be successful, organizations cannot be reactionary – they must view this as an anticipatory process. In his analysis of issues management, Meng (1992) identified a five-stage issues lifecycle encompassing the potential, emerging, current, crisis, and dormant stages of an issue (see Figure 4.1). In simple terms, as the issue moves through the first four stages, it attracts more attention and becomes less manageable from the organization's point of view (Heath & Palenchar, 2009; Meng, 1992).

To borrow from a health care analogy, early detection is the best approach to managing issues, which is in both the organization's and stakeholders' interests. If an organization is able to identify issues before they are triggered by an event, whistleblower, the media, consumers, or any one of the organization's internal or external stakeholders, then the organization has more opportunities to meaningfully address the issue. However, as the issue matures, the number of engaged stakeholders, members of the public, and other influencers expands, and positions on the issue become more entrenched – meaning that the choices available to the organization necessarily shrink (Elsbach, Sutton, & Principe, 1998; Heath & Palenchar, 2009; Kernisky, 1997;

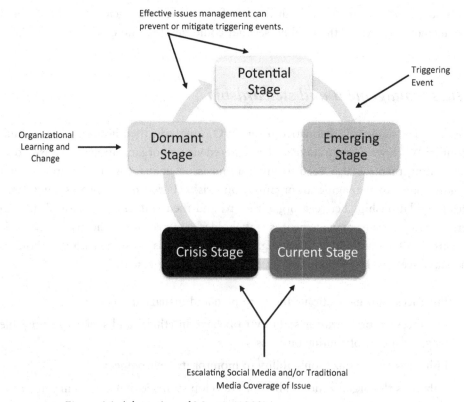

Figure 4.1 Adaptation of Meng's (1992) issues management process

Meng, 1992; Pang, Cropp, & Cameron, 2006; Seeger, Heyart, Barton, & Bultnyck, 2001).

If we think about issues management in complex environments, then organizations should be anticipating stakeholder desires related to the issues and evaluating the potential organizational impact of the issues should they develop into crises. One way to think about the role of issues management is to compare two situations discussed in Box 4.1. The case study compares the changes that accompanied China's hosting of the 2008 Summer Olympics with the emergence of Mad Cow disease in the United States in 2003. In the end, this case study also demonstrates why stakeholder stewardship is in an organization's strategic best interests.

Box 4.1 Case study: Contrasting two approaches to issues management

By Audra Diers-Lawson, Ph.D.

Let us contrast two different approaches to issues management that highlight why it is to an organization's advantage to anticipate stakeholder desires.

The 2008 Beijing Olympics prompted substantial changes in China. One of the examples of laws that were changed were a whole group of safety laws and regulations. Naturally, China knew that it would be in the world's eye in a way that they had not been before. Consequently, the new laws introduced were the outcome of lobbying by various stakeholders, including health and safety agencies as well as car manufacturers. The emerging trend reflected in the laws was increased attention being paid to health and safety concerns in Beijing – including air quality, motor vehicle safety, and traffic reduction.

One of these new laws made retrofitting car sunroofs illegal in Beijing and left a national manufacturer in trouble. The sunroof manufacturer was caught in the crossfire of stakeholder interests and was unable to respond effectively; the outcome was substantial and negative. The manufacturer failed to anticipate the law or its impact, and this meant financial ruin.

By contrast, in the United States Mad Cow disease had been on the issues management radar of the National Cattlemen's Beef Association for years when, in 2003, the first case was identified in the United States. By anticipating the event and mapping out a goal-driven response in advance, the Association was able to respond quickly. This was also helped by the fact that only one infected animal imported from Canada had been identified.

The Association's response was multilayered, including direct consultation with regulators, consumer advocacy groups, and other key stakeholders, as well

as an intensive national and international news media outreach. It also had evaluation measures ready to go – and as a result, beef demand rose by almost 8%
in 2004 and consumer confidence in US beef increased from 88% just before the
event in 2003 to 93% in 2005.

The takeaway from this is that issues management is more than just crisis
avoidance – it is about understanding how social, political, economic, and environmental expectations are shifting and being able to manage the change. When
done well, issues management can lead to increased profitability; when done
poorly, not only can it lead to crisis, but it may mean that an organization simply
cannot function.

Yet, complex environments make all of this incredibly difficult.

The issues management process

If the US National Cattlemen's Beef Association provides us with an example of good
issues management, then we can break it down into a set of assumptions about issues
management and stages in the process.

In order to devote adequate resources to issues management, then organizations
must make four assumptions about issues management.

1 **Strategic business planning:** An organization must assume that issue management
   is essential to good strategic business planning (see, e.g., Elsbach et al., 1998).
   This means that an organization must evaluate its key value proposition, identify
   its stakeholders and the stakes that matter to both the organization and its stakeholders, and then create and implement plans of action that connect all of these
   components (Acquier, Valiorgue, & Daudigeos, 2017; Baldassarre, Calabretta,
   Bocken, & Jaskiewicz, 2017; Heath, 2004).

2 **Social responsibility:** An organization must assume that it is responsible to a variety of stakeholders (Kujala & Korhonen, 2017). However, to whom the organization is responsible will vary by industry, value proposition, and an organization's
   ethics. But this assumption means that the organization believes it has some level
   of social responsibility. Remember that our definition of issue management focused
   on an organization's responsibility to be good stewards of stakeholder interests.

3 **Intelligence:** When I talk about intelligence, naturally I am talking about
   information – and how we use information to make judgments. The assumption
   is that without good intelligence, organizations cannot make good decisions. For
   example, organizations ought to understand key stakeholders and their likely

reactions to situations before making decisions (Hobbins & Enander, 2015). Similarly, organizations ought to understand key situational factors that might influence its ability to respond (Seeger et al., 2001).

4 **Strong defense, smart offense:** Good engagement and communication should be assumed to be an important part of issues management. The process is always grounded by a basic campaign approach emphasizing (a) identifying goals and key audience(s), (b) setting key measurable objectives, (c) developing a well-grounded strategy that will let you meet the measurable objectives, and (d) measurement and evaluation (Elsbach et al., 1998; Heath & Palenchar, 2009; Kernisky, 1997; Ritchie, 2004; Sung & Hwang, 2014).

While there is much work to do in order to enact and maintain an active issues management program within an organization, the process itself is very straightforward. Research from a number of scholars argues the process involves scanning, monitoring, decision-making, and evaluation (Heath & Palenchar, 2009; Palese & Crane, 2002; Regester & Larkin, 2008). So, let us have a look at the process overall and then break it down into each of its individual parts (see Figure 4.2).

Scanning

The first step in effective issues management is to apply both informal and formal research in order to develop actionable intelligence about the organization, its stakeholders, and its operational environment. Put more simply, the scanning phase in

Figure 4.2 Issues management process overview

issues management is ongoing and devoted to collecting and organizing information relevant to the organization. Scanning does not focus on analyzing the information, but instead merely developing a systematic approach for identifying information to analyze. Bridges and Nelson (2000) argue that scanning is important because it ensures the organization is prepared for emergent threats.

The central objective for scanning is to understand the organization's environment, its stakeholders, and the intersection between those (Aldoory, Kim, & Tindall, 2010; Coombs, 2004; Shepard, Betz, & O'Connell, 1997; Sutcliffe, 2001).

Bridges and Nelson (2000) identify four ways to segment an organization's environment in the scanning process:

- **Social** refers to collecting information that monitors an organization's reputation, such as what different stakeholders might be saying or feeling about the organization. For example, this could involve monitoring social media trends related to the organization or industry, conducting questionnaires or interviews with critical stakeholders, or employee satisfaction audits.

- **Economic** refers to collecting information about the economic environment from the local to the global level that reflects the economic trends, issues, and indicators that might affect the organization. For example, this could include monitoring economic publications and forecasts, financial figures for the company and industry or analyzing business news on a regular basis to identify factors likely to affect the organization.

- **Political/regulatory** refers to collecting information about trends or shifts in different administrations, governments, or regulatory environments. An example of the type of regulatory information that could be collected would be tracking new laws that would affect the ways the organization does business. Collecting political information could involve evaluating how a new head of state could influence the operational environment for the organization and monitoring political publications/broadcasts for key themes emerging.

- **Competitive** refers to collecting information about an organization's competitors. This provides intelligence about factors that are affecting the broader industry or specific competitors so that organizations may make strategic decisions about the competitive environment. Examples of this could be monitoring advocacy groups relevant to the industry, tracking news related to events competitors are facing, or identifying global trends within an industry.

From a process viewpoint, scanning is straightforward as it is about gathering information to prepare to analyze it. However, as anyone who has ever started a new project knows, it can be daunting – especially so in this case, if the organization does not have a structured approach to scanning. A critical challenge, at this stage, is information overload – finding so much information that it is not well-organized or systematically collected.

While there are many strategies for managing information overload, there are two broad recommendations to ensure that the scanning process is systematic and manageable.

- **Organizations must assess the information they already have.** There is no point in re-inventing the wheel. Most organizations already have repositories of information, news aggregators, and the like. The key at this point is data reduction, which can involve making lists and creating a simple filing system so that the information is easy to access. One practical recommendation is to create and maintain a database of searchable information. The mechanism to organize the information does not matter – it could be Microsoft Access, Excel, EndNote, or one of the many project-organizing databases. The point should be that the information is searchable and easily available.

- **Organizations must formalize a 'replicable' scanning plan.** Of course, everything that we do in communication needs to be agile, but on a regular basis, there should be an approach to scanning and gathering information that (a) establishes/ uses a clear procedure for getting information on the environment and key stakeholders, (b) has a brief rationale for the procedures so that they are transparent to anyone, (c) identifies the necessary resources that are available, and (d) streamlines the process where possible.

Scanning is often overlooked, but an effective and simple scanning plan can ensure that the best information is getting used so that the organization can monitor issues. To borrow from the adage: Garbage in is garbage out.

Monitoring

Once the routine information is collected in the scanning process, then the work of monitoring the information begins. Monitoring is often paired with scanning, and the two concepts are sometimes used interchangeably; however, it is a conceptually and pragmatically separate step from scanning. When the scanning system reveals an issue that could be emerging or have the potential to emerge, a decision to actively monitor the issue must be made.

There are nearly an infinite number of issues that organizations could monitor; however, no organization has infinite resources; therefore, monitoring is a strategic decision to devote resources to an issue. For that reason, Heath (1997) suggests that monitoring should occur only after a potential issue meets three criteria:

- The issue is growing in legitimacy as signaled by coverage by journalists and/or other opinion leaders in legacy or social media
- The issue offers a quantifiable threat relative to the organization's markets or operations
- The issue is championed by an individual, group, or institution with actual OR potential influence

If an organization is doing a good job of identifying and mapping its stakeholders (see Chapter 5), then the monitoring process is a way to connect issues with relevant stakeholders so that the organization can make informed strategic decisions about the best ways to proceed with risk mitigation. Likewise, organizations need to be able to track issues easily with information available at a glance that can be developed into strategic recommendation reports. In issues management this is often accomplished with a **risk register**. A risk register is just a log or basic database used to identify risks, their severity, and action steps that can be taken. It needs to provide a snapshot to determine what is going on in an organization's environment. Risk registers are meant to be adaptable and living documents updated regularly.

A risk register can be as simple as a Microsoft Excel spreadsheet that formalizes information about potential issues in a way that provides practitioners an at-a-glance summary of issues that organizations are facing. There are many different models and approaches to risk registers; however, they typically identify a number of qualities of issues, including brief descriptions. Risk registers are added to with each of the monitoring, evaluation, and decision-making stages of the issues management process and then used to inform the scanning process. Table 4.1 lists the information that should be captured in the risk register and updated as new intelligence becomes available.

Decision-making

The monitoring phase of the process and creation or updates to the risk register will create an evaluation of particular issues and threats; however, based on categorization and good judgment, we have to begin to allocate proper resources to managing issues. An organization's values and its culture will influence the decision-making process. For example, I would argue that ethical organizations will consider all aspects of costs and benefits. Less ethical organizations consider only profit and loss.

Prioritization is the first component of good decision-making in issues management. It determines which issues demand organizational response and, therefore, the

Table 4.1 Recommended information to capture for risk registers

Process stage	Information category	Brief explanation
Monitoring	Risk title	Provide a brief name for the risk.
	Risk description	Provide a brief description of the risk.
	Category	Identify which category it could affect, including social, economic, political, and competitor.
	Risk category	Categorize the risk. Is it primarily an issue of time, cost, scope, resources, environment, reputation, or another key category?
	Present impact	Is this currently affecting/likely to affect us in the next six months?
	Competitor impact	Is this presently affecting one or more competitor?
	Location risk	Is the operational location(s) likely to be affected?
	Internal or external	Which stakeholders are primarily affected – internal, external, or both?
	Stakeholders involved	Identify the stakeholders likely to be directly involved with issue.
	Stakeholders affected	Regardless of whether they are involved, which stakeholders are likely to be affected by the issue?
	Champions	Regardless of involvement or impact, which stakeholders are likely to champion the issue in the public eye?
	Trigger	What event(s) are likely to happen to trigger the issue's emergence?
Decision-Making	Consequences	What is the likely consequence if the risk becomes an issue? Identify any that apply, such as reputation, sales, emergency losses, strategic alliances, regulatory, or other (specify).
	Probability	Identify the likelihood that the risk will become an issue as low, medium, high, or extreme.
	Severity	Evaluate the risk to the organization's key operations as low, medium, high, or extreme.

(Continued)

Table 4.1 (Continued)

Process stage	Information category	Brief explanation
	Time scale	If the issue emerges, when is the organization likely to see the impacts (immediate, short-term, long-term, or combination)?
	Risk mitigation actions	What can/should the organization do to minimize the likelihood the risk will be triggered?
	Opportunity oosts of risk ritigation	Costs (financial, time, personnel, etc.) that the organization is likely to incur with risk mitigation recommendations.
	Residual Risk	After risk mitigation is enacted, what is the likelihood that the risk will emerge? Low, moderate, high, or extreme
	Risk mitigation owners	Who has to take the lead on risk mitigation (e.g., communications, operations, C-level, HR, etc.)?
	Contingency recommendations	What should be done if the issue emerges?
	Prioritization	What should the priority be to enact risk mitigation actions (low, moderate, high, or extreme)?
Evaluation	Measurable objectives	If action is taken to mitigate this risk, identify two to four specific and measurable objectives to evaluate success of risk mitigation efforts.
	Success threshold	Identify relative levels of success for each objective, and clarify what success means (e.g., minimizing issue emergence, improving reputation, etc.).
	Evaluation scheme	For each measurable objective, identify how it can be concretely measured.
	Issue rank	Rank the known issues listed in this register in terms of priority.
	Sources	What resources have been used to support identification, emergence of issue?
	Comments	Note any other comments to help other groups, departments initiate actions to mitigate risks based on information available

allocation of resources. Although there are many ways to analyze issues using open access and proprietary models, there are four common sense assessments of issues that should guide prioritization.

1 What are the consequences and who will have to face the consequences of the issues?

2 How likely is the issue to affect the organization?

3 How much impact will the issue have? No two issues are equal and should not be treated as such.

4 If there is any impact, when is it likely to occur? In a context of limited resources, sometimes organizations have to balance time scale, severity, and probability.

Prioritization is not a decision that is made once; issues can be moved up or down on an agenda for action or simply back for continued monitoring depending on the prioritization and urgency of the issue. Prioritization is also often determined by the stakeholders involved (Henriques & Sadorsky, 1999).

Second, organizations must assess their **strategic options**. Like any other management discipline, robust issues management strategy emerges from sound data, diverse viewpoints and ingenuity. Obtaining credible information and identifying realistic and measurable objectives provide the foundation for effective anticipatory and responsive strategy development. This is, after all, the core objective of issues management (Ashley & Morrison, 1997; Palese & Crane, 2002).

When an organization is evaluating its options, it has to try to make judgments about the types of scenarios that could happen before it makes decisions. This is why issues management is a research-intensive and information-based process. However, there is also a creative aspect to this process. Issues management analysts need to be able to take existing information and predict realistic situations that could affect the organization. Building on previous research in anticipatory risk management (see Ashley & Morrison, 1997), the decision-making process in issues management has four components:

1 Organizations must identify and choose among different risk mitigation options.

2 Organizations must identify the opportunity costs associated with risk mitigation. That is to say, if the organization allocates resources to mitigate an issue, are there other unintended consequences (positive or negative) that might emerge because of risk mitigation?

3 Organizations must identify the residual risk that remains, even after risk mitigation efforts. No plan will completely eliminate risk and all plans could create other threats, so it is essential that organizations must identify the potential side effects to risk mitigation and evaluate those in comparison with the risk itself.

4   Once risk mitigation decisions are taken, who will own the solution development and implementation? That is to say, who or what department is responsible for executing different elements of the risk mitigation plan?

The final component to the decision-making process is actually **taking action**. It may seem obvious enough, but for anyone who has been around an organization, the space between between decisions to take action and taking action can be quite a cavern. According to issues manager practitioner-expert, Tony Jacques, the greatest barriers to effective issues management are the lack of clear objectives and the unwillingness or inability to act (Jaques, 2009).

For communication practitioners, the action stage should look very familiar because it is based in creating a viable and measurable campaign. This means that to take action effectively, we must:

- Identify clear objectives – like any measurable objective, they should be concrete
- Make contingency recommendations – these must be clear and actionable
- Prioritize risk mitigation actions – we must balance risk and benefits to the actions themselves

The challenge in this process can come in a false-economy approach to decision-making. If we automatically take the less expensive or easier route, we have to ask two questions: Is the organization just going to have to make the more expensive changes later? If so, has the organization opened itself up to additional risks by not taking action? Let me offer you an example: In 2017 the United Kingdom witnessed a terrible fire in a high-rise apartment complex – Grenfell Tower. It turned out that the council, in an effort to make the complex look more attractive (it was low-income housing in a very expensive part of London) paid for cladding (siding) to be installed on the outside of the building. The particular cladding they chose was inexpensive and looked nice. The problem was that if there was a fire, this cladding could cause catastrophic damage – it held heat in and could allow fire to spread in the building's structure. This particular cladding was already illegal in many countries (e.g., the United States and Germany).

Thus, in 2017, when the worst happened – a fire in the 20-plus story building – many people living on the 14th floor and higher had no chance to escape. The loss of life was compounded because fire departments typically recommend for people in high-rise buildings to stay in their apartments in case of fire, because these build-ings are meant to be constructed so that fires are easy to contain. Sadly, the cladding made this recommendation deadly. This is a good example of decision-making that prioritized short-term financial cost against long-term risks. A calculated decision would have been made because the risks of calamity were so low – that is, while the consequences were severe, the probability was low and so in the decision calculus, it seemed a reasonable choice to make. These decisions are common – organizations worldwide weigh these considerations on a regular basis. The decisions balance economic, risk, and ethical evaluations.

It should also be clear at this stage that many of the decisions made and actions taken are beyond the remit of PR and communications professionals. While issues management often starts with public relations professionals, it also has to be a cross-functional task to ensure that the right people are making the decisions. So, while the actions that an organization takes may not be directly related to communication, communications professionals almost always a part of the process because whether the strategy is entirely internal or external, or most likely a combination of both – communication is always a part of the action stage and often involved throughout the decision-making process.

Evaluation

After actions are taken, there is an evaluation stage. The issues management process begins and ends with data or intelligence. At the heart of it, this process – like all strategic communication efforts – should also be a learning process in which we better understand what went well, so that we know what we should replicate in the future and what needs to be addressed now or should be addressed differently in the future. Think of the evaluation stage as the bridge to the ongoing issues management process that wraps up particular actions taken so that the organization can assess and add the outcomes to its scanning, monitoring, and decision-making in the future.

The evaluation stage does not necessarily come last in a sequence. Planning how relative levels of success can be measured, evaluated, and lessons learned developed is an inherent part of each of the stages. However, the evaluation stage formalizes and executes the logics and ethics of enacting recommendations throughout the process. There are three critical components to evaluation: creating measurable objectives, evaluating success, and capturing lessons from successes and failures.

First, setting clear and measurable objectives lays out the thresholds for evaluating the relative success of the issues management process. These should be aligned with the goals set up in the decision-making process, and tied to the risks identified earlier. In short, just as with everything else that we do, we begin by establishing what matters and how we know whether we were successful.

While the details in evaluating the success of issues management initiatives will vary as much as the issues themselves, measurable objectives in issues management should evaluate actions to mitigate the risk and identify the relative success thresholds for risk mitigation actions.

Second, identifying our evaluation scheme identifies the strategy we will use to evaluate our measurable objectives. Practitioners today have access to more measurement tools than ever before; the challenge is to find the tools that best fit the set objectives. For example, measuring the extent and tone of media coverage is meaningful only if one of the pursued objectives is to secure specific media attention in terms of volume, channels, tone, and so on. Other objectives – such as influencing the drafting of legislation, positioning the organization effectively in relation to an industry-wide problem, or correcting allegations about a product or service – all require different metrics. As such, for each objective, the task is to identify how it can be measured and the types of information required. Additionally, how the organization can access the information should also be identified.

Third, capturing lessons learned from failures and successes is vital to informing ongoing organizational strategy. In truth, this is probably the most important in an ongoing issues management program because this informs the other three stages. For what went well, what aspects of the process should be replicated in the future? For what went poorly, what were the problems and how can they be mitigated in the future?

Naturally, lessons learned are not applicable only to issues management; there will also be real tangible management, leadership, communication, and material lessons learned from each issue managed – no matter whether it was poorly managed or effectively managed. When organizations clearly demonstrate that they have listened, made changes, and improved, that carries weight with people (Huzey, Betts, & Vicari, 2014). In short, evaluation must be an authentic activity in which the organization reflects on what it can do better in the future versus simply trying to make itself look good. In the end, issues management cannot be about putting lipstick on a pig.

In review . . .

The purpose of this chapter was to introduce readers to issues management as a concrete process that organizations can and should use to not only manage the complexity of their environment, but to mitigate or minimize issues and crises as they are triggered.

Review your understanding

By the end of this chapter, you should be able to understand and explain the following.

- The concepts of issues management, expectancy violation, issues management, and stewardship

- The assumptions about the issues management process
- The approach to issues management, including:
  - Scanning
  - Monitoring
  - Decision-making
  - Evaluation
- What a risk register is and how it can be approached in issues management

References

Acquier, A., Valiorgue, B., & Daudigeos, T. (2017). Sharing the shared value: A transaction cost perspective on strategic CSR policies in global value chains. *Journal of Business Ethics*, *144*(1), 139–152.

Aldoory, L., Kim, J.-N., & Tindall, N. (2010). The influence of perceived shared risk in crisis communication: Elaborating the situational theory of publics. *Public Relations Review*, *36*(2), 134–140.

Ashley, W. C., & Morrison, J. L. (1997). Anticipatory management: Tools for better decision making. *Futurist*, *31*(5), 47–51.

Baldassarre, B., Calabretta, G., Bocken, N., & Jaskiewicz, T. (2017). Bridging sustainable business model innovation and user-driven innovation: A process for sustainable value proposition design. *Journal of Cleaner Production*, *147*, 175–186.

Breakwell, G. M. (2000). Risk communication: Factors affecting impact. *British Medical Bulletin*, *56*(1), 110–120.

Bridges, J. A., & Nelson, R. A. (2000). Issues management: A relational approach. In E. J. Ki, J. N. Kim., & J. A. Ledingham (Eds.), *Public relations as relationship management: A relational approach to the study practice of public relations* (pp. 95–115). Hillsdale, NJ: Lawrence Erlbaum Associates.

Burgoon, J. K. (1993). Interpersonal expectations, expectancy violations, and emotional communication. *Journal of Language and Social Psychology*, *12*(1–2), 30–48.

Coombs, W. T. (2004). Impact of past crises on current crisis communication: Insights from Situational Crisis Communication Theory. *Journal of Business Communication*, *41*(3), 265–290.

Coombs, W. T. (2014). *Ongoing crisis communication: Planning, managing, and responding.* Thousand Oaks, CA: Sage Publications.

Elsbach, K. D., Sutton, R. I., & Principe, K. E. (1998). Averting expected challenges through anticipatory impression management: A study of hospital billing. *Organization Science*, *9*(1), 68–86.

Freberg, K., & Palenchar, M. J. (2013). Convergence of digital negotiation and risk challenges: Strategic implications of social media for risk and crisis communications. In H. S. N. Al-Deen & J. A. Hendricks (Eds.), *Social media and strategic communications* (pp. 83–100). London: Palgrave Macmillan.

Ginzel, L. E., Kramer, R. M., & Sutton, R. I. (1993). Organizational impression management as a reciprocal influence process: The neglected role of the organizational audience. *Research in Organizational Behavior, 15,* 227–266.

Heath, R. L. (2002). Issues management: Its past, present, and future. *Journal of Public Affairs, 2*(2), 209–214.

Heath, R. L. (2004). Crisis preparation: Planning for the inevitable. In D. P. Millar & R. L. Heath (Eds.), *Responding to crisis: A rhetorical approach to crisis communication* (pp. 33–35). Mahwah, NJ: Lawrence Erlbaum Associates.

Heath, R. L., & Gay, C. D. (1997). Risk communication: Involvement, uncertainty and control's effect on information scanning and monitoring by expert stakeholders. *Management Communication Quarterly, 10*(3), 342–359.

Heath, R. L., & Palenchar, M. J. (2009). *Strategic issues management* (2nd ed.). Thousand Oaks, CA: Sage Publications.

Henriques, I., & Sadorsky, P. (1999). The relationship between environmental commitment and managerial perceptions of stakeholder importance. *Academy of Management Journal, 42*(1), 87–99.

Hobbins, J., & Enander, A. (2015). Citizens and contingencies – Swedish crisis managers' views of the public. *International Journal of Mass Emergencies & Disasters, 33*(3).

Huzey, D., Betts, S. C., & Vicari, V. (2014). Learning the hard way vs. vicarious learning: Post crisis learning for small business. *Journal of Management and Marketing Research, 15,* 1.

Jaques, T. (2009). Issue and crisis management: Quicksand in the definitional landscape. *Public Relations Review, 35*(3), 280–286.

Kernisky, D. A. (1997). Proactive crisis management and ethical discourse: Dow Chemical's issues management bulletins 1979–1990. *Journal of Business Ethics, 16*(8), 843–853.

Kujala, J., & Korhonen, A. (2017). Value-creating stakeholder relationships in the context of CSR. In R. E. Freeman, J. Kujala, & S. Sachs (Eds.), *Stakeholder engagement: Clinical research cases* (pp. 63–85). Cham, Switzerland: Springer.

Meng, M. (1992). Early identification aids issues management. *The Public Relations Journal, 48*(3), 22.

Palese, M., & Crane, T. Y. (2002). Building an integrated issue management process as a source of sustainable competitive advantage. *Journal of Public Affairs, 2*(4), 284–292.

Pang, A., Cropp, F., & Cameron, G. T. (2006). Corporate crisis planning: Tensions, issues, and contradictions. *Journal of Communication Management, 10*(4), 371–389.

Regester, M., & Larkin, J. (2008). *Risk issues and crisis management in public relations: A casebook of best practice.* London: Kogan Page Publishers.

Ritchie, B. W. (2004). Chaos, crises and disasters: A strategic approach to crisis management in the tourism industry. *Tourism Management*, *25*(6), 669–683.

Scott, S. G., & Lane, V. R. (2000). A stakeholder approach to organizational identity. *Academy of Management Review*, *25*(1), 43–65.

Seeger, M. W., Heyart, B., Barton, E. A., & Bultnyck, S. (2001). Crisis planning and crisis communication in the public schools: Assessing post Columbine responses. *Communication Research Reports*, *18*(4), 375–383.

Shepard, J. M., Betz, M., & O'Connell, L. (1997). The proactive corporation: Its nature and causes. *Journal of Business Ethics*, *16*(10), 1001–1011.

Slovic, P. (1987). Perception of risk. *Science*, *236*, 280–285.

Sung, M., & Hwang, J.-S. (2014). Who drives a crisis? The diffusion of an issue through social networks. *Computers in Human Behavior*, *36*, 246–257. doi:10.1016/j.chb.2014.03.063

Sutcliffe, K. M. (2001). Organizational environments and organizational information processing. In F. M. Jablin & L. L. Putnam (Eds.), *The new handbook of organizational communication: Advances in theory, research, and method* (pp. 197–230). Thousand Oaks, CA: Sage Publications.

From friends to frenemies

Mapping an organization's stakeholders

Learning objectives

By the end of this chapter, the reader should:

- Be familiar with a practical tool for mapping stakeholders
- Be able to evaluate the implications of the stakeholder mapping process on issues management and crisis communication

In crisis communication research and practice, the stakeholder perspective is still being developed; yet, it is acknowledged as central to an organization's success in managing both issues and crises, as I have discussed throughout Part 1 and certainly in Chapter 4. In fact, the heart of the stakeholder relationship module is the stakeholder perspective, but the question remains: How do we understand the connections between organizations, issues, and stakeholders in a real-world context?

The purpose of this chapter is to focus on how an organization can map its stakeholders to more effectively prioritize the mutual needs of the organization and stakeholders in a competitive environment. Let us make two very safe assumptions as we proceed:

- No organization has infinite resources
- No organization can perfectly attend to the needs of all of its potential stakeholders at any given time

This is the reality that all organizations face: They must make strategic decisions about how to manage their relationships with different stakeholders who often have radically divergent issues and interests. This is also what complicates the concept of stewardship that is discussed in Chapter 4; while an organization might want to make the best decision for all stakeholders, there can be 'winners' and 'losers' based on an organization's priorities.

Mapping a dynamic stakeholder environment

In Chapter 3, I pointed out that organizations deal with complex environments because they serve a range of stakeholder interests that include internal and external stakeholders. Additionally, organizations face multiple layers of stakeholders, meaning that they serve the stakeholders in their own buildings as well as those potentially on the other side of the world. If we can imagine the overlapping and diverging interests with just a few stakeholders, we might see something like Figure 5.1.

If success in issues and crisis management relies on anticipating stakeholder interests and needs, then simply identifying stakeholders does not provide an organization with actionable intelligence or a way to prioritize stakeholder interests. What is needed is a research-based process that allows an organization to understand its stakeholders and the stakes at any given time, yet is still flexible enough to account for changes in stakeholders and their relationship with the organization.

Stakeholder mapping is a way to begin this process. If we map stakeholders or those groups with an interest in an organization's actions, we can better understand the complexity of a particular organization's environment as well as the risks posed

Figure 5.1 A sample of stakeholder complexity

by that environment and changes within it. This process relies on understanding a few well-researched concepts – stakeholder power, legitimacy, relational history, urgency, and relational valence (Lovejoy, Waters, & Saxton, 2012; Mitchell, Agle, & Wood, 1997; Slabbert & Barker, 2014) – which I will discuss in detail in this chapter.

Stakeholder mapping lets us better understand that when we think about stakeholders, we should not think about them in isolation – it is vital to understand that an organization's stakeholders also themselves have stakeholders. For example, in a 1998 study of the Zapatista movement in Mexico, Schultz (1998) found that the movement's success had less to do with its military strength than it had to do with the strength of its support from individuals and associations that were not explicitly a part of the movement, but a part of the community. These findings suggest that the connections amongst members of a 'community' can be a determining feature in the strength of that community's advocacy for or against an organization (Fawcett et al., 1995).

Stakeholder networks are able to facilitate a number of different types of organizational outcomes, so they have been described as vital resources for any organization (Gulati, 1999). As such, the nature and quality of the connections between an organization and its stakeholders – as well as the ways in which the organization engages its stakeholders – is likely to influence reactions to emergent issues and crises as well as reactions to the organization itself (Barringer & Harrison, 2000; Freeman, 1994; Hossain, Murshed, & Uddin, 2013; Parker, 2008; Wukich & Mergel, 2015). Therefore, interactions with stakeholders never happen in isolation, rather in a web of interactions: Stakeholder groups interact with each other as well as with the organization (Rowley, 1997). But we have to begin somewhere, so we begin with the organization, as in Figure 5.2.

Stakeholder power

Not surprisingly, one of the first factors that ought to be considered in mapping stakeholders is **power**. There are many ways to think about power, from mutual respect to a Machiavellian notion of forcing someone to do something they would not otherwise do. However, most research on power in organizational contexts focuses on whether stakeholders have direct influence over the organization's decisions (see, e.g., Mitchell et al., 1997).

Figure 5.2 Beginning the stakeholder mapping process

In mapping powerful stakeholders, those with greater influence would be mapped on the left half of Figure 5.3 and those with less on the right. A stakeholder can be mapped as powerful if it can impose its influence in a couple of primary manners.

First, it can exert **direct imposition of its will** on the organization. Direct imposition of a stakeholder's will can come through a number of mechanisms, such as regulatory compliance or consumer activism (e.g., boycotts). For example, in the United States several Fox News presenters have lost their jobs over the years because consumers targeted the advertisers on their shows to pressure the network to withdraw advertising dollars from the controversial shows – and this strategy worked. Alternatively, when negotiating opening stores in Southeast Asia, IKEA petitioned the government(s) for improved infrastructure, living wages for anyone connected to the improvements and to IKEA (not just its own employees), and a few other points related to sustainability and employee conditions. Because of the financial benefits to IKEA's presence in these regions, the authorities agreed to IKEA's requests. Likewise, any government can place regulations (e.g., taxes, safety, and so on) on organizations as well. These are all examples of what I mean by the direct imposition of a stakeholder's will on an organization that forces compliance.

Second, stakeholders can impose their will through **utilitarian or practical means**. That is, stakeholders may influence organizations because it is mutually beneficial if the organization meets the stakeholders' requests. Similarly, many companies form strategic alliances with nonprofit or nongovernmental organizations because the nonprofit receives needed money or visibility from the organization and the organization's reputation and reach can be improved through the mutually beneficial relationship. This was the case with the Barcelona Football Club in its partnership with UNICEF. The club provided UNICEF with financial support, and by placing UNICEF's name on its jerseys and having players like Lionel Messi act as spokespersons for the charity,

Figure 5.3 Power in the stakeholder mapping process

the club demonstrated its goodwill and social responsibility. Both organizations win. However, being in that relationship can also mean that each organization is able to influence the other because they are joined by mutual interest and benefit.

Stakeholder legitimacy

Legitimacy should be thought of as an organization's recognition that the stakeholder group has a viable interest in the operation or actions of the organization (see e.g., Mitchell et al., 1997; Rowley, 1997). Legitimacy does not suggest that the organization 'likes' the stakeholders; rather, that it acknowledges that the interest that the stakeholders have in the organization, its actions, and/or its advocacy is fair and valid.

In mapping legitimacy in Figure 5.4, those stakeholders above the horizontal axis would be viewed as having legitimate interests in the organization, whereas those stakeholders that the organization would view as illegitimate would be mapped below the line.

Of course, the social and cultural values that ground the organization will influence whether stakeholder claims are viewed as legitimate or not. For example, in the Nordic countries and Germany, where labor unions often collaborate with companies, the interest that the unions have in the way an organization treats its employees is likely to be viewed as legitimate. By contrast, in countries like the United States (where trade unions are often viewed as adversarial to corporate objectives), the interests that unions have in organizations are much less likely to be viewed as legitimate. Beyond national trends, it is also vital to understand the organizational culture of any organization in order to correctly make determinations about whether the organization would perceive a stakeholder's interest in the organization as legitimate or not.

Figure 5.4 Legitimacy in the stakeholder mapping process

An organization's ethics and values will therefore provide guidance as to how it will interpret any particular stakeholder's interest in its operations (Jensen, 2002; Trice & Beyer, 1993).

Relational history

Relationship history simply asks the question of whether or not an organization directly 'knows' a stakeholder. Those stakeholders who are known to an organization, in this context, are those with whom the organization has had direct dealings and interactions, like their employees, primary consumers or business partners, known regulators, and so on. However, in many cases, organizations may be aware that stakeholders exist but have had no previous dealings with them; in other cases, a stakeholder may have an interest in the organization, but the organization is completely unaware of its existence.

In mapping relational history in Figure 5.5, those stakeholders above the line are those known to the organization – that is, those with whom the organization has had dealings and a proper relationship history. Those stakeholders below the line represent those with whom the organization has no prior direct deals and/or may not be aware have an interest in the organization. It is certainly in an organization's best interests to be aware of as many stakeholders as possible if it is to be successful in stewarding stakeholder interests (Freeman, 1994; Heath, 1994; Scott, Brandow, Hobbins, Nilsson, & Enander, 2015). Therefore, the issues management and stakeholder mapping process should reduce the number of stakeholders that organizations are completely unaware of – but there will always be some that remain.

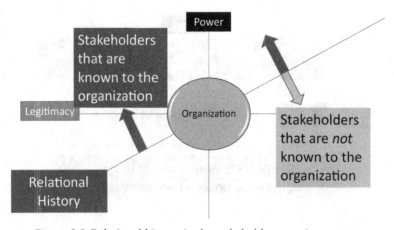

Figure 5.5 Relational history in the stakeholder mapping process

If we think about the way that we use the most public of our social media plat-forms, such as Instagram or Twitter, it can help make relational history clear. If we are active on these social media platforms, we will have followers that we know personally – our friends, family, and colleagues. For the most part, these are the peo-ple that we interact with most often and we know how they are going to react to any particular post that we have. Over time we are also likely to accumulate followers that we have never met – these are people who might like the types of posts or images we share, topics we are interested in, and so forth. It is possible that we could get to know these new people over time, or we may never really get to know them, but what can connect us are mutual interests. In an organizational environment (and not just in social media), there will be people, groups, and organizations that have a connection to an organization but have never made themselves specifically known. Yet, what is likely to activate different groups without a relational history are particular issues. That is also why relational history is more than just whether a stakeholder is known, but whether an organization has a specific relationship with them or not.

Relational valence

Organizations also have stakeholders they like and dislike – their friends and foes. This is where we come back to the distinction that I made earlier with regards to legitimacy: We can recognize a stakeholder's interest as being appropriate based on an organization's mission, but this does not mean that an organization necessarily 'likes' the stakeholder.

In mapping **relational valence** in Figure 5.6, those stakeholders that the organiza-tion prefers to build, manage, and/or repair relationships with would be placed above

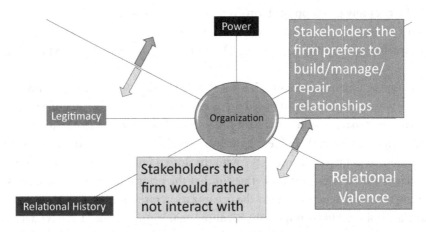

Figure 5.6 Relational valence in the stakeholder mapping process

the line and those stakeholders the organization would rather not interact with would be below the line.

If an organization values a stakeholder - or at least what a positive relationship with the stakeholder offers – then it is going to be more likely to prioritize interactions with the stakeholder and attend to that stakeholder's interests more willingly than those that it does not value (Jaakkola & Alexander, 2014; Jensen, 2002). However, that does not mean that the stakeholders that an organization does not like get ignored; in fact, organizations often seek strategic alliances with stakeholders they may not like because of the value they offer the organization (Daboub, 2002; Das & Rahman, 2010; Heinze, Uhlmann, & Diermeier, 2014). The adage that we should keep our friends close, but our enemies closer is often applied in managing stakeholder relationships. For example, in the oil and gas industry, environmental advocates are probably not the first stakeholders most would guess the industry would 'like'; however, there are increasing numbers of projects and partnerships occurring between the two because of mutual interest. So, relational valence tells us who an organization's most favored stakeholders are, but not necessarily which stakeholders it will interact with the most. Therein lies the key distinction between legitimacy and valance. Both are important to know when mapping stakeholders, but these are the different ways to understanding an organization's disposition towards a stakeholder.

Urgency

Finally, not all stakeholder interests will be viewed equally at any given time by an organization. The previous characteristics of power, legitimacy, history, and valence capture a snapshot of the nature of a relationship between an organization and its stakeholders at any given point. However, one of the principal differences in an organization's motivation to manage stakeholder interests is the timeliness of their interests or **urgency** (Connolly, Conlon, & Deutsch, 1980; Heath, 1994; Mitchell et al., 1997).

In mapping urgency in Figure 5.7, those stakeholders with the most important of interests – which can be defined based on timeliness, severity of impact on stakeholder, or severity of impact on the organization – should be mapped closer to the organization, whereas those stakeholders with less urgency can be placed further from the organization, as depicted in Figure 5.7 with the dotted lines. A stakeholder's urgency is also a matter of the organization's ethics in that the prioritization of competing stakeholder interests will depend on how the organization rates or evaluates the importance of that stakeholder. This is important because organizations cannot always accommodate all stakeholder interests equally. Does an organization define its shareholders as

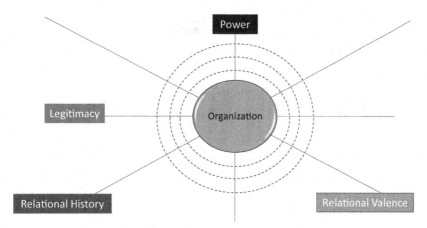

Figure 5.7 Urgency in the stakeholder mapping process

having the most urgency, or its employees or consumers as having the most urgency? The mapping process does not predict how an organization will set its priorities, but it does indicate that prioritization happens.

In this way, as organizations must make strategic choices about resource allocation, urgency can help to identify those stakeholders with concerns that are the most important so that their needs can be met first. For example, in medical triage after any kind of disaster the patients whose injuries are life-threatening are treated first, and so on, until those with only minor injuries are treated. This is necessary to ensure that doctors can manage their time in a way that ensures the greatest survival rate. In an organizational environment, during issues management, understanding stakeholder urgency is a way to help organizations mitigate or even prevent crises from emerging, and in a crisis environment to prioritize which stakeholder interests are managed first.

Classifying stakeholders once they are mapped

Based on this mapping exercise, an organization's stakeholders can be classified as **strategic, desirable, dangerous,** or **moral** (see Figure 5.8). Along with this classification come implications for stakeholder relationship, issue, and crisis management. It is important to note, this process is meant to map an organization's stakeholders at a given moment; as such, it allows organizations to document and track their relationships with critical stakeholders across time with additional mapping exercises.

While the visual map shown in Figure 5.8 is useful as an occasional exercise, for more routine tracking a simple spreadsheet or data base (see Table 5.1) allows

Figure 5.8 Stakeholder classifications in the stakeholder mapping process

Table 5.1 Routine stakeholder mapping with a spreadsheet or database

Stakeholder Name	Date	Internal/ External	Rate the Urgency of Stakeholder Needs 1 (low) to 7 (high)	Power: Does the stakeholder have direct influence over your organization's decision-making? Yes or No	Legitimacy: Do you believe the stakeholder's interest in your organization is appropriate/ necessary? Yes or No	Valence: Is this a stakeholder your organization would prefer to regularly interact with? Yes or No	Relational History: Is this a stakeholder your organization has a history of interacting with? Yes or No

professionals to easily update information, developments, and track all aspects of the organization's relationships with its stakeholders in the context of the organization's strategic objectives, environment, and issues affecting it. This makes the spreadsheet or data base a useful tool for routine stakeholder and issues tracking.

Strategic stakeholders

Strategic stakeholders are those stakeholders that have legitimacy, power, and a clear relational history with the organization, but may not necessarily be liked by the organization. Regardless of the positive or negative valence, these are stakeholders that an organization knows it must work with in order to achieve its key objectives.

For example, a company like Coca-Cola may have a number of stakeholders that it must interact with in order to manage its obligations and achieve its goals, such as its consumers, employees, water conservancy groups, suppliers, and governments. All of these stakeholders require engagement and management, but not all will get the same amount of attention, nor may all be liked by Coca-Cola; yet, depending on the situation and requirements, they are all likely to contribute to Coca-Cola's overall success.

Desirable stakeholders

Desirable stakeholders are those the organization likes and believes have legitimate interests in the business, but may not have a direct relational history with; however, they are also stakeholders that lack direct power over the organization. Identifying what desirable stakeholders care about, and how the organization might be able to support the stakeholder interests in a way that is aligned with the organization's priorities and goals, can create strategic opportunities for organizations.

This kind of alignment of interests between organizations and desirable stakeholders often represents social responsibility initiatives taken on by organizations. For example, Nando's is a popular restaurant chain in the United Kingdom, but was founded in South Africa and has outlets in 35 different countries. It supports a number of charitable endeavors such as fighting malaria and reducing waste that target support for communities in South Africa and other developing regions. This certainly represents an opportunity for the company to improve its reputation, but it also allows the company to build relationships with the communities from which it sources its ingredients (like its chilies) that extend beyond just a formal business relationship. Nando's may not have a strong relationship history with each of the communities, but the stakeholders are readily identifiable.

Moral stakeholders

Moral stakeholders are, by definition, those that an organization does not explicitly have a relationship with and whose concerns are not viewed as legitimate – often because they may not be clear and well defined. We can typically think about these as broadly the 'general public.' Moral stakeholders may not be relevant nor activated until an issue or crisis emerges to which they are connected. At this point, the organization may not be aware of them; however, they are likely to be aware of the organization.

However, while these may not be stakeholders that are segmented and known by an organization, organizations are still likely to communicate with them indirectly through advertising, social media, and networks of relationships with their other known stakeholders. Certainly, in a social media age the proportion of moral stakeholders has probably shrunk because organizations can better define and segment its 'publics' into other categories – especially the desirable stakeholders with whom the organization has no pre-existing relationship. Despite this, the 'public' still remains an important conceptual group because the way that an organization regards the 'public' can provide important information about the organization's values and approach it may take when managing crises that emerge.

Dangerous stakeholders

The final – and sometimes most interesting – stakeholder group are the dangerous stakeholders. These are groups that have power, but are most definitely not liked by the organization nor are their interests in the organization defined as 'legitimate' by the organization. It is also very possible that an organization may not have a clearly defined relational history with all of the groups who could affect or influence it.

One of the critical functions of issues management and risk assessment is to identify groups and issues that could affect the organization and plan for those groups' needs and the issues if they become triggered. As a risk mitigation exercise, understanding an organization's greatest threats is vital if it is to mitigate or at least minimize the impact of emergent issues and crises.

In review . . .

The purpose of this chapter was to introduce readers to a practical and research-grounded approach to developing actionable intelligence about an organization's stakeholders that complements both issues and crisis management. When an organization understands its relationship with its stakeholders, it can better make strategic decisions about the best actions to manage and maintain those relationships over time and during problems and crises. How an organization manages, values, or even defines those relationships is going to be dependent on the organization's culture and ethics.

Review your understanding

By the end of this chapter, you should be able to understand and explain the following.

- Why stakeholder mapping is an important risk and crisis mitigation function for organizations
- Factors influencing an organization's perspective on stakeholders, including:
  - Stakeholder power
  - Stakeholder legitimacy
  - Relational history
  - Relational valence
  - Stakeholder urgency
- Be able to classify and explain the implications of stakeholders once they are mapped as:
  - Strategic stakeholders
  - Desirable stakeholders
  - Moral stakeholders
  - Dangerous stakeholders

References

Barringer, B. R., & Harrison, J. S. (2000). Walking a tightrope: Creating value through interorganizational relationships. *Journal of Management*, 26(3), 367–388.

Connolly, T., Conlon, E. J., & Deutsch, S. J. (1980). Organizational effectiveness: A multiple-constituency approach. *Academy of Management Journal*, 5(2), 211–217.

Daboub, A. J. (2002). Strategic alliances, network organizations, and ethical. *SAM Advanced Management Journal* (Autumn), 40–63.

Das, T. K., & Rahman, N. (2010). Determinants of partner opportunism in strategic alliances: A conceptual framework. *Journal of Business & Psychology*, 25(1), 55–75. doi:10.1007/s10869-009-9132-2

Fawcett, S. B., Paine-Andrews, A., Francisco, V. T., Schultz, J. A., Richter, K. P., Lewis, R. K., . . . Lopez, C. M. (1995). Using empowerment theory in collaborative partnerships for community health and development. *American Journal of Community Psychology*, 23(5), 677–691.

Freeman, R. E. (1994). *Ethical theory and business*. Englewood Cliffs, NJ: Prentice Hall.

Gulati, R. (1999). Network location and learning: The influence of network resources and firm capabilities on alliance formation. *Strategic Management Journal, 20*(3), 394–414.

Heath, R. L. (1994). *Management of corporate communication: From interpersonal contacts to external affairs.* Hillsdale, NJ: Lawrence Erlbaum Associates.

Heinze, J., Uhlmann, E. L., & Diermeier, D. (2014). Unlikely allies: Credibility transfer during a corporate crisis. *Journal of Applied Social Psychology, 44*(5), 392–397. doi:10.1111/jasp.12227

Hossain, L., Murshed, S. T., & Uddin, S. (2013). Communication network dynamics during organizational crisis. *Journal of Informetrics, 7*(1), 16–35. doi:10.1016/j.joi.2012.07.006

Jaakkola, E., & Alexander, M. (2014). The role of customer engagement behavior in value co-creation: A service system perspective. *Journal of Service Research, 17*(3), 247–261. doi:10.1177/1094670514529187

Jensen, M. C. (2002). Value maximization, stakeholder theory, and the corporate objective function. *Business Ethics Quarterly, 12*(2), 235–257.

Lovejoy, K., Waters, R. D., & Saxton, G. D. (2012). Engaging stakeholders through Twitter: How nonprofit organizations are getting more out of 140 characters or less. *Public Relations Review, 38*, 313–318. doi:10.1016/j.pubrev.2012.01.005

Mitchell, R. K., Agle, B. R., & Wood, D. J. (1997). Toward a theory of stakeholder identification and salience: Defining the principle of who and what really counts. *Academy of Management Review, 22*(4), 852–886.

Parker, J. (2008). Using informal networks to encourage change at BP. *Strategic Communication Management, 13*(1), 24–27.

Rowley, T. J. (1997). Moving beyond dyadic ties: A network theory of stakeholder influences. *Academy of Management Review, 22*(4), 887–910.

Schulz, M. S. (1998). Collective action across borders: Opportunity structures, network capacities, and communicative praxis in the age of advanced globalization. *Sociological Perspectives, 41*(3), 587–616.

Scott, D., Brandow, C., Hobbins, J., Nilsson, S., & Enander, A. (2015). Capturing the citizen perspective in crisis management exercises: Possibilities and challenges. *International Journal of Emergency Services, 4*(1), 86–102. doi:10.1108/IJES-12-2014-0024

Slabbert, Y., & Barker, R. (2014). Towards a new model to describe the organisation – Stakeholder relationship-building process: A strategic corporate communication perspective. *Communicatio, 40*(1), 69–97. doi:10.1080/02500167.2014.875481

Trice, H. M., & Beyer, J. M. (1993). *The cultures of work organizations.* Upper Saddle River, NJ: Prentice Hall.

Wukich, C., & Mergel, I. (2015). Closing the citizen-government communication gap: Content, audience, and network analysis of government tweets. *Journal of Homeland Security and Emergency Management, 12*(3), 707–735.

6 Playing the blame game to classify types

Learning objectives

By the end of this chapter, the reader should:

- Understand the influence of 'blame' and crisis severity on attitudes about organizations and crises
- Introduce an approach for classifying crises based on blame

In Chapter 5 I focused on mapping an organization's stakeholders. Not only does this process help throughout the issues management process, but also it provides valuable intelligence if and when crises emerge. Having a strong understanding of our organization's stakeholder networks helps us to understand which stakeholders are going to be activated and in what ways. However, a vital factor that affects stakeholder reaction to crises is, of course, the nature of the crisis itself.

As crises emerge, the type of crisis can reveal much about the risks posed to the organization by the crisis, as well as potential stakeholder reactions to the situation and organization. It can also help guide crisis response strategies (Coombs, 2007; Diers-Lawson, 2017a; Pearson & Mitroff, 1993; Seeger & Ulmer, 2002). Before making practical recommendations about how an organization should respond to the crisis, practitioners have to know what kind of a situation they are managing. Thus, the purpose of this chapter is to focus on a research-grounded approach to classifying crises that will ultimately help us to understand response expectations from different stakeholder groups.

Blame and crisis severity

Why focus on blame and crisis severity? In the field of crisis communication, under-standing the situation is typically viewed as essential for selecting the best response strategy; in particular, the literature defines the attribution of blame for a crisis as a central factor to determine appropriate organizational response (Coombs & Holla-day, 1996, 2002; Hearit, 1999; Pearson & Mitroff, 1993). Blame attribution should be thought of as stakeholder evaluations of the 'fault' for the crisis or the degree to which they hold the organization directly accountable for the crisis (Brown & Ki, 2013; Lee, 2004). Previous literature on blame attribution suggests that blame attribution is essential to understanding the selection of particular messages (Kim, 2013).

In addition, traditional persuasion and psychological theories like the the-ory of planned behavior (Ajzen, 2005) the extended parallel process model (Witte, 1992), or social cognitive theory (Bandura, 1986) all strongly indicate that a stakeholder's perception of the severity of the situation will influence what kinds of messages they find persuasive, especially in situations that are likely to heighten negative emotions like fear and anger. These negative emotions are much more likely to occur during crises because crises create a sense of uncertainty and frustration (Rickard, McComas, Clarke, Stedman, & Decker, 2013) – and if an organization is clearly at fault, that will provide a point of focus for negative emotions. This is a core reason why crises represent a critical threat to an organi-zation's reputation: When negative emotions about an organization are invoked because of a crisis, stakeholders are naturally more likely to blame the organiza-tion (Diers-Lawson, 2017b; Jin, 2009, 2010) and its reputation is likely to suffer. As a result, responders will change their crisis response strategy to adapt to their perception of different levels of stakeholder blame attribution in the situation (Brown & White, 2010; Bundy & Pfarrer, 2015; Kim, Kim, & Cameron, 2009; Ping, Ishaq, & Li, 2015). But from a stakeholder perspective, there are also sub-stantially different stakeholder needs based on the impact a crisis may have in their lives. Thus, understanding blame attribution allows us to both better con-sider stakeholder perception of risks and anticipate crisis response needs (Covello, 2002; Sellnow & Sellnow, 2014).

For these reasons, the research connected to crisis and persuasion tell us that blame and severity make sense as the two most important factors that influence how stakeholders will evaluate crises and the organizations involved with them. Moreover, the types of crises discussed in this chapter represent the four contexts most consis-tently studied in crisis communication management.

Typology of crisis types

Different authors will talk about different typologies for crises. However, for me the types of crises discussed in this chapter not only best complement the body of research connecting crisis, type, stakeholders, and crisis response but also represent a very concrete way to understand crisis type. This approach was first introduced in my chapter in the *Oxford Research Encyclopedia of Intergroup Communication* (Diers-Lawson, 2017a) and was an update on an earlier piece where I introduced a crisis typology (Diers & Tomaino, 2010) based on research from Coombs and Holladay (2012) that introduced reputational crises as distinctive type of crisis. Undoubtedly, as we better understand crises and stakeholder engagement in years to come, we will be better able to fine-tune our discussion. Moreover, it is important to differentiate between primary and secondary crises. A **primary crisis** is the triggering crisis for an organization: What actually caused the crisis's emergence? However, crises are often multilayered, with new and different crises emerging that are directly tied to the primary crisis but are caused by other related factors – including the organization's response to the primary crisis. These are **secondary crises**. The typology presented is equally applicable to both primary and secondary crises, but we will focus most of our discussion on the primary crisis and explore crises as transgressions, events, disasters, and reputational attacks, thus representing the most up-to-date and stakeholder-centric typology.

Transgressions

What is a **transgression**? As the name suggests, the organization is materially to blame for the situation – that is, the organization has done something wrong. While transgressions vary in the potential impact on stakeholders, we should assume some stakeholder perception of severity for any transgression. By far, transgressions are most studied crisis type in the field because they are the basis for the most legislation, most liability, and most likely reputational damage for organizations. I should note that just because an organization commits a transgression, it is not a villain, just that fault is clearly attributable to the organization. Let us examine examples of transgressions from Table 6.1 in more detail to better understand the range of factors to consider with transgressions. While I will not discuss each in detail, there are examples throughout.

As Table 6.1 demonstrates, transgressions range from intentional to unintentional acts, which is why we should not think of organizations that commit transgressions as villains – they may be, but in many cases, there are unintentional acts or carelessness

Table 6.1 Transgression types, definitions, and examples

Illegal corporate behavior	**Definition:** Activities that, regardless of whether they are intentional or unintentional, are illegal and done for the organization's benefit

Examples include:
- Enron's accounting scandal
- Discrimination
- Antitrust violations
- Patent infringement

Technical breakdown accident	**Definition:** An accident that is caused by technology or equipment failure.

Examples include:
- Disappearance Malaysian Airlines Flight MH370
- Collapse of Rana Plaza building in Dhaka, Bangladesh
- Mining accidents
- Industrial accidents

Technical breakdown product recalls	**Definition:** Recall of a product because of technical failure, safety risk, or equipment failure

Examples include:
- Volkswagen emission scandal
- UK horsemeat scandal
- Toyota braking recall
- Wal-Mart pet food recall

Megadamage accidents	**Definition:** A technical breakdown or accident that produces significant environmental damage

Examples include:
- Exxon Valdez crash in Prince William Sound, Alaska
- Union Carbide accident in Bhopal, India
- Chernobyl nuclear power plant meltdown in the USSR

Human breakdown accident/errors	**Definition:** Any industrial accident or crisis caused by human error that does *not* involve corruption or illegal activities.

Examples include:
- Spanish train derailment, driver error cited for the crash
- Financial crisis, the culmination of policies and practices
- Data breach of the UK National Health Service, accidental disclosure of HIV status because of a failure to use 'BCC' in an email
- British Airways delays caused by an engineer disconnecting then connecting a power supply, causing a surge

(Continued)

Misdeed with no injuries	**Definition:** Occurs when management knowingly deceives stakeholders, but no physical injuries result to stakeholders

Examples include:

- Bernie Madoff's Ponzi schemes
- Misreporting of profit or loss
- Deceptive advertising

Misdeed with injuries	**Definition:** Occurs when management knowingly places some stakeholders at risk and some are either injured or killed as a result

Examples include:

- Grenfell Tower in the United Kingdom, cladding responsible for catastrophic fire and loss of life
- Tobacco industry data manipulation on cancer rates caused by smoking
- Unsafe labor practices

that are attributable. But to better understand transgressions, we should explore a few of the examples highlighted in the table.

We should start with the easiest kind of transgression to consider: Corporate behavior where the organization or a public figure has done something illegal and been caught for it. In some cases, illegal behavior may not amount to more than a fine and negative media coverage for an organization. Much of the difference in crisis impact will depend on whether people feel the illegal act can affect them individually.

However, in some cases, the behavior not only brings down an organization but also fundamentally changes laws because of the severity of impact on stakeholders. In 2001, the US Securities and Exchange Commission (SEC) brought charges against Enron for some of the worst ethics and legal violations that have been documented. These charges not only bankrupted the company, but also irreparably harmed Arthur Anderson, one of the largest auditing firms in the world. But more than that, it resulted in fundamental changes to accounting law and procedure that had ripple effects around the world. Illegal behavior can result in both serious material and reputational problems for organizations or even entire industries.

A second example of a transgression is some kind of technical breakdown or accident. In these cases, the organization does not necessarily do anything wrong; however, the crisis is ultimately the organization's responsibility because its property, technology, or equipment failure caused the crisis. These can be some of the deadliest and life-changing transgressions. A clear example is the 2015 disappearance of Malaysian Airlines Flight MH370. However, a list of major accidents that have affected people would include the Chernobyl disaster in the Ukraine during the 1980s; the

1984 explosion of a pesticide plant run by Union Carbide in Bhopal, India, that killed around 4,000 people; or more recently the collapse of a textiles factory in Dhaka, Bangladesh, that killed about 1,100 workers and injured another 2,500. In each of these cases, there was a clear and measurable attribution of blame to the organizations, often centering on safety standards, regardless of whether there was any kind of malicious intent – the impact of these incidents was so severe, they demanded attention.

Another type of technical breakdown is the product recall. In the case of recalls, a systematic defect is found in a product or brand and a recommendation is made that the products be returned. Allianz, which specializes in global specialty insurance services, has found a steady rise in recalls over time (Allianz, 2017). The rising numbers of recalls can be attributed to better safety regulation, the rise of the complexity of global supply chains, improved consumer awareness, and social media engagement. The Allianz report also indicates that the average cost of any recall is $1.65 million, with the most affected industries being automotive and food. Yet most recalls do not trigger a major crisis for organizations; the severity of impact of the recalls is often small and not covered extensively in the media.

This is where blame attribution and perceived severity is clearest. One of the most problematic recent recalls was the Volkswagen emissions scandal. In 2015 it was discovered that the company had misrepresented its emissions trials, and 550,000 vehicles sold in the United States alone were recalled. This resulted in a $14.7 billion settlement to compensate car owners and address the environmental harm done (Bartlett, Naranjo, & Plungis, 2017). In part, the scale and scope of the global product recall influenced the impact; however, because the Volkswagen brand had been synonymous with quality and integrity for decades, public expectations of the company were fundamentally violated. While the Volkswagen case is an extreme example, it helps to illustrate the impact of blame attribution and perceived severity based on expectancy violation on crisis impact.

Events

The second type of crisis includes organizational events where blame attribution is likely more complex and where perceived severity and personal impact will dramatically affect the perception of the events. Events can be triggered by actions an organization takes (e.g., layoff) in response to a situation. There may not necessarily be a 'wrong' that the organization has committed, but that does not absolve organizations of blame in terms of stakeholder perception. Like transgressions, organizational events assume that at least some stakeholders are meaningfully affected by the crisis. However, unlike transgressions, the material blame for the crisis is typically less clear. That said, events still directly involve and affect the organization and its stakeholders.

Table 6.2 summarizes key examples of events found across the research on crisis communication.

What is particularly important about organizational events is the degree to which different stakeholder groups attribute blame to the organization, largely based on perceived personal impact (i.e., severity); this will often be telling about the likely

Table 6.2 Event types, definitions, and examples

Mergers and failed mergers	**Definition:** The combination (or failure to combine) of two or more organizations

Examples include:
- Attempted merger of Skype and eBay
- Lloyd's Bank and TSB merger
- Failed merger of Quaker Oats and Snapple
- Daimler-Benz and Chrysler

Strikes and industrial iction	**Definition:** The threat of or stoppage of work at an organization by a union or group of workers with specific objectives

Examples include:
- British miner's strike
- Indian communication workers' strike
- National Hockey League lockout of players
- Palestinian general strike in support of political prisoners hunger strike
- Iranian truck driver's strike

Economic downturns	**Definition:** When downturns in the economy force organizations to take action in order to protect the organization's survivability

Examples include:
- Rising unemployment
- Low consumer confidence Downsizing
- Layoffs

Workplace violence	**Definition:** Being attacked in the workplace by current or former members of the organization (may affect a number of different types of stakeholders)

Examples include:
- UKIP members' altercation at the European Parliament
- Crash of German Wings flight by its co-pilot
- Post office shootings
- School shootings
- Sexual harassment

outcomes of the crisis. It also helps us to better understand the connections between our stakeholder maps, issues management, and crisis response. Let us examine some of the examples of these types of events identified in Table 6.2 to illustrate some of the challenges connected with events crises.

One of the common types of event crises that organizations face are mergers – whether successful or failed. These catch peoples' interest because of what they mean for both internal and external stakeholders. For example, in the 1990s, in the United Kingdom, Lloyds Bank and TSB merged. Then, in 2013, the two companies were forced to split to meet competition rules and regulations – leaving millions of customers transferred to a new company overnight. While all of the customers were offered the same accounts, terms, and conditions, the changes created both reputational problems as well as initial infrastructure problems. For employees, the question was whether there would be redundancies (i.e., downsizing). In this case, the split cost about 9,000 employees their jobs across the United Kingdom (Ahmed, 2013). Not surprisingly, mergers and failed mergers can have a host of legal, consumer, and employee issues that can evolve into crises with the potential for very different levels of blame attribution, depending on stakeholder perspective.

Speaking of labor, labor-related crises such as strikes force us to ask this question: Who is really 'in crisis'? Certainly, strikes are crises for the organization affected by the industrial action, but it does not necessarily end there. Strikes may represent just another evolution of an ongoing crisis for employees, but also can be triggers of crisis for government(s), and unions as well. With labor action, the critical question is, where do users of the organization as well as the general public place blame for the inconveniences or problems caused as a result of the action?

In some countries, unions and organizations work very closely together on a regular basis and have very positive relationships. However, in many countries, the relationship between unions and organizations is adversarial and publics are often divided by the issue. In the United States, this attitude can be different state-by-state, as the United States has 'right to work' states that fundamentally eliminate legal protections for industrial action as well as states that support labor laws recognizing unions.

In the United Kingdom, the history is likewise checkered, with a strong tradition of union membership and identification as well as examples like Margaret Thatcher's Conservative Government, which used violent police actions to break up the Miner Strikes in the 1980s. More recently, the junior doctor's strike was a good example of modern challenges for labor action. In this case, the doctors were striking against the government, but showed strong support for their organization, the National Health Service (NHS). Media coverage of the strike was divided – as well as public opinion – so the strike was a crisis for multiple groups, with the NHS, the Conservative Government, and doctors' unions all trying to manage public perception, and to improve their own reputations, while managing blame attribution.

Conflicts between stakeholders and organizations can also result in violence – and depending on what country that people live and work in, there is a reality of violence in the workplace ranging from sexual harassment to shootings. In most cases, the organization itself is not directly to blame for these situations and is often one of the victims of them; however, these cases are organizational events because the organization can be held accountable, and blame assigned by stakeholders. One example of this was a 2016 altercation between United Kingdom Independence Party (UKIP) members of the European Parliament, Steven Woolfe and the aptly named Mike Hookem. Certainly, it is a transgression on the part of the boxing parliamentarians, but for their party and the EU parliament, it is an organizational event – something that happened that these organizations had to manage and where blame could be attributed by some stakeholders. It was also certainly an event that received a healthy chunk of news coverage and required a response by the organizations affected. From the ridiculous to the life changing, organizational events represent a threat to potentially multiple organizations, groups, and public figures affected by them.

Clearly, events are not always initiated internally by decisions that the organization takes or as a consequence of changing internal relationships. External factors also can create crises for organizations. For example, between the mid-1980s and 2008 much of the West experienced consistent economic growth. Of course, different organizations and industries have had ups and downs. However, since the economic crash of 2008, and changes caused by the emergence and growing dominion of the digital economy, there have been many industries and organizations facing economic downturns that force them to take action. We certainly witnessed this in the global banking crash and saw a number of models for dealing with it ranging from Iceland's people's bailout to the US banking bailout and everything in between.

However, one industry that has faced increasing problems is the retail industry. As traditional retail driven by shop locations is being minimized or replaced by the digital marketplace, a lot of companies have had to start making different types of decisions. For example, beginning in 2013, Swedish retailer H&M has faced a lot of challenges, from downsizing its labor force to announcing in 2017 that, because of shifts toward the digital marketplace, it would not be opening as many new stores in new locations.

From a crisis communication side, events may not always lead directly to crises if they are well-managed; however, they can lead to crises as consumer confidence begins to slide or employee satisfaction erodes and as media coverage grows.

Thus there are three critical questions that we learn about crises from events are:

- Who is in crisis?
- Is the event caused by internal decisions or a response to external conditions?
- How will blame be attributed across the different, often competing, stakeholders involved in the crisis?

Reputational crises

Sohn and Lariscy (2014) distinguish between reputational crises and other types of crises by first pointing out that just because a crisis may affect an organization's reputation, it does not mean that the crisis itself is reputational. Instead, they argue that reputational crises are events that focus specifically on a threat to stakeholder perceptions and collective estimates of the qualities of an organization. As such, reputational crises are typically viewed as having low severity; while the relationship risk is real, the risks are unlikely to be life-changing. As such, Sohn and Laricy (2014) identify three conditions that have to be met for a crisis to be considered reputational:

- Reputational crises are different than reputational problems because there are specific events that trigger the crisis. These triggers can be the direct result of an interaction between any stakeholder group (e.g., employees, consumers, members of a brand community, critics, etc.) and the organization in person or online. They can also be the result of advocacy or claims made against the organization that have not yet been documented.

- The threat to the organization has to be credible to distinguish the reputational crisis from a reputational problem – organizations can have bad reputations and still be very successful. Crises, by definition, represent a threat to some aspect of the organization's viability in its present state.

- By emphasizing the collective nature of an organization's reputation, it suggest that whatever the reputational crisis is, it affects a more global evaluation of the worth, appropriateness, or value of the organization to one or more stakeholder.

These characteristics also suggest that reputational crises may not be universally viewed as crises because they can be specific to different groups. What one stakeholder group finds as a 'red line' may not affect the perception of the organization by other stakeholder groups. Considering the discussion of event-type crises, this is why asking the question 'who is in crisis' is an important part of understanding the nature of crises, because it is not always as clear as we might assume. Table 6.3 identifies the most common types of reputational crises.

We will take a look at a couple of types of reputational crises and examples of them to help apply these criteria. However, in a world of 'alternative facts,' organizations must also more actively manage rumors, online activism, consumer engagement, and varying levels of 'fan' support and criticism (Claeys & Cauberghe, 2015; Rhee & Yang, 2014; Veil, Reno, Freihaut, & Oldham, 2015)

Rumors about organizations, for example, are nothing new – these can be internal rumors about downsizing, changes, and the like or they can be viral rumors that

Table 6.3 Reputational crisis types, definitions, and examples

Paracrisis	**Definition:** Potentially high-frequency, low-impact crises, ranging from complaints to social media gaffes

Examples include:
- Unmonitored selfies in a Walkers Crisps competition for Champions League tickets (United Kingdom)
- Customer service complaints – especially those that go viral
- Complaints about company in social media

Rumor	**Definition:** Circulation of false information designed to hurt the organization

Examples include:
- Rumor that Apple CEO Steve Jobs had a heart attack (United States)
- Rumor that Procter & Gamble has ties to the Church of Satan (United States)
- Rumor that Corona beer was made with urine (United States)
- Bananas can give people SARS (China)

Challenge	**Definition:** Confrontation by disgruntled stakeholders claiming the organization has acted wrongly

Examples include:
- Taco Bell lawsuit over erroneous claims about beef content in tacos (United States)
- Boycotts
- Activism/pressure groups

Shifting political attitudes	**Definition:** As political attitudes change, different products, services, values, etc. become less desirable to stakeholders

Examples include:
- Dick's Sporting Goods announces scaling back gun business (United States)
- Honda decides to close its UK operations because of Brexit
- Emergence of the Sino-Africa Community of Common Destiny for investment and support

emerge. For example, in 2008 a viral rumor emerged that the Apple CEO (the late Steve Jobs) had a heart attack. This was picked up in the United States by CNN. Apple's stock dropped by 10% in ten minutes, then recovered somewhat but was valued at 3% lower by the session closing for the day (Hargreaves, 2008). Of course, the price rebounded because the rumor was an easy one to respond to; however, it was investigated by the SEC to see whether it emerged as a way for unscrupulous investors to profit. This turned out not to be the case, but this shows that rumors can often be difficult to manage and can represent a serious risk to an organization.

Apple certainly is not the only organization that manages rumors. For example, Coca-Cola has a section on its website designed to push back against rumors that circulate about the company – from those about the company using bug-based dyes to Coke causing Alzheimer's. Likewise, Procter & Gamble has ongoing efforts to manage claims that it is a front for Satanists – even having won a $19.3 million settlement against Amway for spreading the rumor in 2007 (The New York Times, 2007).

In a general recognition that organizations are increasingly facing crises that are different from other types of crises, Coombs and Holladay (2012) coined the term 'paracrises' to refer to complaints against an organization that gain some traction in online or traditional media outlets, thus describing them as potentially high-frequency, but low-impact events. Organizations must respond to and manage these complaints, but unlike most other types of crises, the risk is reputational and is unlikely to trigger fundamental change in the organization or industry. In a social-media rich environment, organizations are increasingly getting used to managing complaints. In talking with people in industry, the general sense is that for every piece of positive feedback they receive about their company, they are likely to get about 20 complaints. For the most part, they do not escalate – but when they do they can create interesting challenges for organizations.

Disasters

When this typology was first considered, the lines between levels of blame attribution seemed easy to draw between events that organizations would be held accountable for, might be held accountable for, and could not be held accountable for. However, as crisis research has developed, it has become clear that these lines are subjective. What is hopefully clear in this typology is that crises can best be classified on a continuum of blame attribution, from situations where full blame attribution for the primary crisis can be placed at the organization's door to situations where no blame for the primary crisis can be reasonably attributed to the organization. As we move from the debatable domain of events and even reputational crises into disasters, it should be clear that no reasonable blame attribution could be made on an organization based on the emergence of a disaster; however, disasters also carry risk for organizations depending on how they respond. Thus, aside from the direct material problems created by the disaster, much of the crisis risk associated with disasters is connected to secondary crises stemming from the organization's response to the disaster. Moreover, because disasters are likely to be severe – both in terms of material impact and perceived severity – they also carry much risk for organizations and stakeholders. Table 6.4 summarizes the most typical types of disasters that organizations face.

Table 6.4 Disaster crisis types, definitions, and examples

Natural disasters & Epidemics	**Definition:** Naturally occuring events that harm the organization and/or its stakeholders

- **Examples include:**
  - Floods
  - Earthquakes
  - Tsunamis
  - Diseases

Terrorism and external violence	**Definition:** Actions, often violent, by those outside an organization, with an array of impacts ranging from different stakeholders affected, infrastructure, collapse in demand, etc.

- **Examples include:**
  - Charlie Hebdo attacks in Paris
  - Planned Parenthood shooting in Colorado (United States)
  - Christchurch, New Zealand mosque shooting
  - Easter bombing of Christians in Sri Lanka

Aside from blame attribution, what makes disasters different from other types of crises is the degree to which both organizations and stakeholders alike can be affected by these events, which are completely out of their locus of control.

Obviously, natural disasters affect organizations and stakeholders alike. However, just because no organization can control the weather, it does not mean that people and organizations cannot be prepared for them – which is how organizations are judged in the wake of disasters. As a crisis type, research associated with disasters has grown considerably amongst crisis communication researchers since Hurricane Katrina hit New Orleans in August 2005, demonstrating that a lack of hurricane preparation and poor response by different governmental agencies cost lives and money. However, since the 2011 Fukushima nuclear disaster and the 2015 Ebola crisis, researchers and practitioners have really focused on the intersection of disaster management and crisis communication. A lot of research has focused not just on traditional mechanisms for response, but also the means for communicating with those affected by disasters. This reflects the modern reality that social media is a vital way of not only communicating with publics but also getting live updates about what is happening during disasters.

Disasters pose unique challenges from a crisis communication context because so many of them are global and demand serious reconsideration of policy and approach in their wake. For example, after the Fukushima disaster, governments across Europe – including Switzerland, Austria, and Germany – have reflected on nuclear energy and reconsidered the risks to the environment and their populations, ultimately deciding to phase out their nuclear energy programs in favor of other alternative energy sources. However, countries like the United Kingdom and France continue to develop nuclear energy. Debates about disasters and disaster response are complex and challenging in their aftermath; however, the immediate crisis response is also often complex as well because of the fear-based responses that disasters evoke. We will be talking more about stakeholder emotion later in this book, but suffice it to say that strong emotional responses make crisis communication even more challenging.

One of the unique challenges for disasters and other similar types of crises is how to accommodate the mourning process for the families of those whose lives have been lost and for those who have been dramatically affected by the events. This is especially difficult when the crises occur outside of the victims' own country. Kjell Brataas offers an important practitioner perspective on this type of situation (see Box 6.1).

Box 6.1 Practitioner perspective: Victims across borders

By Kjell Bratass

In most cases, disasters have international implications that challenge those people whose task it is to help victims, the bereaved, and survivors. Language barriers and cultural differences need to be taken into account, and oftentimes family members want to travel to the city where their loved ones died or are in a hospital. To prepare for this, several governments have prepared leaflets that can be handed out or downloaded. They contain information about where to turn for help, procedures for contacting hospitals, or listings of consulates and embassies.

Victims of crime or terror abroad often face challenges that last weeks, months, and even years after the event took place. The return of personal belongings takes longer when border crossings are involved, and in some instances human remains of the same person will be found and identified at various times during the investigation. Depending on where the disaster occurred and where the bereaved live, funeral parlors in each country might have to be involved – meaning possible delays, paperwork, and costs.

When a person is killed in a disaster abroad, the bereaved do not have the same opportunity to visit the site or a local memorial. Such visits are often part of the healing process, and many family members find it comforting to put down flowers or light a candle at a physical memorial. Other countries can therefore learn from the United Kingdom, which in 2017 opened a National Memorial to British Victims of Overseas Terrorism at the National Memorial Arboretum in Lichfield, Staffordshire England.

After the tsunami in Asia in 2004, I was part of a team from the Norwegian government that organized the unprecedented task of bringing victims' families to Thailand to see where their loved ones had died. Participants could choose between travelling in May or in October of 2005, and they were allowed much leeway regarding personal choices and what to do during the weeklong visit. For two days, minivans (with a guide in each) were available, and a common memorial service was conducted the last evening. This was a logistical challenge, but participants later reported that the visits to Thailand had been useful in their mourning processes. All expenses were paid by the Norwegian government.

When we are talking about crises that evoke fear, we must also talk about terrorist attacks and external violence in the context of disasters. This is one of the more under-studied types of crises in the field; yet, this is an area where crisis communication can probably offer some of the most direct benefits.

Of course, issues of social violence and terror attacks remain on people's minds these days because of the litany of attacks from many different groups in many different countries. However, the Charlie Hebdo attacks in Paris were noteworthy, from a communication perspective, for a host of reasons. Hebdo as an organization was obviously targeted because of its politics, but this offers a profound example of how events outside the organization's control can affect people's identities, attitudes, and even behaviors. In response to the crisis, Hebdo maintained that it was going to be undeterred by the events and it would remain controversial. However, emerging around the attacks and in response to it seemed to be a shift in public sentiment beyond Europe and beyond in both pro-social and potentially antisocial ways. In pro-social contexts, we saw evidence of a public sentiment of solidarity and people organizing themselves online to try to offer safe houses in the wake of violence that re-emerged in subsequent attacks in Belgium and the United Kingdom. However, in more challenging social contexts, we have also seen a resurgence of anti-immigration and nationalist movements. Organizations – ranging from local to multinational businesses through government and nongovernmental organizations – are then left to not only try to plan for eventualities but also to manage communication and public sentiment connected to these affecting everything from their public relations to employment practices.

In review . . .

The purpose of this chapter was to provide a straightforward way to classify the type of crisis an organization may face based on the reasonable blame that can both materially

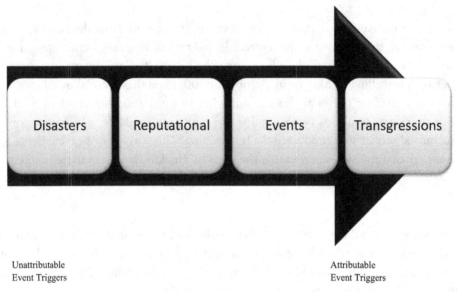

Unattributable
Event Triggers

Attributable
Event Triggers

Figure 6.1 Continuum of crisis type based on reasonable blame attribution

and arguably be attributed to it and then consider the potential for material or perceived severity from a stakeholder perspective as a way to predict the risk posed to an organization by different types of crises. As such, we have established that we can understand different types of crises based on a continuum of blame attribution from those crises that have virtually no attributable blame at the point that the crisis is triggered to those where blame is clearly attributable to the organization at the point of trigger (see Figure 6.1).

Review your understanding

By the end of this chapter, you should be able to understand and explain the following.

- The impact of blame and crisis severity on stakeholder attitudes about crises and organizations
- Understand the difference between primary and secondary crises
- Be able to define and offer examples of each of the types of crises discussed:
  - Transgressions
  - Events
  - Reputational
  - Disasters

> • Be able to explain the continuum of crisis blame attribution and its implications on likely stakeholder attitudes

References

Ahmed, K. (2013, 1/7/2019). Welcome back, TSB, as bank splits from Lloyds. *The Telegraph*. Retrieved from www.telegraph.co.uk/finance/newsbysector/banksandfinance/10293493/Welcome-back-TSB-as-bank-splits-from-Lloyds.html. Accessed July 10, 2019.

Ajzen, I. (2005). *Explaining intentions and behavior: Attitudes, personality, and behavior* (Vol. 2). Berkshire, England: McGraw-Hill Education.

Allianz. (2017). *Product recall: Managing the impact of the new risk landscape*. Munich, Germany. Retrieved from www.agcs.allianz.com/assets/PDFs/Reports/AGCS_ProductRecallReport.pdf

Bandura, A. (1986). *Social foundations of thought and action: A social cognitive theory*. Englewood Cliffs, NJ: Prentice Hall.

Bartlett, J. S., Naranjo, M., & Plungis, J. (2017). *Guide to the Volkswagon emissions recall: An FAQ with everything you need to know about the VW 'Dieselgate.'* Retrieved from www.consumerreports.org/cro/cars/guide-to-the-volkswagen-dieselgate-emissions-recall-

Brown, K. A., & Ki, E.-J. (2013). Developing a valid and reliable measure of organizational crisis responsibility. *Journalism & Mass Communication Quarterly*, 90(2), 363–384. doi:10.1177/1077699013482911

Brown, K. A., & White, C. L. (2010). Organization – Public relationships and crisis response strategies: Impact on attribution of responsibility. *Journal of Public Relations Research*, 23(1), 75–92.

Bundy, J., & Pfarrer, M. D. (2015). A burden of responsibility: The role of social approval at the onset of a crisis. *Academy of Management Review*, 40(3), 345–369. doi:10.5465/amr.2013.0027

Claeys, A.-S., & Cauberghe, V. (2015). The role of a favorable pre-crisis reputation in protecting organizations during crises. *Public Relations Review*, 41(1), 64–71. doi:10.1016/j.pubrev.2014.10.013

Coombs, W. T. (2007). Protecting organization reputation during a crisis: The development and application of situational crisis communication theory. *Corporate Reputation Review*, 10(3), 163–176.

Coombs, W. T., & Holladay, S. (2012). The paracrisis: The challenges created by publicly managing crisis prevention. *Public Relations Review*, 38, 408–415. doi:10.1016/j.pubrev.2012.04.004

Coombs, W. T., & Holladay, S. J. (1996). Communication and attributions in a crisis: An experimental study in crisis communication. *Journal of Public Relations Research*, 8(4), 279–295.

Coombs, W. T., & Holladay, S. J. (2002). Helping crisis managers protect their reputational assets: Initial tests of the Situational Crisis Communication Theory. *Management Communication Quarterly*, 16(2), 165–186.

Covello, V. T. (2002). *Message mapping, risk and crisis communication*. Paper presented at the Invited paper presented at the World Health Organization Conference on Bio-terrorism and Risk Communication, Geneva, Switzerland.

Diers, A. R., & Tomaino, K. (2010). Comparing strawberries and quandongs: A cross-national analysis of crisis response strategies. *Observatorio*, 4(2), 21–57.

Diers-Lawson, A. (2017a). Crisis communication. In *Oxford research encyclopedia of communication*. Oxford University Press. Retrieved from http://communication.oxfordre.com/view/10.1093/acrefore/9780190228613.001.0001/acrefore-9780190228613-e-397. doi:10.1093/acrefore/9780190228613.013.397

Diers-Lawson, A. (2017b). Will they like us when they're angry? Antecedents and indicators of strong emotional reactions to crises among stakeholders. In S. M. Croucher, B. Lewandowska-Tomaszczyk, & P. Wilson (Eds.), *Conflict, mediated message, and group dynamics* (pp. 81–136). Lanham, MD: Lexington Books.

Hargreaves, S. (2008, 1/7/2019). Apple's stock hit by Web rumor. *CNN Money*. Retrieved from http://money.cnn.com/2008/10/03/technology/apple/. Accessed July 10, 2019.

Hearit, K. M. (1999). Newsgroups, activist publics, and corporate apologia: The case of Intel and its Pentium chip. *Public Relations Review*, 25(3), 291–308.

Jin, Y. (2009). The effects of public's cognitive appraisal of emotions in crises on crisis coping and strategy assessment. *Public Relations Review*, 35(3), 310–313.

Jin, Y. (2010). Making sense sensibly in crisis communication: How publics' crisis appraisals influence their negative emotions, coping strategy preferences, and crisis response acceptance. *Communication Research*, 37(4), 522–552. doi:10.1177/0093650210368256

Kim, J., Kim, H. J., & Cameron, G. T. (2009). Making nice may not matter: The interplay of crisis type, response type and crisis issue on perceived organizational responsibility. *Public Relations Review*, 35(1), 86–88.

Kim, S. (2013). Corporate ability or virtue? Relative effectiveness of prior corporate associations in times of crisis. *International Journal of Strategic Communication*, 7(4), 241–256. doi:10.1080/1553118X.2013.824886

Lee, B. K. (2004). Audience-oriented approach to crisis communication: A study of Hong Kong consumers' evaluation of an organizational crisis. *Communication Research*, 31(5), 600–618.

Pearson, C. M., & Mitroff, I. (1993). From crisis prone to crisis prepared: A framework for crisis management. *Academy of Management Executive*, 7(1), 48–59.

Ping, Q., Ishaq, M., & Li, C. (2015). Product harm crisis, attribution of blame and decision making: An insight from the past. *Journal of Applied Environmental and Biological Sciences*, 5(5), 35–44.

Rhee, H. T., & Yang, S.-B. (2014). Consumers' emotional reactions to negative publicity and crisis management in the health care industry: A multiple case study of Lipitor and Oxyelite Pro. *Social Science Computer Review*, 32(5), 678–693. doi:10.1177/0894439314525901

Rickard, L. N., McComas, K. A., Clarke, C. E., Stedman, R. C., & Decker, D. J. (2013). Exploring risk attenuation and crisis communication after a plague death in Grand Canyon. *Journal of Risk Research*, 16(2), 145–167. doi:10.1080/13669877.2012.725673

Seeger, M., & Ulmer, R. R. (2002). A post-crisis discourse of renewal: The cases of Malden Mills and Cole Hardwoods. *Journal of Applied Communication Research*, 30(2), 126–142.

Sellnow, D. D., & Sellnow, T. L. (2014). The challenge of exemplification in crisis communication. *Journal of Applied Communications*, 98(2), 53–65.

Sohn, Y., & Lariscy, R. W. (2014). Understanding reputational crisis: Definition, properties, and consequences. *Journal of Public Relations Research*, 26(1), 23–43. doi:10.1080/1062 726X.2013.795865

The New York Times. (2007). *Procter & Gamble wins $19 million in Satanism suit*. Retrieved from www.nytimes.com/2007/03/20/business/worldbusiness/20iht-satan.4966053.html

Veil, S. R., Reno, J., Freihaut, R., & Oldham, J. (2015). Online activists vs. Kraft foods: A case of social media hijacking. *Public Relations Review*, 41(1), 103–108. doi:10.1016/j. pubrev.2014.11.017

Witte, K. (1992). Putting the fear back into fear appeals: The extended parallel process model. *Communication Monographs*, 59, 329–349.

PART 3

Internal stakeholders and organizational factors: Evaluating the organization's crisis capacity

In the first two parts of this textbook, I have looked outside the organization in order to learn about the field of crisis communication, introduce a stakeholder relationship management perspective, and evaluate the risks that organizations face. However, understanding crisis management is an outside-in and inside-out area of practice. We must place our organizations within their overall operational environment, but if we fail to understand the internal organizational realities crisis management is likely to also fail.

For that reason, Part 3 explores an organization's internal capacity to respond effectively to crises. I will explore the organizational factors that constrain and enable its internal stakeholders to manage information, teams, and situations. I will also explore how these capacities can be more effectively built within organizations as well. Understanding organizational capacity is also important because, as I have mentioned already, an organization's relationships with its employees is vital to manage if organizations are to be successful in managing risk and responding to crises. Chapter 7 will define organizational capacity by focusing on the challenges of crisis management, exploring crisis history, and defining what it takes to be successful in crisis management. Chapter 8 will focus on building crisis capacity by focusing on the employee experience with crises and their organizations. Finally, Chapter 9 will explore the leadership challenge for organizations in crisis.

7 Defining crisis capacity in a modern environment

Learning objectives

By the end of this chapter, the reader should:

- Better understand the relationship between crisis management and crisis communication
- Be able to use theory to analyze organizational capacity for stakeholder relationship management
- Evaluate the influence of industry of organizational capacity to respond to crises

In Part 2 I focused on understanding the intersection of stakeholders and crises. However, in this section, I look inside the organization to better understand what can influence how effectively an organization *can* respond to crises. Just as organizations do not exist in vacuums, crisis management and crisis communication are not only about the environment and stakeholders outside the organization, but also about those within the organization who make decisions and execute strategy.

For this reason, I will adopt an inside-out approach to crisis response. I will begin by examining the concept of organizational capacity relative to crisis management, then explore the challenges of crisis management. How does an organization's crisis history and its industry affect its capacity to answer this question: What does success in crisis response really take?

Crisis management and crisis response

In Chapter 2, I differentiated between crisis management, as the material response to the crisis, and crisis communication, as the focus on stakeholder relationship management. I also introduced Loosemore's (1999) theory of crisis management, which identifies the four essential crisis management challenges:

- Internal power struggles
- Linking communication to efficiency instead of value
- Capacity of crises to encourage conflict
- Crisis emergence discouraging collective responsibility

While Loosemore's theory of crisis management has been influential in the last couple of decades, one of the key elements that his identification of the challenges and factors influencing successful crisis management demonstrates is that effective communication is likely to predict the success or failure of crisis response efforts. Internally, managing our teams and organizations relies on creating a productive work environment. Externally, the same themes focus stakeholder identification with the organization and goodwill towards it, despite the crisis.

The Jet2 case study in Box 7.1 demonstrates some of the quintessential differences between crisis management and communication as well as the importance of building the organization's capacity to communicate effectively during crises.

Box 7.1 Case study: "They don't care about you people at all"; when crisis management works but communication fails

By Audra Diers-Lawson, Ph.D.

One of the emerging pressure points for organizations in crisis is how often and clearly they communicate with those directly affected by the situation. An organization may be managing a crisis effectively, but without communicating that information to invested stakeholders, they risk creating a secondary crisis. For example, one of the principal criticisms of Malaysian Airlines regarding the disappearance of Flight 370 in 2014 was the perception that the airline failed to meet the information update needs of the families affected.

For those who travel, minor flight delays are common; however, they are likely to create stress and concern. As I was getting ready to begin work on this textbook, I happened to take a Jet2CityBreak in Prague, Czech Republic, to meet with friends and was returning on the late Sunday evening flight to the United Kingdom.

Because of severe weather in the United Kingdom, the Sunday afternoon and evening flights between Leeds and Prague were delayed and then cancelled.

What did Jet2 do to manage the passenger crisis?

From a crisis management perspective, Jet2 seemed to meet its obligations. As a vacation package passenger, I received preferential treatment compared to flight-only passengers. That meant that Jet2 booked me into a hotel until I could arrange for a flight home. Flight-only passengers had to manage their own accommodations, but from reports they were also re-booked once customer service was open again on Monday morning.

The secondary crisis: Crisis communication failure

Take a look at the timeline: For as decent a job that the company did in ultimately getting people home, its communication was abysmal. It was clear from watching the airport and Jet2 ground staff in Prague that they were receiving no information from Jet2. In fact, the first that the agents at the check-in desk heard that the flight was cancelled was from a passenger who received a status update online. This was then confirmed with the airport, though with no additional information.

Once everyone learned the flight would be cancelled, Jet2 was not readily available for anyone – including ground staff, the local travel company, or the passengers. Not surprisingly, this led to considerable frustration. In fact, after more than two hours of trying to connect to Jet2 to get instructions for vacation-package and flight-only passengers, one of the local agents exclaimed, "I don't know what to tell you, flight-only passengers – Jet2 doesn't care about you. They don't care about you people at all."

Let that sink in: The core message at the moment when people were feeling most uncertain and frustrated was that the company did not care about those directly affected by the delay. Regardless of whether that was true, as the flight-only passengers began to disperse, this was the thought in their minds as they had to find their own accommodations and return flights.

For those of us on the vacation package, at least we were 'cared for' enough to finally get to a hotel with the promise of contact. At that point we learned

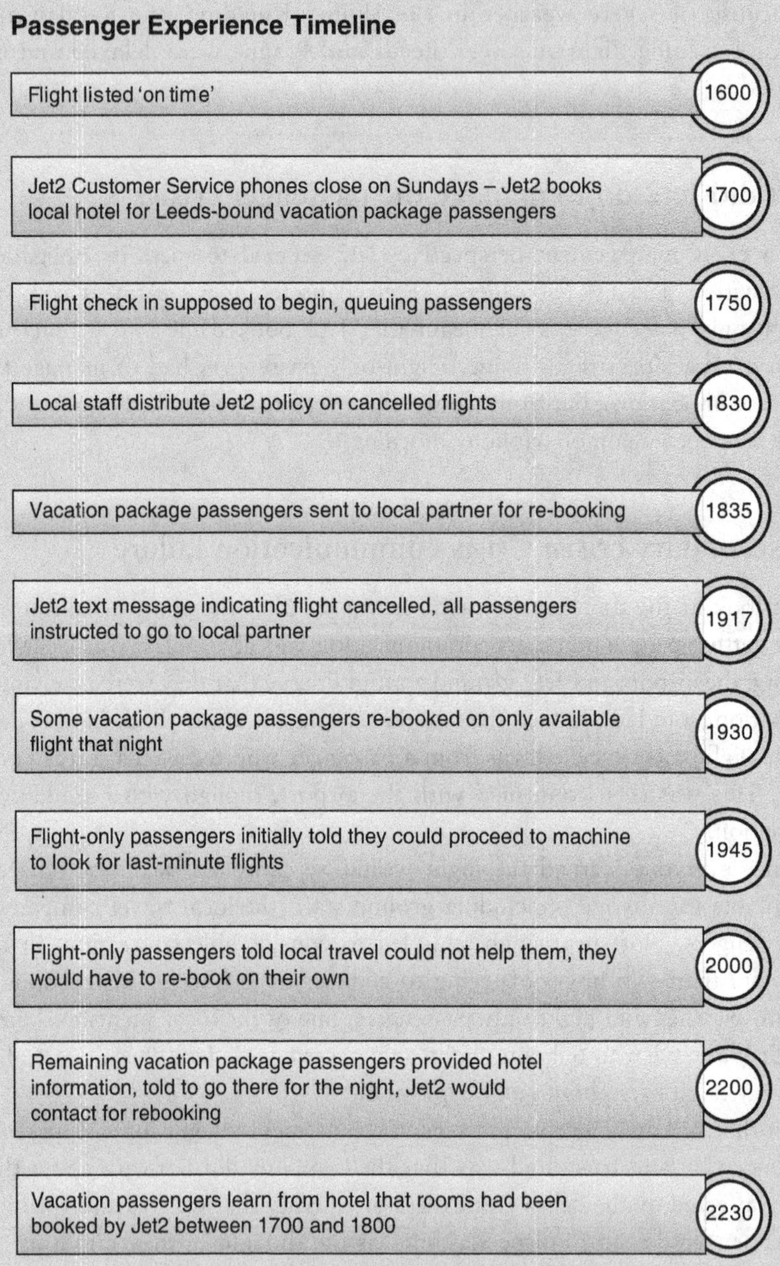

Passenger Experience Timeline

Flight listed 'on time'	1600
Jet2 Customer Service phones close on Sundays – Jet2 books local hotel for Leeds-bound vacation package passengers	1700
Flight check in supposed to begin, queuing passengers	1750
Local staff distribute Jet2 policy on cancelled flights	1830
Vacation package passengers sent to local partner for re-booking	1835
Jet2 text message indicating flight cancelled, all passengers instructed to go to local partner	1917
Some vacation package passengers re-booked on only available flight that night	1930
Flight-only passengers initially told they could proceed to machine to look for last-minute flights	1945
Flight-only passengers told local travel could not help them, they would have to re-book on their own	2000
Remaining vacation package passengers provided hotel information, told to go there for the night, Jet2 would contact for rebooking	2200
Vacation passengers learn from hotel that rooms had been booked by Jet2 between 1700 and 1800	2230

Figure 7.1 Jet2 passenger experience timeline

that Jet2 had contacted the hotel to book the rooms for us about five hours earlier.

Between 5:00 p.m. and midnight, the only direct communication that everyone received from Jet2 was a single text message:

Dear <insert passenger name> Jet2.com and Jet2holidays regrets to advise that due to operational issues flight LS197 to Leeds Bradford has been cancelled. Jet2.com apologises for the inconvenience caused by these circumstances which are beyond our control. Customers should speak to <local partner> staff for further information. We would like to thank you for your patience and understanding at this time and apologise for the disruption caused.

In the end, the primary crisis was an unavoidable event – there were severe storms in the United Kingdom. Jet2 also met its contractual obligations to passengers. Though its crisis management was not seamless in its decision-making and problem solving, the genuine failure was a lack of timely communication, information dissemination, instructions for passengers, and messaging for local responders.

As I was navigating my own experience with Jet2, what occurred to me was a phrase that I heard from passengers, the local staff, Jet2, and in the media: This particular route had never had a situation like this before. It seemed to be that everyone was treading into new waters and was unprepared for both the situation and its timing (a Sunday night once the central customer service offices were closed).

What the Jet2 case also highlights is that crisis management is increasingly seen as a public relations (PR) function (Stacks, 2004), something that is consistent with the research trends across applied fields like medicine and health, the STEM fields (science, technology, engineering, and math), management and business, as well as industry-based research discussed in Chapter 1 (see Figures 1.4–1.9). In all of these applied fields, crisis communication has been increasingly linked with risk assessment, information management, crisis management, crisis planning, and training. Why? Because as Stacks (2004) argues:

Crisis management planning is actually a corporate communication plan that seeks to manage various public perceptions of the crisis. An effective crisis management plan is a well thought out campaign that seeks to reduce any negative impact, while generating positive outcomes during a crisis period.

(p. 38)

Because I have already been talking about issues and crisis management in the context of the stakeholder relationship model, Stacks's argument should make sense. He is suggesting that crisis management, from a structural perspective, should look like any other strategic campaign that an organization can develop and implement – one that has: strategic objectives, devises an aligned strategy to meet those objectives, executes them effectively, and then evaluates the effectiveness of the campaign.

This lets us de-mystify the strategy component of crisis communication so that we are focusing on structures and strategy with which we are already familiar.

Organizational capacity for crisis response

If we begin with the assumption that building crisis response is similar to building any other campaign, and that communication professionals are integral to that process, then specifically what does it take to define an organization's capacity for effective crisis response? Stacks's (2004) multidimensional model of PR provides some good criteria for organizational capacity.

Effective crisis management is inextricably linked with communication

Stacks's model argues that effective crisis management has three distinctive qualities. First, **effective crisis management ensures that PR functions are institutionalized.** This means that in order for crisis management to be successful, communication professionals need to be included as an equal part of the strategic decision-making team. This does not mean that the communication professional is responsible for solving the material problem (if there is one) associated with the crisis, but it does mean that in a cross-functional team it is essential to have communication expertise as part of the process.

Stacks's argument about the importance of having communication expertise in crisis management is not unique. For example, Chen's (2009) analysis of the Chinese government's response to the 2008 Sichuan earthquake demonstrated that when communication was institutionalized – that is, made an inherent part of strategic decision-making process – the government's capacity to respond to the crisis was substantially improved. Chen compared these findings to the relatively lower levels of strategic decision-making institutionalization across Europe and North America and argued that when PR falls into mere supporting or advisory roles, the organization's capacity for effective crisis response is reduced. But the Chinese case is not the only one that points to the importance of institutionalizing the PR function as part of building capacity for crisis response. In fact, reflections on the failures of the US Government's crisis response during Hurricane Katrina (Comfort, 2007) – as well as reflections on the post 9/11 era and case studies across industries like the public sector, financial services, travel and tourism, fast food, and manufacturing – demonstrate that the institutionalization of communication within crisis management and decision-making is essential to the success of crisis management and corporate strategy (Campiranon & Scott, 2014; Frandsen & Johansen, 2009; Jindal, Laveena, & Aggarwal, 2015; McLaughlin, 2002, p. 870; Miller & Horsley, 2009; Takamatsu, 2014).

Second, effective crisis management must take into account the **type of organization** the plan will manage. Crisis planning and management for corporate firms, nonprofits, governments, schools, and so on all need to be customized to the particular organization and particular circumstances in which the organization is operating (Stacks, 2004). For example, after the 2010 BP deep-water oil rig explosion in the Gulf of Mexico, one of the embarrassing realities that came to light was that just about all of the major oil companies – not just BP – had problematic crisis plans. In the congressional hearings on the explosion, this was cited as one of the reasons that the material problems were slow to be addressed: Very simply, the industry did not have the right resources ready to deploy.

No matter the particular situational factors, Stacks's argument focuses on the impact of tailored crisis plans and crisis management as essential to success. This has been demonstrated across industries like financial services, where unique information needs and efforts to rebuild trust and confidence in financial organizations were central after the 2008 financial collapse (DiStaso, 2010). Consistently, the narrative is that industry and organization-centered strategies are essential to success (Bowen & Zheng, 2015; Conkey, 2004; Kal-kausar, Rafida, Nurulhusna, Alina, & Mashitoh, 2013; Maresh & Williams, 2007). We will come back to the question of how the type of organization affects crisis management shortly, because one of the critical assumptions in crisis response is that the type of organization influences crisis reactions – both in terms of the organization's likelihood to react as well as stakeholders' reactions to the organization.

Third, effective crisis management **develops specific targeted messaging**. Tailored communication is nothing new, but in the context of crisis response, organizations have to ensure that their crisis responses are aligned with their current practices and stakeholder concerns about the crisis (Stacks, 2004). In terms of capacity building, this suggests that the crisis management team needs to be directly connected with all communications activities. In a study of the best ways to help manage a major natural hazard, Steelman and McCaffrey (2013) found that the process of wildfire management – that is, making decisions that affect the strategy for fighting the wildfires themselves – was improved when there was evidence of good information management and communication practices before and during the fires. This enabled manages to more readily adapt to the changeable conditions in the wildfires and help improve the response and efficacy of the response. This wildfire example is not just a great metaphor for most crises, but it demonstrates that even in situations where the material management of the situation is about a physical response to the situation, good communication with targeted and focused messaging is essential. One of the reasons for this is that crisis management requires adaptive information-rich responses to facilitate both internal and external stakeholder actions to help manage the situation, risk, and relationships (Steelman & McCaffrey, 2013). But more than that, in an era where information seeking is high and information sharing happens across platforms, it is vital that organizations be viewed as credible sources of information for all key stakeholders (Park & Cameron, 2014; Utz, Schultz, & Glocka, 2013; van Zoonen & van der Meer, 2015).

Crisis capacity defined

If we take these three qualities of good crisis management into account – that an organization has institutionalized its communication function, it adapts its crisis response to its own needs, and that it develops aligned and targeted messaging – then organizations should adopt a management structure that focuses on stakeholders, facilitates a good flow of communication, and allows excellence in adaptation to the situation.

Initially, Stacks (2004) argues that organizations must have the physical organizational structures in place in order to respond to crises. In their work on corporate governance in the context of crises, Alpaslan, Green, and Mitroff (2009) demonstrate that if organizations adopt a stakeholder model of corporate governance, this will improve their ability to be more proactive and accommodating in crisis management. They suggest that every aspect of corporate governance should focus on the needs of stakeholder responsibility, including everything from contract development to management behaviors. Their core argument is that organizations following these principles are more likely to avert crises or at least mitigate their impact. This supports Heath's (1998) body of research indicating that good crisis management emphasizes an **integrated management approach for organizational decision-making** that involves prevention, mitigation, actual response, and recovery and explicitly includes advisory personnel, internal and external communications personnel, and functional management teams linking normal operations and crisis response. This suggests that as a crisis emerges, instead of assembling a crisis response team, the team is already in place and has been working together across routine activities as well as risk mitigation and crisis management activities.

There are several benefits for organizations with management structures that facilitate this kind of ongoing risk mitigation, stakeholder-centered strategy, and cross-functional decision-making.

- First, the obvious one – risk mitigation activities (e.g., issues management) minimize or eliminate crises before they emerge and improves crisis response.

- This kind of integrated management improves organizational learning and is especially beneficial for small and medium-sized organizations that are least able to weather significant crises (Huzey, Betts, & Vicari, 2014).

- These structures improve the purposeful exchange of information within and between organizations, the media, and other stakeholders before during and after crises (Johansson & Härenstam, 2013).

- It can help to improve the coordination of crisis management between often competing interests in organizations. There is often a disconnect between communication recommendations for responding to issues and crises and legal recommendations for response. When the organization's decision-making process is set up to facilitate coordination between departments and interests within the organization, competing and contradictory recommendations can be minimized both improving the material response and reputational outcomes (Martinelli & Briggs, 1998).

In short, when an organization's structure and management approach integrates issues and crisis response as routine, it provides a source of sustainable competitive advantage that allows organizations to move from being crisis prone to crisis prepared (Palese & Crane, 2002; Pearson & Mitroff, 1993). More than that, this kind of an integrated management approach not only builds the capacity of the organization to respond to crises but also to perform more ethically before, during, and after crises (Folkes & Karmins, 1999; Kim, 2013; Simola, 2003, 2005).

Organizations, industries, and crisis capacity

To put it simply, an organization's crisis capacity is also influenced by the type of organization that it is and the industry that it is in (Stacks, 2004). But why is this? Why does the type of organization affect crisis response so much?

In part, we have to consider an organization's industry because the influences of structure, infrastructure, relationships, social environments, and stability are often strongly related to the industry that an organization is in. An industry is likely to influence an organization's experience with crises as well as its reaction to them. As such, industry contributes to an organization's capabilities, identity, and even its reputation. This is no more clearly evidenced than in the banking industry after the financial crash of 2008, when the industry's reputation created credibility problems throughout the industry – no matter the particular financial institution (DiStaso, 2010).

But also, there is good evidence that the industry influences an organization's communication needs and opportunities when the organization is in crisis (Sellnow & Sarabakhsh, 1999). Research suggests there are two ways that industry is often considered in terms of its influence.

- **Industries affect organizations and their experience with crises.** For example, Elsbach's (1994) analysis of the California cattle industry examined the construction and effectiveness of verbal accounts across the industry as it faced different crises. One industry that is often studied is the airline industry, with research centering on crisis response to specific events or broad industry reactions to changing conditions (Goyal & Negi, 2014; Greer & Moreland, 2003, p. 619). There are similar findings across different industries such as travel and tourism, automobile, manufacturing, financial, sports/entertainment, and technology industries.

- When industry is considered in crisis communication, we can find clear evidence of differences in communication needs based on those organizations that are in **crisis prone versus non-crisis prone industries.** Previous research has identified seven industries as crisis-prone: finance and insurance; professional, scientific, and technical services, information (e.g., telecommunications, computer software, and hardware); transportation and warehousing; manufacturing; mining; and travel (Coombs & Holladay, 2004; Diers & Tomaino, 2010; Millar, 2004). Consistently, these findings suggest that a history of crisis changes the ways that organizations react to crises.

In review . . .

In the end, it is important to remember that while crisis management and crisis communication are not the same, they are inextricably linked. The data for the last 15–20 years very clearly indicates that in organizations where communications or PR functions are an integrated part of the decision-making, management, and strategy processes, those organizations are significantly better able to prepare for and respond to crises. Thus, as we talk about capacity building for improved crisis response in Part 3 of this book, we must remember that when organizations adopt a stakeholder model for governance, this not only shifts the ethical and social responsibility obligations of those organizations away from a purely self-focus but also improves their capacity for mitigating and managing crises. Put simply, a stakeholder model for governance places communication as a part of the decision-making process and not merely an add-on advisory role.

Review your understanding

By the end of this chapter, you should be able to understand and explain the following.

- The differences between crisis management and crisis response
- What organizational capacity for crisis response includes:
  - The inextricable link between crisis management and crisis communication
  - Definition of crisis capacity
  - Benefits of building crisis capacity
- Influence of industry on crisis capacity

References

Alpaslan, C., Green, S., & Mitroff, I. (2009). Corporate governance in the context of crises: Towards a stakeholder theory of crisis management. *Journal of Contingencies & Crisis Management*, 17(1), 38–49.

Bowen, S. A., & Zheng, Y. (2015). Auto recall crisis, framing, and ethical response: Toyota's missteps. *Public Relations Review*, 41(1), 40–49. doi:10.1016/j.pubrev.2014.10.017

Campiranon, K., & Scott, N. (2014). Critical success factors for crisis recovery management: A case study of Phuket hotels. *Journal of Travel & Tourism Marketing*, 31(3), 313–326. doi:10.1080/10548408.2013.877414

Chen, N. (2009). Institutionalizing public relations: A case study of Chinese government crisis communication on the 2008 Sichuan earthquake. *Public Relations Review*, 35, 187–198.

Comfort, L. K. (2007). Crisis management in hindsight: Cognition, communication, coordination, and control. *Public Administration Review*, 67(S1), 189–197.

Conkey, H. (2004). National crisis communication arrangements for agricultural emergencies. *The Australian Journal of Emergency Management*, 19(3), 43.

Coombs, W. T., & Holladay, S. J. (2004). Reasoned action in crisis communication: An attribution theory-based approach to crisis management. In D. P. Millar & R. L. Heath (Eds.), *Responding to crisis: A rhetorical approach to crisis communication* (pp. 95–115). Mahwah, NJ: Lawrence Erlbaum Associates.

Diers, A. R., & Tomaino, K. (2010). Comparing strawberries and quandongs: A cross-national analysis of crisis response strategies. *Observatorio*, 4(2), 21–57.

DiStaso, M. W. (2010). Industry in crisis: The communication challenge in the banking industry. *Public Relations Journal*, 4(1), 1–17.

Elsbach, K. D. (1994). Managing organizational legitimacy in the California cattle industry: The construction and effectiveness of verbal accounts. *Administrative Science Quarterly*, 39, 57–88.

Folkes, V. S., & Karmins, M. A. (1999). Effects of information about firms' ethical and unethical actions on consumers' attitudes. *Journal of Consumer Psychology*, 8(3), 243–259.

Frandsen, F., & Johansen, W. (2009). Institutionalizing crisis communication in the public sector: An explorative study in Danish municipalities. *International Journal of Strategic Communication*, 3(2), 102–115.

Goyal, R., & Negi, D. (2014). Impact of global economic crisis on airline industry. *International Journal of Commerce, Business and Management*, 3(2), 297–301.

Greer, C. F., & Moreland, K. D. (2003). United Airlines' and American Airlines' online crisis communication following the September 11 terrorist attacks. *Public Relations Review*, 29, 427–441.

Heath, R. L. (1998). Dealing with the complete crisis – The crisis management shell structure. *Safety Science*, 30(1), 139–150.

Huzey, D., Betts, S. C., & Vicari, V. (2014). Learning the hard way vs. vicarious learning: Post crisis learning for small business. *Journal of Management and Marketing Research*, 15, 1.

Jindal, S., Laveena, L., & Aggarwal, A. (2015). A comparative study of crisis management-Toyota v/s General Motors. *Scholedge International Journal of Management & Development*, 2(6), 1–12.

Johansson, A., & Härenstam, M. (2013). Knowledge communication: A key to successful crisis management. *Biosecurity and Bioterrorism: Biodefense Strategy, Practice, and Science*, 11(S1), S260–S263. doi:10.1089/bsp.2013.0052

Kal-kausar, M., Rafida, A. N., Nurulhusna, N., Alina, A., & Mashitoh, A. S. (2013). Crisis communication and management on food recall in the Malaysian Food Industry. *Middle-East Journal of Scientific Research*, 13, 54–60. doi:10.5829/idosi.mejsr.2013.16.s.100210

Kim, S. (2013). Corporate ability or virtue? Relative effectiveness of prior corporate associations in times of crisis. *International Journal of Strategic Communication*, 7(4), 241–256. doi:10.1080/1553118X.2013.824886

Loosemore, M. (1999). A grounded theory of construction crisis management. *Construction Management and Economics*, 17, 9–19.

Maresh, M., & Williams, D. (2007). *Toward an industry-specific crisis response model: A look at the oil crises of British Petroleum and Phillips Petroleum*. Paper presented at the National Communication Association, Chicago, IL.

Martinelli, K. A., & Briggs, W. (1998). Integrating public relations and legal responses during a crisis: The case of Odwalla, Inc. *Public Relations Review*, 24(4), 443–465.

McLaughlin, S. (2002). Sept. 11: Four views of crisis management. *Public Relations Strategist*, 8(1), 22–28. doi:105666336

Millar, D. P. (2004). Exposing the errors: An examination of the nature of organizational crises. In D. P. Millar & R. L. Heath (Eds.), *Responding to crisis: A rhetorical approach to crisis communication* (pp. 19–35). Mahwah, NJ: Lawrence Erlbaum Associates.

Miller, B. M., & Horsley, J. S. (2009). Digging deeper: Crisis management in the coal industry. *Journal of Applied Communication Research*, 37(3), 298–316.

Palese, M., & Crane, T. Y. (2002). Building an integrated issue management process as a source of sustainable competitive advantage. *Journal of Public Affairs*, 2(4), 284–292.

Park, H., & Cameron, G. T. (2014). Keeping it real: Exploring the roles of conversational human voice and source credibility in crisis communication via blogs. *Journalism & Mass Communication Quarterly*, 91(3), 487–507. doi:10.1177/1077699014538827

Pearson, C. M., & Mitroff, I. (1993). From crisis prone to crisis prepared: A framework for crisis management. *Academy of Management Executive*, 7(1), 48–59.

Sellnow, T., & Sarabakhsh, M. (1999). Crisis management in the hospitality industry. *Hospitality Review*, 17(1), 6.

Simola, S. (2003). Ethics of justice and care in corporate crisis management. *Journal of Business Ethics*, 46(4), 351–361.

Simola, S. (2005). Concepts of care in organizational crisis prevention. *Journal of Business Ethics*, 62, 341–353. doi:10.1007/s10551-005-3069-9

Stacks, D. W. (2004). Crisis management: Toward a multidimension model of public relations. In D. P. Millar & R. L. Heath (Eds.), *Responding to crisis: A rhetorical approach to crisis communication* (pp. 37–49). Mahwah, NJ: Lawrence Erlbaum Associates.

Steelman, T. A., & McCaffrey, S. (2013). Best practices in risk and crisis communication: Implications for natural hazards management. *Natural Hazards*, 65(1), 683–705.

Takamatsu, M. (2014). The Okinawa tourism crisis Management initiatives. *International Journal of Event Management Research*, 8(1), 19–34.

Utz, S., Schultz, F., & Glocka, S. (2013). Crisis communication online: How medium, crisis type and emotions affected public reactions in the Fukushima Daiichi nuclear disaster. *Public Relations Review*, 39(1), 40–46.

van Zoonen, W., & van der Meer, T. (2015). The importance of source and credibility perception in times of crisis: Crisis communication in a socially mediated era. *Journal of Public Relations Research*, 27(5), 371–388. doi:10.1080/1062726X.2015.1062382

8 | Building crisis capacity from the inside out

Learning objectives

By the end of this chapter, the reader should:

- Be able to critically reflect on the influence of an organization's character, its perspective on social responsibility, and culture as part of its capacity to respond to crises
- Consider employees as internal stakeholders, vital to crisis response capacity building
- Evaluate employee hard and soft skills needed to build crisis response capacity
- Understand the role of simulation in capacity building

In Chapter 7 I reflected on the differences between crisis management and crisis response and defined organizational capacity with regard to an organization's ability to effectively manage a crisis. I also focused on the importance of good communication throughout. However, the most critical component to understanding crisis capacity is to evaluate how it can be built from the inside out. Though external stakeholders see an organization's response, the quality of that response depends on its internal stakeholders.

As I continue the focus in Part 3 on developing an inside-out approach to crisis response, I argue that an organization's ability to effectively manage crises and a stakeholder approach to crisis response requires us to think about employees as vital stakeholders. More than that, I also argue that if an organization wants to build its capacity to respond effectively, it must critically reflect on developing its employees' skills in both the hard and soft skills required for effective crisis response.

Organizational culture, social responsibility, and crisis capacity

In the discussion of the stakeholder relationship model (SRM) in Chapter 3, several of the factors influencing the relationships between organizations, issues, and stakeholders focused on an organization's values either directly or indirectly. For example, in stakeholders' evaluations of the organization's connection with an issue, the degree to which stakeholders believe the organization demonstrates positive intention, concern, and commitment to the issue will influence their attitude towards the organization (Lacey, Kennett-Hensel, & Manolis, 2015). Similarly, in the connections that stakeholders make with the issues themselves, their existing attitudes and values affect their emotional involvement with the issue and thus interest in seeing the organization act (Ajzen, 2005; van der Meer & Verhoeven, 2014). Of course, when stakeholders perceive their values are congruent with an the organization's, then the organization is going to be viewed as more trustworthy (Freberg & Palenchar, 2013; Ki & Brown, 2013). What the SRM suggests then, is that not only do an organization's culture and values influence how stakeholders see their relationship with the organization but also its capacity to effectively respond to crises.

Organizational culture

In order to understand an organization's crisis capacity, we must understand its culture. In the context of crisis, organizational culture is vital because it not only functions to help stakeholders – both internal and external – cope with the uncertainty of crisis but also potential chaos created by it (Dolan, Garcia, & Auerbach, 2003; Hurley, Gillespie, Ferrin, & Dietz, 2013; Jindal, Laveena, & Aggarwal, 2015; Langer & Thorup, 2006).

In their seminal work on organizational culture, Trice and Beyer (1993) talk about two components to culture: An organization's ideology and its forms. From a social science perspective, ideology is difficult to measure and describe because it focuses on our shared systems of beliefs, values, and norms. However, Trice and Beyer (1993) argue that by examining what an organization does, people can understand (and make judgements about) an organization's culture and its values. The forms of organizational culture are observable ways that members of any culture express their identity. Figure 8.1 summarizes Trice and Beyer's conceptualization of the forms of organizational culture.

When organizations try to argue that they are ethical, sustainable, and socially responsible – before, during, or after crises – stakeholders look for evidence that would confirm or deny the organization's self-description. This is one of the reasons that an organization's history of crisis (Coombs, 2004; Kim, 2013; Maresh & Williams, 2007), its pre-crisis reputation (Claeys & Cauberghe, 2015; Coombs & Holladay, 2006; Lyon & Cameron, 2004; Turk, Jin, Stewart, Kim, & Hipple, 2012), the strength of its brand community (Brown & Billings, 2013), and its corporate heritage in social responsibility (Balmer, Blombäck, & Scandelius, 2013; Coombs & Holladay, 2015; Kim & Lee, 2015; Vanhamme & Grobben, 2009) can all affect how stakeholders interpret an organization's actions. Each of these can be readily interpreted as evidence of an organization's culture and more broadly its ideology.

This is one of the most important reasons that developing an organization's capacity for crisis response must begin with a critical examination of its culture and how its actions are interpreted by all of its stakeholders – internal and external. This kind of analysis can begin with simple SWOT or PESTLE analyses, with an issues management protocol as I have already discussed, but a comparison of what the organization says it believes in and what its stakeholders think it believes in provides insight into the opportunities and limitations in its crisis response argument.

Let me give you a brief example. BP is a company with a long and problematic crisis history – like most companies in the oil and gas industry. However, before the 2010 explosion in the Gulf of Mexico, there had been a number of damaging incidents in the United States and around the world. This was one of the reasons that then CEO

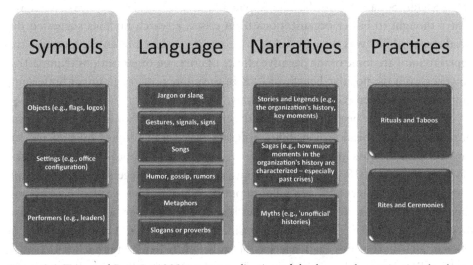

Figure 8.1 Trice and Beyer's (1993) conceptualization of the forms of organizational culture

Tony Hayward became the CEO in the first place; he had a good history for safety within BP and that was his core mission as CEO – to improve its safety performance. When the explosion and the massive oil leak happened in April, 2010 BP's crisis response messaging and actions were excellent (Diers-Lawson & Pang, 2016; Diers, 2012; Diers & Donohue, 2013). Yet, in part because of some clumsy engagement by the company's leaders and because of its crisis history, very few people believed BP's sincerity. Why? There was too much 'evidence' available in the public sphere that could be interpreted as demonstrating the company did not care, was not interested in safety, and was socially irresponsible.

Social responsibility

Should BP have responded differently? Definitely not. A socially responsible and ethical response to the crisis provides evidence for future judgements about the company. But this poses a challenge to crisis response. So, let us take a step backwards and briefly consider the role and impact of social responsibility on an organization's capacity to respond to crises.

Today organizations are increasingly expected to be socially responsible, with active corporate social responsibility (CSR) programs (Tench, Sun, & Jones, 2014). Business cases for CSR argue it creates value by enhancing a business's integrative capacity by focusing on the interrelationships between shareholders, stakeholders, and society (Graafland & Smid, 2019; Kurucz, Colbert, & Wheeler, 2008). Unfortunately, the direct relationship between CSR and the performance of a firm is tenuous at best, with findings directly linking to financial performance problematic (Barnett, 2019; Saeidi, Sofian, Saeidi, Saeidi, & Saaeidi, 2015). At the very least, CSR was always thought to buffer organizations from crises; research findings suggested that social responsibility was strongly linked with a more positive pre-crisis reputation that helped to mitigate some of the negative effects of crises on organizations (Kim, 2013). However, even the positive benefit of CSR in the context of reputational buffering is now being questioned (Coombs & Holladay, 2015).

While there have been debates about the efficacy of the outcomes of CSR programs for organizations, social responsibility programs have been adopted by most modern firms because they assume it will help to create value and appeal with stakeholders (Habib & Hasan, 2019; Morgeson, Aguinis, Waldman, & Siegel, 2013). Contemporary thought also places CSR as a pillar of public relations (PR) because social responsibility improves a brand's reputation and identity, customer relations, and purchase intention, and it encourages consumer/business engagement and collaboration (Cornelissen, 2014). The core challenge for the stakeholder-based approach is that there can be a disconnection between the socially responsible identity that the organization communicates about and any number of alternative or competing versions about the organization's identity, depending on the stakeholders asked (Crane & Glozer, 2016).

If all of this is true, then why is social responsibility not the panacea for building crisis response capacity? One good explanation is, as Coombs and Holladay (2015) would suggest, a crisis can violate stakeholders expectations about an organization and thus create greater frustration and anger. I have no doubt this is part of the challenge. However, my own research on social responsibility also suggests that stakeholders make evaluations about the authenticity of CSR behaviors (i.e., how much stakeholders connect CSR activities with judgments about the organization's core values or its ideology) in order to evaluate how they feel about the organization (Diers-Lawson, Coope, & Tench, 2018). Doug Ashwell's case study (see Box 8.1) provides a good example of this point.

Box 8.1 Case study: Questioning Fonterra's authenticity

By Doug Ashwell

In 2013, Fonterra, New Zealand's largest dairy exporter, conducted a multimillion dollar recall of some of its milk powder suspected of being contaminated with botulism. Later tests revealed no botulism was present. However, the recall and subsequent issues with Fonterra's inability to speedily trace where all the milk powder had been sold detrimentally affected the company's image both internationally and locally – an image already tarnished by two previous food safety issues in 2008 and 2013.

The first, in 2008, occurred when Sanlu, a Chinese subsidiary company of Fonterra, was found to be adding melamine to milk powder to boost protein levels. The milk powder was then used to manufacture infant milk formula, causing approximately 300,000 infants to suffer kidney damage and killing six. Fonterra's second food safety issue in 2013 resulted from residues of dicyandiamide (DCD), a fertilizer aid, being found in some of its milk products. The discovery saw the destruction of 130,000 tons of milk powder in Sri Lanka worth nearly $700,000. In addition to these problems and the botulism recall, the intensification of dairy farming and subsequent effluent run-off is blamed for increasing degradation of the water quality in New Zealand waterways. Being the biggest dairy producer in the country means that Fonterra is the main target of those who blame dairy farming for the degradation of New Zealand waterways.

Since the botulism crisis, and as a response to these issues, Fonterra has embarked on a television advertising campaign. Some advertisements feature two-time world champion All Black captain, Richie McCaw, a New Zealand icon. In the advertisements McCaw states that Fonterra is taking its products to the world, and this makes him proud and keen to give his support to Fonterra farmers. More recent advertisements highlight medical applications of Fonterra products, including the production of high-quality lactose used in asthma inhalers worldwide.

Despite these good news stories and McCaw's support, the advertisements have been heavily criticized as nothing more than a charm offensive by Fonterra. Different groups, including Greenpeace, have used social media to criticize the advertising campaign, arguing it attempts to distract people from the continued pollution of New Zealand waterways caused by intensive dairy farming. This reading of the advertisements seems borne out by a 2018 New Zealand's Ministry for Primary Industries survey that found only half those surveyed held a positive image of dairy farming, with the other half citing the poor environmental performance and pollution of waterways by dairy farming as their reason for being negative towards the industry.

This result suggests Fonterra's advertising efforts to improve its image have failed because the major issue in the public's mind – Fonterra's track record on environmental pollution – is being ignored. Acknowledging the issue and illustrating how the company is working with farmers to alleviate pollution of water ways could be a better strategy – a strategy that might appear more genuine to the public than the current advertising campaign.

The Fonterra case demonstrates that amplifying socially responsible actions is simply not enough to build crisis capacity or even a good reputation. So, if we get practical about this, then how can organizational culture and social responsibility help build capacity? From new focus group conversations and a questionnaire to a broader participant group that I have developed in recently, it seems that the pathway to building crisis capacity via appealing to values requires (see Figure 8.2):

1   Building stakeholder belief that their voice is heard by the organization – if stakeholders like or dislike the organization, it matters.

2   Focusing on local community-based engagement. More so than helping people in far-off places, it is more believable when organizations treat their own employees and communities well.

3   Already having a good reputation. This is the double-edged sword; If an organization does not have a good reputation, then its CSR efforts are probably not going to be as effective. However, consistently behaving ethically builds reputation over time and thus makes subsequent CSR efforts more believable.

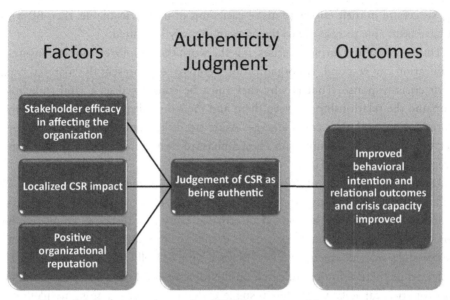

Figure 8.2 Pathway to improving CSR's impact on crisis response capacity

Building crisis capacity with employees as internal stakeholders

I have suggested that stakeholder judgments about an organization's culture and its CSR efforts are going to influence how well it is able to respond to a crisis and how believable its responses are going to be. I have also shown a pathway for organizations to help build their values-oriented capacity for crisis response, but that is not the only way that an inside-out approach to crisis capacity building should be explored. It is also imperative that employees be treated as strategic and vital stakeholders in order to ensure that organizations can effectively respond to crises.

Let me come back to the case of BP's explosion in the Gulf of Mexico to help make the point. In 2014, I had the occasion to hear Brian Gilvary – BP's dhief financial officer (CFO) during the crisis – speak about his experience in crisis response and talk with him about it. As CFO, Gilvary was a long way from the oil spill in the Gulf of Mexico, but his group's work was essential to BP's response. BP had to free up tens of millions of dollars very quickly in order to not only fund the process to stop the spill and clean it up, but also ensure those affected could receive the support they needed. He talked about the hardest part of getting the job done: Keeping his team focused. Everyone was profoundly emotional about the loss of life, the continuing risks, and the personal attacks they were receiving as employees of BP because of the situation. We will come back to crisis leadership in the next chapter, but had Gilvary's team not been successful in their efforts to make vast sums of money available, then BP would not have been able to respond to the crisis in the way it wanted.

This is the point: During all crises, it is the work that employees do that ensures an organization can respond. An organization's employees represent the material capacity for crisis response. That is why they must be considered as a vital stakeholder group and the relationship between them and their organization managed effectively before, during, and after crises emerge. Aside from the material response employees offer, they also are an organization's best ambassadors and front line of the defense for its reputation (Riddell, 2013).

Despite this, the field of crisis communication has some limitations in its understanding of the role and importance of employees during crises (Heide & Simonsson, 2015; Riddell, 2013). In the context of crisis capacity and response, employees have been on the periphery of our investigations despite their importance for an organization to successfully manage emergent crises (Mazzei, Kim, & Dell'Oro, 2012; Riddell, 2013).

So, while there is limited research on the topic of employees and crisis communication or crisis capacity, what there is suggests that employee reactions are likely to be influenced by several factors. For example, Promsri (2014) discussed that perceptions of poor crisis preparedness can lead to poor morale, productivity, and productivity. Moreover, employee voice and emotion has been connected to employee decisions during crises (Edwards, Lawrence, & Ashkanasy, 2016). Also, effective communication and information sharing can help to safeguard trust relationships within an organization during crises (Mazzei & Ravazzani, 2014). This leads us to some very specific recommendations for improving crisis response capacity that focus on the hard and soft skills needed for organizations to respond to crises more effectively.

Hard and soft skills needed to build crisis capacity

In the context of crises, there are specific skill sets that need to be developed. Lalonde and Roux-Dufort (2013) suggest that effective crisis response requires three levels of knowledge:

- **Conceptual or theoretical** – understanding previous research and theory related to crisis
- **Practical** – gaining experience in the issues management process and responding to crises
- **Reflective** – being able to evaluate performance, outcomes, and best practices for the future

Recognizing these needs, in the last several years, there has been a growing engagement between the academic and practitioner crisis communities, with improved exchanges of knowledge and experience in the classroom, at conferences, and in practice. Though students often challenge the salience and practicality of theory-based learning, good theory informs good practice and vice versa. As a testament to the dual importance of practice and theory, I would say this: Practitioners in crisis communication have challenged the academic community in recent years to develop and test more predictive theory to inform their own crisis decision-making. I would argue that, in our field, the recognition of the importance of both theory and practice is wide-spread.

Theoretical, practical, and reflective knowledge come in many shapes and sizes. These can range from news management and media relations to interpersonal and team skills, to business administration, and even to information technology (Zamoum, 2013). This is also why crisis response capacity is not just a domain of the communications professional but represents a multidisciplinary endeavor where technical specialists ranging from management to communication to IT must take on more strategic and managerial roles, not just those most directly related to their technical or specialist skills (Heide & Simonsson, 2014).

More than this, research connected to learning and training consistently recognize that improving decision-making skills in moments of stress is critical if organizations and professionals are to build their crisis capacity (Simola, 2014; Tipuric, Skoko, Jugo, & Mesin, 2013). Simola (2014) points out that practice makes perfect (or at least better) – especially when it comes to making ethical decisions during crises. Likewise, Frisby, Sellnow, Lane, Veil, and Sellnow (2013) point out that improving practitioner's self-efficacy, or their confidence in their ability to react well during crises is vital to improving crisis performance and capacity. This would also address Promsri's (2014) research that employees want good crisis preparedness on the organization's part.

These skill sets complement findings across a number of reports related broadly to the PR field. The research findings and trends remain relatively clear – what drives excellence in public relations is consistent – content, technology, and reputation (Cook & Holmes, 2016; Education, 2015; Holmes Report, 2015; Zerfass, Moreno, Tench, Verčič, & Verhoeven, 2017). These reports identify a number of core traits (see Figure 8.3), and skills (see Figure 8.4) that professionals entering the field should have.

If we take these as starting points blending conceptual, practical, and reflective knowledge bases, adding in the distinctive multidisciplinary crisis knowledge discussed, then we can better understand that organizations must build capacity and crisis preparation from the inside out.

Simulation's role in crisis capacity building

Here is the sticking point for professionals: How do we get practice? How do we test ourselves outside of a 'real' crisis? All professionals can and should certainly build

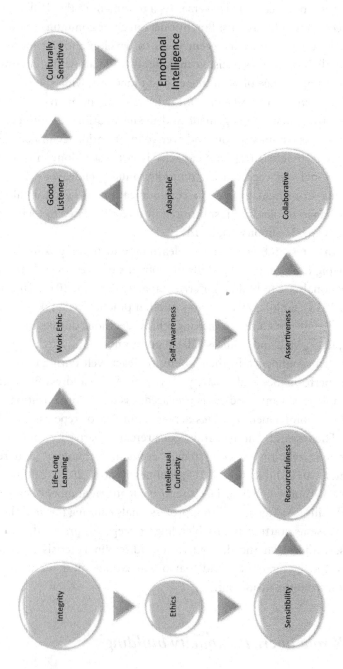

Figure 8.3 Traits needed by PR practitioners (Education, 2015)

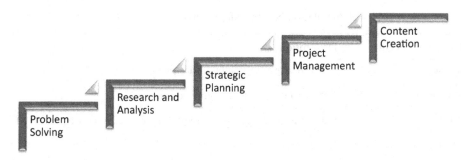

Figure 8.4 Skills needed by PR practitioners (Education, 2015)

conceptual and theoretical knowledge during their studies at university, in certification programs, or by keeping up with the latest research and practice in the field – but who lets people loose on a crisis so that students and professionals alike can improve their practical and reflective skills?

An increasing number of practitioners and educators across fields from business and communication to scientific fields highlight the importance of simulation for capacity building. A *Harvard Business Review* article in 2016 points out that while 'corporate tryouts' are still in their infancy, they are an increasingly popular way to screen candidates through the interview process because they are able to see them in action (Carey & Smith, 2016). As a result, they are being increasingly used from the C-suite to entry-level positions.

Consultancies and firms are increasingly using simulations to improve performance – both internally and with their clients. When we look at the offerings from management and communications consultancies, there are an increasing number of these companies using simulation-based training to improve firms' competencies. KPMG, for example, highlights simulation-based training and assessment as a part of its key service offerings, suggesting that rehearsal mitigates problems and risks later.

The research on simulation-based learning and training establishes a number of skills or learning benefits from simulations. Most of the relevant research on capacity building for organizations centers on learning in a business or communications context. Table 8.1 highlights a summary of the critical benefits offered from experiencing simulations as part of capacity building for organizations (Avramenko, 2012). Not surprisingly, when we compare these findings with the key skills and traits needed in the field of communication more broadly (see Figures 8.3 and 8.4), we find a pretty strong overlap. This is why so many more organizations are using simulation to build capacity.

One of the reasons that good simulation-based learning is able to do all this is that it targets **efficacy** (Sellnow et al., 2015). Efficacy is the belief in our ability to perform a specific action as well as the prediction of what will happen when we perform the action (Bandura, 1982, 1986, 1997). Bandura (1986) separated these expectations

Table 8.1 Simulation benefits adapted from Avramenko (2012)

Simulation benefits	Description
Teamwork	Collaboration, especially under pressure
Motivation	Offers an enjoyable learning experience
Risk-free	Students/organizations can experiment without consequences of bad decisions
Variety	Provides a different learning environment
Experiential	Provides action feedback to learners
Cost-effective	Alternative to real-life practice, high effectiveness compared to other approaches
Critical thinking	Enhances critical management thinking skills
Simplified reality	Focuses attention on specific elements by the simplification of the real world
Learning by comparison	Allows learners to compare their performance against each other, industry expectations, real-life data
Negotiation skills	Supports argumentation skills development to negotiate decisions
Time management	Provides practice of working towards deadlines
Independent learning	Applies theories, encourages students to think

into two distinctive types of efficacy: **Self-efficacy** and **outcome or response efficacy**. He defined self-efficacy as the conviction that a person can successfully execute the behavior required to produce the desired outcomes. The outcome or response efficacy refers to a person's estimation that a given behavior will lead to desirable outcomes. For example, one of the biggest reasons cited as a reason for low voter turnout in elections is that people often do not believe their vote will matter. In this case, their concern is not about whether they can successfully vote (self-efficacy), but about whether voting will result in a worthwhile outcome (response efficacy).

Why do we care so much about efficacy when we are talking about capacity building for crisis response? Very simply, because it substantially affects human behavior. For example, it governs choices about the behaviors that we will attempt: The lower our self-efficacy, the less likely we are to try a behavior (no one likes feeling like they are failing). As a result, it influences our simple motivation to act and really becomes a self-fulfilling prophecy.

Yet, when we target improving self-efficacy as a part of capacity building – especially in a crisis context – then we find that it is not difficult to improve employees' willingness and ability to act decisively and ethically across a number of business domains, but especially in crises (Avramenko, 2012; Cowton & Cummins, 2003; Hall & Ko, 2014; Helsloot, 2005; Sellnow et al., 2015; Shifflet & Brown, 2006; Springer & Borthick, 2004).

The pathway from simulations, to improving self-efficacy, and increasing crisis capacity exists because:

1 Simulations provide a "mastery experience" (Bandura, 1982; 1986; 1997). This is how we answer the question I posed earlier: How do we improve capacity without turning people loose on crises they are not ready for? We simulate the crisis experience to give them a chance to make mistakes, bad decisions, good decisions, and the like.

2 It allows professionals the opportunity to model their behaviors and gain vicarious experience (Bandura, 1982; 1986; 1997). Simulations can not only provide practical mastery experience, but also provide a reflective opportunity as well. This can come with critical reflections on a person's own performance as well as viewing how other people performed in the same or similar situations and developing best practices. More than just a case study, a simulation provides a more immersive experience.

3 It involves social persuasion as a tool for skill development (Bandura, 1982; 1986; 1997). What I mean by this is that people can be encouraged to improve their performance and offered feedback on their performance in a low-stakes context. Because of the practical and reflective nature of simulations, people are primed for feedback to improve their performance.

In an issues and crisis management context, simulation development also just makes sense because it supports module learning objectives like demonstrating the ability to critically evaluate and prioritize issues in complex and competitive international environments. It provides feedback on employing a stakeholder relationship management approach to managing risk. It allows learners to experience how to apply theory to crisis response decision-making so that they can articulate ethical and culturally appropriate crisis response recommendations. In short, it solves the chicken-and-egg question in crisis communication: How can we get experience if we do not have any?

My own students who have experienced simulations in our classes have said the following:

● The simulation experience helped them to learn more about issues and crisis management
● It allowed them to work on strategy development skills
● They gained experience in decision-making

- They had a good team/collaboration experience
- They felt challenged by the pressure and situation
- It improved their hard skills in issues and crisis management

I will leave you with this statement from one student who had been through a full-year internship before taking an issues and crisis management class. The student reflected on simulations and crisis capacity for organizations this way:

> During my placement year there were a few major crises. Personally, I think they were not handled as well as they could have been. And I think a big reason for this is that they were not effectively undergoing issues management.
>
> I think in future roles I would be able to sell the benefits of investing in issues management. I also think that even if a formal issues management process was not in place it if I am working in a corporate communications type role I could carry out the issues management process once a month or so. This would give me the edge as a practitioner to be able to see what could be coming internally or externally for the organization and be on top of any issues.

In review . . .

There are two sides to internal capacity building for crises. On the organizations' part, it is important for organizations to be ethical, to develop their reputation, and to generally be socially responsible. However, it is essential that their stakeholders – both internal and external – see this as authentic for it to help them weather crises more effectively. Likewise, capacity building is also about ensuring that employees – in our case especially those in the communications specialty – also have the capacity to respond. Lalonde and Roux-Dufort's (2013) analysis that effective crisis response requires conceptual or theoretical knowledge, practical experience, and reflection grounds our discussion of the key traits and skills required in the field of PR and corporate communications broadly, and complements the value in participating in (as employees) or offering (as organizations) simulations as a part of the capacity building process.

Review your understanding

By the end of this chapter, you should be able to understand and explain the following.

- The role that values and ideology play in an organization's capacity to respond to crises including:

- ○ Organizational culture – its ideology and forms
- ○ Using social responsibility to build crisis capacity:
  - ■ The pathway to building authentic social responsibility initiatives
  - ■ The challenge of reputation and crisis capacity
- The importance of building capacity within an organization
- Three levels of knowledge required for effective crisis response
  - ○ Connections between crisis capacity and overall PR field needs
  - ○ The role of simulation in building capacity

References

Ajzen, I. (2005). *Explaining intentions and behavior: Attitudes, personality, and behavior* (Vol. 2). Berkshire, England: McGraw-Hill Education.

Avramenko, A. (2012). Enhancing students' employability through business simulation. *Education + Training, 54*(5), 355–367.

Balmer, J. M., Blombäck, A., & Scandelius, C. (2013). Corporate heritage in CSR communication: A means to responsible brand image? *Corporate Communications: An International Journal, 18*(3), 362–382. doi:10.1108/CCIJ-07-2012-0048

Bandura, A. (1982). Self-efficacy mechanism in human agency. *American Psychologist, 37*(2), 122–147.

Bandura, A. (1986). *Social foundations of thought and action: A social cognitive theory.* Englewood Cliffs, NJ: Prentice Hall.

Bandura, A. (1997). *Self-efficacy: The exercise of control.* New York, NY: Freeman.

Barnett, M. L. (2019). The business case for corporate social responsibility: A critique and an indirect path forward. *Business & Society, 58*(1), 167–190.

Brown, N. A., & Billings, A. C. (2013). Sports fans as crisis communicators on social media websites. *Public Relations Review, 39*(1), 74–81.

Carey, D., & Smith, M. (2016, April 22). How companies are using simulations, competitions, and analytics to hire. *Harvard Business Review.* Retrieved from http://hbr.org/2016/04/how-companies-are-using-simulations-competitions-and-analytics-to-hire. Accessed July 10, 2019.

Claeys, A.-S., & Cauberghe, V. (2015). The role of a favorable pre-crisis reputation in protecting organizations during crises. *Public Relations Review, 41*(1), 64–71. doi:10.1016/j.pubrev.2014.10.013

Commission on Public Relations Education. (2015). *Commission on Public Relations Education industry-educator summit on public relations education.* Retrieved from www.instituteforpr.org/wp-content/uploads/CPRE20Summit20Summary20Report20July202015.pdf

Cook, F., & Holmes, P. (2016). *Global communications report*. Retrieved from www.holmes report.com/docs/default-source/default-document-library/2016-global-communications-report.pdf?sfvrsn=2

Coombs, T., & Holladay, S. (2015). CSR as crisis risk: Expanding how we conceptualize the relationship. *Corporate Communications: An International Journal, 20*(2), 144–162. doi:10.1108/CCIJ-10-2013-0078

Coombs, T. W., & Holladay, S. J. (2006). Unpacking the halo effect: Reputation and crisis management. *Journal of Communication Management, 10*(2), 123–137.

Coombs, W. T. (2004). Impact of past crises on current crisis communication: Insights from Situational Crisis Communication Theory. *Journal of Business Communication, 41*(3), 265–290.

Cornelissen, J. (2014). *Corporate communication: A guide to theory and practise*. London: Sage Publications.

Cowton, C. J., & Cummins, J. (2003). Teaching business ethics in UK higher education: Progress and prospects. *Teaching Business Ethics, 7*(1), 37–54.

Crane, A., & Glozer, S. (2016). Researching corporate social responsibility communication: Themes, opportunities and challenges. *Journal of Management Studies, 53*(7), 1223–1252.

Diers, A. R. (2012). Reconstructing stakeholder relationships using 'corporate social responsibility' as a response strategy to cases of corporate irresponsibility: The case of the 2010 BP spill in the Gulf of Mexico. In R. Tench, W. Sun, & B. Jones (Eds.), *Corporate social irresponsibility: A challenging concept* (Vol. 4, pp. 177–206). Bingley, UK: Emerald.

Diers, A. R., & Donohue, J. (2013). Synchronizing crisis responses after a transgression: An analysis of BP's enacted crisis response to the Deepwater Horizon crisis in 2010. *Journal of Communication Management, 17*(3), 252–269.

Diers-Lawson, A., Coope, K., & Tench, R. (2018). *Why can CSR seem like putting lipstick on a pig? Comparing practitioner and consumer perspectives to understand why CSR often fails to meet its objectives*. Paper presented at the European Public Relations, Education, and Research Association (EUPRERA) Annual Conference, Aarhus, Denmark.

Diers-Lawson, A., & Pang, A. (2016). Did BP atone for its transgressions? Expanding theory on 'ethical apology' in crisis communication. *Journal of Contingencies and Crisis Management, 24*(3), 148–161.

Dolan, S. L., Garcia, S., & Auerbach, A. (2003). Understanding and managing chaos in organisations. *International Journal of Management, 20*(1), 23–35.

Edwards, M. S., Lawrence, S. A., & Ashkanasy, N. M. (2016). How perceptions and emotions shaped employee silence in the case of "Dr. Death" at Bundaberg hospital. In N. M. Askanasy, C. E. J. Hartel, & W. J. Zerbe (Eds.), *Emotions and organizational governance* (pp. 341–379). Bingley, UK: Emerald Group Publishing Limited.

Freberg, K., & Palenchar, M. J. (2013). Convergence of digital negotiation and risk challenges: Strategic implications of social media for risk and crisis communications. In H.

S. N. Al-Deen & J. A. Hendricks (Eds.), *Social media and strategic communications* (pp. 83–100). London: Palgrave Macmillan.

Frisby, B. N., Sellnow, D. D., Lane, D. R., Veil, S. R., & Sellnow, T. L. (2013). Instruction in crisis situations: Targeting learning preferences and self-efficacy. *Risk Management, 15*(4), 250–271. doi:10.1057/rm.2013.7

Graafland, J., & Smid, H. (2019). Decoupling among CSR policies, programs, and impacts: An empirical study. *Business & Society, 58*(2), 231–267.

Habib, A., & Hasan, M. M. (2019). Corporate social responsibility and cost stickiness. *Business & Society, 58*(3), 453–492.

Hall, O. P., & Ko, K. (2014). Learning assurance using business simulations applications to executive management education. *Developments in Business Simulation and Experiential Learning, 33*.

Heide, M., & Simonsson, C. (2014). Developing internal crisis communication: New roles and practices of communication professionals. *Corporate Communications: An International Journal, 19*(2), 128–146.

Heide, M., & Simonsson, C. (2015). Struggling with internal crisis communication: A balancing act between paradoxical tensions. *Public Relations Inquiry, 4*(2), 223–255. doi:10.1177/2046147X15570108

Helsloot, I. (2005). Bordering on reality: Findings on the bonfire crisis management simulation. *Journal of Contingencies and Crisis Management, 13*(4), 159–169.

Holmes Report. (2015). *Social media changes leave gaps in PR education.* Retrieved from www.holmesreport.com/research/article/social-media-changes-leave-gaps-in-pr-education.

Hurley, R. F., Gillespie, N., Ferrin, D. L., & Dietz, G. (2013). Designing trustworthy organizations. *MIT Sloan Management Review, 54*(4), 75.

Jindal, S., Laveena, L., & Aggarwal, A. (2015). A comparative study of crisis management-Toyota v/s General Motors. *Scholedge International Journal of Management & Development, 2*(6), 1–12.

Ki, E.-J., & Brown, K. A. (2013). The effects of crisis response strategies on relationship quality outcomes. *Journal of Business Communication, 50*(4), 403–420. doi:10.1177/00219 43613497056

Kim, H.-S., & Lee, S. Y. (2015). Testing the buffering and boomerang effects of CSR practices on consumers' perception of a corporation during a crisis. *Corporate Reputation Review, 18*(4), 277–293. doi:10.1057/crr.2015.18

Kim, S. (2013). Corporate ability or virtue? Relative effectiveness of prior corporate associations in times of crisis. *International Journal of Strategic Communication, 7*(4), 241–256. doi:10.1080/1553118X.2013.824886

Kurucz, E. C., Colbert, B. A., & Wheeler, D. (2008). The business case for corporate social responsibility. In A. Crane, A. McWilliams, D. Matten, J. Moon, & D. S. Siegel (Eds.), *The Oxford handbook of corporate social responsibility* (pp. 83–112). New York, NY: Oxford University Press.

Lacey, R., Kennett-Hensel, P. A., & Manolis, C. (2015). Is corporate social responsibility a motivator or hygiene factor? Insights into its bivalent nature. *Journal of the Academy of Marketing Science, 42*(3). doi:10.1007/s11747-014-0390-9

Lalonde, C., & Roux-Dufort, C. (2013). Challenges in teaching crisis management connecting theories, skills, and reflexivity. *Journal of Management Education, 37*(1), 21–50. doi:10.1177/1052562912456144

Langer, R., & Thorup, S. (2006). Building trust in times of crisis: Storytelling and change communication in an airline company. *Corporate Communications: An International Journal, 11*(4), 371–390.

Lyon, L., & Cameron, G. T. (2004). A relational approach examining the interplay of prior reputation and immediate response to a crisis. *Journal of Public Relations Research, 16*(3), 213–241.

Maresh, M., & Williams, D. (2007). *Toward an industry-specific crisis response model: A look at the oil crises of British Petroleum and Phillips Petroleum.* Paper presented at the National Communication Association, Chicago, IL.

Mazzei, A., Kim, J.-N., & Dell'Oro, C. (2012). Strategic value of employee relationships and communicative actions: Overcoming corporate crisis with quality internal communication. *International Journal of Strategic Communication, 6*(1), 31–44.

Mazzei, A., & Ravazzani, S. (2014). Internal crisis communication strategies to protect trust relationships: A study of Italian companies. *International Journal of Business Communication,* 1–19. doi:10.1177/2329488414525447

Morgeson, F. P., Aguinis, H., Waldman, D. A., & Siegel, D. S. (2013). Extending corporate social responsibility research to the human resource management and organizational behavior domains: A look to the future. *Personnel Psychology, 66*(4), 805–824.

Promsri, C. (2014). Thai employees' perception towards organizational crisis preparedness. *Mediterranean Journal of Social Sciences, 5*(14), 41. doi:10.5901/mjss.2014.v5n14p41

Riddell, P. (2013). Rallying the troops: Crisis communication and reputation management in financial services. *Journal of Brand Strategy, 2*(3), 222–227.

Saeidi, S. P., Sofian, S., Saeidi, P., Saeidi, S. P., & Saaeidi, S. A. (2015). How does corporate social responsibility contribute to firm financial performance? The mediating role of competitive advantage, reputation, and customer satisfaction. *Journal of Business Research, 68*(2), 341–350.

Sellnow, D. D., Lane, D., Littlefield, R. S., Sellnow, T. L., Wilson, B., Beauchamp, K., & Venette, S. (2015). A receiver-based approach to effective instructional crisis communication. *Journal of Contingencies and Crisis Management, 23*(3), 149–158. doi:10.1111/1468-5973.12066

Shifflet, M., & Brown, J. (2006). The use of instructional simulations to support classroom teaching: A crisis communication case study. *Journal of Educational Multimedia and Hypermedia, 15*(4), 377.

Simola, S. (2014). Teaching corporate crisis management through business ethics education. *European Journal of Training and Development, 38*(5), 483–503. doi:10.1108/EJTD-05-2013-0055

Springer, C. W., & Borthick, A. F. (2004). Business simulation to stage critical thinking in introductory accounting: Rationale, design, and implementation. *Issues in Accounting Education*, 19(3), 277–303.

Tench, R., Sun, W., & Jones, B. (2014). *Communicating corporate social responsibility: Perspectives and practice*. Bingley, UK: Emerald Group Publishing.

Tipuric, D., Skoko, B., Jugo, D., & Mesin, M. (2013). Crisis management dilemmas: Differences in attitudes towards reactive crisis communication strategies among future business professionals in Croatia. *Montenegrin Journal of Economics*, 9(2), 27.

Trice, H. M., & Beyer, J. M. (1993). *The cultures of work organizations*. Upper Saddle River, NJ: Prentice Hall.

Turk, J. V., Jin, Y., Stewart, S., Kim, J., & Hipple, J. R. (2012). Examining the interplay of an organization's prior reputation, CEO's visibility, and immediate response to a crisis. *Public Relations Review*, 38(4), 574–583. doi:10.1016/j.pubrev.2012.06.012

van der Meer, T. G., & Verhoeven, J. W. (2014). Emotional crisis communication. *Public Relations Review*, 40(3), 526–536. doi:10.1016/j.pubrev.2014.03.004

Vanhamme, J., & Grobben, B. (2009). "Too good to be true!". The effectiveness of CSR history in countering negative publicity. *Journal of Business Ethics*, 85(2), 273–283.

Zamoum, K. (2013). Teaching crisis management in Arab universities: A critical assessment. *Public Relations Review*, 39(1), 47–54. doi:10.1016/j.pubrev.2012.09.005

Zerfass, A., Moreno, Á., Tench, R., Verčič, D., & Verhoeven, P. (2017). *European Communication Monitor 2017. How strategic communication deals with the challenges of visualisation, social bots and hypermodernity. Results of a survey in 50 countries*. Brussels: EACD and EUPRERA; Berlin: Quadriga Media Berlin.

9 | The leadership challenge for organizations in crisis

Learning objectives

By the end of this chapter, the reader should:

- Be able to examine the differences between crisis management and crisis leadership
- Identify the roles that leaders serve during crises for different stakeholders
- Reflect on the challenges of crisis leadership

In Chapter 8 I focused on the two pathways to building crisis capacity: Building the organization's capacity and building its employees' capacity. In Chapter 8 I also talked about what BP's chief financial officer, Brian Gilvary, said about his job as a corporate leader through the crisis: The hardest part was keeping his employees positive, focused, and able to ensure the company's success.

I am going to pick back up with that theme in Chapter 9 as the critical leadership challenges that organizations in crisis face are discussed. There can be no doubt that a leader plays a pivotal role in the management and containment of a crisis. This chapter will differentiate between crisis management and crisis leadership, and explore the different kinds of roles that leaders must play – all the while exploring the challenges of crisis leadership.

Leadership and management are different constructs

In this chapter, I will make one vital assumption: While leadership and management are both important during crises, they are different constructs. Throughout the book,

Management	Leadership
• A function	• Relationship
• Planning	• Talent
• Budgeting	• Motivating
• Evaluating	• Coaching
• Facilitating	• Trust

Figure 9.1 Summary of the critical concerns in management versus leadership

I have discussed the importance of crisis management; however, if I adopt an inside-out approach to stakeholder engagement, then leadership is vital to success in managing and responding to crises. Most business literature separates management and leadership functions along simple lines: Leadership is about relationships and relationship building; management is functional. Figure 9.1 summarizes the critical differences between management and leadership functions.

Fener Cevik and Finance (2015) point out that there are four critical objectives in crisis management:

● Identifying how the crisis type could influence pivotal aspects of the organization like finance to ensure that as a crisis emerges, pivotal aspects are not adversely affected

● Helping the management team identify and assess the sources of the crisis

● Forming a strategy to end a crisis

● Strategizing how to improve the organization post-crisis

Their analysis complements others like Wooten and James (2008), who argue that effective crisis management is characterized by four elements: Speed of response, an effective crisis management plan, adequacy of resources, and good communication. I will come back to the crisis plan in Part 5 of this text. However, these are all essential functions in crisis response, but they do not necessarily reflect what good crisis leadership actually represents.

Core crisis leadership roles

If we think about leadership as a relational function, this is one of the reasons that great leaders also tend to be great communicators. This is probably a reason that both industry and academic research focuses so heavily on leaders as spokespeople for their organizations during crises. For example, one analysis focuses on the eight lessons that leaders can learn and the importance of having leaders practice communication scenarios, setting expectations, getting media training, and such (Spaeth, 2010). When we begin to explore the research focusing on the more specific roles that leaders serve during crises, we see several different roles that leaders have to carry out: Psychological roles to reaffirm and inspire (Sandler, 2009), functional roles to direct and manage the material needs in a crisis (i.e., getting the right people in the right places) (Alder, 1997), and public relations (PR) roles. Let us take a detailed look at each of these core crisis leadership roles.

Psychological and emotional role

Leaders serve a vital psychological and emotional role for stakeholders – both inside and outside the organization. Remember, crises heighten peoples' sense of uncertainty, thus raising fears and anxieties (Alder, 1997; Loosemore, 1998; Rickard, McComas, Clarke, Stedman, & Decker, 2013).

Why does the psychological and emotional role matter?

Good crisis leadership should **serve to reduce fears and anxiety** (Griffin-Padgett & Allison, 2010; Liu, Liao, & Wei, 2015; Parmenter, 2010; Quirke, 2009; Sandler, 2009). But the psychological and emotional function goes beyond mere reassurance: **Good crisis leaders are able to build trust amongst their critical stakeholders** in the organization's ability to meaningfully address the problem (Parmenter, 2010). Sandler's (2009) research indicates that stakeholders demand a leader who will follow through on they/their promises, seems transparent, gives credit where it is due, and is generous with their criticisms (i.e., they do not seek to scapegoat their subordinates or other agencies). In order to build trust, good leaders must also demonstrate decisiveness while allowing others to participate; in other words, good crisis leaders often demonstrate characteristics of servant leadership characterized by an other-orientation to support their stakeholders' psychological safety (Liu et al., 2015; Parmenter, 2010).

If good crisis leaders are able to demonstrates themselves to be trustworthy, then – as well as reducing fear and anxiety – one of the outcomes of being trustworthy is that leaders are also to **generate optimism about the future in times of crisis** (Griffin-Padget & Allison, 2010; Sandler, 2009). We have seen this executed for decades, from Winston Churchill's World War II radio addresses through to President Bill Clinton's responses to the terrorist attacks in Oklahoma City, to President Barack Obama's responses to gun violence in the United States, and more recently into the way that leaders have responded to the attacks in Belgium, Germany, France, London, and Manchester – there is a defiance and rhetoric of survival that generates optimism in the face of adversity. Good leadership is about inspiring people.

151

We contrast this against people who have been less effective crisis leaders. For me, one of the worst examples of this psychological and emotional role had to have been President George Bush after 9/11. I remember listening to his first public statement – I was on my way to work. The two key messages that he sent were that the world was ever more uncertain, and that the United States would seek retribution. I think that he was probably trying to acknowledge the struggle and offer a rallying cry, but his rhetoric on that day and beyond focused on messages of "We have a lot to be afraid of, but we're going to go after them." There was really nothing offered that made people feel better. It was more of an 'Old Testament justice' appeal, but it failed to generate optimism for the future – and I would argue this shaped a dark American identity for the next decade.

Behaviors to enact the psychological and emotional role of crisis leadership

If the psychological and emotional role is a tricky one to maneuver, it becomes complicated because not only is there a rhetorical aspect to leadership but there is also a behavioral one. It is one thing to offer reassuring messages, but a leader's behaviors in the midst of a crisis must also support and match their rhetoric (Parmenter, 2010; Quirke, 2009; Sandler, 2009). This is not about knee-jerk reactions, but stakeholders do expect good leaders to **demonstrate prompt and considered action** during a crisis that backs up their rhetoric in order to be reassured the crisis will be positively and meaningfully resolved (Griffin-Padgett & Allison, 2010; Paraskevas, Altinay, McLean, & Cooper, 2013; Sandler, 2009). This is one of the reasons why effective crisis planning is going to help an organization to respond to a crisis effectively: It gives the leader a pre-considered set of actions that hopefully need only minor adaptations, so those first press conferences in which they give information are ones where something is actually happening – and the leader is not just punting the ball down the pitch for a while.

All of this, though – from meeting people's expectations for what leaders should deliver during crises to understanding their behaviors – also requires **honest and consistent communication** (Hargis & Watt, 2010; Jamal & Bakar, 2015; Parmenter, 2010; Sandler, 2009). Notice the first part of this: The honesty bit. People can take bad news, especially when it is delivered in a way that meets the goals we have already talked about, but it has to be honest. It used to be that organizations could be a bit strategically ambiguous; they could try to shift the blame a bit, obscure the issues, and generally be a bit sleazy – and people would take that. Today's information consumers, though. simply do not accept it. When we dig into the crisis communication research from the 1990s, we see a lot of discussion about the strategic ambiguity tactic, but these days, people's expectations have simply shifted.

The other part of honest and consistent communication is that in a 24/7 news cycle, people expect updates from the organization. This is tough sometimes; as a crisis is unfolding, it can be several hours before anything more is known about the situation. The problem is that the media does not just leave stories until there is new information: If the crisis is big enough for instant coverage, then the media is going to look at all possible angles and fish until they have something. This is one of the reasons that today's organizational leader needs to be an effective communicator. It is to an organization's advantage to be available to the media and to those affected – to keep a consistent flow of communication internally and externally.

For example, the disappearance of the Malaysian Airlines flight that was bound for China has been largely viewed as a failure because the families of the passengers perceived a lack of communication from its leaders. While the airline did regular updates a few times a day, the frequency of the updates and available information did not meet the anxiety and information needs of those affected by the crisis. Worse yet, all of the communication was done by spokespersons and not the leaders themselves; the company was not talking about the process they were following to find the flight; and for the largely Chinese families affected, it seemed like Malaysian Airlines was not being forthcoming. The reality was just that there little to report, but that did not matter because the stakeholders' emotional needs were not being met.

Connecting with stakeholder emotional needs is also a critical leadership behavior during crises (Sandler, 2009). In their analysis of the mayors of New Orleans after Hurricane Katrina and New York after 9/11 Griffin-Padget and Allison (2010) found that these leaders were incredibly effective in the psychological and emotional role because their messaging consistently communicated the values that everyone had in common and highlighted their priority on everyone's safety. But connecting with stakeholder emotional needs is not only important for external stakeholders, it is also vital for internal ones as well. Liu et al. (2015) argue that a leader's job is to help manage a team environment for psychological safety in order to build an organizational context to manage challenging situations.

Finally, in order to meet the psychological and emotional needs of their stakeholders during a crisis, **leaders need to be inspiring**. This is more than just making people feel good: Good crisis leaders need to make their stakeholders feel like they are connected to the success of the crisis being managed – internal stakeholders especially (Parmenter, 2010; Sandler, 2009). Of course, when we are talking about inspiration, we are talking about charismatic leadership and people who lead their companies through challenging times (Jamal & Bakar, 2015). Certainly, Steve Jobs was an example of a charismatic leader, but he was not the only one in the technology industry who was. During the 1990s, the semiconductor manufacturing industry was struggling to be competitive. At this time Robert Noyce created a cross-company research consortium – basically getting competitors to agree to collaborate on research to improve semiconductors – called SEMATECH. Because of his approach to leadership, Noyce was able to inspire competitors to collaborate, improve their products, and be more globally competitive (Beyer & Browning, 1999). Leaders like Noyce are able to be successful advocates within their organizations, and also outside of them, because the same characteristics that draw people to them within their organizations also tend to make them appealing to media outlets and to other kinds of stakeholders.

Functional role

We have to remember that leaders must serve more than an emotional role – they must also serve functional roles. That is not to say that the same person necessarily needs to be the emotional and functional leader. In many cases, we find that people who are excellent in serving the psychological and emotional roles of crisis leadership (like Robert Noyce) may not be the best functional leaders. Other organizational representatives may be better at addressing the details of the material crisis; therefore, understanding the functional role is also about recognizing different aptitudes as a part of modern organizational leadership as well.

What are the qualities of functional leadership during crises?

One of the first qualities of the functional role of leadership is that leaders need the **legitimate authority to act in a crisis**. This is more than just being the boss; for example, President Donald Trump had a massive amount of power conferred to him because of his office. However, the question about his legitimacy to act in a crisis is not conferred through the office, rather through his credibility. As such, it is worth talking about what power is. When we are talking about power, we are talking about more than just a Machiavellian ability to force people to do things that they would not ordinarily do. Let us have a quick look at the five classical bases of social power (French, Raven, & Cartwright, 1959). It is important to note that no single leader necessarily needs to embody all of these, but most powerful leaders will have multiple sources of power because it makes them appealing to different types of people.

1 **Reward power:** Ask these questions: Who signs your bonus check? Does that motivate you? The easiest way to think about reward power is a Pavlovian response: If I am training my dog, to reinforce the good behavior that I am trying to encourage, I offer him a reward for behaving. In a crisis context, when organizations are struggling to solve a problem, sometimes they will offer rewards for crowdsourcing solutions. This is a positive way to get people to focus on problems through incentivizing solutions. Employee reward schemes, bonuses, and even customer reward schemes are all ways of harnessing reward power.

2 **Coercive power:** This is what we often think of in terms of power – what I just called a Machiavellian view of power – where people perform because the leader holds some power of negative consequences over them. In traditional classrooms, when I am marking, I hold coercive power over my students. If they fail to perform to my expectations, I can give them a bad grade, which might affect them negatively beyond just my class. This can be an effective way to get what we want out of people – fear of negative consequences. In cases of crisis, because crises produce fear, this can be harnessed effectively to get various stakeholders focused on finding solutions. Yet, the peculiarity of fear is that it has to be wielded very carefully because there is what we call a 'curvilinear relationship' between fear and motivation: Fear motivates only to a certain point. When we increase the fear beyond the point where people can cope, it serves as a demotivator: People will either just not act or act exactly opposite of what we want. Think about revolutions, mutinies, takeovers – a lot of times these happen because the fear stops working. Crises can be incredibly overwhelming, so coercive power can be used, but it should be used cautiously.

3 **Legitimate power:** We must consider stakeholders' perceptions that the leader has the authority and a legitimate right to prescribe behavior for them. Think about the age-old child's cry of rebellion – "You're not the boss of me!" In this case, it is not about whether the leader can reward or punish us; it is about whether we recognize and accept their authority. This comes from the belief that a person has the formal right to make demands, and to expect others to be compliant and obedient. A president, prime minister or monarch typically has legitimate power. So does a chief executive officer (CEO), a religious minister, or a fire chief. Electoral mandates, social hierarchies, cultural norms, and organizational structure all provide the basis for legitimate power. This type of power, however, can be unpredictable and unstable. With the loss of title or position, legitimate power can instantly disappear, because people were influenced by the position held rather than by the leader. Also, the scope of a leader's legitimate power is limited to situations that others believe they have a right to control. If a fire chief tells people to stay away from a burning building, for example, they will likely listen. But if their tries to make two people act more courteously toward one another, odds are just as good that they will ignore the instruction.

4 **Referent power:** This emerges because a leader is liked and respected; the leader is someone with whom others identify. Celebrities have referent power, which is why they can influence everything from what people buy to which politician they elect. Take, for example, Kylie Jenner's tweet that she did not use Snapchat anymore, effectively wiping $1.3 billion (USD) from the company's stock value (BBC News, 2018). In a workplace, a person with referent power often makes everyone feel good, so their tends to have a lot of influence. In crisis contexts, it can be really useful because these are leaders other people want to hear from, see, and follow.

5 **Expert power.** When a leader has the knowledge and skills that enable them to to understand a situation, suggest solutions, use solid judgment, and generally outperform others, people will listen to, trust, and respect what the leader says. In the context of a crisis, this is the source of power that can be the most compelling: We want to have faith in the knowledge and experience of the people in charge of the situation, and trust that they actually know what they are doing.

Ideally, in a crisis, for a leader to have legitimate authority to act, they should be able to demonstrate all five sources of power. Leaders must be in a position to make decisions (legitimate power). They should be credible sources of authority on the organization and the situation (expert power), but they should also be respected and liked (referent power). More than that, because of the immediate need to act in a crisis, it is also helpful to wield the ability to reward (reward power) and punish people (coercive power); however, given the needs we have already discussed in terms of the psychological and emotional role of leadership, these types of social power should be exerted cautiously.

If a leader has a solid base of power, then – hopefully clearly aided by an effective crisis plan – they are able to **create or implement the appropriate procedures** to respond to the crisis. Because of the power they have, effective leaders are able to get compliance so that when they say that x, y, and z need to happen, they do (Alder, 1997).

One of the challenges in moments of crisis is that people can be easily sidetracked by the situation. Part of the functional role of leaders is also to keep people on track, so that they are not focused on the uncertainty of the situation and the response strategy is actually executed (Paraskevas et al., 2013; Parmenter, 2010). This works at the organizational level, stakeholder level, and certainly at the level of the group. When we have talked about group roles, this is one of the critical roles during crisis preparation and management for the crisis team – focusing on response integrity and effective team engagement (Hwang & Cameron, 2008; King, 2002; Parmenter, 2010). There are three functional roles that crisis leaders must serve to be effective during crises.

First, the functional role of leadership is an inside-out role as well because one of the critical components to functional crisis leadership is **effectively managing relationships with people** (Hwang & Cameron, 2008). So, effective crisis leaders are able to build perceptions of justice for all stakeholders. Of course, this does not mean that stakeholders are always going to get what they want, but the process for managing stakeholder needs to be transparent and fair – and leaders have a lot to do with creating and communicating this impression. It is for this reason that Hwang and Cameron (2008) found that a leader's style matters, and accommodative and democratic styles of leadership resulted in the most positive evaluations of crisis leadership.

Second, because of their leadership role, one of the most important functional tasks that leaders have is to build long-term group relationships both within the organization and also (importantly) with outside groups (Paraskevas et al., 2013; Parmenter, 2010; Ucelli, 2002; Ulmer, 2001). As I have mentioned, crises tend to bring together groups with very different interests – including corporations, government agencies, nonprofits, health organizations, environmental advocacy groups, research groups such as universities, and consumer groups. All of these types of stakeholders may not have interacted previously; however, a crisis can result in collaborations between these groups. So, a critical role for a leader during a crisis is to be an effective boundary-spanner (Fischbacher-Smith, 2014) so that once the connection to these stakeholders is made, (when possible) they are maintained. These stakeholders can often represent important partners in the future for issue management, innovation, and managing new rules and regulations.

Third, along these lines in a modern organizational environment, leaders must develop a participative culture within an organization, and between an organization and its stakeholders, is an important functional role that leaders can serve in order to optimize the opportunities for good crisis response. Because stakeholders are looking to leaders, it can be a way to reaffirm or even develop two-way engagement from decision-makers to interested stakeholders.

In short, managing relationships with people – the PR role – is a vital part of the functional leadership process during crises (Hargis & Watt, 2010; Jamal & Bakar, 2015; Ucelli, 2002).

Public relations role

If the concept of crisis leadership is challenging to define, the research on the communicative function of those leaders is not. For example, most of the contemporary research focusing on organizational transgressions emphasizes the importance of communicating sincerity and regret, and trying to help restore faith in the company and the actions it takes in order to manage the crisis (Coombs & Holladay, 2002; Griffin-Padgett & Allison, 2010; Wesseling, 2008). In fact, an analysis of New York's Mayor Rudy Giuliani after 9/11 and New Orleans's Mayor Ray Nagin after Hurricane Katrina demonstrated a process of 'restorative rhetoric': An initial reaction, assessment of the crisis, articulating blame, messages of healing and forgiveness, and corrective action (Griffin-Padget & Allison, 2010). In general, this suggests that while leaders' messaging after a crisis will emphasize pro-social strategies, there is also a possibility of seeing defensive responses to address issues of blame and criticism. However, unlike a mayor who is serving the public, the corporate leader is also serving their company's financial health; therefore, we should also look for messaging that emphasizes their role as the guardians and promoters of their company's image (Ginzel, Kramer, & Sutton, 1993).

This leads us to more traditional PR roles for leaders – and one of the first questions that we have to ask is whether the CEO should be the spokesperson. Conventional wisdom generally says yes, but with a caveat. In serious crises, all stakeholders expect to hear from the boss, but that does not necessarily mean that their is going to be the only spokesperson (Carroll & Hatakenaka, 2001). The CEO has to be seen and heard from, but they have other jobs to do as well and so their presence has to be managed. But this also is moderated by the timing of the crisis and its severity (Lucero, Kwang, & Pang, 2009).

By timing, what I mean is that the CEO is probably not the first person from the organization that the public or media will hear from. If that is the case, this signals that is a major crisis. This can certainly serve to escalate perceptions of severity and so has to be considered. In addition, there's some degree of debate about having CEOs address all crises, because their words on the crisis can make it seem more important, garner additional media coverage, and the like. Nonetheless, if a crisis is severe they certainly have to be heard from (Pines, 2000).

Within the PR function, managing media coverage is a vital PR role that a leader must serve during a crisis. I will discuss agenda setting and its importance in a crisis context in Chapter 17, but in the context of leadership, Schultz, Kleinnijenhuis, Oegema, Utz, and Van Atteveldt (2012) focuses on the concept of agenda building – something that organizational actors use to try to influence stakeholder impressions of not only organizations involved in crises but also the issues themselves. In their work, Oliveira and Murphy (2009) found that because leaders are the faces of an organization in crisis, one of their most important roles was controlling the messaging and ultimately the types of stories covered in the media. Their findings suggest that consistency and repetition of theme are at the heart of a corporate leader's ability to shape the way a crisis is covered. While the leader can expect to take the brunt of the anger from the public in the case of a serious transgression (Ingenhoff & Sommer, 2010), they can still build an agenda. This suggests that organizations and journalists co-create the crisis narrative. If the organization builds a narrative that is consistent and credible, it is more likely to be used in the media coverage of the crisis (Liu, 2015; Veil & Ojeda, 2010).

In review . . .

If we adopt an inside-out approach to crisis response, then few concepts demonstrate the importance of balancing internal and external stakeholder concerns more than leadership. In differentiating between management and leadership, then exploring the three core roles that crisis leaders must play, I have suggested that crisis leadership is a complex concept. But it is also important to note that it is very possible that different organizational leaders may take on different roles during a crisis. To suggest that every leader must be all things to all people at once is a relatively naïve proposition to make. While all of the roles must be addressed, organizations should expect to use multiple leaders throughout the crisis, ranging from their corporate leadership, their CEO (or equivalent), to functional leaders as they are relevant to the material problems of the crisis.

Review your understanding

By the end of this chapter, you should be able to understand and explain the following.

- The critical differences between management and leadership:
  - The implications of these differences in a crisis context
- Core crisis leadership roles
  - Psychological and emotional role:
    - The three reasons this role matters
    - The four behaviors related to this role
  - Functional role:
    - The three qualities of functional leadership during crises
    - The five bases of social power
    - The three ways that effective crisis leaders manage relationships with people
  - PR role:
    - The balance between pro-social and defensive communication
    - Consideration of when the CEO should be the spokesperson
    - Agenda building functions of leaders

References

Alder, G. (1997). Managing environmental uncertainty with legitimate authority: A comparative analysis of the Mann gulch and storm king mountain fires. *Journal of Applied Communication Research*, 25(2), 98–115.

BBC News. (2018, 16/4/2019). Kylie Jenner 'sooo over' Snapchat – And shares tumble. Retrieved from www.bbc.co.uk/news/business-43163544. Accessed August, 8, 2019.

Beyer, J. M., & Browning, L. D. (1999). Transforming an industry in crisis: Charisma, routinization, and supportive cultural leadership. *Leadership Quarterly, 10*(3), 483–520.

Carroll, J. S., & Hatakenaka, S. (2001). Driving organizational change in the midst of crisis. *Mt. Sloan Management Review* (Spring), 70–79.

Coombs, W. T., & Holladay, S. J. (2002). Helping crisis managers protect their reputational assets: Initial tests of the Situational Crisis Communication Theory. *Management Communication Quarterly, 16*(2), 165–186.

Fener, T., & Cevik, T. (2015). Leadership in crisis management: Separation of leadership and executive concepts. *Procedia Economics and Finance, 26*, 695–701.

Fischbacher-Smith, D. (2014). Organisational ineffectiveness: Environmental shifts and the transition to crisis. *Journal of Organizational Effectiveness: People and Performance, 1*(4), 423–446. doi:10.1108/JOEPP-09-2014-0061

French, J., Raven, B., & Cartwright, D. (1959). The bases of social power. *Classics of Organization Theory, 7*, 311–320.

Ginzel, L. E., Kramer, R. M., & Sutton, R. I. (1993). Organizational impression management as a reciprocal influence process: The neglected role of the organizational audience. *Research in Organizational Behavior, 15*, 227–266.

Griffin-Padgett, D., & Allison, D. (2010). Making a case for restorative rhetoric: Mayor Rudolph Giuliani and Mayor Ray Nagin's response to disaster. *Communication Monographs, 77*(3), 376–392. doi:10.1080/03637751.2010.502536

Hargis, M., & Watt, J. D. (2010). Organizational perception management: A framework to overcome crisis events. *Organizational Development Journal, 28*(1), 73–87.

Hwang, S., & Cameron, G. T. (2008). Public's expectation about an organization's stance in crisis communication based on perceived leadership and perceived severity of threats. *Public Relations Review, 34*(1), 70–73.

Ingenhoff, D., & Sommer, K. (2010). Trust in companies and in CEOs: A comparative study of the main influences. *Journal of Business Ethics, 95*(3), 339–355.

Jamal, J., & Bakar, H. A. (2015). The mediating role of charismatic leadership communication in a crisis: A Malaysian example. *International Journal of Business Communication*, 1–25. doi:10.1177/2329488415572782

King, G. I. (2002). Crisis management and team effectiveness: A closer examination. *Journal of Business Ethics, 41*, 235–249.

Liu, H. (2015). Constructing the GFC: Australian banking leaders during the financial 'crisis.' *Leadership, 11*(4), 424–450. doi:10.1177/1742715015584537

Liu, S.-M., Liao, J.-Q., & Wei, H. (2015). Authentic leadership and whistleblowing: Mediating roles of psychological safety and personal identification. *Journal of Business Ethics, 131*(1), 107–119.

Loosemore, M. (1998). Reactive crisis management in construction projects: Patterns of communication and behaviour. *Journal of Contingencies and Crisis Management*, 6(1), 23–34.

Lucero, M., Kwang, A. T., & Pang, A. (2009). Crisis leadership: When should the CEO step up? *Corporate Communications: An International Journal*, 14(3), 234–248.

Oliveira, M., & Murphy, P. (2009). The leader as the face of a crisis: Philip Morris' CEO's speeches during the 1990's. *Public Relations Research*, 21(4), 361–380.

Paraskevas, A., Altinay, L., McLean, J., & Cooper, C. (2013). Crisis knowledge in tourism: Types, flows and governance. *Annals of Tourism Research*, 41, 130–152. doi:10.1016/j.annals.2012.12.005

Parmenter, D. (2010). Crisis leadership: 10 lessons from Sir Shackleton. *Leadership Excellence*, 27(6), 6.

Pines, W. L. (2000). Myths of crisis management. *Public Relations Quarterly*, 45(3), 15–17.

Quirke, B. (2009). Steering leaders out of a crisis using effective communication. *Strategic Communication Management*, 14(1), 24–27. doi:1930082341

Rickard, L. N., McComas, K. A., Clarke, C. E., Stedman, R. C., & Decker, D. J. (2013). Exploring risk attenuation and crisis communication after a plague death in Grand Canyon. *Journal of Risk Research*, 16(2), 145–167. doi:10.1080/13669877.2012.725673

Sandler, C. (2009). The psychological role of the leader in turbulent times. *Strategic HR Review*, 8(3), 30–35.

Schultz, F., Kleinnijenhuis, J., Oegema, D., Utz, S., & Van Atteveldt, W. (2012). Strategic framing in the BP crisis: A semantic network analysis of associative frames. *Public Relations Review*, 38(1), 97–107.

Spaeth, M. (2010). BP's oil spill: Eight lessons for leaders. *Leadership Excellence*, 27(10), 19.

Ucelli, L. (2002). The CEO's "how to" guide to crisis communications. *Strategy and Leadership*, 30(2), 21–24.

Ulmer, R. R. (2001). Effective crisis management through established stakeholder relationships: Malden Mills as a case study. *Management Communication Quarterly*, 14(4), 590–615.

Veil, S. R., & Ojeda, F. (2010). Establishing media partnerships in crisis response. *Communication Studies*, 61(4), 412–429.

Wesseling, Y. (2008). *Communication of moral emotions during an organizational crisis: Differential effects of an ashamed CEO and a regretful CEO*. Paper presented at the International Communication Association, Montreal, Quebec, Canada.

Wooten, L. P., & James, E. H. (2008). Linking crisis management and leadership competencies: The role of human resource development. *Advances in Developing Human Resources*, 10(3), 352–379.

PART 4

Stakeholder factors: Shifting from the inside out

In the first three parts of this textbook, the focus has been outside the organization in order to learn about the field of crisis communication, introduce a stakeholder relationship management perspective, and evaluate the risks that organizations face. However, because understanding crisis management is an outside-in and inside-out area of practice, organizations were also placed within their overall operational environments by examining the organizational factors that enable and improve crisis response.

Now, in Part 4 I shift away from an organizational perspective to focus on what motivates stakeholders to act, attitudes that shape how they experience crises, and how their view of the organization shapes their reactions to crises. In Part 4 I will explore the detail connected to the stakeholder relationship management model introduced in Chapter 3 in greater detail. I begin with Chapter 10 that explores culture, emotion, and persuasion in the context of crisis communication. I continue in Chapter 11 by evaluating how issue-related attitudes influence stakeholder reactions to crises. And I wrap up our exploration in Chapter 12 by turning the stakeholder gaze onto the organization to develop a deeper understanding of how building strong relationships with stakeholders is a vital to weathering the storm of crises.

10 The missing link of stakeholder attitudes to understand crisis communication

Learning objectives

By the end of this chapter, the reader should:

- Evaluate crises and crisis response from a stakeholder, not organizational perspective
- Analyze the influence of culture on stakeholder reactions to crisis
- Develop awareness of crises as emotional events for stakeholders

In Part 4 the focus moves away from the organization directly to stakeholder attitudes and a deep exploration and discussion of the stakeholder relationship model (SRM) is provided as it was introduced in Chapter 3.

In this chapter, I will explore the foundations of stakeholder attitudes. This chapter gives us the opportunity to briefly discuss the ways in which traditional persuasion models, culture, and emotion inform our understanding of stakeholder attitudes about crises. In short, the central point to keep in mind as you read this chapter is: **Organizations that fail to understand stakeholder attitudes that affect both the organization and the stakeholder are less likely to be effective in issue mitigation or crisis response.**

Persuasion's contribution to understanding stakeholder attitudes

Not surprisingly, the field of crisis communication is very diverse – not only because the types of crises that we try to understand are global and diverse but also because

Figure 10.1 The stakeholder relationship management model

the field is still developing. I wanted to get a better understanding of where the field had come from as a way of arguing where the field would go and so, as I discussed in the opening chapter of the book, I reviewed the broad body of journal articles published on crisis communication from 1953 to 2015 (Diers-Lawson, 2017a). Of those 690 journal articles that I reviewed, about 270 were practical or descriptive – that is, they had no theory connected to them. Of the 415 that remained, nearly one-fifth used some combination of psychological, persuasion, or risk-based theories to guide their research and analysis. For the most part, the application of these theories focused on better understanding of stakeholder attitudes and how those attitudes might inform crisis response. Moreover, in the last five or so years, we have seen the development of crisis-specific theories that apply these types of attitudinal constructs within the crisis context. For this reason, it is important to have a strong understanding of the types of theories and attitudinal constructs that are informing the development of the field.

Do not worry, we are not going to be reviewing every psychological, persuasion, and risk theory applied in crisis communication – I want to highlight the key constructs and theories that are shaping our understanding of stakeholder attitudes, culture, and emotion within crisis communication. But, as I discussed in Chapter 3, focusing on the formation of attitudes is consistent with most approaches in persuasion research where theories, like the health belief model or extended parallel process model, emphasize the importance of understanding the implications of constructs such as **perceived susceptibility, severity, beliefs, demographics,** and **perceived efficacy** as key predictors of reactions to stimuli and situations (Rosenstock, Strecher, & Becker, 1988; Witte, 1992; Witte & Allen, 2000). Similarly, theories like the theory of planned behavior assume that people typically behave sensibly and that our intentions to act (or not) are directly related to our existing attitudes, social norms, and perceived situational control (Ajzen, 2005). In fact, these findings do align with some important research that has been done analyzing emotions in crisis communication that found that, for example, stakeholder perceptions of their own control over situations and **uncertainty perceptions** affected not only the emotional reactions to crises but also their attitudes and actions towards the organizations in crisis (Jin, Liu, Anagondahalli, & Austin, 2014; McDonald & Cokley, 2013; Mou & Lin, 2014). Let us take a brief look at four persuasion models to better understand what grounds them and pushes the SRM to focus on these factors.

Theory of planned behavior

I begin with Ajzen's (2005) **theory of planned behavior** (TPB) shown in Figure 10.2 and work backwards in the figure. To understand why people behave the way they do, the first step is to identify their behavioral intention – that is, what they plan to do. Across most areas of human behavior research, this is a proxy for behavior: While we do not always do what we intend, if we do not intend to act in a particular way we probably will not do it. In most areas of integrated marketing communications research and practice, we also measure purchase intention when we are talking about consumers and (more broadly) stakeholder behavioral intention when we are talking about other stakeholders. Ajzen's research found that attitudes, subjective norms, and perceive behavioral control all influence people's behavioral intention. He defines **attitudes** as beliefs about the outcomes of particular behaviors plus whether people think those are good outcomes. The **subjective norm** is functionally like peer pressure or social desirability bias, which makes people want to feel socially acceptable. This is

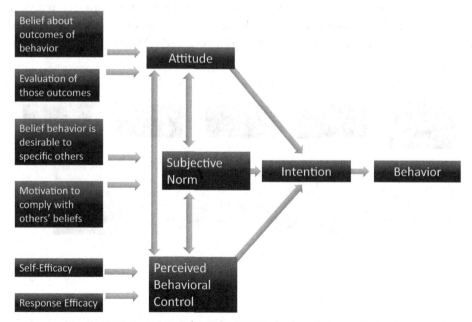

Figure 10.2 Summary of Ajzen's (2005) theory of planned behavior

made up by stakeholder beliefs that their behaviors are desirable to people whose opinions they care about, *as well as* how motivated stakeholders are to comply with others' beliefs. Finally, **perceived behavioral control** is about people's evaluation of whether they think they can perform a particular behavior (self-efficacy), *as well as* whether that behavior will lead to desirable ends (response efficacy) – as we discussed in Chapter 8. Ajzen also argues that attitudes, subjective norms, and perceived behavioral control all influence each other as well.

Elaboration likelihood model

Next, I move to Petty and Cacioppo's (1986) **elaboration likelihood model** (ELM) (see Figure 10.3). ELM looks complicated but is pretty straightforward. The core question the theory asks is: How do people react to messages they are exposed to? The theory suggests there are two routes: First, if it is related to a topic that people are very interested in or concerned about, they are more likely to be highly involved. This means that they are motivated to process it. Second, if people have the ability to process the message and enact the behavior, then – because they are highly involved – it shapes their behavioral intent and thus the desired action.

However, the theory acknowledges that not everyone is always going to be really interested or engaged with messages they come across. Sometimes we have to catch their attention. If you have seen the Disney movie *Up*, then think about the dog that befriends the main characters – any time that he thinks he sees a squirrel, it catches his attention and he runs off. This is the heart of the low-involvement route in ELM: It suggests that if people are not already highly involved with an issue, then we must

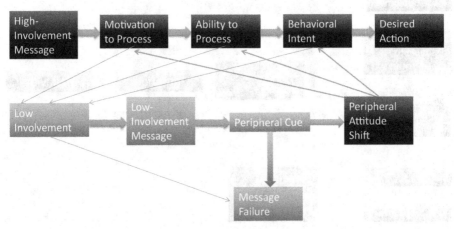

Figure 10.3 Summary of Petty and Cacioppo's (1986) elaboration likelihood model

catch their attention with a peripheral cue (i.e., our squirrel moment). If the peripheral cue is successful, then we become interested in the message and can be pushed into the high-involvement route. If it is not successful, then the message is likely to fail. The objective is, therefore, catching the viewer's attention with a good message and motivating them to pay attention.

Health belief model

The **health belief model** (HBM) was developed in the 1950s by social psychologists to try to predict and design messages to improve healthy behaviors. The model uses some familiar concepts in that the persuader tries to influence behavioral intention and believing that attitudes and efficacy are vital parts of the persuasion process. However, instead of focusing on primarily social cues like TPB or whether people are interested in a message like ELM, this theory adds in characteristics of the target audience (i.e., **demographics**) and importantly **perceived threat**, which asks about people's evaluations of whether they perceive the threat as severe enough for them to care – that is, the threat could negatively affect people and whether those people believe those threats could affect them or their susceptibility to the threats (Rosenstock et al., 1988). HBM also points out that in order for people to change their behaviors, there needs to be some kind of trigger or **cue to action** in order to motivate people to take on new behaviors.

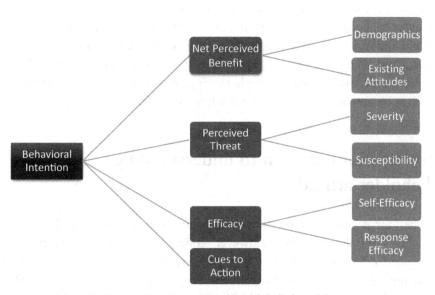

Figure 10.4 Summary of health belief model

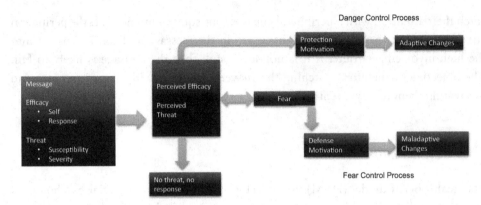

Figure 10.5 Summary of Witte's (1992; 1996; 2000) extended parallel process model

Extended parallel process model

Finally, Witte's (1992, 1996) **extended parallel process model** (EPPM) builds on the HBM by not only refining our understanding of the influence of threats but also focusing on the role of strategic messaging in the process. At the core of the model are messages that people are exposed to (e.g., information about a threat, a campaign message meant to motivate people to change, etc.), efficacy, and threat. However, Witte's research found a curvilinear relationship between the introduction of 'fear' and people's behavioral motivations. What this means is that fear motivates people to act – this is what she called the **danger control process** and is a useful tool to help ensure that people take precautions to avoid undue risk or harm. However, there is a point at which people can be overstimulated by fear, and instead of motivating us to act, it has almost the opposite effect: We become defensive, often to the point that we actively avoid acknowledging that the risk exists. This is what Witte called the **fear control response,** and it leads to people making poor decisions about how to protect themselves because all they want is for the fear to go away.

Emotion's contribution to understanding stakeholder attitudes

With the four persuasion theories we can begin to better understand what shapes stakeholder attitudes in crises. However, concepts like threat, efficacy, message involvement, subjective norms, perceived behavioral controls, and behavioral intention are not merely individualized concepts. They are grounded in emotion. The theories discussed in this chapter align with some important research that has been done analyzing emotions in crisis communication. Researchers have found, for example, that stakeholder perceptions of their own and organizations' control over situations and uncertainty affect not only emotional reactions to crises but also attitudes and actions towards the organizations in crisis (Jin et al., 2014; McDonald & Cokley, 2013; Mou & Lin, 2014).

At their heart, crises can be incredibly emotional for organizations and stakeholders alike, and there can be a lot of emotionally charged communication (van der Meer & Verhoeven, 2014). Though our understanding of the role that emotion plays in crisis is still developing, there is an increasing recognition that emotional reactions affect the outcomes of crises (Hajibaba, Gretzel, Leisch, & Dolnicar, 2015). For example, my own research has demonstrated that stakeholder beliefs about their own susceptibility, efficacy, and severity to a situation have substantially and negatively affected how angry they were likely to be both about the issue and the organization at the onset of a crisis (Diers-Lawson, 2017b).

However, some of the most vital work advancing the field's understanding of emotion and crises has emerged from Jin and her research partners over the last several years. For example, Jin et al.'s (2014) research to develop the **social-mediated crisis communication model** (SMCC) provides instrumental insight into understanding the measures of emotions and types of emotional reactions to crises.

In the context of stakeholder relationship management, SMCC very clearly links stakeholder attitudes about crisis issues and the organization to the production of emotional reactions to the crises. As such, because of the unique nature of relationship management in the organizational/stakeholder context (as compared to the interpersonal context), key findings from the SMCC help to support a stakeholder relationship management approach to understanding the antecedents of emotion and crisis. For example, the research finds that there is a strong positive relationship between attributions of blame and anger – that is, the more stakeholders attribute blame to an organization for a crisis, the more likely they are to be very angry about the situation (Jin, 2009, 2010; Jin et al., 2014). Similarly, in research about food safety, Mou and Lin (2014) found positive relationships between perceived incident awareness, factual awareness, risk perception, emotional reactions to previous actions, and reduced perceived control over the situation with increased emotional responses to the situation. In particular, Mou and Lin (2014) found that the negative emotions produced increased stakeholders' perception of risk and their likelihood to take action.

Factors influencing strong emotional reactions to crises

In a global environment, there are several individual factors identified in different studies as influencing emotional reactions to crises. One important study of individual factors within the tourism industry focused on 'crisis resistant tourists' – that is, those people whose attitudes and planned behaviors were less likely to be affected by emerging crises. Hajibaba et al. (2015) found that people who are more likely to take risks, travel more, and be actively involved in travel planning, are younger, are interested in a number of other activities, and have a number of personal and lifestyle preferences were all less likely to perceive substantial risk from individual crises. This suggests that we must assume that individual factors like **gender, age, income,** and **experience with the crisis issue,** as well as **attitudes about the crisis issue,** are likely to influence emotional reactions to crises.

In addition, there is increasing evidence to suggest that media use is likely to influence peoples' reactions to crises. We must better understand how **traditional and social media use** – both reading and posting – influence emotional reactions to crises (Brummette & Sisco, 2015; Brynielsson, Johansson, Jonsson, & Westling, 2014; Kim & Cameron, 2011; Pace, Balboni, & Gistri, 2014; Utz, Schultz, & Glocka, 2013; Yin, Feng, & Wang, 2015). Based on the previous research, we should expect there to be a connection between use, posting, and strong emotions. In fact, McDonald and Cokley's (2013) taxonomy of emotional reactions to expect online found that there were two key ways to classify reactions: Problem focused and emotion focused. In particular, they found a number of online behaviors indicating direct action taken against the 'offending' organization, ranging from different word-of-mouth (WOM) behaviors to boycotts, reduced product usage, and buying alternative brands. As such, these findings suggest that there are many individual factors that help us to understand and predict emotions in reaction to crises.

Culture's contribution to understanding stakeholder attitudes

When we dig into emotion, we do not have to go too far before we begin to see the real impact that culture is likely to have on stakeholder reactions to crises. For example, many of the indicators of an organization's reputation – like its trustworthiness (Sohn & Lariscy, 2014), values (Austin, Liu, & Jin, 2014; Falkheimer & Heide, 2015), or even brand appeal (Brown, Brown, & Billings, 2015) – represent stakeholder judgments rooted in culture and similar enduring identities (Scollon, Diener, Oishi, & Biswas-Diener, 2004) as well as existing attitudinal constructs like uncertainty avoidance (Coombs, 2008; Siew-Yoong Low, Varughese, & Pang, 2011). Understanding cultural identities is important because they give people the sense of belonging, provide guidelines for behavior, and instill a sense of morality or identity (Moran, Abramson, & Moran, 2014). Identities can range from **national, social, cultural,** and religious, to **political identities**, and often influence a host of attitudes, including our understanding of situations as well as our belief that we can control our surroundings (Ajzen, 2005; Bandura, 1986; Hajibaba et al., 2015; Ratten & Ratten, 2007; Yum & Jeong, 2014).

Today, crises typically have cultural components – no matter whether we are discussing challenges within countries (Olofsson, 2007) or we are discussing global crises (Gurman & Ellenberger, 2015). For example, increasing globalization poses unique challenges for practitioners, as many do not feel prepared to handle multicultural crises or adapt their response strategies across different cultures (de Fatima Oliveira, 2013). In fact, in Zhao's (2014) discussion of crisis communication in a global context, she suggests that nationalist, statist, classist, and often even cultural analyses are often too static rather than relational and dynamic. There have also been a number of examples of multinational organizations that have failed to effectively respond to crises in an international environment because they have chosen strategies that were culturally 'tone deaf' (An, Park, Cho, & Berger, 2010), for example, the disappearance of the Malaysian Airlines flight that was discussed earlier demonstrated that the airline failed to meet the information expectations of the families of the passengers who were mostly Chinese.

Thus, **intercultural crisis communication** (ICC) research represents an important development in both the fields of intercultural communication and crisis communication, as intercultural issues fuel many of the conflicts at all levels of society and crises are increasingly global. Moreover, insights into cultural differences can help researchers and practitioners to understand variations in blame attribution and communication needs for organizations in crisis (Kouabenan, Medina, Gilibert, & Bouzon, 2001).

Unfortunately, much of crisis communication theory is based on a Western-oriented paradigm, and there is little reference to its cross-cultural aspects (Haruta & Hallahan, 2003). However, that issue has begun to be meaningfully addressed in research and practice. Of course, one way to conceptualize culture is in terms of nationality, which is emerging as a common operationalization of culture in many crisis communication studies (An et al., 2010; Lyu, 2012). As such, in recent years there has been an increasing recognition of the importance of national identity in crisis communication (Chen, 2009; Molleda, Connolly-Ahern, & Quinn, 2005; Rovisco, 2010). However, that is not the only way to define and describe the impact that culture can have on stakeholder reactions to crises.

Globally, one of the most important cultural factors shaping crises and conflicts is religion (An et al., 2010; Goby & Nickerson, 2015; Haruta & Hallahan, 2003; Jindal, Laveena, & Aggarwal, 2015; Palmer-Silveira & Ruiz-Garrido, 2014; Taylor, 2000). There is a strong body of research suggesting that religion or **religiosity** – which is an indicator of how much religious identifications influence decision-making – influences people's attitudes and perceptions (Moran, Abramson, & Moran,

2014; Ursanu, 2012). Additionally, Croucher's (2013) research indicates that conflict management (a construct related to crises) is influenced by religion as well. Though this is an emergent area for issues and crisis research, case studies indicate that stakeholders are likely to react more negatively when crises or their related issues violate stakeholders' religious beliefs (Al-Hyari, Alnsour, Al-Weshah, & Haffar, 2012; Jaques, 2015).

For example, in one crisis study connecting religion and crisis, Al-Hyari et al. (2012) found that in largely Muslim countries, if the crisis was seen to be connected with their faith, respondents perceived it as more severe and were more likely to support boycotts of the organization in crisis. Using the same concept as Al-Hyari et al. (2012), Jaques (2015) compared Islam with Arab nations' collectivistic culture and the results from case studies. Jacques found that organizations involved in issues violating Islam's religious beliefs were expected to apologize even when the crises were not that severe. This suggests that in cultures with strong religious identifications, perceptions of crisis severity and response expectations might be affected. However, other findings suggest that religion should be evaluated separately from national culture, because religious and national identities may be different (Cohen & Hill, 2007) and individualism or collectivism dimension may be extracted from the religion itself (Lindridge, 2010).

Depending on the nature of the crisis, understanding cultural values applying common cultural dimensions like **individualism, collectivism, uncertainty avoidance, power distance, masculininty,** and **ethical ideology** (Leonidou, Leonidou, & Kvasova, 2013) or other values-based identifies like **political identities** (Zeri, 2014) is necessary if we are to fully understand stakeholder attitudes about issues and organizations. Though this is challenging, for crisis communication, the good news is that multinational organizations may able to manage or even avoid crises by communicating more effectively with local populations based on what is important to them (Hoffmann, Röttger, Ingenhoff, & Hamidati, 2015; Taylor, 2000).

In review . . .

This chapter has explored the foundations of stakeholder attitudes in crisis, beginning with some of the most informative persuasion theory that identifies key attitude formation factors we most often explore in crisis communication. Because crises are inherently emotional events for stakeholders and organizations, we discussed the emotional factors that influence crisis communication, then discussed the role of culture in crisis communication as well as a number of different cultural influencers that affect how stakeholders experience and react to crises.

Review your understanding

By the end of this chapter, you should be able to understand and explain the following.

- Persuasion's contribution to understanding stakeholder attitudes:
  - The concepts of susceptibility, severity, efficacy, subjective norm, and perceived behavioral control
  - Summarize the following persuasion theories:
    - TPB
    - ELM
    - HBM
    - EPPM

- Emotion's contribution to understanding stakeholder attitudes:
  - Summarize the SMCC
  - Factors influencing strong emotional reactions to crises, including demographics and media use
- Culture's contribution to understanding stakeholder attitudes:

  - Summarize the impact of cultural factors on organizations in crisis
  - Identify and briefly explain how national identity or religion influence crisis experiences for stakeholders

References

Ajzen, I. (2005). *Explaining intentions and behavior: Attitudes, personality, and behavior* (Vol. 2). Berkshire, England: McGraw-Hill Education.

Al-Hyari, K., Alnsour, M., Al-Weshah, G., & Haffar, M. (2012). Religious beliefs and consumer behaviour: From loyalty to boycotts. *Journal of Islamic Marketing, 3*(2), 155–174.

An, S. K., Park, D. J., Cho, S., & Berger, B. (2010). A cross-cultural study of effective organizational crisis response strategy in the United States and South Korea. *International Journal of Strategic Communication, 4*(4), 225–243.

Austin, L. L., Liu, B. F., & Jin, Y. (2014). Examining signs of recovery: How senior crisis communicators define organizational crisis recovery. *Public Relations Review, 40*(5), 844–846. doi:10.1016/j.pubrev.2014.06.003

Bandura, A. (1986). *Social foundations of thought and action: A social cognitive theory*. Englewood Cliffs, NJ: Prentice Hall.

Brown, N. A., Brown, K. A., & Billings, A. C. (2015). "May no act of ours bring shame": Fan-enacted crisis communication surrounding the Penn State sex abuse scandal. *Communication & Sport, 3*(3), 288–311. doi:10.1177/2167479513514387

Brummette, J., & Sisco, H. F. (2015). Using Twitter as a means of coping with emotions and uncontrollable crises. *Public Relations Review, 41*(1), 89–96.

Brynielsson, J., Johansson, F., Jonsson, C., & Westling, A. (2014). Emotion classification of social media posts for estimating people's reactions to communicated alert messages during crises. *Security Informatics, 3*(1), 7.

Chen, N. (2009). Institutionalizing public relations: A case study of Chinese government crisis communication on the 2008 Sichuan earthquake. *Public Relations Review, 35*, 187–198.

Cohen, A. B., & Hill, P. C. (2007). Religion as culture: Religious individualism and collectivism among American Catholics, Jews, and Protestants. *Journal of Personality, 75*(4), 709–742.

Coombs, T. W. (2008). The future of crisis communication from an international perspective. In T. Noting & A. Thießen (Eds.), *Krisenmanagement in der Mediengesellschaft* (pp. 275–287). Wiesbaden, Germany: VS Verlag für Sozialwissenschaften.

Croucher, S. M. (2013). Religion and conflict: An emerging field of inquiry. In J. G. Oetzel & S. Ting-Toomey (Eds.), *The SAGE handbook of conflict communication: Integrating theory, research, and practice* (pp. 563–584). Thousand Oaks, CA: Sage Publications.

de Fatima Oliveira, M. (2013). Multicultural environments and their challenges to crisis communication. *International Journal of Business Communication, 50*(3), 253–277. doi:10.1177/0021 943613487070

Diers-Lawson, A. (2017a). Crisis communication. In *Oxford research encyclopedia of communication*. Oxford University Press. Retrieved from http://communication.oxfordre.com/view/10.1093/acrefore/9780190228613.001.0001/acrefore-9780190228613-e-397. doi:10.1093/acrefore/9780190228613.013.397

Diers-Lawson, A. (2017b). Will they like us when they're angry? Antecedents and indicators of strong emotional reactions to crises among stakeholders. In S. M. Croucher, B. Lewandowska-Tomaszczyk, & P. Wilson (Eds.), *Conflict, mediated message, and group dynamics* (pp. 81–136). Lanham, MD: Lexington Books.

Falkheimer, J., & Heide, M. (2015). Trust and brand recovery campaigns in crisis: Findus Nordic and the horsemeat scandal. *International Journal of Strategic Communication, 9*(2), 134–147. doi:10.1080/1553118X.2015.1008636

Goby, V. P., & Nickerson, C. (2015). The impact of culture on the construal of organizational crisis: Perceptions of crisis in Dubai. *Corporate Communications: An International Journal, 20*(3), 310–325.

Gurman, T. A., & Ellenberger, N. (2015). Reaching the global community during disasters: Findings from a content analysis of the organizational use of Twitter after the 2010 Haiti earthquake. *Journal of Health Communication*, 20(6), 687–696. doi:10.1080/10810730. 2015.1018566

Hajibaba, H., Gretzel, U., Leisch, F., & Dolnicar, S. (2015). Crisis-resistant tourists. *Annals of Tourism Research*, 53, 46–60. doi:10.1016/j.annals.2015.04.001

Haruta, A., & Hallahan, K. (2003). Cultural issues in airline crisis communications: A Japan-US comparative study. *Asia Journal of Communication*, 13(2), 122–150.

Hoffmann, J., Röttger, U., Ingenhoff, D., & Hamidati, A. (2015). The rehabilitation of the "nation variable": Links between corporate communications and the cultural context in five countries. *Corporate Communications: An International Journal*, 20(4), 483–499.

Jaques, T. (2015). Cadbury and pig DNA: When issue management intersects with religion. *Corporate Communications: An International Journal*, 20(4), 468–482.

Jin, Y. (2009). The effects of public's cognitive appraisal of emotions in crises on crisis coping and strategy assessment. *Public Relations Review*, 35(3), 310–313.

Jin, Y. (2010). Making sense sensibly in crisis communication: How publics' crisis appraisals influence their negative emotions, coping strategy preferences, and crisis response acceptance. *Communication Research*, 37(4), 522–552. doi:10.1177/0093650210368256

Jin, Y., Liu, B. F., Anagondahalli, D., & Austin, L. (2014). Scale development for measuring publics' emotions in organizational crises. *Public Relations Review*, 40(3), 509–518. doi:10.1016/j.pubrev.2014.04.007

Jindal, S., Laveena, L., & Aggarwal, A. (2015). A comparative study of crisis management-Toyota v/s General Motors. *Scholedge International Journal of Management & Development*, 2(6), 1–12.

Kim, H. J., & Cameron, G. T. (2011). Emotions matter in crisis: The role of anger and sadness in the publics' response to crisis news framing and corporate crisis response. *Communication Research*, 38(6), 826–855. doi:10.1177/0093650210385813

Kouabenan, D. R., Medina, M., Gilibert, D., & Bouzon, F. (2001). Hierarchical position, gender, accident severity, and causal attribution. *Journal of Applied Social Psychology*, 31(3), 553–575.

Leonidou, L. C., Leonidou, C. N., & Kvasova, O. (2013). Cultural drivers and trust outcomes of consumer perceptions of organizational unethical marketing behavior. *European Journal of Marketing*, 47(3/4), 525–556.

Lindridge, A. (2010). Are we fooling ourselves when we talk about ethnic homogeneity? The case of religion and ethnic subdivisions amongst Indians living in Britain. *Journal of Marketing Management*, 26(5–6), 441–472.

Lyu, J. C. (2012). A comparative study of crisis communication strategies between Mainland China and Taiwan: The melamine-tainted milk powder crisis in the Chinese context. *Public Relations Review*, 38(5), 779–791.

McDonald, L. M., & Cokley, J. (2013). Prepare for anger, look for love: A ready reckoner for crisis scenario planners. *PRism*, 10(1), 1–11.

Molleda, J. C., Connolly-Ahern, C., & Quinn, C. (2005). Cross-national conflict shifting: Expanding a theory of global public relations management through quantitative content analysis. *Journalism Studies*, 6(1), 87–102.

Moran, R. T., Abramson, N. R., & Moran, S. V. (2014). *Managing cultural differences*. Oxford, UK: Routledge.

Mou, Y., & Lin, C. A. (2014). Communicating food safety via the social media: The role of knowledge and emotions on risk perception and prevention. *Science Communication*, 36(5), 593–616. doi:10.1177/1075547014549480

Olofsson, A. (2007). Crisis communication in multicultural societies: A study of municipalities in Sweden. *International Journal of Mass Emergencies and Disasters*, 25(2), 145–172.

Pace, S., Balboni, B., & Gistri, G. (2014). The effects of social media on brand attitude and WOM during a brand crisis: Evidences from the Barilla case. *Journal of Marketing Communications*, 1–14. doi:10.1080/13527266.2014.966478

Palmer-Silveira, J. C., & Ruiz-Garrido, M. F. (2014). Examining US and Spanish annual reports crisis communication. *Business and Professional Communication Quarterly*, 1–17. doi:10.1177/2329490614543176

Petty, R. E., & Cacioppo, J. T. (1986). Message elaboration versus peripheral cues. In R. E. Petty & J. T. Cacioppo (Eds.), *Communication and persuasion* (pp. 141–172). New York, NY: Springer.

Ratten, V., & Ratten, H. (2007). Social cognitive theory in technological innovations. *European Journal of Innovation Management*, 10(1), 90–108. doi:10.1108/14601060710720564

Rosenstock, I. M., Strecher, V. J., & Becker, M. H. (1988). Social learning theory and the health belief model. *Health Education and Behavior*, 15(2), 175–183. doi:10.1177/109019818801500203

Rovisco, M. (2010). One Europe or several Europes? The cultural logic of narratives of Europe views from France and Britain. *Social Science Information*, 49(2), 241–266. doi:10.1177/0539018409359844

Scollon, C. N., Diener, E., Oishi, S., & Biswas-Diener, R. (2004). Emotions across cultures and methods. *Journal of Cross-cultural Psychology*, 35(3), 304–326.

Siew-Yoong Low, Y., Varughese, J., & Pang, A. (2011). Communicating crisis: How culture influences image repair in Western and Asian governments. *Corporate Communications: An International Journal*, 16(3), 218–242.

Sohn, Y., & Lariscy, R. W. (2014). Understanding reputational crisis: Definition, properties, and consequences. *Journal of Public Relations Research*, 26(1), 23–43. doi:10.1080/1062726X.2013.795865

Taylor, M. (2000). Cultural variance as a challenge to global public relations: A case study of the Coca-Cola scare in Europe. *Public Relations Review*, 26(3), 277–293.

Ursanu, R. (2012). Models for ascertaining the religiosity's effects on the consumer's behaviour. *Anuarul Institutului de Cercetari Economice*, 21(1), 17.

Utz, S., Schultz, F., & Glocka, S. (2013). Crisis communication online: How medium, crisis type and emotions affected public reactions in the Fukushima Daiichi nuclear disaster. *Public Relations Review, 39*(1), 40–46.

van der Meer, T. G., & Verhoeven, J. W. (2014). Emotional crisis communication. *Public Relations Review, 40*(3), 526–536. doi:10.1016/j.pubrev.2014.03.004

Witte, K. (1992). Putting the fear back into fear appeals: The extended parallel process model. *Communication Monographs, 59*, 329–349.

Witte, K. (1996). Generating effective risk messages: How scary should your risk communication be? *Communication Yearbook, 18*, 229–254.

Witte, K., & Allen, M. (2000). A meta-analysis of fear appeals: Implications for effective public health campaigns. *Health Education and Behavior, 27*(5), 591–615. doi:10.1177/109019810002700506

Yin, J., Feng, J., & Wang, Y. (2015). Social media and multinational corporations' corporate social responsibility in China: The case of ConocoPhillips oil spill incident. *IEEE Transactions on Professional Communication, 58*(2), 135–153. doi:10.1109/TPC.2015.2433071

Yum, J.-Y., & Jeong, S.-H. (2014). Examining the public's responses to crisis communication from the perspective of three models of attribution. *Journal of Business and Technical Communication, 29*(2), 159–183. doi:10.1177/1050651914560570

Zeri, P. (2014). Political blogosphere meets off-line public sphere: Framing the public discourse on the Greek crisis. *International Journal of Communication, 8*, 17.

Zhao, Y. (2014). Communication, crisis, & global power shifts: An introduction. *International Journal of Communication, 8*, 26.

Issue-related attitudes influencing stakeholder reactions to crises

Learning objectives

By the end of this chapter, the reader should:

- Evaluate crises and crisis response by understanding stakeholder reactions to crisis issues
- Develop a stronger understanding of the assumptions that stakeholders may make about crisis issues that organizations face

In Chapter 10, I explored the foundations of stakeholder attitudes. In this chapter I will still focus on stakeholder attitudes, but focus more directly on the factors that influence stakeholder evaluations of crisis severity and blame on evaluations of an organization's competence, commitment, and clear association towards managing those issues. In short, I will begin to focus on those issue-related factors that most influence how stakeholders evaluate an organization's performance and intentions during crises.

Situational crisis communication theory, crisis severity, and blame

In Chapter 3, I introduced the types of judgments that stakeholders make about an organization's connection to the issues relevant to a crisis. Then in Chapter 6 I discussed severity and blame in the context of evaluating the types of crisis an organization may face. However, in this chapter, I focus on severity and blame in the context of how stakeholders make evaluations about organizations in crisis and how that influences their judgments about the organization's fitness and intentions for crisis recovery.

As I mentioned in Chapter 6, understanding the situation is essential for selecting the best response strategy. The literature defines the attribution of blame for a crisis as a central factor to determine appropriate organizational response (Coombs & Holladay, 1996, 2002; Hearit, 1999; Kim, 2013; Pearson & Mitroff, 1993). In fact, Coombs' (1995, 2007) **situational crisis communication theory** (SCCT) is dominant in the study of crisis communication (Ha & Boynton, 2014; Kim, Choi, Reber, & Kim, 2014). SCCT is informed by the attribution theory and assumes that people make attributions for the causes of negative and unexpected events (Weiner, 1985, 2006) and subsequently experience an emotional reaction, which serves as a motivation for their actions (Coombs, 2007). However, instead of focusing on SCCT's application in selecting response strategies in this chapter, I adapt it to better understand how stakeholders will evaluate the crisis and organization.

Crisis severity

Crisis severity describes the perception of the importance of the crisis (Goby & Nickerson, 2015). The more severe the crisis is judged to be, the more that stakeholders are likely to pay attention to it and believe that it will affect them directly (Haas-Kotzegger & Schlegelmilch, 2013). Crisis severity can also affect the selection of crisis responses (Heath, 2002) and the crisis responsibility attributions (Coombs, 1998, p. 2546; Coombs & Holladay, 2002; Laufer & Coombs, 2006). Crisis severity can be considered both in terms of 'real' damage in a crisis (Coombs, 1998), or from a stakeholder perspective as perceived damage or risk created by a crisis (Gygax, Bosson, Gay, & Ribordy, 2010; Hwang & Cameron, 2008; van der Plight, 1998). Just as in the context of persuasion, severity connects with susceptibility in order to produce a stakeholder's overall judgment about the threat that the stakeholder faces from a crisis.

Blame attribution

SCCT-based research also suggests that understanding blame attribution is crucial for understanding potential outcomes of the crisis and crisis response effectiveness (Coombs, 2004, 2006; Coombs & Holladay, 2015; Kim & Sung, 2014; Schwarz, 2012). **Blame attribution** is an evaluation of the degree to which stakeholders believe that an organization has control over a particular issue. Blame attribution is one of the most important predictors of stakeholder attitudes about an organization after a crisis. It is a core concept in SCCT, and it is also applied in other related crisis communication research connecting to other factors like corporate social responsibility, crisis history, and ethics (Kim, 2013; Ping, Ishaq, & Li, 2015).

In part, we can think about blame attribution as the potential threat to an organization's reputational. **Reputational threat** is a multi-step process combining evaluations of severity and blame attribution that is followed by considering situational intensifiers such as the organization's history of crises (Coombs, 2007; Maresh & Williams, 2007) and its reputation (Coombs, 2007; Sisco, Collins, & Zoch, 2010; van Zoonen & van der Meer, 2015). For example, previous research suggests that higher perceptions of blame attribution result in greater reputational damage for crises (e.g., Coombs & Holladay, 1996; Kim, 2014; Schwarz, 2012). All of this generates emotions on the part of the stakeholders that influences their understanding of the situation as well as their interpretation of the organization's crisis response (Choi & Lin, 2009; McDonald & Cokley, 2013). When the perception towards the organization is more negative, the greater the responsibility attributed on the organization, and thus the greater the reputational threat created by the crisis (Weiner, 1985). As such, better understanding of the factors that serve as intensifiers to a crisis is vital to better understanding the attribution of blame and the reputational risk that crises carry with them.

Competence, commitment, and clear association

Questions about how stakeholders assign blame to organizations have been asked since the 1970s, with Schwartz and Ben David's (1976) analysis of blame, ability, and denial of responsibility in the face of emergencies. Evaluations of an organization's competence in crisis management is, by contrast, a newer evolution in the field's understanding of this relationship that has emerged in analyses such as my own analysis of the BP crisis in the Gulf of Mexico (Diers, 2012) or Sohn and Lariscy's (2014) discussion of reputational crises. While competence had long been considered from the crisis management perspective, it has not always been considered from the stakeholder perspective. **Competence** asks whether or not stakeholders judge that the organization has the capacity to successfully address the issue (de Fatima Oliveira, 2013; Hyvärinen & Vos, 2015; Sohn & Lariscy, 2014).

Positive intention, concern, and **commitment** all represent value judgments stakeholders make regarding the authenticity of the organization's interest in the issue (Huang, 2008). As I discussed in Chapter 8, stakeholder evaluations of an organization's intentions toward an issue are largely governed by their evaluation of the authenticity of the organization's actions. This is why positive intention is often connected with hygiene-motivation theory (Lacey, Kennett-Hensel, & Manolis, 2015), suggesting that if a stakeholder believes an organization's intentions to be authentic when it comes to social responsibility, then they will most likely view the organization's connection to the issue as positive and productive. However, if stakeholders believe the organization's interest in an issue is inauthentic, then it does not matter how good the organization's behaviors, it is unlikely to positively influence their judgments about the organization's intentions towards the issue.

Finally, **clear association** also matters. If stakeholders believe there is a logical connection between an issue and the organization's core business or mission, then the organization's interest in the issue is more compelling to the stakeholder and can thus change the stakeholder's judgement about the organization, particularly after a crisis emerges (Claeys & Cauberghe, 2015; Coombs & S. Holladay, 2015; De Bruycker & Walgrave, 2014; Kernisky, 1997; Knight & Greenberg, 2002). Clear association not only improves the judgements stakeholders make about the organization and the issue, but also – broadly speaking – improves the organization's credibility (Heinze, Uhlmann, & Diermeier, 2014; Pang, Begam Binte Abul Hassan, & Chee Yang Chong, 2014; Park & Cameron, 2014).

What makes stakeholders particularly angry during crises, and how do we know?

If we take what we know about blame, severity, competence, commitment, and clear association into account, then we should have a pretty good picture of what frustrates stakeholders during crises. In the previous chapter I talked about crises as emotional experiences for stakeholders. Not surprisingly, crises can also generate a lot of anger towards organizations. In fact, anger is one of the primary emotions investigated in crisis communication – and it turns out we know a lot about how organizations anger stakeholders and how we know that they are angry.

Jin's research (2009, 2010, 2014) clearly indicates that perceptions of the "controllability of the crisis" is likely to generate stakeholder anger. The more perceived control that an organization is believed to have, the more likely a crisis is to produce anger because the organization is seen as being able to have prevented the crisis in these cases. Thus, the question of an organization's perceived competence is likely to affect stakeholder anger as one indicator of perceived control. Likewise, in these situations we also see a clear indicator of whether stakeholders are angry: They are more likely to blame the organization for the crisis (Jin, 2009, 2010). Therefore, we can think of **perceived control** as being a combination of blame attribution and competence.

If stakeholders believe the organization could reasonably have controlled the situation leading to the crisis and that makes them angry, then the degree to which they feel helpless will only intensify the situation. Of course, this brings us back to efficacy. In Bandura's (1997) discussion of **social cognitive theory**, he suggests that interactions between individual attitudes of control (i.e., efficacy) and external influences like the organization's perceived control are going to interact to intensify stakeholder reactions. Think about it this way: It is bad enough knowing that we cannot do anything about a situation, but knowing that the situation could have been avoided? That is to say, knowing that those who had the ability to change the situation would drive most people to the point of frustration (to put it mildly). Thus, in considering factors that produce anger in a crisis context, the stakeholder relationship model provides a framework for considering both antecedents and indicators of emotion together to more fully understand the complex dynamics of stakeholder relationships with organizations, issues, and crises (Diers, 2012).

There are also other causes and indicators of stakeholder anger towards organizations found in previous research. For example, Choi and Lin (2009) and Rhee and Yang (2014) found that an **increased exposure to a crisis** also increased the likelihood of stakeholder anger at organizations in crisis. These findings suggest that organizations with a history of crises were also more likely to be met with greater levels of stakeholder anger – particularly if the crisis was viewed as more controllable. Further, Kim (2013) found that previous beliefs about a company were most likely to influence attitudes about that company. Likewise, Coombs (2004) and Maresh and Williams (2007) have drawn similar conclusions across different industries.

As such, knowing stakeholder **prior attitudes about the organization and/or industry** should help us know just how angry stakeholders are likely to be. Prior experiences within an industry or with a crisis can potentially create a 'negative communication dynamic,' suggesting that two of the critical indicators of stakeholder anger could be **negative word-of-mouth** (nWOM) (Coombs & Holladay, 2007; S. Kim, 2014; McDonald & Cokley, 2013; Pace, Balboni, & Gistri, 2014; Yin, Feng, & Wang, 2015) as well as reduced **purchase intention** after a crisis (Coombs & Holladay, 2007; Ping et al., 2015; Sellnow et al., 2015; Yum & Jeong, 2014).

In review . . .

When we are trying to understand how stakeholders judge organizations in relation to the issues that both the organizations and the stakeholders are trying to confront – and we can make no mistake, they are judging the organizations – then we have to consider not only how much control stakeholders judge an organization to have over a situation but also their evaluations of the organization's disposition to the crisis. That is, do stakeholders believe organizations can affect the organization's own futures, and do the organizations genuinely care to do so?

> ### *Review your understanding*
>
> By the end of this chapter, you should be able to understand and explain the following.
>
> - How crisis blame and severity are linked with stakeholder attitudes about crisis issues:
>   - Be able to summarize SCCT and its connection with attribution theory
>   - Identify how blame and severity are connected with reputational threat
> - How stakeholder evaluations of an organization's competence, commitment, and clear association with crisis issues
>
>   - Articulate the relationship between these and stakeholder anger
>   - Address how perceived control connects competence and blame attribution
>   - Identify other factors influencing stakeholder anger at organizations in crisis

References

Bandura, A. (1997). *Self-efficacy: The exercise of control*. New York, NY: Freeman.

Choi, Y., & Lin, Y.-H. (2009). Consumer response to crisis: Exploring the concept of involvement in Mattel product recalls. *Public Relations Review*, *35*(1), 18–22.

Claeys, A.-S., & Cauberghe, V. (2015). The role of a favorable pre-crisis reputation in protecting organizations during crises. *Public Relations Review*, *41*(1), 64–71. doi:10.1016/j.pubrev.2014.10.013

Coombs, T., & Holladay, S. (2015). CSR as crisis risk: Expanding how we conceptualize the relationship. *Corporate Communications: An International Journal*, *20*(2), 144–162. doi:10.1108/CCIJ-10-2013-0078

Coombs, W. T. (1995). Choosing the right words the development of guidelines for the selection of the "appropriate" crisis-response strategies. *Management Communication Quarterly*, *8*(4), 447–476.

Coombs, W. T. (1998). An analytic framework for crisis situations: Better responses from a better understanding of the situation. *Journal of Public Relations Research*, *10*(3), 177–191.

Coombs, W. T. (2004). Impact of past crises on current crisis communication: Insights from Situational Crisis Communication Theory. *Journal of Business Communication*, *41*(3), 265–290.

Coombs, W. T. (2006). The protective powers of crisis response strategies: Managing reputational assets during a crisis. *Journal of Promotion Management, 12*(3/4), 241–260. doi:10.1300/J057v12n03_13

Coombs, W. T. (2007). Protecting organization reputation during a crisis: The development and application of situational crisis communication theory. *Corporate Reputation Review, 10*(3), 163–176.

Coombs, W. T., & Holladay, S. (2007). The negative communication dynamic: Exploring the impact of stakeholder affect on behavioral intentions. *Journal of Communication Management, 11*(4), 300–312.

Coombs, W. T., & Holladay, S. J. (1996). Communication and attributions in a crisis: An experimental study in crisis communication. *Journal of Public Relations Research, 8*(4), 279–295.

Coombs, W. T., & Holladay, S. J. (2002). Helping crisis managers protect their reputational assets: Initial tests of the Situational Crisis Communication Theory. *Management Communication Quarterly, 16*(2), 165–186.

Coombs, W. T., & Holladay, S. J. (2015). Public relations' "relationship identity" in research: Enlightenment or illusion. *Public Relations Review, 41*(5), 689–695. doi:10.1016/j.pubrev.2013.12.008

De Bruycker, I., & Walgrave, S. (2014). How a new issue becomes an owned issue. Media coverage and the financial crisis in Belgium (2008–2009). *International Journal of Public Opinion Research, 26*(1), 86–97.

de Fatima Oliveira, M. (2013). Multicultural environments and their challenges to crisis communication. *International Journal of Business Communication, 50*(3), 253–277. doi:10.1177/0021943613487070

Diers, A. R. (2012). Reconstructing stakeholder relationships using 'corporate social responsibility' as a response strategy to cases of corporate irresponsibility: The case of the 2010 BP spill in the Gulf of Mexico. In R. Tench, W. Sun, & B. Jones (Eds.), *Corporate social irresponsibility: A challenging concept* (Vol. 4, pp. 177–206). Bingley, UK: Emerald.

Goby, V. P., & Nickerson, C. (2015). The impact of culture on the construal of organizational crisis: Perceptions of crisis in Dubai. *Corporate Communications: An International Journal, 20*(3), 310–325.

Gygax, P. M., Bosson, M., Gay, C., & Ribordy, F. (2010). Relevance of health warnings on cigarette packs: A psycholinguistic investigation. *Health Communication, 25*, 397–409. doi:10.1080/10410236.2010.483334

Ha, J. H., & Boynton, L. (2014). Has crisis communication been studied using an interdisciplinary approach? A 20-year content analysis of communication journals. *International Journal of Strategic Communication, 8*(1), 29–44. doi:10.1080/1553118X.2013.850694

Haas-Kotzegger, U., & Schlegelmilch, B. (2013). Conceptualizing consumers' experiences of product-harm crises. *Journal of Consumer Marketing, 30*(2), 112–120.

Hearit, K. M. (1999). Newsgroups, activist publics, and corporate apologia: The case of Intel and its Pentium chip. *Public Relations Review, 25*(3), 291–308.

Heath, R. L. (2002). Issues management: Its past, present, and future. *Journal of Public Affairs, 2*(2), 209–214.

Heinze, J., Uhlmann, E. L., & Diermeier, D. (2014). Unlikely allies: Credibility transfer during a corporate crisis. *Journal of Applied Social Psychology, 44*(5), 392–397. doi:10.1111/jasp.12227

Huang, Y. (2008). Trust and relational commitment in corporate crises: The effects of crisis communicative strategy and form of crisis response. *Journal of Public Relations Research, 20*, 297–327.

Hwang, S., & Cameron, G. T. (2008). Public's expectation about an organization's stance in crisis communication based on perceived leadership and perceived severity of threats. *Public Relations Review, 34*(1), 70–73.

Hyvärinen, J., & Vos, M. (2015). Developing a conceptual framework for investigating communication supporting community resilience. *Societies, 5*(3), 583–597. doi:10.3390/soc5030583

Jin, Y. (2009). The effects of public's cognitive appraisal of emotions in crises on crisis coping and strategy assessment. *Public Relations Review, 35*(3), 310–313.

Jin, Y. (2010). Making sense sensibly in crisis communication: How publics' crisis appraisals influence their negative emotions, coping strategy preferences, and crisis response acceptance. *Communication Research, 37*(4), 522–552. doi:10.1177/0093650210368256

Jin, Y. (2014). Examining publics' crisis responses according to different shades of anger and sympathy. *Journal of Public Relations Research, 26*(1), 79–101. doi:10.1080/1062726X.2013.848143

Kernisky, D. A. (1997). Proactive crisis management and ethical discourse: Dow Chemical's issues management bulletins 1979–1990. *Journal of Business Ethics, 16*(8), 843–853.

Kim, S. (2013). Corporate ability or virtue? Relative effectiveness of prior corporate associations in times of crisis. *International Journal of Strategic Communication, 7*(4), 241–256. doi:10.1080/1553118X.2013.824886

Kim, S. (2014). What's worse in times of product-harm crisis? Negative corporate ability or negative CSR reputation? *Journal of Business Ethics, 123*(1), 157–170.

Kim, S., & Sung, K. H. (2014). Revisiting the effectiveness of base crisis response strategies in comparison of reputation management crisis responses. *Journal of Public Relations Research, 26*(1), 62–78. doi:10.1080/1062726X.2013.795867

Kim, S.-Y., Choi, M.-I., Reber, B. H., & Kim, D. (2014). Tracking public relations scholarship trends: Using semantic network analysis on PR Journals from 1975 to 2011. *Public Relations Review, 40*(1), 116–118. doi:10.1016/j.pubrev.2013.11.017

Knight, G., & Greenberg, J. (2002). Promotionalism and subpolitics: Nike and its labor critics. *Management Communication Quarterly, 15*(4), 541–570.

Lacey, R., Kennett-Hensel, P. A., & Manolis, C. (2015). Is corporate social responsibility a motivator or hygiene factor? Insights into its bivalent nature. *Journal of the Academy of Marketing Science, 42*(3). doi:10.1007/s11747-014-0390-9

Laufer, D., & Coombs, W. T. (2006). How should a company respond to a product harm crisis? The role of corporate reputation and consumer-based cues. *Business Horizons, 49*(5), 379–385.

Maresh, M., & Williams, D. (2007). *Toward an industry-specific crisis response model: A look at the oil crises of British Petroleum and Phillips Petroleum.* Paper presented at the National Communication Association, Chicago, IL.

McDonald, L. M., & Cokley, J. (2013). Prepare for anger, look for love: A ready reckoner for crisis scenario planners. *PRism, 10*(1), 1–11.

Pace, S., Balboni, B., & Gistri, G. (2014). The effects of social media on brand attitude and WOM during a brand crisis: Evidences from the Barilla case. *Journal of Marketing Communications*, 1–14. doi:10.1080/13527266.2014.966478

Pang, A., Begam Binte Abul Hassan, N., & Chee Yang Chong, A. (2014). Negotiating crisis in the social media environment: Evolution of crises online, gaining credibility offline. *Corporate Communications: An International Journal, 19*(1), 96–118. doi:10.1108/CCIJ-09-2012-0064

Park, H., & Cameron, G. T. (2014). Keeping it real: Exploring the roles of conversational human voice and source credibility in crisis communication via blogs. *Journalism & Mass Communication Quarterly, 91*(3), 487–507. doi:10.1177/1077699014538827

Pearson, C. M., & Mitroff, I. (1993). From crisis prone to crisis prepared: A framework for crisis management. *Academy of Management Executive, 7*(1), 48–59.

Ping, Q., Ishaq, M., & Li, C. (2015). Product harm crisis, attribution of blame and decision making: An insight from the past. *Journal of Applied Environmental and Biological Sciences, 5*(5), 35–44.

Rhee, H. T., & Yang, S.-B. (2014). Consumers' emotional reactions to negative publicity and crisis management in the health care industry: A multiple case study of Lipitor and Oxyelite Pro. *Social Science Computer Review, 32*(5), 678–693. doi:10.1177/0894439314525901

Schwartz, S., & Ben David, A. (1976). Responsibility and helping in an emergency: Effects of blame, ability and denial of responsibility. *Sociometry*, 406–415.

Schwarz, A. (2012). How publics use social media to respond to blame games in crisis communication: The Love Parade tragedy in Duisburg 2010. *Public Relations Review, 38*(3), 430–437. doi:10.1016/j.pubrev.2012.01.009

Sellnow, D. D., Lane, D., Littlefield, R. S., Sellnow, T. L., Wilson, B., Beauchamp, K., & Venette, S. (2015). A receiver-based approach to effective instructional crisis communication. *Journal of Contingencies and Crisis Management, 23*(3), 149–158. doi:10.1111/1468-5973.12066

Sisco, H. F., Collins, E. L., & Zoch, L. M. (2010). Through the looking glass: A decade of Red Cross crisis response and situational crisis communication theory. *Public Relations Review, 36*(1), 21–27.

Sohn, Y., & Lariscy, R. W. (2014). Understanding reputational crisis: Definition, properties, and consequences. *Journal of Public Relations Research*, 26(1), 23–43. doi:10.1080/1062726X.2013.795865

van der Plight, J. (1998). Perceived risk and vulnerability as predictors of precautionary behavior. *British Journal of Health Psychology*, 3, 1–14.

van Zoonen, W., & van der Meer, T. (2015). The importance of source and credibility perception in times of crisis: Crisis communication in a socially mediated era. *Journal of Public Relations Research*, 27(5), 371–388. doi:10.1080/1062726X.2015.1062382

Weiner, B. (1985). An attributional theory of achievement motivation and emotion. *Psychological Review*, 92(4), 548.

Weiner, B. (2006). *Social motivation, justice, and the moral emotions: An attributional approach*. Mahwah, NJ: Psychology Press.

Yin, J., Feng, J., & Wang, Y. (2015). Social media and multinational corporations' corporate social responsibility in China: The case of ConocoPhillips oil spill incident. *IEEE Transactions on Professional Communication*, 58(2), 135–153. doi:10.1109/TPC.2015.2433071

Yum, J.-Y., & Jeong, S.-H. (2014). Examining the public's responses to crisis communication from the perspective of three models of attribution. *Journal of Business and Technical Communication*, 29(2), 159–183. doi:10.1177/1050651914560570

Organization-related attitudes influencing stakeholder reactions to crises

12

Learning objectives

By the end of this chapter, the reader should:

- Evaluate crises and crisis response by understanding how stakeholders view the organization
- Develop a stronger understanding of the influence that a healthy relationship between an organization and its stakeholders has on an organization's ability to be successful after a crisis

Chapter 11 focused on stakeholder attitudes that influence their judgements about how the organization in crisis is handling the issue by focusing on the effects of crisis severity and blame on evaluations of an organization's competence, commitment, and stakeholder judgments of the organization's clear association towards managing those issues. In this chapter I will focus on better understanding the building blocks of the stakeholder's relationship with an organization.

The stakeholder relationship model as a recursive process

This is the last chapter in Part 4 because it builds on the other two. While I like to think of the stakeholder relationship model (SRM) as a love triangle focusing on two-way relationships between stakeholders, issues, and the organization, if we are trying

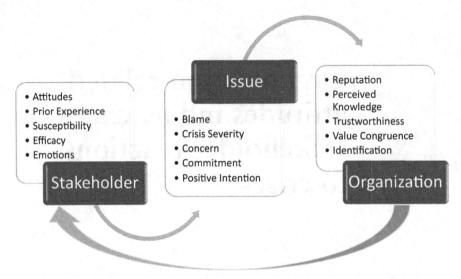

Figure 12.1 Thinking about the SRM as a recursive process

to understand the factors that build up stakeholders' expectations for their relationship with an organization, we can also view the SRM as a recursive process as well.

Figure 12.1 demonstrates what I mean. If we start on the left with the stakeholder, as we did in Chapter 10, then we lay the foundations, understanding that when crises occur stakeholders' existing attitudes, experience with the organization, perceptions of susceptibility, efficacy, and reaction to the crisis provide a context for how they react to the issue. Based on their existing attitudes, stakeholders make judgements about the issue and the organization's relationship to that issue (in the middle box), assessing blame, evaluating the severity of the crisis, and then judging the organization's position on the crisis, as discussed in Chapter 11. Those attitudes then inform their judgements about the organization and their relationship to the organization (in the final box on the right). That loops around to influence their attitudes. As such, our task in this chapter is understanding what drives different kinds of evaluations of the organization in crisis.

Understanding stakeholder evaluations of organizations in crisis

Stakeholder attitudes towards organizations in crisis represent the relationship in SRM that has been studied the most in crisis communication. Often treated as an outcome of a crisis, these judgments have been assessed across multiple fields of study, from communication and marketing to industry-specific studies in such diverse areas as health care and tourism. If researchers and practitioners want to understand this relationship, they should analyze changes to an organization's reputation using the immense body of research ranging from the evolution of image restoration in the 1990s (Benoit, 1995) to studies of reputational crises themselves (Carroll, 2009) to experimental evaluations of factors evaluating the impact of crises on reputation (Kim & Lee, 2015). However, I have found that other factors – such as stakeholders' perceived knowledge of the organization – not only changed under different crisis circumstances but also influenced stakeholders' overall perception of the crisis (Diers, 2012). For example, if a crisis made stakeholders feel like they had less knowledge about an organization, they were more likely to evaluate the organization negatively. Evaluations of stakeholder attitudes towards organizations also tend to invoke more personal feelings about organizations, like stakeholder assessments of whether an organization is fundamentally trustworthy (Freberg & Palenchar, 2013), or whether they believe the organization in crisis has values that are congruent to their own (Koerber, 2014), or even whether they feel strong relationship satisfaction (Ki & Brown, 2013) or loyalty to the organization in crisis (Helm & Tolsdorf, 2013).

Legitimacy and stakeholder evaluations of organizations

There is a well-established research and practice base for understanding stakeholder evaluations of organizations that is important to know before we can talk about it in the crisis context directly. As Jones (1995) points out, it is in an organization's interests to manage different stakeholders well, exhibiting behaviors that are trusting, trustworthy, and cooperative. Therefore, organizations that want to maintain a competitive advantage cannot just be opportunistic. This is the point that I made in Chapter 8 with regard to organizations creating crisis capacity by being authentic in their social responsibility and ethical stances. But this also means that stakeholder relationships are challenging: In a web of relationships, stakeholders may not only identify with a particular organization, but with each other; therefore, they have power in the ability to marshal resources and create and enact shared realities (Scott, Brandow, Hobbins, Nilsson, & Enander, 2015; Scott & Lane, 2000). Balancing those identities and needs can create conflict based on tension and pressures between issues of social responsibility, fiscal responsibility, and legislative/regulatory responsibility (Amba-Rao, 1993; Reich, 1998).

As discussed in Chapter 5, when an organization or group is viewed as 'legitimate,' it is viewed as having socially acceptable policies and behaviors. Evaluations of organizational legitimacy have long been connected with stakeholder relationship management as well as crisis communication (Elsbach & Sutton, 1992; Matejek & Gössling, 2014; Palazzo & Scherer, 2006; Pittroff, 2014; Veil, Reno, Freihaut, & Old-ham, 2015). Legitimacy is necessary to justify corporate activities, maintain support, 'win' important political decisions (e.g., permits and legislation), and act in socially permissible, desirable, proper, and culturally consistent ways (Meznar & Nigh, 1993; Samkin, Allen, & Wallace, 2010; Suchman, 1995). Legitimate organizational behavior can lead to the perception of an organization's trustworthiness, recognizability, reputation, image, history of socially responsible action, and expertise (Haley, 1996; King & Whetten, 2008; Sirgy, 2002). As such, legitimacy is based on a process of gaining, maintaining, and even having to regain these perceptions (Massey, 2001; Palazzo & Scherer, 2006). Finally, legitimacy can also be defined in terms of an ethical or legal model where governing industrial standards or laws might automatically denote stakeholders and organization's claims as legitimate (Diers-Lawson & Pang, 2016; Simola, 2005).

Much of our understanding of organizational legitimacy comes in the crisis communication literature. During crises, however, the question about legitimacy changes somewhat to considering what stakeholders might do as a result of the crisis and how the crisis changes the stakeholders' attitudes towards the organization.

Building blocks of the stakeholder relationship with organizations

In Chapter 3, I examined five critical building blocks for understanding the relationship between organizations and stakeholders:

- Reputation
- Trustworthiness
- Value congruence
- Perceived knowledge
- Identification (i.e., relationship satisfaction and loyalty)

Reputation

Reputation represents stakeholder perceptions of how an organization has behaved across its functional domains, in particular how well it treats its stakeholders (Coombs, 2007). There is no shortage of studies highlighting the importance of a good reputation before a crisis (Helm & Tolsdorf, 2013; Kim, 2014). But what makes for a good reputation? As it turns out, previous research identifies five factors that directly influence an organization's reputation.

1 Its overall **appeal** to stakeholders (Avraham, 2015; Brown, Brown, & Billings, 2015; Folkes & Karmins, 1999; Huber, Vollhardt, Matthes, & Vogel, 2010), which is related to the degree to which the organization and/or its products/services are likeable or desirable

2 The degree to which the organization is viewed as **socially responsible**, which not only includes authentic corporate social responsibility (CSR) initiatives, but also broader evaluations of its ethical behavior (Balmer, Blombäck, & Scandelius, 2013; Bowen & Zheng, 2015; Coombs & Holladay, 2015; Lacey, Kennett-Hensel, & Manolis, 2015; Shanahan & Seele, 2015)

3 An evaluation of the quality of the organization's **values** and whether those values are evidenced in the organization's actions (Austin, Liu, & Jin, 2014; Falkheimer & Heide, 2015; Ott & Theunissen, 2015)

4 Whether the organization itself is viewed as a **credible source of information** – especially about the crisis (Heinze, Uhlmann, & Diermeier, 2014; Pang, Begam Binte Abul Hassan, & Chee Yang Chong, 2014; Park & Cameron, 2014)

5 Whether stakeholders believe it will survive the crisis as a viable organization (Hargis & Watt, 2010)

In Chapter 11, I introduced reputational threat as a multi-step process that combines evaluations of severity and blame attribution and is followed by considering situational intensifiers like the organization's history of crises (Coombs, 2004, 2007; Maresh & Williams, 2007) and its reputation (Coombs, 2004, 2007; Sisco, Collins, & Zoch, 2010; van Zoonen & van der Meer, 2015). This means that reputational threat can also be discussed in terms of stakeholder perceptions of damage or risk created by different types of crises (Gygax, Bosson, Gay, & Ribordy, 2010; Hwang & Cameron, 2008; van der Plight, 1998). So, in addition to considering reputational threat as damage or risk of damage to the five factors affecting the organization's reputation identified, it can also be caused by negative stakeholder assessments of the following:

1 Its **competence** in managing the crisis issue (Diers, 2012; Sohn & Lariscy, 2014), as discussed in Chapter 11

2 Its **trustworthiness** (Diers, 2012; Trettin & Musham, 2000), which will be discussed in detail next

An organization's reputation represents a judgment that stakeholders make about what they can expect from the organization. Previous research demonstrates that different types of crises produce different types of damage to an organization's reputation and loss of trust from its stakeholders. For example, Kim, Ferrin, Cooper, and Dirks (2004) found that violations of integrity are more damaging than violations of competence because an integrity violation points to a moral failure versus a personnel or procedural failure.

In Chapter 4, I introduced expectancy violation theory (EVT) in the discussion of why crises can cause problems for organizations in a complex environment. Let us take a look at EVT again in terms of how it affects stakeholder evaluations of the organization's reputation as well. In a context where publics are increasingly building expectations for behavior on organizations based on their existing reputation, EVT is the bridge to explain why we often see negative reactions to crises: An organization may have violated its stakeholders' expectations for it (Millar, 2004; Sellnow & Seeger, 2013). This is also one of the reasons why Coombs and Holladay (2015) identify CSR as a potential risk to an organization's reputation with the emergence of a crisis – if the company's reputation is built upon 'being good' and it is found out to have committed a transgression, then its reputation has further to fall. If we think about the Volkswagen emissions scandal that emerged in 2015, when the company was found to have falsified its tests, the company's reputation was seriously damaged because its reputation had been based on integrity and quality.

Trustworthiness

Underlying reputation and this process of assessing reputational threat is a more fundamental concept – an organization's trustworthiness (Mal, Davies, & Diers-Lawson, 2018; Trettin & Musham, 2000). Shockley-Zalabak, Morreale, and Hackman (2010) describe trust in organizations broadly as evaluations of the organization's positive expectations about the intent and behaviors of the organization. Further, Mayer, Davis, and Schoorman (1995) argue that to be trusted an organization must have integrity – that is, its stakeholders must believe the organization's values are aligned with their own (Austin & Jin, 2015; Falkheimer & Heide, 2015). Naturally, this is also related to assessments of an organization's social responsibility, which is an important factor affecting its reputation (Coombs & Holladay, 2015; Kim & Lee, 2015).

As a side note, at this point it should be clear why the SRM focuses on the two-way connections between factors that influence the relationships between organizations, stakeholders, and issues. As we dig into these relationships, we can really begin to see how connected they are. This is one of the reasons that managing relationships with stakeholders, especially through crises, is challenging: There are a lot of factors to take into consideration in balancing the material crisis, stakeholder needs, ethics, and strategic response to the crisis.

But no matter whether we view this as a process or two-way interaction, previous research demonstrates that different types of crises produce different types of damage to the stakeholder's relationship with the organization, including both a loss of reputation and of trust. For example, Kim et al. (2004) found that violations of integrity are more damaging than violations of competence, because the integrity violation points to a moral failure versus a personnel or procedural failure. Kramer and Lewicki (2010) emphasize that violations of trust are often based in unmet expectations such as broken promises, the inability to perform, or behaviors that are misaligned with core values.

Value congruence

In Chapter 10 I argued that values and identity shape how stakeholders react to crises, but at this point it should be clear they also shape how stakeholders react to organizations as well. **Value congruence** represents the degree to which stakeholders see a similarity between their own values and the values demonstrated by the organization (Koerber, 2014). This is why an organization's culture, as it is manifested in the demonstrable forms of its ideology (see Chapter 8) and its social responsibility initiatives, should be considered as contributing to an organization's crisis capacity: As long as the organization's behavior is well-aligned with the values that its stakeholders hold, then the stakeholder's perception of their relationship with the organization should remain relatively undamaged.

Value congruence also helps to explain why organizations can experience crises yet also experience seemingly few negative effects of those crises: If the organization's crisis response is aligned with the stakeholders' values, then the crisis does not threaten the relationship. For example, several years ago, Bayer aspirin had a short-lived campaign in the United States targeting women who have back pain as part of its broader campaign for "all of life's little pains." As a way to try to build the campaign's narrative, Bayer explained that it is natural for mothers to experience back pain from picking up children, doing household chores and so on. Bayer tried to inject a bit of humor into the campaign by using a double-entendre to refer to "all of life's little pains" as being both back pain and the toddlers depicted in the commercial. Several hundred mothers signed a letter of complaint to the company suggesting they were offended by the suggestion their child could be a pain – apparently, they were unmoved by the humor. Instead of dismissing their complaint, the company issued a personal apology to each of the signatories and pulled the campaign. Though this cost Bayer money, the same group of mothers paid them back with praise and appreciation for the company's sensitivity to their concerns. In this way, what Bayer successfully communicated to this group and to the broader US public was that the company genuinely cared about the same things their consumers did – and even if it cost the the company money, it would protect its consumers' interests. In short, Bayer's response to the reputational crisis demonstrated strong value congruence. Instead of damaging the relationship, the crisis improved it.

Perceived knowledge

In the Bayer case, by demonstrating value congruence, the company was able to connect or re-connect its values with its stakeholders. The messages of appreciation for Bayer's response also seemed to re-affirm what the mothers had thought about the company before the campaign. Had Bayer's response been different, aside from losing value congruence, it is also possible that the company could have shaken these stakeholders' confidence in what they 'knew to be true' about the company. As has been discussed throughout the book (see Chapter 10 for a refresher), efficacy underpins most of our decisions and actions. Yet, crises are challenging because they create uncertainty (Rickard, McComas, Clarke, Stedman, & Decker, 2013). For organizations experiencing crises, this is problematic because many of the indicators of stakeholders' relationship with an organization rely on their confidence in the organization's trustworthiness and value congruence, as we have just discussed. But trustworthiness and value congruence represent stakeholder judgments that are rooted in enduring identities like culture (Scollon, Diener, Oishi, & Biswas-Diener, 2004) and in existing attitudinal constructs like uncertainty (Coombs & Holladay, 2008; Siew-Yoong Low, Varughese, & Pang, 2011).

Efficacy and identity are important because they not only give us a sense of belonging and morality, but they also provide expectations for behavior and give us confidence about how we should think and act (Moran, Abramson, & Moran, 2014). However, a crisis can threaten what we think we know about an organization. Consistently, I have found that if a crisis makes stakeholders feel like they have less knowledge about an organization, they are more likely to evaluate the organization in crisis more negatively. In most cases, this is one of the strongest predictors of the stakeholder's evaluation of the organization. If it significantly changes, then it is a good indicator of a change in the way stakeholders see their relationship with the organization – either positively or negatively.

Identification

When stakeholders view their relationship with an organization as satisfactory (Ki & Brown, 2013) they will often feel loyal to the organization (Helm & Tolsdorf, 2013). This is akin to the concept of identification. Though identification is usually framed in terms of how members of an organization feel about it, in a modern and social media context, it is just as applicable to other stakeholders as well. Dutton, Dukerich, and Harquail (1994) explored the self-organization connection and found that no matter the stakeholder – internal or external – having a positive image led to greater stakeholder attachment to the organization. Organizational identification focuses on how attached stakeholders are to the organization. Attachment forms when stakeholders connect their own self-concept (e.g., values) with the organization. This produces perceptions of mutual connectedness, loyalty, and satisfaction with the organization. This grounds an identification continuum where at its most positive stakeholders see themselves cooperating with the organization in a range of ways to co-create the value of the organization in the public sphere (Chandler & Lusch, 2015; Jaakkola & Alexander, 2014).

Alternatively, if the identification is negative, stakeholders may see themselves as adversaries, actively working against the brand (Swaminathan, Page, & Gurhan-Canli, 2007). I will address both of these ends of the continuum in Chapter 13 as I explore brand communities and counter branding. In a crisis context, the challenge is how to ensure that stakeholders view their relationship as cooperative and not adversarial – but should the identification with the organization change, that suggests a meaningful change in the nature of the relationship caused by the crisis.

In review . . .

To help us better understanding the building blocks for the relationship between stakeholders and organizations, this chapter has positioned organization-related attitudes as being built from the stakeholders' evaluations of the issues affecting the organization and the stakeholders together. With this deeper understanding of the nature of the relationships between organizations, stakeholders, and issues, we can now really begin to focus on the message factors and how to go about responding to a crisis in a way that helps the organization manage these often tricky and sometimes fragile relationships.

Review your understanding

By the end of this chapter, you should be able to understand and explain the following.

- How the SRM can be both a bidirectional model and a recursive process.
- Have developed a stronger understanding of what affects a stakeholder's relationship with an organization in crisis

  - Summarize the connection between legitimacy and stakeholder evaluations of organizations
  - Summarize and explain the five building blocks of the stakeholder's relationship with organizations:

    - Reputation
    - Trustworthiness

- Value congruence
- Perceived knowledge
- Identification

References

Amba-Rao, S. C. (1993). Multinational corporate social responsibility, ethics, interactions and Third World governments: An agenda for the 1990s. *Journal of Business Ethics, 12*(7), 553–573.

Austin, L., & Jin, Y. (2015). Approaching ethical crisis communication with accuracy and sensitivity: Exploring common ground and gaps between journalism and public relations. *Public Relations Journal, 9*(1), 2.

Austin, L. L., Liu, B. F., & Jin, Y. (2014). Examining signs of recovery: How senior crisis communicators define organizational crisis recovery. *Public Relations Review, 40*(5), 844–846. doi:10.1016/j.pubrev.2014.06.003

Avraham, E. (2015). Destination image repair during crisis: Attracting tourism during the Arab Spring uprisings. *Tourism Management, 47*, 224–232.

Balmer, J. M., Blombäck, A., & Scandelius, C. (2013). Corporate heritage in CSR communication: A means to responsible brand image? *Corporate Communications: An International Journal, 18*(3), 362–382. doi:10.1108/CCIJ-07-2012-0048

Benoit, W. L. (1995). Sears' repair of its auto service image: Image restoration discourse in the corporate sector. *Communication Studies, 46*(1–2), 89–105.

Bowen, S. A., & Zheng, Y. (2015). Auto recall crisis, framing, and ethical response: Toyota's missteps. *Public Relations Review, 41*(1), 40–49. doi:10.1016/j.pubrev.2014.10.017

Brown, N. A., Brown, K. A., & Billings, A. C. (2015). "May no act of ours bring shame": Fan-enacted crisis communication surrounding the Penn State sex abuse scandal. *Communication & Sport, 3*(3), 288–311. doi:10.1177/2167479513514387

Carroll, C. (2009). Defying a reputational crisis – Cadbury's salmonella scare: Why are customers willing to forgive and forget? *Corporate Reputation Review, 12*(1), 64–82.

Chandler, J. D., & Lusch, R. F. (2015). Service systems: A broadened framework and research agenda on value propositions, engagement, and service experience. *Journal of Service Research, 18*(1), 6–22. doi:10.1177/1094670514537709

Coombs, T., & Holladay, S. (2015). CSR as crisis risk: Expanding how we conceptualize the relationship. *Corporate Communications: An International Journal, 20*(2), 144–162. doi:10.1108/CCIJ-10-2013-0078

Coombs, W., & Holladay, S. J. (2008). Comparing apology to equivalent crisis response strategies: Clarifying apology's role and value in crisis communication. *Public Relations Review, 34*(3), 252–257. doi:10.1016/j.pubrev.2008.04.001

Coombs, W. T. (2004). Impact of past crises on current crisis communication: Insights from situational crisis communication theory. *Journal of Business Communication (1973), 41*(3), 265–289.

Coombs, W. T. (2007). Protecting organization reputation during a crisis: The development and application of situational crisis communication theory. *Corporate Reputation Review, 10*(3), 163–176.

Diers, A. R. (2012). Reconstructing stakeholder relationships using 'corporate social responsibility' as a response strategy to cases of corporate irresponsibility: The case of the 2010 BP spill in the Gulf of Mexico. In R. Tench, W. Sun, & B. Jones (Eds.), *Corporate social irresponsibility: A challenging concept* (Vol. 4, pp. 177–206). Bentley, UK: Emerald.

Diers-Lawson, A., & Pang, A. (2016). Did BP atone for its transgressions? Expanding theory on 'ethical apology' in crisis communication. *Journal of Contingencies and Crisis Management, 24*(3), 148–161.

Dutton, J. E., Dukerich, J. M., & Harquail, C. V. (1994). Organizational images and member identification. *Administrative Science Quarterly, 39*(2), 239–264.

Elsbach, K. D., & Sutton, R. I. (1992). Acquiring organizational legitimacy through illegitimate actions: A marriage of institutional and impression management theories. *Academy of Management Journal, 33*(4), 699–738.

Falkheimer, J., & Heide, M. (2015). Trust and brand recovery campaigns in crisis: Findus Nordic and the horsemeat scandal. *International Journal of Strategic Communication, 9*(2), 134–147. doi:10.1080/1553118X.2015.1008636

Folkes, V. S., & Karmins, M. A. (1999). Effects of information about firms' ethical and unethical actions on consumers' attitudes. *Journal of Consumer Psychology, 8*(3), 243–259.

Freberg, K., & Palenchar, M. J. (2013). Convergence of digital negotiation and risk challenges: Strategic implications of social media for risk and crisis communications. In H. S. N. Al-Deen & J. A. Hendricks (Eds.), *Social media and strategic communications* (pp. 83–100). London: Palgrave Macmillan.

Gygax, P. M., Bosson, M., Gay, C., & Ribordy, F. (2010). Relevance of health warnings on cigarette packs: A psycholinguistic investigation. *Health Communication, 25,* 397–409. doi:10.1080/10410236.2010.483334

Haley, E. (1996). Exploring the construct of organization as source: Consumers' understandings of organizational sponsorship of advocacy advertising. *Journal of Advertising, 25,* 19–36.

Hargis, M., & Watt, J. D. (2010). Organizational perception management: A framework to overcome crisis events. *Organizational Development Journal, 28*(1), 73–87.

Heinze, J., Uhlmann, E. L., & Diermeier, D. (2014). Unlikely allies: Credibility transfer during a corporate crisis. *Journal of Applied Social Psychology, 44*(5), 392–397. doi:10.1111/jasp.12227

Helm, S., & Tolsdorf, J. (2013). How does corporate reputation affect customer loyalty in a corporate crisis? *Journal of Contingencies and Crisis Management, 21*(3), 144–152. doi:10.1111/1468-5973.12020

Huber, F., Vollhardt, K., Matthes, I., & Vogel, J. (2010). Brand misconduct: Consequences on consumer-brand relationships. *Journal of Business Research*, *63*, 1113–1120. doi:10.1016/j.jbusres.2009.10.006

Hwang, S., & Cameron, G. T. (2008). Public's expectation about an organization's stance in crisis communication based on perceived leadership and perceived severity of threats. *Public Relations Review*, *34*(1), 70–73.

Jaakkola, E., & Alexander, M. (2014). The role of customer engagement behavior in value co-creation: A service system perspective. *Journal of Service Research*, *17*(3), 247–261. doi:10.1177/1094670514529187

Jones, T. M. (1995). Instrumental stakeholder theory: A synthesis of ethics and economics. *Academy of Management Review*, *20*(2), 404–438.

Ki, E.-J., & Brown, K. A. (2013). The effects of crisis response strategies on relationship quality outcomes. *Journal of Business Communication*, *50*(4), 403–420. doi:10.1177/0021943613497056

Kim, H.-S., & Lee, S. Y. (2015). Testing the buffering and boomerang effects of CSR practices on consumers' perception of a corporation during a crisis. *Corporate Reputation Review*, *18*(4), 277–293. doi:10.1057/crr.2015.18

Kim, P. H., Ferrin, D. L., Cooper, C. D., & Dirks, K. T. (2004). Removing the shadow of suspicion: The effects of apology versus denial for repairing competence-versus integrity-based trust violations. *Journal of Applied Psychology*, *89*(1), 104.

Kim, S. (2014). What's worse in times of product-harm crisis? Negative corporate ability or negative CSR reputation? *Journal of Business Ethics*, *123*(1), 157–170.

King, B. G., & Whetten, D. A. (2008). Rethinking the relationship between reputation and legitimacy: A social actor conceptualization. *Corporate Reputation Review*, *11*(3), 192–207. doi:10.1057/crr.2008.16

Koerber, D. (2014). Crisis communication response and political communities: The unusual case of Toronto mayor Rob Ford. *Canadian Journal of Communication*, *39*(3).

Kramer, R. M., & Lewicki, R. J. (2010). Repairing and enhancing trust: Approaches to reducing organizational trust deficits. *Academy of Management Annals*, *4*(1), 245–277.

Lacey, R., Kennett-Hensel, P. A., & Manolis, C. (2015). Is corporate social responsibility a motivator or hygiene factor? Insights into its bivalent nature. *Journal of the Academy of Marketing Science*, *42*(3). doi:10.1007/s11747-014-0390-9

Mal, C. I., Davies, G., & Diers-Lawson, A. (2018). Through the looking glass: The factors that influence consumer trust and distrust in brands. *Psychology & Marketing*, *35*(12), 936–947.

Maresh, M., & Williams, D. (2007). *Toward an industry-specific crisis response model: A look at the oil crises of British Petroleum and Phillips Petroleum*. Chicago, IL: National Communication Association.

Massey, J. E. (2001). Managing organizational legitimacy: Communication strategies for organizations in crisis. *Journal of Business Communication*, *38*(2), 153–170.

Matejek, S., & Gössling, T. (2014). Beyond legitimacy: A case study in BP's "green lashing." *Journal of Business Ethics*, *120*(4), 571–584.

Mayer, R. C., Davis, J. H., & Schoorman, F. D. (1995). An integrative model of organizational trust. *Academy of Management Review*, *20*(3), 709–734.

Meznar, M. B., & Nigh, D. (1993). Managing corporate legitimacy: Public affairs activities, strategies and effectiveness. *Business and Society*, *32*(1), 30–44.

Millar, D. P. (2004). Exposing the errors: An examination of the nature of organizational crises. In D. P. Millar & R. L. Heath (Eds.), *Responding to crisis: A rhetorical approach to crisis communication* (pp. 19–35). Mahwah, NJ: Lawrence Erlbaum Associates.

Moran, R. T., Abramson, N. R., & Moran, S. V. (2014). *Managing cultural differences*. Oxford, UK: Routledge.

Ott, L., & Theunissen, P. (2015). Reputations at risk: Engagement during social media crises. *Public Relations Review*, *41*(1), 97–102. doi:10.1016/j.pubrev.2014.10.015

Palazzo, G., & Scherer, A. G. (2006). Corporate legitimacy as a deliberation: A communicative framework. *Journal of Business Ethics*, *667*(1), 71–88. doi:10.1007/s10551-006-9044-2

Pang, A., Begam Binte Abul Hassan, N., & Chee Yang Chong, A. (2014). Negotiating crisis in the social media environment: Evolution of crises online, gaining credibility offline. *Corporate Communications: An International Journal*, *19*(1), 96–118. doi:10.1108/CCIJ-09-2012-0064

Park, H., & Cameron, G. T. (2014). Keeping it real: Exploring the roles of conversational human voice and source credibility in crisis communication via blogs. *Journalism & Mass Communication Quarterly*, *91*(3), 487–507. doi:10.1177/1077699014538827

Pittroff, E. (2014). Whistle-blowing systems and legitimacy theory: A study of the motivation to implement whistle-blowing systems in German organizations. *Journal of Business Ethics*, *124*(3), 399–412.

Reich, R. B. (1998). The new meaning of corporate social responsibility. *California Management Review*, *40*(2), 8–18.

Rickard, L. N., McComas, K. A., Clarke, C. E., Stedman, R. C., & Decker, D. J. (2013). Exploring risk attenuation and crisis communication after a plague death in Grand Canyon. *Journal of Risk Research*, *16*(2), 145–167. doi:10.1080/13669877.2012.725673

Samkin, G., Allen, C., & Wallace, K. (2010). Repairing organisational legitimacy: The case of the New Zealand police. *Australasian Accounting Business & Finance Journal*, *4*(3), 23–45. doi:2170715441

Scollon, C. N., Diener, E., Oishi, S., & Biswas-Diener, R. (2004). Emotions across cultures and methods. *Journal of Cross-cultural Psychology*, *35*(3), 304–326.

Scott, D., Brandow, C., Hobbins, J., Nilsson, S., & Enander, A. (2015). Capturing the citizen perspective in crisis management exercises: Possibilities and challenges. *International Journal of Emergency Services*, *4*(1), 86–102. doi:10.1108/IJES-12-2014-0024

Scott, S. G., & Lane, V. R. (2000). A stakeholder approach to organizational identity. *Academy of Management Review*, *25*(1), 43–65.

Sellnow, T. L., & Seeger, M. W. (2013). *Theorizing crisis communication* (Vol. 4). Oxford, UK: John Wiley & Sons.

Shanahan, F., & Seele, P. (2015). Shorting ethos: Exploring the relationship between Aristotle's ethos and reputation management. *Corporate Reputation Review*, 18(1), 37–49. doi:10.1057/crr.2014.19

Shockley-Zalabak, P. S., Morreale, S., & Hackman, M. (2010). *Building the high-trust organization: Strategies for supporting five key dimensions of trust* (Vol. 7). Oxford, UK: John Wiley & Sons.

Siew-Yoong Low, Y., Varughese, J., & Pang, A. (2011). Communicating crisis: How culture influences image repair in Western and Asian governments. *Corporate Communications: An International Journal*, 16(3), 218–242.

Simola, S. (2005). Concepts of care in organizational crisis prevention. *Journal of Business Ethics*, 62, 341–353. doi:10.1007/s10551-005-3069-9

Sirgy, M. J. (2002). Measuring corporate performance by building on the stakeholders model of business ethics. *Journal of Business Ethics*, 35(3), 143–163.

Sisco, H. F., Collins, E. L., & Zoch, L. M. (2010). Through the looking glass: A decade of Red Cross crisis response and situational crisis communication theory. *Public Relations Review*, 36(1), 21–27.

Sohn, Y., & Lariscy, R. W. (2014). Understanding reputational crisis: Definition, properties, and consequences. *Journal of Public Relations Research*, 26(1), 23–43. doi:10.1080/1062726X.2013.795865

Suchman, M. C. (1995). Managing legitmacy: Strategic and institutional approach. *Academy of Management Review*, 20(3), 571–610.

Swaminathan, V., Page, K. L., & Gurhan-Canli, Z. (2007). "My" brand or "our" brand: The effects of brand relationship dimensions and self-construal on brand evaluations. *Journal of Consumer Research*, 34(2), 248–259. doi:10.1086/518539

Trettin, L., & Musham, C. (2000). Is trust a realistic goal of environmental risk communication? *Environment and Behavior*, 32(3), 410–427.

van der Plight, J. (1998). Perceived risk and vulnerability as predictors of precautionary behavior. *British Journal of Health Psychology*, 3, 1–14.

van Zoonen, W., & van der Meer, T. (2015). The importance of source and credibility perception in times of crisis: Crisis communication in a socially mediated era. *Journal of Public Relations Research*, 27(5), 371–388.

Veil, S. R., Reno, J., Freihaut, R., & Oldham, J. (2015). Online activists vs. Kraft foods: A case of social media hijacking. *Public Relations Review*, 41(1), 103–108. doi:10.1016/j.pubrev.2014.11.017

PART 5

Message factors: Crisis response that focuses on stakeholder needs

It might seem odd that we have gone through four parts in this textbook and are only now coming to crisis response. Yet without a strong and clear understanding of what it means to adopt a stakeholder perspective; how to evaluate stakeholders, risks, and crisis types; how to develop an organization's capacity for effective crisis response; and what helps to predict the relationship between stakeholders, issues, and organizations it would be a fool's errand to try to create crisis response strategy. This is the reason why both practitioners and academics in this field look for research-based answers to the question of how to best respond to and manage crises.

In Part 5, I lay out the critical components to crisis response. I begin in Chapter 13 by exploring the realities of crisis response in multi-platform and multi-actor environments. We live in an increasingly connected environment where networks of people from around the world interact on a daily basis. This makes for a challenging but interesting dynamic for organizations to try to manage. Then in Chapter 14 I explore the reasonable options that organizations have for responding, and I lay out a taxonomy of crisis response tactics. In this chapter, I make the point that there is no one-size-fits-all type of crisis response, despite what we may hope. In Chapter 15 I explore some of the dominant theories used to create or select different crisis strategies. More broadly, in this chapter I explore the role of theory in practice and how it can be used as a shortcut to drafting good crisis response and risk management messaging. Finally, in Chapter 16 I bring all of this together to discuss how to strategically plan for crisis response.

13 | The realities of crisis response in multi-platform, multi-actor environments

Learning objectives

By the end of this chapter, the reader should:

- Be able to deconstruct the challenges of complex message environments and competing stakeholder interests for crisis response
- Have a better understanding of the changing nature of crises and crisis communication in a modern context

In Chapter 12 I suggested that we can classify stakeholder perceptions of their relationships with organizations along a continuum from cooperative to adversarial depending the convergence of their own attitudes, issues affecting both the organization and stakeholder, and stakeholder views of their relationship with the organization itself. In this chapter, I will explore the implications of that continuum (see Figure 13.1) by discussing the challenges of multi-platform and multi-actor environments. Recall that in Chapter 5, when I discussed how organizations could map their stakeholders, I pointed out that one of the reasons to map an organization's stakeholders was not only to classify the stakeholders themselves but also to begin to consider the networks of relationships amongst stakeholders as a way of identifying potential risks and opportunities to manage issues before they become crises. This chapter extends that discussion by directly examining the complexities for organizations that interact with their own brand communities and manage their adversaries.

Figure 13.1 Continuum of stakeholder relationships with organizations

Communities and co-creation of crisis response

When stakeholders view their relationship with an organization generally positively, they might feel they have a **cooperative relationship,** which is characterized by a perception of a shared reality between the stakeholders and the organization that is characterized by trust, openness, involvement, investment, and commitment – thus engendering a sense of loyalty between the organization and the stakeholder (Atkins & Lowe, 1994; Jaakkola & Alexander, 2014; Sirdeshmukh, Singh, & Sabol, 2002). Some studies suggest that when crisis response is executed well, it can strengthen stakeholder trust, loyalty, and commitment to a brand (Huang, 2008) while others have found that the response strategy does not have such an impact (Ki & Brown, 2013). However, what does remain consistent across the body of crisis and crisis response research is that building trustworthy organizations with good reputations and a positive history of interaction is consistently predictive of improved crisis outcomes (Hurley, Gillespie, Ferrin, & Dietz, 2013; Kim, 2014). We also happen to live in the social media age where organizations increasingly recognize the importance of meaningful engagement with stakeholders across social media outlets, and where the social media manager has even been identified as the gatekeeper to an organization's reputation (Jiang, Luo, & Kulemeka, 2016; Moretti & Tuan, 2015).

Brand communities

It is important to talk about the **brand community.** Muniz and O'Guinn (2001) found that members of brand communities, like traditional communities, demonstrate a shared consciousness, rituals, and traditions, as well as a sense of moral responsibility to their brands. Where brand communities emerge, they are social phenomena with distinctive social structures and manifest in virtual contexts, just like face-to-face contexts, where people demonstrate identification and satisfaction with the brand community (Woisetschläger, Hartleb, & Blut, 2008).

There are four characteristics of successful brand communities.

- Well-organized and well-structured brand communities reinforce **brand loyalty** (McAlexander, Schouten, & Koenig, 2002; Muniz & O'Guinn, 2001)

- Brand communities create **communities of consumption** characterized by joint values, patterns, and habits, meaning that consumers join brand communities to interact with people who share similar experiences and passions for a particular brand (Boorstin, 1965; Woisetschläger et al., 2008)

- Brand communities create a **psychological sense of community** characterized by trust, support, and satisfaction of mutual needs (Sarason, 1974; Woisetschläger et al., 2008)

- Brand communities **encourage stakeholder interaction** and, when successful, create strong influence and involvement across channels (Woisetschläger et al., 2008)

Not surprisingly, the rise of social media has amplified and virtually institutionalized the need for organizations to actively participate in their own brand communities (Kaplan & Haenlein, 2010). Many people think that social media–based brand communities are just the transfer of traditional brand communities (with the same characteristics and markers) online for the social media generation. The truth is that the new forms of brand communities are a lot more interesting and complex. It is vital to remember that social media–based brand communities are distinct from traditional online communities because of their commercial nature, shared common interests, and the dedication and even love of their members towards a particular brand (Albert, Merunka, & Valette-Florence, 2013). According to Laroche, Habibi, Richard, and Sankaranarayanan (2012) social media–based brand communities are characterized as "sites which provide the user with a sense of freedom and allow them to converse in various languages, topics and issues, and which foster an environment that allows for the free flow of information" (p. 1757).

Virtual communities and the co-creation of crisis response

If all of this sounds familiar, then you have read Part 4. But when it comes to crisis, brand communities matter. Not only is it possible to mitigate the negative impact of some crises with a strong brand community, but also brand communities are an organization's first line of defense, for two reasons: They want to hear the organization's side of the story or are at least willing to consider it (DiStaso, Vafeiadis, & Amaral, 2015), and they are likely to defend the organization (Brown & Billings, 2013).

An example of this was what happened after Adidas's 2016 Valentine's Day Instagram post when the company posted a picture of two women's legs and feet in Adidas shoes and the simple caption, "The love you take is equal to the love you make." Though the post generally received positive feedback, not surprisingly, there were a minority of responses that were negative and focused on criticisms of homosexuality and the portrayal of homosexual relationships by the brand. Generally, Adidas did not offer much response to the situation, but the stakeholders identifying with the community certainly did. Of course, the company would have expected negative feedback, but it allowed its brand community to activate those aligned with the values communicated in the post to defend the company and the post. This is a very concrete demonstration of how not only brand communities, but also extended stakeholder networks can be activated in the co-creation of shared values, issue mitigation, and even crisis response.

If we shift out of a brand community context and focus more directly on crisis response, when organizations face serious crises, like BP's 2010 spill in the Gulf of Mexico, we are increasingly finding that companies and stakeholders co-create the narrative about the situation on social media, and that the dialogue developed between an organization and its stakeholders will influence an organization's overall response to crises (Chewning, 2015; Diers, 2012; Diers & Donohue, 2013). In BP's case, it had no social media community before the April explosion. That is, it had a Facebook account, but no posts and did not even have Twitter account – in short, BP had no social media strategy or engagement before the explosion in the Gulf. Yet, in the year after the explosion, it was very clear that a brand community been created and that it demonstrated each of the aforementioned characteristics of a brand community. However, what my analysis of BP's brand community demonstrated was that unlike the findings of most analyses of brand communities, where attitudes towards the organization are homogenous, BP's Facebook community had varying attitudes about the company, ranging from being supporters to being detractors; yet, the people interacting were generally familiar with one another and behaved as a community. While it is possible that the genesis of the community – a major disaster – could shape the nature of the community, I would suggest that when we talk about brand communities before, during, or after crises, organizations have to be prepared for their community's members to have different opinions about the organization and its performance.

The BP example also demonstrates that framing the discussion in terms of brand communities alone does not fully encompass the nature of social support and engagement that happens as a result of crises. In fact, it demonstrates that meaning is co-created during crises, which both affects how those affected by crises seek communities of support and how they can also emerge into communities of advocacy. Kjell Brataas's practitioner perspective on victim communities of support and advocacy (see Box 13.1) provides a good example of how these communities emerge and engage with organizations in crisis, governments, and most importantly the people directly affected by the crisis.

Box 13.1 Practitioner perspective: Victim communities of support and advocacy

By Kjell Bratass

Norway is a country where support groups have played a major role in the aftermath of tragedies. The country has experienced oil rigs capsizing, train crashes and aircraft accidents, a tsunami (in Asia), and terror in Oslo and on Utoya. After most of these events, support groups have formed that have tried – with various ability and influence – to be an important voice for victims.

Right after a tragic event, support groups function as a physical (and nowadays digital) way of connecting with others. In such a group, members can discuss pressing matters and talk to people in a similar situation. Such peer support is important, and many victims find that it is easier to talk to a support group member instead of talking to family or friends who do not have the same experience and reference points. In the first few days after a tragedy, support groups can also shine light on practical matters and give advice on topics such as funeral arrangements, media coverage, and financial questions.

Many support groups continue to exist for years and even decades after the tragedy occurred that spurred their formation. For many members, an important reason is that they want to *change something* – so that what happened to them or their family member does not happen again. Several support groups therefore work actively for stricter gun control or improved aviation safety.

Support groups are often hindered by internal discussions and disagreements. Membership itself can become a sore point, as there might be various views regarding who can belong to such a group. Should it be a group for the bereaved only, or should also other types of victims – who may have 'only' seen what happened – also be included? Other topics of frequent discussions are media handling, financial questions, and playing the 'blame game.' Having an outside adviser – for example, a psychiatrist or an HR expert – might therefore be a good idea if the support group struggles to focus and come to consensus.

One month after the terror attacks in Oslo and on Utoya that took the lives of 77 individuals on July 22, 2011, a support group was formally organized with the help of the Norwegian Red Cross. The mostly young people who had attended the youth camp of the Labor party on Utoya came from all over Norway, and *local* support groups therefore also played an important role in the months and years following the tragedy. Funded mostly by the government, they offered practical support and advice regarding topics such as psychological follow-up and the widely publicized court case. They also had their say in questions regarding vigils and anniversaries, research projects, and various movies being produced about the attack. Members had many discussions about the *timing* of some of these projects, and controversy erupted regarding the groups' political focus, questions about the release of pictures of victims, and physical memorials near Utoya.

Seven years after the attacks in Norway, the national support group is active and engaged in a variety of projects. At the beginning of 2018, 1,665 individuals were registered as members. It continues to receive a yearly funding of NOK 5 million (about £460,000).

In the context of risk, issue, and crisis management, one of the strongest reasons for organizations to pay attention to and engage with their brand community and other stakeholders, like support groups, is because it gives them an opportunity to develop more agile and timely messaging to manage public sentiment (Freberg, Saling, Vidoloff, & Eosco, 2013; Hosseinali Mirza, de Marcellis-Warin, & Warin, 2015; Ott & Theunissen, 2015). In addition, we are increasingly seeing evidence that communities on social media are vital for disaster response because they enable people to communicate with one another, get timely information, initiate search and rescue operations, and provide emotional support to one another in ways that are otherwise impossible and that literally save lives (Cho, Jung, & Park, 2013; Dufty, 2015; Gurman & Ellenberger, 2015; Houston et al., 2015; Lachlan, Spence, & Lin, 2014; Slavkovikj, Verstockt, Van Hoecke, & Van de Walle, 2014; Verroen, Gutteling, & Vries, 2013; Xiao, Huang, & Wu, 2015).

Adversarial stakeholder relationships and counter branding

The importance of brand communities and social media engagement is that they allow organizations that understand their value proposition and their stakeholders to take calculated risks. Nike's use of Colin Kaepernick in its 30th anniversary "Just do it" campaign demonstrates the complexities of a modern organizational environment, risk management, and the use of advocacy to create and counter social, organizational, and political challenges. Kaepernick became a household name in the United States not for his performance as a National Football League (NFL) quarterback but for his social statement during the 2016–2017 season of kneeling for the US national anthem (which is played before the start of every NFL football game). For many Americans, including the NFL and US President Donald Trump, this marked a sign of enormous disrespect towards the United States. For Kaepernick, it represented a statement against racial injustice and police brutality. Clearly, when Nike launched its campaign in 2018 it got a lot of attention with predictions that it would hurt the company's profits. However, that has clearly not been the case, with the company's online sales growing and estimates of $6 billion worth of sales attributable to the campaign itself globally (BBC News, 2018).

So, why does a campaign that was risky garner global attention for a sport that is mostly irrelevant outside of North American (and a few places in Europe)? Consider the narrative, the timing, and the subject matter. Nike is able to position itself as an adversary to issues that reasonable people would oppose: Racial injustice and police brutality. But more than that, the company was able to indirectly criticize a globally unpopular political figure – President Trump – while also potentially creating a reputational problem for another organization (the NFL). This campaign exemplifies the complexities of a modern multi-platform, multi-actor environment, but also lets me introduce the concept of counter branding into the domain of issues and risk management as well as crisis response.

But let us take a step back to focus on what counter branding demonstrates – an adversarial relationship between stakeholders and organizations. In this case, both Kaepernick and Nike are positioning themselves as stakeholders to the NFL and President Trump. When we think of **adversarial relationships** between stakeholders and organizations, we should think of those typically characterized by antagonism, opposition, asymmetry of power, and perceived risk (Folkes & Karmins, 1999; Veil, Reno, Freihaut, & Oldham, 2015).

Counter branding, risk, issues management, crisis, and complex environments

In recent years, arguments for the use of counter branding approaches in social marketing campaigns have been growing because of an increased urgency to address public health issues. Arguments spurred by research on anti-smoking campaigns demonstrate that negative advertising (i.e., attacks on organizations or industries or attacks on the behavior) is an effective public health tool in promoting behavioral change (Apollonio & Malone, 2009; Eisenberg, Ringwalt, Driscoll, Vallee, & Gullette, 2004; Evans, Price, & Blahut, 2005; Farrelly, Davis, Haviland, Messeri, & Healton, 2005; Pralea, 2011; Terblanche-Smit & Terblanch, 2011).

When we think of **branding**, we think of building positive relationships between stakeholders and the targeted company, product, service, or even behavior (Evans et al., 2005; Pralea, 2011). When we think of **counter branding,** we should think about it as a negative messaging strategy attempting to harm existing positive relationships or simply to build adversarial relationships between stakeholders and the targeted company, product, service, or even behavior (Apollonio & Malone, 2009).

Counter branding to change stakeholder relationships with organizations

Counter branding is not new – as a distinctive competitive strategy, it appeared in 7-Up's 1967 campaign that branded itself as the "uncola" (Williams, 2005). We have seen it applied in a host of contexts over the years, from commercial applications by competitors, to political advertising, and certainly traditional social protest and advocacy campaigns like those to stop fracking in the United States and the United Kingdom. The underlying assumption in counter branding is that, "no matter how big a brand might be in the public's mind, there's always an open spot for the exact opposite" (Williams, 2005, np).

One of the most successful examples of counter branding is the American Legacy Foundation's Truth.com campaign (Apollonio & Malone, 2009). In 1997, the four largest tobacco companies in the United States were successfully sued and had to pay more than $200 billion over 25 years. As a result, the American Legacy Foundation was created in order to try to target and reduce teen smoking, as one of its principal objectives. Instead of only targeting the health-related behavior, the Truth.com ads also targeted the tobacco industry because consumers prefer to support brands who share their values. The Legacy campaign emphasized 'truth' as its brand, suggesting the messages promoting cigarettes were lies. It built arguments that the messages that the tobacco industry offered were incomplete, misleading, and inaccurate representations of both cigarettes and smoking. These strategies were effective: Campaign analyses demonstrated a significant reduction in youth smoking as a result of this multifaceted approach (Eisenberg et al., 2004; Farrelly et al., 2005).

If we take the Truth.com campaign out of a health context and put it into a crisis context, what the Legacy foundation was able to do was create a very successful reputational crisis (see Chapter 6 for a refresher on reputational crises) for the tobacco industry. More than just a message strategy, counter branding represents the opposite side of the advocacy coin to brand communities. Instead of supporting the organization, stakeholders can just as easily advocate against it. This was the case in the critics of the Adidas Valentine Day's Instagram post and certainly with Nike's "Just do it" campaign critics. Moreover, this can happen within a brand community, as I found evidence of in the BP brand community on Facebook. Functionally, we should think of activism of any kind 'against' an organization as counter branding because it represents stakeholders trying to shape other stakeholders' attitudes about an organization to such an extent that it changes the dynamic in the relationship between the stakeholder and the organization. The degree to which organizations respond to the reputational attacks will depend on the risk they believe the counter branding represents to relationships with the organization's stakeholders.

Activism and counter branding

In recent years, there have been a growing number of examples of activism and counter branding that have threatened the relationships between organizations and their vital stakeholders. These have forced responses from and even changes to organizations. For example, Veil et al.'s (2015) discussion of how social media activists used counter branding techniques to force Kraft into making product changes in its macaroni and cheese brand suggests not only that counter branding can successfully create risk for organizations, but also that organizations will act to protect their brands. Similarly, other research has found that parody social media accounts, hoaxes, and fake news constitute viable threats to organizations because they can worsen the relationship between stakeholders and organizations and such accounts are often triggered by the evolution of crises (Wan, Koh, Ong, & Pang, 2015).

Yet a challenge for organizations is how to decide which of these threats they should respond to, if any, and how they should respond. For example, in 2014 an offensive tagline – "Serving shit to scum for over 70 years" – appeared on Greggs's Wikia profile summary when people did a Google search for the British bakery chain. Of course, Greggs had nothing to do with it, and the culprits were never found – but, not surprisingly, this is one piece of counter branding that required a response. The Greggs social media team responded to thousands of Twitter messages in such a humorous way that the talk became about how well Greggs responded, as opposed to talking about the offensive tagline. The team not only used humor but also pulled Google into the conversation, to demonstrate a credible response and to clearly state the problem was not their fault. The full conversation helped to diffuse the situation demonstrated goodwill on both Greggs's and Google's part in managing the situation:

Greggs's initial tweet: "Hey @GoogleUK, fix it and they're yours!!! #FixGreggs" and was accompanied by a photograph of a platter of doughnuts being served.

Google's response: "Sorry @GreggstheBakers, we're on it. Throw in a sausage roll and we'll get it done ASAP. #fixgreggs"

Greggs's final word: "@GoogleUK WE LOVE YOU GOOGLE!!!!"

Of course, the example demonstrates that humor can be an effective strategy, especially on social media, as it captures attention and helps people/organizations stand out from all the digital 'noise' (Fraustino & Ma, 2015). But beyond the response strategy, the Greggs case also demonstrates the complexity of modern organizational environments, where organizations must manage multiple relationships at a time – and often through contexts, complaints, and advocacy that are difficult to predict.

Whistleblowing and counter branding

In the last six decades, there has been a growing and diverse body of research on crises; however, the voice that is often forgotten in this body of research is that of the whistleblower. We seldom get a glimpse into the employee experience, their decisions to stay silent or blow the whistle, and what happens to them after the crisis emerges (Chen & Lai, 2014; Edwards, Lawrence, & Ashkanasy, 2016; Heide & Simonsson, 2015). Yet, this is an important act of counter branding: The stakeholder is not just complaining about an organization, but making serious accusations about their own organization that have likely been ignored internally, so they take them outside the organization in order to ensure the problems or risks are addressed.

This underscores a point that Frandsen and Johansen (2016) make suggesting that crises are challenging because they represent the intersection of many stakeholder voices and perspectives on an organization and situation. Thinking about **whistleblowing** as another form of counter branding helps us to better understand the relationships between crisis issues, stakeholders, and the organization are multilayered and semi-fluid. When an employee decides to bring public attention to an internal problem within an organization, the question of blame attribution is both easy and difficult to answer. It is easy because it is a transgression – a situation where the organization has clearly done something wrong (Diers-Lawson, 2017). Yet, because it has been triggered by a whistleblower, other stakeholders – both within and outside the organization – may not view the whistleblower as a hero; rather, they may view him or her as a villain . . . or at least a problem to deal with. This makes blame attribution less of a question of the facts of a situation and more of a question of perception and competing interests.

Whistleblowing also represents a fundamental breakdown in the relationship between one organizational stakeholder – one of its members – and the organization, with the repercussions of that relationship breakdown played out in the public eye. Chen and Lai (2014) found that the intention to blow the whistle represented a relatively rational ethical decision-making framework wherein the whistleblower balanced the moral intensity of the situation against the potential harms and social pressures that confronted them after signaling organizational transgressions. These findings are consistent with a number of studies examining the employee perspective on whistleblowing finding that organizational and contextual factors shape employee perceptions and emotion, and ultimately predict whistleblowing or silence in the face of transgressions (Edwards et al., 2016; Grimm, Choo, Horvath, & Nitta, 2016; Liu, Liao, & Wei, 2015; Mesmer-Magnus & Viswesvaran, 2005).

Whistleblowing also provides an important and often ignored narrative about transgressions in organizations – the emotional journey that employees take through the crisis, no matter whether they are whistleblowers or trying to make sense of the events as they unfold. In crisis communication, we often focus exclusively on external stakeholders and ignore the employee voices and perspectives, which are vital to managing issues and crises alike (Heide & Simonsson, 2015; Mazzei, Kim, & Dell'Oro, 2012; Mazzei & Ravazzani, 2014). As such, the question of how an organization could manage a crisis may be better understood in the context of whistleblowing as it affords an opportunity to evaluate the quality of relationships between organizations and many different kinds of stakeholders during and after a crisis. One of the vital lessons learned in whistleblowing is how complex, challenging, and changeable crises are once we begin to consider the environments in which organizations operate. Organizations and organizational actors are subject to a lot of pressures because they serve multiple stakeholders at any given time (Connolly, Conlon, & Deutsch, 1980; Frooman, 1999). These stakeholders range vastly and can include groups like employees, customers or clients, regulators, competitors, and the like.

Where Frandsen and Johansen (2016) describe crises as the intersection of different voices and perspectives, we should probably be thinking of crises as cases where organizations have failed to meet at least one important stakeholder's expectations of the organization.

In review . . .

In this chapter we have seen both the constructive and destructive power of the increasingly complex and competitive environments in which stakeholders and organizations interact. As we begin to consider how organizations can and should respond to crises, we have to consider the overall quality of potentially many different stakeholder relationships with an organization, the strength of its brand community, the platform(s) on which it communicates, and certainly its adversaries, before we can begin to consider the specific messaging that an organization should use to manage risks, issues, and crises.

Review your understanding

By the end of this chapter, you should be able to understand and explain the following.

- How communities influence the creation of crisis response messages:
  - The implications of cooperative relationships with stakeholders
  - Brand communities:
    - Brand loyalty
    - Communities of consumption
    - Psychological sense of community
    - Stakeholder interaction
  - Co-creation of crisis response:
    - Lessons learned from Adidas, BP, and Nike
- Adversarial stakeholder relationships and counter branding:
  - What is counter branding?
    - Lessons learned from 7-Up and Truth.com about counter branding
    - Lessons learned from Greggs
  - Whistleblowing and counter branding:
    - Its implications for different stakeholder relationships
    - Its implications for blame attribution

References

Albert, N., Merunka, D., & Valette-Florence, P. (2013). Brand passion: Antecedents and consequences. *Journal of Business Research*, 66(7), 904–909.

Apollonio, D. E., & Malone, R. E. (2009). Turning negative into positive: Public health mass media campaigns and negative advertising. *Health Education Research*, 24(3), 483–495. doi:10.1093/her/cyn046

Atkins, M., & Lowe, J. (1994). Stakeholders and the strategy formation process in small and medium enterprises. *International Small Business Journal*, 12(3), 12–25.

BBC News. (2018, 19/4/2019). Nike sales defy Kaepernick ad campaign backlash. Retrieved from www.bbc.co.uk/news/business-45472399

Boorstin, D. J. (1965). The Americans: The national experience. *Vintage*, 2(358), 454.

Brown, N. A., & Billings, A. C. (2013). Sports fans as crisis communicators on social media websites. *Public Relations Review, 39*(1), 74–81.

Chen, C. P., & Lai, C. T. (2014). To blow or not to blow the whistle: The effects of potential harm, social pressure and organisational commitment on whistleblowing intention and behaviour. *Business Ethics: A European Review, 23*(3), 327–342.

Chewning, L. V. (2015). Multiple voices and multiple media: Co-constructing BP's crisis response. *Public Relations Review, 41*(1), 72–79. doi:10.1016/j.pubrev.2014.10.012

Cho, S. E., Jung, K., & Park, H. W. (2013). Social media use during Japan's 2011 earthquake: How Twitter transforms the locus of crisis communication. *Media International Australia, 149*(1), 28–40.

Connolly, T., Conlon, E. J., & Deutsch, S. J. (1980). Organizational effectiveness: A multiple-constituency approach. *Academy of Management Journal, 5*(2), 211–217.

Diers, A. R. (2012). Reconstructing stakeholder relationships using 'corporate social responsibility' as a response strategy to cases of corporate irresponsibility: The case of the 2010 BP spill in the Gulf of Mexico. In R. Tench, W. Sun, & B. Jones (Eds.), *Corporate social irresponsibility: A challenging concept* (Vol. 4, pp. 177–206). Bingley, UK: Emerald.

Diers, A. R., & Donohue, J. (2013). Synchronizing crisis responses after a transgression: An analysis of BP's enacted crisis response to the Deepwater Horizon crisis in 2010. *Journal of Communication Management, 17*(3), 252–269.

Diers-Lawson, A. (2017). Crisis communication. In *Oxford research encyclopedia of communication*. Oxford University Press. Retrieved from http://communication.oxfordre.com/view/10.1093/acrefore/9780190228613.001.0001/acrefore-9780190228613-e-397. doi:10.1093/acrefore/9780190228613.013.397

DiStaso, M. W., Vafeiadis, M., & Amaral, C. (2015). Managing a health crisis on Facebook: How the response strategies of apology, sympathy, and information influence public relations. *Public Relations Review, 41*(2), 222–231. doi:10.1016/j.pubrev.2014.11.014

Dufty, N. (2015). The use of social media in countrywide disaster risk reduction public awareness strategies. *Australian Journal of Emergency Management, 30*(1), 12.

Edwards, M. S., Lawrence, S. A., & Ashkanasy, N. M. (2016). How perceptions and emotions shaped employee silence in the case of "Dr. Death" at Bundaberg hospital. In N. M. Ashkanasy, C. E. J. Hartel, & W. J. Zerbe (Eds.), *Emotions and organizational governance* (pp. 341–379). Bingley, UK: Emerald Group Publishing Limited.

Eisenberg, M., Ringwalt, C., Driscoll, D., Vallee, M., & Gullette, G. (2004). Learning from truth: Youth participation in field marketing techniques to counter tobacco advertising. *Journal of Health Communication, 9*, 223–231. doi:10.1080/10910730490447066

Evans, W. D., Price, S., & Blahut, S. (2005). Evaluating the truth brand. *Journal of Health Communication, 10*, 181–192. doi:10.1080/10810730590915137

Farrelly, M. C., Davis, K. C., Haviland, M. L., Messeri, P., & Healton, C. G. (2005). Evidence of a dose-response relationship between the 'truth' antismoking ads and youth smoking prevalence. *American Journal of Public Health*, 95(3), 425–431. doi:10.2105/AJPH 2004.049692

Folkes, V. S., & Karmins, M. A. (1999). Effects of information about firms' ethical and unethical actions on consumers' attitudes. *Journal of Consumer Psychology*, 8(3), 243–259.

Frandsen, F., & Johansen, W. (2016). *Organizational crisis communication: A multivocal approach*. London: Sage Publications.

Fraustino, J. D., & Ma, L. (2015). CDC's use of social media and humor in a risk campaign – "Preparedness 101: Zombie apocalypse." *Journal of Applied Communication Research*, 43(2), 222–241. doi:10.1080/00909882.2015.1019544

Freberg, K., Saling, K., Vidoloff, K. G., & Eosco, G. (2013). Using value modeling to evaluate social media messages: The case of Hurricane Irene. *Public Relations Review*, 39(3), 185–192. doi:10.1016/j.pubrev.2013.02.010

Frooman, J. (1999). Stakeholder influence strategies. *Academy of Management Journal*, 24(2), 191–205.

Grimm, V., Choo, L., Horvath, G., & Nitta, K. (2016). Whistleblowing and diffusion of responsibility: An experimental investigation, Beiträge zur Jahrestagung des Vereins für Socialpolitik 2016: Demographischer Wandel - Session: Social Norms and Diffusion of Responsibility, No. G21-V2, ZBW - Deutsche Zentralbibliothek für Wirtschaftswissenschaften, Leibniz-Informationszentrum Wirtschaft, Kiel und Hamburg.

Gurman, T. A., & Ellenberger, N. (2015). Reaching the global community during disasters: Findings from a content analysis of the organizational use of Twitter after the 2010 Haiti earthquake. *Journal of Health Communication*, 20(6), 687–696. doi:10.1080/10810730.2015.1018566

Heide, M., & Simonsson, C. (2015). Struggling with internal crisis communication: A balancing act between paradoxical tensions. *Public Relations Inquiry*, 4(2), 223–255. doi:10.1177/2046147X15570108

Hosseinali Mirza, V., de Marcellis-Warin, N., & Warin, T. (2015). Crisis communication strategies and reputation risk in the online social media environment. *International Journal of Business and Social Science*, 6(5).

Houston, J. B., Hawthorne, J., Perreault, M. F., Park, E. H., Goldstein Hode, M., Halliwell, M. R., . . . McElderry, J. A. (2015). Social media and disasters: A functional framework for social media use in disaster planning, response, and research. *Disasters*, 39(1), 1–22. doi:10.1111/disa.12092

Huang, Y. (2008). Trust and relational commitment in corporate crises: The effects of crisis communicative strategy and form of crisis response. *Journal of Public Relations Research*, 20, 297–327.

Hurley, R. F., Gillespie, N., Ferrin, D. L., & Dietz, G. (2013). Designing trustworthy organizations. *MIT Sloan Management Review*, 54(4), 75.

Jaakkola, E., & Alexander, M. (2014). The role of customer engagement behavior in value co-creation: A service system perspective. *Journal of Service Research*, 17(3), 247–261. doi:10.1177/1094670514529187

Jiang, H., Luo, Y., & Kulemeka, O. (2016). Social media engagement as an evaluation barometer: Insights from communication executives. *Public Relations Review*, 42(4), 679–691.

Kaplan, A. M., & Haenlein, M. (2010). Users of the world, unite! The challenges and opportunities of social media. *Business Horizons*, 53(1), 59–68.

Ki, E.-J., & Brown, K. A. (2013). The effects of crisis response strategies on relationship quality outcomes. *Journal of Business Communication*, 50(4), 403–420. doi:10.1177/002194 3613497056

Kim, S. (2014). The role of prior expectancies and relational satisfaction in crisis. *Journalism & Mass Communication Quarterly*, 91(1), 139–158. doi:10.1177/1077699013514413

Lachlan, K. A., Spence, P. R., & Lin, X. (2014). Expressions of risk awareness and concern through Twitter: On the utility of using the medium as an indication of audience needs. *Computers in Human Behavior*, 35, 554–559. doi:10.1016/j.chb.2014.02.029

Laroche, M., Habibi, M. R., Richard, M.-O., & Sankaranarayanan, R. (2012). The effects of social media based brand communities on brand community markers, value creation practices, brand trust and brand loyalty. *Computers in Human Behavior*, 28(5), 1755–1767.

Liu, S.-M., Liao, J.-Q., & Wei, H. (2015). Authentic leadership and whistleblowing: Mediating roles of psychological safety and personal identification. *Journal of Business Ethics*, 131(1), 107–119.

Mazzei, A., Kim, J.-N., & Dell'Oro, C. (2012). Strategic value of employee relationships and communicative actions: Overcoming corporate crisis with quality internal communication. *International Journal of Strategic Communication*, 6(1), 31–44.

Mazzei, A., & Ravazzani, S. (2014). Internal crisis communication strategies to protect trust relationships: A study of Italian companies. *International Journal of Business Communication*, 1–19. doi:10.1177/2329488414525447

McAlexander, J. H., Schouten, J. W., & Koenig, H. F. (2002). Building brand community. *Journal of Marketing*, 66(1), 38–54.

Mesmer-Magnus, J. R., & Viswesvaran, C. (2005). Whistleblowing in organizations: An examination of correlates of whistleblowing intentions, actions, and retaliation. *Journal of Business Ethics*, 62(3), 277–297.

Moretti, A., & Tuan, A. (2015). The social media manager as a reputation's gatekeeper: An analysis from the new institutional theory perspective. *International Journal of Sales, Retailing and Marketing*, 4, 153–167. ISSN: 2045-810X.

Muniz, A. M., & O'Guinn, T. C. (2001). Brand community. *Journal of Consumer Research*, 27(4), 412–432.

Ott, L., & Theunissen, P. (2015). Reputations at risk: Engagement during social media crises. *Public Relations Review*, 41(1), 97–102. doi:10.1016/j.pubrev.2014.10.015

Pralea, A. R. (2011). Branding in health marketing. *Bulletin of the Transilvania University of Brasov*, 4(2), 65–72.

Sarason, S. B. (1974). *The psychological sense of community: Prospects for a community psychology*. San Francisco, CA: Jossey-Bass.

Sirdeshmukh, D., Singh, J., & Sabol, B. (2002). Consumer trust, value, and loyalty in relational exchanges. *Journal of Marketing, 66*, 15–37.

Slavkovikj, V., Verstockt, S., Van Hoecke, S., & Van de Walle, R. (2014). Review of wildfire detection using social media. *Fire Safety Journal, 68*, 109–118. doi:10.1016/j.firesaf.2014.05.021

Terblanche-Smit, M., & Terblanch, N. S. (2011). HIV/Aids marketing communication and the role of fear, efficacy and cultural characteristics in promoting social change. *Journal of Public Affairs, 11*(4), 279–286.

Veil, S. R., Reno, J., Freihaut, R., & Oldham, J. (2015). Online activists vs. Kraft foods: A case of social media hijacking. *Public Relations Review, 41*(1), 103–108. doi:10.1016/j.pubrev.2014.11.017

Verroen, S., Gutteling, J. M., & Vries, P. W. (2013). Enhancing self-protective behavior: Efficacy beliefs and peer feedback in risk communication. *Risk Analysis, 33*(7), 1252–1264. doi:10.1111/j.1539-6924.2012.01924.x

Wan, S., Koh, R., Ong, A., & Pang, A. (2015). Parody social media accounts: Influence and impact on organizations during crisis. *Public Relations Review, 41*(3), 381–385. doi:10.1016/j.pubrev.2015.01.002

Williams, R. H. (2005, March 14). The benefits of counter-branding. *Entrepreneuer*. Retrieved from www.entrepreneur.com/article/76476. Accessed July 16, 2019.

Woisetschläger, D. M., Hartleb, V., & Blut, M. (2008). How to make brand communities work: Antecedents and consequences of consumer participation. *Journal of Relationship Marketing, 7*(3), 237–256.

Xiao, Y., Huang, Q., & Wu, K. (2015). Understanding social media data for disaster management. *Natural Hazards, 79*(3), 1663–1679. doi:10.1007/s11069-015-1918-0

One size seldom fits all

A taxonomy of crisis response tactics

Learning objectives

By the end of this chapter, the reader should:

- Identify the variety of crisis response tactics identified in crisis communication literature
- Judge which response tactics should be used in different situations

When I was working on my Ph.D. in the early 2000s, the field of crisis communication was still finding a strong identity and trying to describe crisis communication more completely. What had emerged in the field was a relatively long list of possible crisis response tactics that organizations could use with different theories suggesting different lists. Yet, there was no definitive list nor theory to recommend the most sensible strategic use and combination of those tactics.

Fast-forward nearly 20 years and while we have a fairly complete list of tactics, there is still not a parsimonious roadmap for organizations to use to respond to different situations. This is not for the lack of trying, but, as the chapters to this point have identified, crises are complex, stakeholder judgments about crises and organizations affected by them are complex, and at this point I am not convinced there is a definitive way to effectively identify plug-and-play strategies to respond to crises. I am also relatively convinced that anyone who tells you there is understands very little about the complexities affecting stakeholder attitudes in crises – because as much as we can say that stakeholders have some very specific needs (e.g., good, clear information and uncertainty management) during crises, organizations must be agile to respond to different and often competing stakeholder interests across many different platforms during any given situation. This is why there are many different theories that can be applied to guide crisis response; each attends to different types of situational, stakeholder, or organizational needs. While creating a boilerplate template for responding to different types of crises will have value in offering organizations a starting point for initial crisis response, as we will discuss in Chapter 16, it is important to acknowledge that is just a starting point for organizations, not a destination.

With that very substantial proviso in mind, let us explore the crisis response tactics that organizations can choose from and some of the situational and organizational factors that can influence the types of tactics that should be used in different situations.

Taxonomy of crisis response tactics

Crisis response tactics or strategies have been studied for more than 20 years, with several taxonomies emerging, including Benoit's (1997) summary of image repair tactics, Coombs's (2007) discussion of tactics used in situational crisis communication theory, and Mohamed, Gardner, and Paolillo's (1999) taxonomy of organizational impression management tactics, along with a host of individual studies identifying different individual tactics. The result of my work (Diers-Lawson, 2017; Diers, 2009; Diers & Tomaino, 2010) – spent trying to identify as many different tactics as possible in case studies and separate taxonomies of crisis communication – is that more than 40 distinctive response tactics across eight categories can be used in a nearly infinite number of combinations in order to respond to a crisis (see Table 14.1).

Brief summary of the categories

Table 14.1 provides a definition for each of the tactics identified and the key authors who first identified and described the particular tactics. However, instead of focusing on the 44 tactics individually, it is more useful to focus on the categories or what the different groups have in common. In my view, there are eight categories for the tactics identified across the crisis communication literature.

1 **Self-enhancement tactics:** These focus on making the organization look good, despite the crisis, through traditional marketing or image advertising techniques. Not all marketing and image advertising strategies are related to crisis response, but when it is used to directly respond to a crisis across paid media channels, and then it fits into this category.

2 **Routine communication tactics:** Similar to self-enhancement tactics, these may also be used to address crises where the organization focuses on its mission or

Table 14.1 Taxonomy of crisis response tactics potentially used by organizations

Tactic category	Tactic	Tactic description	Example key author(s)
Self-enhancement	Marketing	Emphasize product quality, prices, safety, promotions	Heath (1994), Proto and Supino (1999), Scott and Lane (2000)
	Image advertising	Provide information to make the organization look positive; framing an issue for the stakeholders	Heath (1994, 1998), Scott and Lane (2000)
Routine communication	Communication of mission/ vision	Issue communications emphasizing organizational goals/mentioning mission/ vision	Heath (1994)
	Annual reports	Report monetary assets, liabilities, future liabilities, interest in cooperation to increase market value	Heath (1994), Proto and Supino (1999)
	Newsletters	Report monetary gains, attention to stakeholder concerns	Fiol (1995), Heath (1994), Proto and Supino (1999)
Framing the crisis	Accounts	Develop a dominant narrative, use the narrative to explain the problem	Kauffman (2001), Massey (2001), Mohamed et al. (1999)
	Information dissemination	Deliver information regarding the issue to educate, often with the goal of increasing stakeholder sense of empowerment	Martinelli and Briggs (1998), Rowan (1996), Sellnow (1993), Slovic (1987)
	Issue salience	Communicate importance, often useing risk or fright factors and/or scientific discourse	Bennett (1998), Sellnow (1993), Slovic (1987), Williams and Olaniran (1998)
	Preconditioning	Influence stakeholders regarding the organization's position on a crisis and their opinions about the organization by downplaying damage, putting act in a more favorable context, or attacking accusers	Benoit (2004, 1997), Sturges (1994)

(Continued)

Table 14.1 (Continued)

Tactic category	Tactic	Tactic description	Example key author(s)
Framing the organization	Ingratiation	Expend efforts to create a positive image by reminding stakeholders of past good works or qualities	Coombs and Schmidt (2000)
	Organizational promotion	Present the organization as being highly competent, effective, successful	Marra (1998), Mohamed et al. (1999)
	Issue management	Release issue diagnosis, advocacy advertising	Cheney and Christensen (2001), Gonzales-Herrero and Pratt (1998), Hayes and Patton (2001)
	Supplication	Portray the organization as dependent on others in effort to solicit assistance	Mohamed et al. (1999)
	Organizational handicapping	Make task success appear unlikely in order to have ready-made case for failure	Mohamed et al. (1999)
	Bolstering	Separate the organization from the crisis by emphasizing past accomplishments, stressing good traits	Benoit and Czerwinski (1997), Benoit (2004), Coombs and Schmidt (2000), Kauffman (2001), Sellnow and Brand (2001)
Anti-social or defensive	Noncompliance	Organization cannot/does not choose to act	Henriques and Sadorsky (1999)
	disclaimers	Give explanations prior to an action that might be embarrassing to ward off negative implications to image	Mohamed et al. (1999)
	Defensive compliance	Indicate that actions are driven by compliance or requirements	Henriques and Sadorsky (1999)
	Evasion of responsibility	De-emphasize role in blame by emphasizing lack of control over events, emphasizing accident, or emphasizing good intentions	Benoit (2004, 1997), Benoit and Czerwinski (1997), Coombs and Holladay (2002), Coombs and Schmidt (2000), Henderson (2003), Ray (1999)

(Continued)

Tactic category	Tactic	Tactic description	Example key author(s)
	Shifting the blame	Shift or minimize responsibility for fault (the most defensive strategy)	Benoit (2004), Benoit (1997), Coombs and Holladay (2002), Coombs and Schmidt (2000), Ray (1999)
	Simple denial	Communicate that the organization did not perform the act	Benoit and Czerwinski (1997), Benoit (2004), Coombs and Schmidt (2000)
	Strategic ambiguity	Do not releasing many details, keep stories consistent	Sellnow and Ulmer (1995), Ulmer and Sellnow (2000), Sellnow and Ulmer (2004)
	Intimidation	Represent the organization as powerful or dangerous, willing and able to adversely affect those who oppose its efforts	Mohamed et al. (1999)
	Minimization	Emphasize that the act or event is not serious	Benoit (1997, 2004), Benoit and Czerwinski (1997), Coombs and Schmidt (2000)
	Transcendence	Emphasize more important considerations	Benoit and Czerwinski (1997); Benoit (2004)
Accommodative	Corrective action/compensation	Make an effort to 'correct' actions adversely affecting others (can include announcements of recall or offers of compensation)	Benoit (1997, 2004), Benoit and Czerwinski (1997), Coombs and Holladay (2002), Coombs and Schmidt (2000), Henderson (2003), Martinelli and Briggs (1998), Mohamed et al. (1999), Ray (1999)
	Apologia	Communicate contrition, admission of blame including remorse and requests for pardon, mortification	Benoit (1997, 2004), Benoit and Czerwinski (1997), Coombs and Holladay (2002), Coombs and Schmidt (2000), Hearit (1999), Henderson (2003), Martinelli and Briggs (1998), Mohamed et al. (1999)

(Continued)

Table 14.1 (Continued)

Tactic category	Tactic	Tactic description	Example key author(s)
Accommodative (continued)	Compassion	Communicate concern for well-being/safety of public; help people psychologically cope with crisis	Martinelli and Briggs (1998), Mohamed et al. (1999), Sturges (1994)
	Offering reassurances	Assert that problems are corrected ("This will never happen again.")	Henderson (2003)
	Eliciting Sympathy	Asking stakeholders to feel sorry for the organization because of what happened	Ray (1999)
	Transparency	Emphasize complete compliance, openness to inquiry, requesting information seeking	Greer and Moreland (2003), Kauffman (2001), Sellnow and Brand (2001), Sellnow and Ulmer (1995), Williams and Olaniran (1998)
	Volunteering	Seek stakeholder involvement with the organization as a means of resolving the crisis	Gregory (2000)
Excellence/ renewal	Dialogic	Emphasizie openness and willingness to engage about the issue	Das and Teng (1998), Milliman Clair, and Mitroff (1994), Williams and Olaniran (1998)
	Exemplification	Portray the organization as having integrity, social responsibility, moral worthiness	Benoit and Czerwinski (1997), Henriques and Sadorsky (1999), Marra (1998)
	Pro-social behavior	Engage in actions to atone for transgression and persuade stakeholders of positive identity	Mohamed et al. (1999), Sellnow and Brand (2001)
Interorga- nizational relationships	Blaring Others	Identify negative link to undesirable other	Mohamed et al. (1999)

(Continued)

Tactic category	Tactic	Tactic description	Example key author(s)
	Blasting	Exaggerate negative features of an undesirable other	Mohamed et al. (1999), Sellnow and Brand (2001)
	Burying	Obscure or disclaim a positive link to an undesirable other	Mohamed et al. (1999)
	Blurring	Obscure or disclaim a negative link to a favorable other	Mohamed et al. (1999)
	Belittling	Minimize traits or accomplishments of a negatively linked other; attack accuser's credibility	Benoit and Czerwinski (1997), Coombs and Schmidt (2000), Mohamed et al. (1999)
	Boosting	Minimize undesirable features of a positively linked other	Mohamed et al. (1999)
	Boasting	Proclaim a positive link to a desirable other	Mohamed et al. (1999)
	Burnishing	Enhance desirable features of a positively linked other	Mohamed et al. (1999)
	Collaboration	Emphasize desire to change and work with another organization to resolve the crisis	Henriques and Sadorsky (1999), Martinelli and Briggs (1998), Milliman et al. (1994)

vision as a part of responding to a crisis or even uses outlets like their annual reports or employee newsletters to directly discuss the crisis. Often these meant to reassure stakeholders about the situation and the organization.

3 **Tactics that frame the crisis:** Shifting focus from tactics that can be applied to crises to crisis-specific tactics, these focus on framing the crisis. This category can involve a range of messages that summarize the situation, provide status updates, discuss the importance of the situation to the stakeholders or the organization, and try to account for the nature of the situation.

4 **Tactics that frame the organization:** Organizations may frame themselves by emphasizing their ability or inability to prevent or manage the situation. That is,

in framing the organization instead of focusing on the situation, the organization may choose to focus on its role in a way that works to give context to stakeholders about what it can or cannot do.

5   **Anti-social or defensive tactics:** In many cases, anti-social or defensive tactics are risky ways to respond to crises because their focus is to minimize blame attribution with a range of tactics from strategic ambiguity to denial to obfuscation to fairly aggressive tactics like intimidation.

6   **Accommodative tactics:** Organizations may choose to be very pro-social in their crisis response approaches by apologizing, focusing on repairing the problems, communicating empathy, or at the very least showing that they have nothing to hide.

7   **Excellence or renewal tactics:** In some circumstances, organizations may choose to demonstrate their excellence by promoting dialogue with stakeholders, discussing the organization's leadership in the time of crisis, or emphasizing its corporate social responsibility (CSR).

8   **Emphasizing interorganizational relationships:** Organizations may also choose to emphasize positive or negative interorganizational relationships to either try to borrow credibility from positively viewed partners, distance themselves from other organizations with a negative reputation, or even directly attack organizations as a way of shifting attention away from themselves.

Common patterns of crisis response

As I said in the introduction to this chapter, there is no definitive approach to combining these tactic categories or individual tactics within them. In many cases, to develop their response to crises across platforms organizations select many different tactics to use in various combinations. There are four common patterns that seem to emerge across a number of different studies of organizations in crisis.

1   **Defensive strategies** often incorporating some kind of minimization of the problem, explanations of the situation to help clarify the organization's role, denial of responsibility – in other words, image-protection messages (Choi, 2012; Diers & Donohue, 2013; Park & Cameron, 2014)

2   **Accommodative strategies** often including an apology, emphasis on empathy for those affected, and certainly demonstrating a commitment towards solving the problem (Chang, Tsai, Wong, Wang, & Cho, 2015; Diers-Lawson & Pang, 2016; DiStaso, Vafeiadis, & Amaral, 2015)

3   **Image-oriented responses** focusing on promoting the organization without any negativity found in the defensive responses but also without apology and accommodation (Diers & Donohue, 2013; Seeger & Griffin-Padgett, 2010)

4   **Status updates** recognizing that a critical component to managing communication with stakeholders during a crisis is providing information to them (Choi, 2012; Snoeijers, Poels, & Nicolay, 2014)

Ethical apology in crisis response

As we consider the many different ways that organizations can respond to crises, it is also important to consider that even when organizations say the right things, it may not always work – at least in the short term. Ethical apology is an example of an accommodative strategy that a colleague and I have identified (Diers-Lawson & Pang, 2016). The strategy packages some important lessons about long-term stakeholder relationship management, ethics, and the importance for organizations to be realistic; sometimes crises will hurt their stakeholder relationships, especially transgressions.

Today, organizations and prominent individuals who are accused of wrongdoing increasingly face pressure to apologize to stakeholders in order to maintain a good image, because it is "morally the correct action" (Benoit & Pang, 2008) and to diffuse some of the anger and hostility directed at them (Hearit, 1994). Research has found that although apology is the most effective crisis strategy (Kim, Avery, & Lariscy, 2009), it is often accompanied by affirmative statements such as those where the organization accepts responsibility (Pace, Fediuk, & Botero, 2009) or demonstrates corrective action (Blaney, Benoit, & Brazeal, 2002), and it can work to atone for the transgression (Jerome, 2008). Unfortunately, as Bauman (2011) argues, research exploring ethical approaches to managing crisis response is not well developed. As a result, it may not come across as authentic to an organization. Authenticity, as discussed in Chapter 8, is vital if stakeholders are going to give credit to the organization for its 'good works' or – in the case of crisis response – its efforts to make up for the damage the crisis has caused.

The question is: What should an authentic apology look like? As we dug into the literature on apology, it quickly became clear that ethical frameworks underlie any relationship-based apology framework. We identified three from research on business ethics and crisis communication that provide good explanations for what an apology 'ought' to look like.

1   **Ethics of care perspective:** Simola (2003, 2005) defines ethical action in crises as doing what is right for those affected by the crisis. Thus, adopting an ethics of care approach during a crisis focuses on maintaining and improving relationships after

231

the crisis. However, in order to do this, organizations must not only acknowledge the harm, apologize, and act to resolve the problem, but also demonstrate that they cares about those affected (Bauman, 2011).

2 **Atonement theory:** Across analyses of CSR, ethics, and crisis response, the question of an organization's ethical authenticity often means that stakeholder judge whether the organization's messages or behaviors are motivated by genuine interest (Bauman, 2011; Botan, 1997; Koesten & Rowland, 2004; Lacey, Kennett-Hensel, & Manolis, 2015). The problem with determining whether an organization's actions are 'authentic' or are merely efforts to improve its image is that it can include supposition about an organization's intent. Atonement theory (Jerome, 2008; Koesten & Rowland, 2004) suggests that to atone transgressors must: acknowledge the wrongdoing and ask for forgiveness, demonstrate an attitude of change or relationship renewal, identify steps to ensure the change will happen, and do this in a very public manner.

3 **Apologetic ethics framework:** In addition to considering the ethics and believability of the messaging, we must also focus on the specific content and contextual factors influencing whether ethical apologies are viewed as authentic. Hearit and Borden's (2006) framework suggests that in order to be believable, the manner of apology must be judged to be sincere and well-timed, addressing all stakeholders – not just an organization's strategic stakeholders. Additionally the content of apology must be thorough and stakeholder centered.

Put together, we suggested that the model of ethical apology (see Figure 14.1) requires the manner to be appropriate (i.e., highlighting the source of apology, context, and timing). Then, it requires the content to be tailored to the stakeholders, and to be effective in acknowledging the wrongdoing, being empathetic to those affected, and demonstrating action to correct the situation. Finally, the stakeholders will evaluate whether or not the apology has been effective and believable. Based on our analysis (Diers-Lawson & Pang, 2016), the critical lessons learned about apology are as follows.

1 Apologizing too early and too often can hurt the perceived sincerity of the apology

2 Apologies without communicating empathy make the apology less believable

3 Organizations that need to apologize (i.e., those committing transgressions) should communicate acknowledgement, empathy, and action together rather than in phases across a crisis

4 Defensive response strategies – even when used in very different contexts and focused on very different stakeholders than those affected (e.g., courts of law, Congressional hearings, etc.) – may negatively affect the believability of the apology

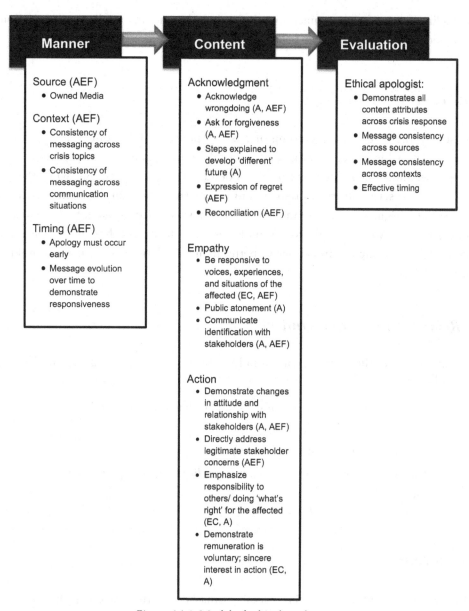

Figure 14.1 Model of ethical apology

5 Organizations need to focus on the credibility of the message, which involves effective timing and who is apologizing, regardless of whether the content is ethical

What we found gives good insight into why a lot of organizations' apologies to crises fail – they come across as inauthentic. This provides an important broader guideline for crisis communication: It is vital that no matter how organizations respond, the response must be believable.

In review . . .

Based on the field's understanding of crisis response, at this point we can provide a list of possible ingredients (i.e., the tactics), some common strategies used crisis response, and some guidelines for what does and does not work. But while there is no definitive set of strategies that organizations should use in different situations, we should begin to understand that if we are mindful of stakeholder needs and interests, then we can begin to assemble response strategies that serve their interests – and thus help organizations to better manage relationships with stakeholders during crises.

Review your understanding

By the end of this chapter, you should be able to understand and explain the following:

- The eight broad categories of tactics, key characteristics, and examples of each
- Four common patterns of crisis response
- The model of ethical apology and its implications for apology and authenticity

References

Bauman, D. C. (2011). Evaluating ethical approaches to crisis leadership: Insights from unintentional harm research. *Journal of Business Ethics*, *98*(2), 281–295. doi:10.1007/s10551-010-0549-3

Benoit, W. L. (1997). Image repair discourse and crisis communication. *Public Relations Review*, *23*(2), 177–187.

Benoit, W. L., & Pang, A. (2008). Crisis communication and image repair discourse. In T. L. Hansen-Horn & B. D. Neff (Eds.), *Public relations: From theory to practice* (pp. 244–261). Boston, MA: Pearson.

Blaney, J. R., Benoit, W. L., & Brazeal, L. M. (2002). Blowout! Firestone's image restoration campaign. *Public Relations Review, 28*(4), 379–392.

Botan, C. (1997). Ethics in strategic communication campaigns: The case for a new approach to public relations. *Journal of Business Communication, 34*(2), 188–203.

Chang, H. H., Tsai, Y.-C., Wong, K. H., Wang, J. W., & Cho, F. J. (2015). The effects of response strategies and severity of failure on consumer attribution with regard to negative word-of-mouth. *Decision Support Systems, 71*, 48–61.

Choi, J. (2012). A content analysis of BP's press releases dealing with crisis. *Public Relations Review, 38*, 422–429. doi:10.1016/j.pubrev.2012.03.003

Coombs, W. T. (2007). Protecting organization reputation during a crisis: The development and application of situational crisis communication theory. *Corporate Reputation Review, 10*(3), 163–176.

Diers, A. R. (2009). *Strategic crisis response: The strategic model of organizational crisis communication.* Saarbrücken, Germany: VDM Verlag.

Diers, A. R., & Donohue, J. (2013). Synchronizing crisis responses after a transgression: An analysis of BP's enacted crisis response to the Deepwater Horizon crisis in 2010. *Journal of Communication Management, 17*(3), 252–269.

Diers, A. R., & Tomaino, K. (2010). Comparing strawberries and quandongs: A cross-national analysis of crisis response strategies. *Observatorio, 4*(2), 21–57.

Diers-Lawson, A. (2017). Crisis communication. In *Oxford research encyclopedia of communication.* Oxford University Press. Retrieved from http://communication.oxfordre.com/view/10.1093/acrefore/9780190228613.001.0001/acrefore-9780190228613-e-397. doi:10.1093/acrefore/9780190228613.013.397

Diers-Lawson, A., & Pang, A. (2016). Did BP atone for its transgressions? Expanding theory on 'ethical apology' in crisis communication. *Journal of Contingencies and Crisis Management, 24*(3), 148–161.

DiStaso, M. W., Vafeiadis, M., & Amaral, C. (2015). Managing a health crisis on Facebook: How the response strategies of apology, sympathy, and information influence public relations. *Public Relations Review, 41*(2), 222–231. doi:10.1016/j.pubrev.2014.11.014

Hearit, K. M. (1994). Apologies and public relations crises at Chrysler, Toshiba, and Volvo. *Public Relations Review, 20*(2), 113–125.

Hearit, K. M., & Borden, S. L. (2006). *Crisis management by apology: Corporate response to allegations of wrongdoing.* New York, NY: Routledge.

Jerome, A. M. (2008). Toward prescription: Testing the rhetoric of atonement's applicability in the athletic arena. *Public Relations Review, 34*(2), 124–134. doi:10.1016/j.pubrev.2008.03.007

Kim, S., Avery, E., & Lariscy, R. (2009). Are crisis communicators practicing what we preach? An evaluation of crisis response strategy analyzed in public relations research from 1991 to 2009. *Public Relations Review, 35*(4), 446–448. doi:10.1016/j.pubrev.2009.08.002

Koesten, J., & Rowland, R. C. (2004). The rhetoric of atonement. *Communication Studies*, *55*, 68–88.

Lacey, R., Kennett-Hensel, P. A., & Manolis, C. (2015). Is corporate social responsibility a motivator or hygiene factor? Insights into its bivalent nature. *Journal of the Academy of Marketing Science*, *42*(3). doi:10.1007/s11747-014-0390-9

Mohamed, A. A., Gardner, W. L., & Paolillo, J. G. P. (1999). A taxonomy of organizational impression management tactics. *Advances in Competitiveness Research*, *7*(1), 108–128.

Pace, K., Fediuk, T. A., & Botero, I. C. (2009). The acceptance of responsibility and expressions of regret in organizational apologies after a transgression. *Corporate Communications: An International Journal*, *15*(4), 410–427. doi:10.1108/13563281011085510

Park, H., & Cameron, G. T. (2014). Keeping it real: Exploring the roles of conversational human voice and source credibility in crisis communication via blogs. *Journalism & Mass Communication Quarterly*, *91*(3), 487–507. doi:10.1177/1077699014538827

Seeger, M. W., & Griffin-Padgett, D. R. (2010). From image restoration to renewal: Approaches to understanding postcrisis communication. *Review of Communication*, *10*(2), 127–141. doi:10.1080/1535859090354526

Simola, S. (2003). Ethics of justice and care in corporate crisis management. *Journal of Business Ethics*, *46*(4), 351–361.

Simola, S. (2005). Concepts of care in organizational crisis prevention. *Journal of Business Ethics*, *62*, 341–353. doi:10.1007/s10551-005-3069-9

Snoeijers, E. M., Poels, K., & Nicolay, C. (2014). #universitycrisis: The impact of social media type, source, and information on student responses toward a university crisis. *Social Science Computer Review*, *32*(5), 647–661. doi:10.1177/0894439314525025

Table references

Bennett, P. (1998). *Communicating about risks to public health: Pointers to good practice.* Department of Health. Retrieved from www.bvsde.paho.org/tutorial6/fulltext/pointers. pdf. Accessed August 8, 2019.

Benoit, W. L. (1997). Image repair discourse and crisis communication. *Public Relations Review*, *23*(2), 177–187.

Benoit, W. L. (2004). Image restoration discourse and crisis communication. In D. P. Millar & R. L. Heath (Eds.), *Responding to crisis: A rhetorical approach to crisis communication* (pp. 263–280). Mahwah, NJ: Lawrence Erlbaum Associates.

Benoit, W. L., & Czerwinski, A. (1997). A critical analysis of USAir's image repair discourse. *Business Communication Quarterly*, *60*(3), 38–57.

Cheney, G., & Christensen, L. T. (2001). Organizational identity: Linkages between internal and external communication. In F. M. Jablin & L. L. Putnam (Eds.), *The new handbook of organizational communication: Advances in theory, research, and methods* (pp. 231–269). Thousand Oaks, CA: Sage Publications.

Coombs, W. T., & Holladay, S. J. (2002). Helping crisis managers protect their reputational assets: Initial tests of the Situational Crisis Communication Theory. *Management Communication Quarterly*, *16*(2), 165–186.

Coombs, W. T., & Schmidt, L. (2000). An empirical analysis of image restoration: Texaco's racism crisis. *Journal of Public Relations Research*, *12*(2), 163–178.

Das, T. K., & Teng, B.-S. (1998). Between trust and control: Developing confidence in partner cooperation in alliances. *Academy of Management Review*, *23*(3), 491–513.

Fiol, C. M. (1995). Corporate communications: Comparing executives' private and public statements. *Academy of Management Journal*, *38*(2), 522–536.

Gonzales-Herrero, A., & Pratt, C. B. (1998). Marketing crises in tourism: Communication strategies in the United States and Spain. *Public Relations Review*, *24*(1), 83–97.

Greer, C. F., & Moreland, K. D. (2003). United Airlines' and American Airlines' online crisis communication following the September 11 terrorist attacks. *Public Relations Review*, *29*, 427–441.

Gregory, R. (2000). Using stakeholder values to make smarter environmental decisions. *Environment*, *42*(5), 34.

Hayes, D., & Patton, M. (2001). Proactive crisis-management strategies and the archaeological heritage. *International Journal of Heritage Studies*, *7*(1), 37–58.

Hearit, K. M. (1999). Newsgroups, activist publics, and corporate apologia: The case of Intel and its Pentium chip. *Public Relations Review*, *25*(3), 291–308.

Heath, R. L. (1994). *Management of corporate communication: From interpersonal contacts to external affairs*. Hillsdale, NJ: Lawrence Erlbaum Associates.

Heath, R. L. (1998). Dealing with the complete crisis – The crisis management shell structure. *Safety Science*, *30*, 139–150.

Henderson, J. C. (2003). Communicating in a crisis: Flight SQ 006. *Tourism Management*, *24*, 279–287.

Henriques, I., & Sadorsky, P. (1999). The relationship between environmental commitment and managerial perceptions of stakeholder importance. *Academy of Management Journal*, *42*(1), 87–99.

Kauffman, J. (2001). A successful failure: NASA's crisis communications regarding Apollo 13. *Public Relations*, *27*(4), 437–449.

Marra, F. J. (1998). Crisis communication plans: Poor predictors of excellent crisis public relations. *Public Relations Review*, *24*(4), 461–475.

Martinelli, K. A., & Briggs, W. (1998). Integrating public relations and legal responses during a crisis: The case of Odwalla, Inc. *Public Relations Review*, *24*(4), 443–465.

Massey, J. E. (2001). Managing organizational legitimacy: Communication strategies for organizations in crisis. *Journal of Business Communication*, *38*(2), 153–170.

Milliman, J., Clair, J. A., & Mitroff, I. (1994). Environmental groups and business organizations: Conflict or cooperation? *SAM Advanced Management Journal*, *59*(2), 41–47.

Mohamed, A. A., Gardner, W. L., & Paolillo, J. G. P. (1999). A taxonomy of organizational impression management tactics. *Advances in Competitiveness Research*, 7(1), 108–128.

Proto, M., & Supino, S. (1999). The quality of environmental information: A new tool in achieving customer loyalty. *Total Quality Management*, s679.

Ray, S. (1999). *Strategic communication in crisis management: Lessons from the airline industry*. Westport, CT: Quorum Books.

Rowan, F. (1996). The high stakes of risk communication. *Preventive Medicine*, 25, 26–29.

Scott, S. G., & Lane, V. R. (2000). A stakeholder approach to organizational identity. *Academy of Management Review*, 25(1), 43–65.

Sellnow, T. L. (1993). Scientific argument in organizational crisis communication: The case of Exxon. *Argumentation and Advocacy*, 30(1), 28–43.

Sellnow, T. L., & Brand, J. D. (2001). Establishing the structure of reality for an industry: Model and anti-model arguments as advocacy in Nike's crisis communication. *Journal of Applied Communication Research*, 29(3), 278–296.

Sellnow, T. L., & Ulmer, R. R. (1995). Ambiguous argument as advocacy in organizational crisis communication. *Argumentation and Advocacy*, 31(3), 138–151.

Sellnow, T. L., & Ulmer, R. R. (2004). Ambiguity as an inherent factor in organizational crisis communication. In D. P. Millar & R. L. Heath (Eds.), *Responding to crisis: A rhetorical approach to crisis communication* (pp. 251–262). Mahwah, NJ: Lawrence Erlbaum Associates.

Slovic, P. (1987). Perception of risk. *Science*, 236, 280–285.

Sturges, D. L. (1994). Communicating through crisis: A strategy for organizational survival. *Management Communication Quarterly*, 7, 297–316.

Ulmer, R. R., & Sellnow, T. L. (2000). Consistent questions of ambiguity in organizational crisis communication: Jack in the Box as a case study. *Journal of Business Ethics*, 25(2), 143–156.

Williams, D. E., & Olaniran, B. A. (1998). Expanding the crisis planning function: Introducing elements of risk communication to crisis communication practice. *Public Relations Review*, 24(3), 387–402.

15 Comparing theories of crisis response

Learning objectives

By the end of this chapter, the reader should:

- Understand the role of theory in developing crisis response strategies
- Identify the major classifications of theory used in crisis communication
- Better appreciate that crisis communication is a genuinely interdisciplinary and applied field of study

Whenever I can, I like to attend the International Risk and Crisis Communication Conference in Florida. I know, there are worse places to be in early March than central Florida. But one of the things that I really appreciate about this conference is that it has a great combination of academics and practitioners in attendance. This is something that we are working on encouraging in Europe as well because the interchange between the groups only improves the community's working and theoretical knowledge about risk and crisis communication.

So, in 2016 I was sitting in a keynote panel discussion where very distinguished academics were talking about their experiences in talking to people affected by crises, capturing these moving stories, and better understanding the tactics that failed in different crises. Then one of the practitioners asked a very simple question couched in an important critique of the field that went something like this: "It is great that you are able to capture these narratives, but where are the predictive theories that would really help us design message strategies to be more successful in handling crises?" The question was followed by a murmur of agreement from practitioners around the room. This was not the first time that I had heard a practitioner expressing appreciation for theory and research in risk and crisis communication; in fact, across the domains of communication practice I would argue that risk and crisis practitioners are some of the more research friendly and theoretically driven. It was, though, was the first time that I had heard such a public frustration with the state of theory-building in risk and crisis communication.

My initial reaction was to agree with the practitioner's assessment about the state of theory in the field, but this question also prompted me to take a deep dive into the state of risk and crisis research to answer this guy's question for myself. What I found was that while there is still work to be done in terms of theory building in risk and crisis communication – this is true of any field, but especially one like ours that is still in the process of 'institutionalizing' itself – there is a rich body of theory that we can tap into, if we only know where to look and how to approach the decisions that need to be made to have theory-driven practice.

To this point, I have introduced a number of theories. I began with the theory organizing the whole text – the stakeholder relationship model (SRM) – but have also discussed interpersonal theories like expectancy violation, persuasion theories like the extended parallel process model (EPPM), and crisis theories like situational crisis communication theory. I am pretty confident that everyone has survived to this point. The fact of the matter is that when we talk about theory, a lot of people tune out: They believe that theory is only for the nerds wearing jackets with leather elbow pads, sitting in academic ivory towers.

So, before you start flipping pages and getting the bare bones of what you need to study for a quiz or test, or to apply in a project, let me try to persuade you that to be a good practitioner you should have a deep understanding of theory. After that, I will offer a broad overview of the types of theory that are applied in the cross-disciplinary research in risk and crisis communication. I am not going to introduce all of the theories that have been used – that would be a textbook by itself and we have several good texts that focus on theory in crisis communication, such as Sellnow and Seeger's *Theorizing Crisis Communication* as well as a great number of collections of essays incorporating different authors discussing the theories they have developed, researched, and applied, such as *The Handbook of Crisis Communication, Social Media and Crisis Communication*, or *The Handbook of International Crisis Communication Research*. Instead, we are going to focus on developing theoretical approaches to crisis response and how to find and choose the right theories to suit the organization's needs and objectives.

Theory-informed practice improves performance

There are a lot of leather elbow-pad reasons to appreciate and use theory in research, but let us be practical about this. In the 'real world,' when organizations spend money on any communication campaign, any social responsibility program, and any stakeholder-related research, we have to show a **return on the investment** (ROI) that the organization has made. If the expenditures do not show a direct ROI (e.g., increased profit/donations/votes) or impact on an organization's **key performance indicators** (KPIs), then there is little evidence that the money has been wisely spent. In a crisis context, we already know the stakes are high for organizations in terms of the material, reputational, and relational risks posed. Thus, my basic argument is that it is fundamentally irresponsible not to do everything that we can to optimize success in achieving ROI, KPI, relational, and situational objectives.

But how does theory connect to this point? Think of theory like a playbook used in sports. When sports managers put together their playbooks, what they are doing is taking all of their experience, factoring in their team's strengths and weaknesses, factoring in their opposition's strengths and weaknesses, and then developing a strategy that they think will help them win. What grounds the playbook is a lot of data. Sports team spend a lot of money to:

- Hire the best coach or manager they can afford – one whose experience and decision-making has been proven to be sound and one who has a vision for the team that complement's the team's goals
- Evaluate their own players each day, week, or season
- Scout new players
- Scout other teams for their game strategies, their players
- Develop strategy from all of this

The movie *Moneyball* with Brad Pitt was the story of how the Oakland A's team and then-manager Billy Beane fundamentally changed the way that the game of baseball was managed in the United States. The 'old style' of management was not data-driven nor theoretically grounded, but what Beane demonstrated was that identifying a theory and data-driven strategy towards player acquisition and management improved performance.

Not a sports fan? That's fine. This is the same thing that happens in the entertainment industry when a new television series or movie is put together, beginning with the director. This is the same process that is used in product development and so on and so forth. Why? Because we are talking about massive amounts of money and a lot of expectations.

What is theory?

Theory is both a prediction about what will happen in the future as well as a summary of what has happened in the past. All good theory is based on tangible evidence. If we think about the playbook analogy, then why would a coach recommend a particular formation or play? In most cases it worked in the past and is expected to work in the future. But that does not mean that the playbook always stays the same; as time goes on, the playbook is updated when better information is available or different plays prove more successful.

This is what theory does. We use theories in our everyday lives; we just seldom label them as 'theory.' Let us say that you go to your regular bus stop every day for a week and every day the bus is five to ten minutes later than the posted timetable. What are reasonable explanations for this?

- The bus company cannot maintain a timetable
- There might be roadworks temporarily delaying the bus
- The timetable may have changed, but the posted schedule has not been updated
- The traffic at the time of day is consistently slow, meaning the optimal timetable cannot be maintained

Any of these could be a reasonable explanation, but what you do in response to the pattern that you have noticed with the perpetually late bus? You could just surmise that you did not need to leave your house for an additional five to ten minutes, get some extra sleep, have breakfast, or something else. This would be a reasonable action to take and would represent a rudimentary theory that you have formed: The bus is not going to be on time. You can test to see if that works out for you the following week. If everything works out, you can conclude that your prediction was true and plan accordingly.

However, an incomplete prediction may also mean that you end up missing your bus. A better approach to determining whether you hit that snooze button one more time would be to figure out which explanation (or combination of them) was most likely to be true. If there were roadworks, then knowing when they were going to end would tell you when you needed to go out early again. If the start of the school day meant that traffic was heavier in your area, then knowing when school was or was not in session could let you better predict when the bus would be on time or late, and so on.

This is all that research-based theory is: We collect data about real events, attitudes, judgments and situations, and then analyse them to identify consistent and verifiable patterns that allow us to make predictions. Then, over time, we test these theories in different contexts to see if those predictions work out in slightly different contexts or with different groups. Developing good theory takes time – as in years – but this is why theory-based decision-making and strategy generally improves performance. It builds on our mistakes, our successes, and our knowledge from the past in order to make reasonable predictions about the future. It also is able to account for the strange and bizarre circumstances that lead to excellent or terrible outcomes as being different from normal, because it pools together many different experiences to define what is 'typical' and 'atypical.' Because theory, especially in risk and crisis communication, is built from what happens in 'the real world,' it gives us a playbook that helps us make better predictions about how our organizations should manage risk or respond to crises. It lets us have better ROI and impact our KPIs more positively.

What are the theoretical options in risk and crisis communication?

The short answer to this question is – a lot. In my deep dive into the crisis communication literature between 1953 and 2015, analyzing 690 different journal articles, I found more than 90 distinctive theories directly applied to academic research – and this is not an exhaustive list. While the 690 journal articles represent a substantial proportion of the articles published across these six decades, there are articles that I did not capture in the study. In the four years since, there have certainly been additional theories developed or applied. These theories can be broken down into three broad groups:

● Risk and crisis theories

● Communication theories

● Theories from complementary fields of study

Risk and crisis theories

Over the last few decades, a number of risk and crisis theories have been developed. These can be broken down into three broad sub-groups (see Figure 15.1).

Risk-oriented theories focus most on risk mitigation – that is, reducing the likelihood that crises will happen at all or if they happen either stakeholders or organizations will be better prepared for them. A few examples of these include:

○ The internalization, distribution, explanation, and action (IDEA) model (Sellnow et al., 2015) is one good example of a risk-oriented theory. This is a stakeholder-centered model with the goal of getting people to take precautions to either avoid or minimize the impact of events like natural disasters or disease on themselves or their businesses.

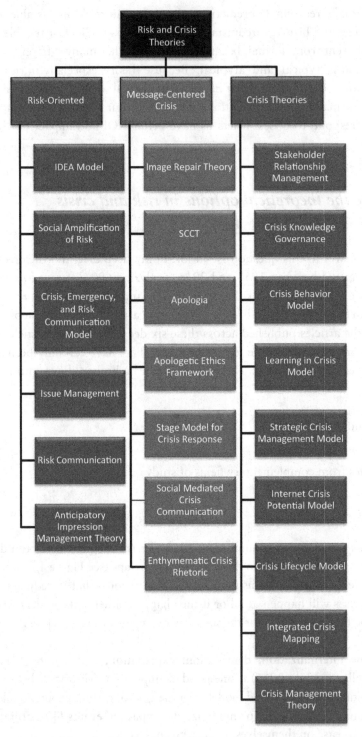

Figure 15.1 Risk and crisis theories applied in crisis communication research

- o   The **social amplification of risk framework** (Kasperson et al., 1988) is also a stakeholder-centered model. It tries to explain why people can misjudge the potential negative impact of risks, which ultimately affects their willingness or ability to take precautionary measures to avoid them. They found that the ways risks are discussed in the media, cultural groups, and interpersonal networks affects how much risk people perceive.

- o   A final example from this category is the **crisis, emergency, and risk communication model (CERC)** (Reynolds & Seeger, 2005) which focuses on the intersection of health communication and complex events like disasters. The theory's objective is to identify the kinds of communication activities that are appropriate for various stages of disasters or crises in order to help manage the total situation from pre- to post-crisis stages.

Surprisingly, **message-centered crisis theories** are not at the heart of much of the crisis communication research that occurs. In fact, two of the core theories most commonly applied (i.e., 17% of the time in the crisis literature that I identified) in crisis communication research – image repair theory and situational crisis communication theory – are both good examples of message-centered theories. I discussed the apologetic ethics framework in Chapter 14. Collectively, these theories make specific recommendations about the types of message strategies that should be enacted across different kinds of crises and with different types of audiences. A few examples of these include:

- o   **Image repair theory (IRT)** (Benoit, 1997) is one of the first genuine crisis communication theories that helped establish crisis communication as a distinctive area of study. IRT argues that one of the core functions of crisis communication is to repair the damage done to an organization's image and that responses must take into account the nature of the crisis before developing its strategy. The theory, therefore, makes a number of situational recommendations about crisis response strategy.

- o   **Situational crisis communication theory (SCCT)** (Coombs, 2006) has also made a meaningful contribution to the development and institutionalization of crisis communication. As we have discussed, SCCT focuses on addressing situational factors, like blame attribution, that influence how stakeholders evaluate particular crisis response strategies arguing that "managers make informed choices about crisis response strategies based upon theoretically derived and empirically tested evidence" (Coombs, 2006, p. 255).

- o   **Social-mediated crisis communication** (Liu, Fraustino, & Jin, 2015) blends media richness theory, cross-platform crisis communication, and stakeholder reactions to messages in order to better understand stakeholder information needs, information sharing, and messaging in disaster contexts. This is a particularly innovative example of message theory because it directly includes social media and legacy media engagement as a part of active crisis response.

- **Crisis theories** represent a diverse and multidisciplinary group of theories that help organizations to diagnose the specific risks and problems that issues and crises create for them (e.g., the stakeholder relationship management model), learn from crises, and know what to expect throughout the crisis lifecycle. Aside from SRM, a few examples of these include:
  - **Internet crisis potential** (Conway, Ward, Lewis, & Bernhardt, 2007) is a marketing-based model that focuses on the ways that organizations should use online monitoring in order to improve their agility in issue identification and crisis response.
  - **Integrated crisis mapping model** (Jin & Pang, 2010) provides a mechanism for organizations to analyze social media – especially Twitter – in order to gauge public sentiment about the organization and the crisis and then inform the construction of messages to help stakeholders emotionally cope with crises.
  - **Crisis management theory** (R. Heath, 1998) provides a multidisciplinary shell structure meant to provide in integrated management approach to crisis management. Heath argues that using a central management hub with coordinated activities connecting personnel, communication, internal communication, image management, and situational response offers organizations the best approach for successfully managing crises.

Communication theories

Not surprisingly, a substantial proportion of the crisis communication research that I reviewed also applies traditional communication theories (see Figure 15.2) to understand, evaluate, and develop crisis response strategy. I have already discussed a number of these throughout this book, like expectancy violation theory (EVT), credibility, and the EPPM. These can be broken down into five sub-groups. I will address the broad contributions across the sub-groups rather than providing specific examples of these theories.

- **Traditional public relations (PR) and communication theories** are commonly used in crisis communication because the principles governing stakeholder relationship management are aligned with the work in interpersonal communication, PR, and organizational communication. For example, I discussed how EVT helps us to understand how stakeholders might react if a crisis shakes their view of an

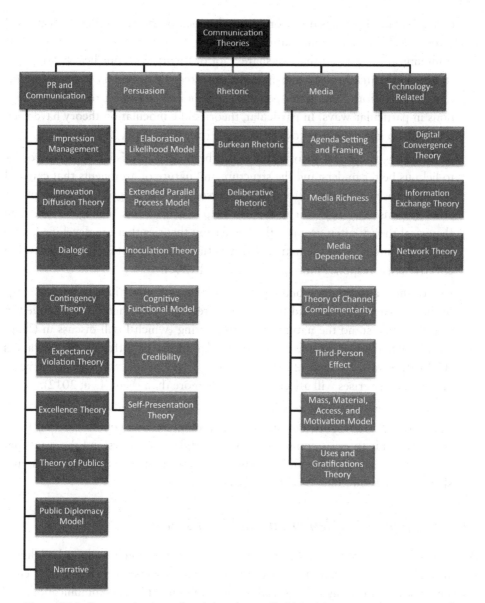

Figure 15.2 Communication-related theories applied in crisis communication research

organization's image or culture. But theories like contingency theory help practitioners and researchers alike to consider what factors must be taken into consideration when planning a response to any situation.

- I have also already spent a considerable amount of time (see, e.g., Chapter 10) discussing the importance of **persuasion theories** in understanding and predicting factors that influence stakeholder reactions to both crises and crisis response messages. Good persuasion theory grounds much of the messaging strategy used across the field of communication – not just in crisis situations. Yet, in crisis communication we find that we share a lot of theory with our health campaign colleagues because health campaigns and crisis response often try to manage emotions, expectations, and better persuade stakeholders to act or respond to situations in particular ways. In particular, theories like **inoculation theory** have been used to help industries improve their image over time (Kim, 2013).

- Additionally, **rhetorical theories** have also been used in crisis response in order to help us better understand the structure and nature of arguments that can and should be used to respond to crises. If persuasion theory grounds much of the crisis response strategy that is used to help organizations manage crises, then rhetorical theory often grounds the persuasion theories that are developed, so it is useful to understand the nature and structure of argument if we are to develop effective crisis response messages (R. L. Heath, 2006).

- One of the realities of responding to crises is that organizations have to manage media – owned, earned, and bought. As a result, **media theories** are applied in order to understand the nature of agenda setting (which I will discuss in Chapter 17), what drives people to use particular media in different circumstances (Holbert, Kwak, & Shah, 2003), and what drives people to make judgements about whether crises will affect other people more than them (Lyu, 2012).

- Of course, if we are going to talk about media theories, we also have to acknowledge the important contributions that **technology-related communication theories** have made to crisis communication by helping us understand the ways that social media has fundamentally changed the way that we collect, process, and share information (Sung & Hwang, 2014).

Theories from complementary fields of study

As I pointed out in Chapter 1, the field of crisis communication is an interdisciplinary field of study with research occurring across the STEM fields (science, technology, engineering, and math), management, social sciences and humanities, communication, and a number of applied industries. In Chapter 1 I also argued that if we want to understand what crisis communication is, we must be reading broadly across domains of practice in order to prepare us for practice. Likewise, we must also be drawing from fields that complement what communication does, in order to build and apply theory in different types of crises as well. For example, a lot of the most innovative analyses and theories related to social media and crisis communication – theories that contribute to saving lives during disasters – comes from the field of computer science because these researchers are able to dig into networks most effectively. Moreover, it should not be surprising that the field of psychology makes substantial contributions in theory and practice within crisis communication as well. However, in terms of identifying particular theories driving crisis response and analysis, there are five fields of study that I found most contribute to our research (see Figure 15.3): psychology and learning, organizational, marketing and advertising, management and leadership, and cultural studies.

Developing theory-informed crisis response

Any of these theories can make an important contribution to issues, risk, and crisis response depending on the nature of the circumstances, stakeholders, issues, and organization. But that's the critical challenge – trying to figure out how to develop theory-informed crisis response. Being familiar with any of the theories across thee three categories does not mean that we can use them well.

I go back to my opening sports analogy of building a great playbook. This is something that Benoit (1997) and Coombs (2006) both talked about as they introduced their theories – the importance of having a sound strategy for building a successful response to a crisis. So, how do we translate the sports analogy into theory-informed crisis response? It is about good decision-making. In Chapter 16 I talk about strategically planning crisis response messages, but let us first review what was discussed throughout this book. The stakeholder relationship management model is a decision-making diagnostic tool to help organizations evaluate what they need to do to effectively manage their stakeholder relationships during a crisis.

Using theory to build crisis capacity

Why do sports teams hire the best managers and players that they can? They do this to give themselves the best advantage they can have before the game or match starts. This is what organizational capacity building does, as I discussed in Part 3 of this textbook. If an organization goes through the process of evaluating its culture, its staff, and its leadership in order to evaluate its crisis readiness, to respond to a crisis, or to recover from a crisis, then it likely that it will have to address organizational and management or leadership issues. It may even have to make adaptations in its approach to brand management or cultural competence.

If this is where the biggest areas of need are for an organization, then the organization should consider those types of theories (see Figure 15.3) that would target capacity building, such as using theories from disciplines like decision-making, organizational change, learning, leadership, cultural competence, cultural trauma, or social

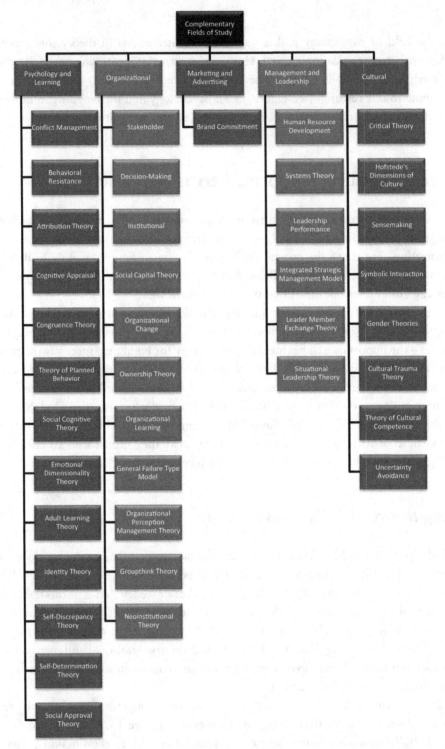

Figure 15.3 Theories from complementary disciplines applied in crisis communication research

marketing to help guide the strategy that they developed in order to meet the specific objectives identified in a needs assessment.

More than that, crisis capacity building is also about issues management, so organizations might also need to initiate a strategy to mitigate risk for themselves or their stakeholders. Doing this ahead of time, as I have discussed, would better enable an organization to help respond to and manage a crisis if it should occur. Depending on the type of organization, stakeholders, or types of risk, this could range from applying theories like anticipatory impression management to build an organization's reputation in anticipation of negative events or helping to prepare the stakeholders themselves for crises by applying the IDEA model (see Figure 15.1). In either direction, these types of strategic objectives are also helping to build capacity. Applying these theories give organizations a playbook to plan and anticipate the types of ROI they can expect for these activities.

Finally, as part of crisis capacity building, organizations should get to know their stakeholders better – both internally and externally. Internally, using the playbooks provided by theories like leader member exchange, organizational learning, organizational perception management theory, or behavioral resistance theory, or conflict management theory can provide organizations with meaningful intelligence on their internal stakeholders and therefore how effectively the organization can respond to changing circumstances (see Figure 15.3), as I discussed in Part 4. Externally, applying the psychology and learning theories like attribution theory, emotional dimensionality theory, or social approval theory (see Figure 15.3) or certainly persuasion theories like self-presentation theory or the EPPM, can help organizations piece together their stakeholders' attitudes, as I discussed in Chapter 10.

Using theory to choose crisis response strategies

In Chapter 14, I identified eight categories of tactics and more than 40 individual tactics that organizations could choose to respond to crises – but how should an organization pick the best tactics to use (see Figures 15.1 and 15.2)? Fortunately for those of us in the broad field of corporate communication, this should be our wheelhouse of strength, but it can still be difficult. If we understand our organization's capacity and we have done our work with the stakeholder relationship management model that I have laid out throughout the book, then it is simply a matter of identifying which stakeholder, issue, and organization-related concepts are going to matter in a situation and identifying the plays (i.e., theories) that are going to help us choose the best tactics. This is what the sports teams are doing when they evaluate their own players and scout other teams – they are laying the groundwork to build their own team's strategy before, throughout, and after their season ends.

For example, if an organization has a good reputation but has committed a transgression, then a theory like the apologetic ethics framework is a natural fit because it is most effective when the organization has done something wrong but has a great reputation. If, however, an organization is responding to a disaster and it needs its stakeholders to be able to manage their fear effectively – meaning it needs to focus on building efficacy and telling stakeholders what to do in order to keep themselves safe – then a theory like the EPPM could be the most effective.

However, unless we have done our work ahead of time with our crisis capacity building, it is much more difficult to quickly identify the best play to help manage both organizational and stakeholder interests. In a crisis context, being quick and decisive is vital to being viewed as a credible source of information and getting to help set the agenda for the crisis response. In the next chapter, I will discuss strategically planning crisis response messages, I will provide an example of a crisis plan to help direct the decisions that organizations can follow ahead of time to plan their initial crisis response.

In review . . .

We have taken a look at the three categories of theory most commonly applied to risk and crisis communication in order to introduce the core themes across them. We have also talked about what it means to develop theory-informed crisis response – both as a crisis capacity building activity as well as a crisis response activity. In the end, good theory gives practitioners a playbook to follow. Yes, sometimes playbooks have to be re-written or even set aside in exceptional circumstances, but all good managers and leaders know that in order to demonstrate ROI, help an organization meet its KPIs, and – most importantly in the crisis context – manage their organization's relationships with its stakeholders, having a strategically sound starting point will improve its team's performance.

Review your understanding

By the end of this chapter, you should be able to understand and explain the following.

- The role of theory in practice
- Crisis communication theories:
  - Risk-centered theories
  - Message-centered theories
  - Crisis theories

- Communication theories:
  - PR and communication theories
  - Persuasion theories
  - Rhetorical theories
  - Media theories
  - Technology-based theories

- Theories from complementary fields:
  - Psychological theories
  - Organizational theories
  - Marketing theories
  - Management and leadership theories
  - Cultural theories

- What it means to develop a theory-informed crisis response:
  - Using theory to build crisis capacity
  - Using theory to choose crisis response strategies

References

Benoit, W. L. (1997). Image repair discourse and crisis communication. *Public Relations Review*, 23(2), 177–187.

Conway, T., Ward, M., Lewis, G., & Bernhardt, A. (2007). Internet crisis potential: The importance of a strategic approach to marketing communications. *Journal of Marketing Communication*, 13(3), 213–228. doi:10.1080/13527260601086462

Coombs, W. T. (2006). The protective powers of crisis response strategies: Managing reputational assets during a crisis. *Journal of Promotion Management*, 12(3/4), 241–260. doi:10.1300/J057v12n03_13

Heath, R. L. (1998). Dealing with the complete crisis – The crisis management shell structure. *Safety Science*, 30(1), 139–150.

Heath, R. L. (2006). A rhetorical theory approach to issues management. In C. L. Botan & V. Hazleton (Eds.), *Public relations theory II* (pp. 63–100). London: Routledge.

Holbert, R. L., Kwak, N., & Shah, D. V. (2003). Environmental concern, patterns of television viewing, and pro-environmental behaviors: Integrating models of media consumption and effects. *Journal of Broadcasting & Electronic Media*, 47(2), 177–196.

Jin, Y., & Pang, A. (2010). Future directions of crisis communication research: Emotions in crisis – The next frontier. In W. T. Coombs & S. J. Holladay (Eds.), *Handbook of crisis communication* (pp. 677–682). Oxford, UK: Wiley-Blackwell.

Kasperson, R. E., Renn, O., Slovic, P., Brown, H. S., Emel, J., Goble, R., . . . Ratick, S. (1988). The social amplification of risk: A conceptual framework. *Risk Analysis, 8*(2), 177–187.

Kim, S. (2013). Does corporate advertising work in a crisis? An examination of inoculation theory. *Journal of Marketing Communications, 19*(4), 293–305. doi:10.1080/13527266. 2011.634430

Liu, B. F., Fraustino, J. D., & Jin, Y. (2015). Social media use during disasters: How information form and source influence intended behavioral responses. *Communication Research, 43*(5), 626–646. doi:10.1177/0093650214565917

Lyu, J. C. (2012). How young Chinese depend on the media during public health crises? A comparative perspective. *Public Relations Review, 38*(5), 799–806.

Reynolds, B., & Seeger, M. W. (2005). Crisis and emergency risk communication as an integrative model. *Journal of Health Communication, 10*(1), 43–55.

Sellnow, D. D., Lane, D., Littlefield, R. S., Sellnow, T. L., Wilson, B., Beauchamp, K., & Venette, S. (2015). A receiver-based approach to effective instructional crisis communication. *Journal of Contingencies and Crisis Management, 23*(3), 149–158. doi:10.1111/1468-5973.12066

Sung, M., & Hwang, J.-S. (2014). Who drives a crisis? The diffusion of an issue through social networks. *Computers in Human Behavior, 36*, 246–257. doi:10.1016/j.chb.2014.03.063

16 Strategically planning crisis response messages

Learning objectives

By the end of this chapter, the reader should:

- Be able to discuss crisis response in the context of crisis planning, risk management, and issues management
- Use a campaign-based model for planning crisis response and adapting to 'live' situations
- Learn how to create an adaptable crisis plan

In the previous three chapters in this section, I have addressed the realities of crisis response in multi-platform competitive message environments, I introduced the broad range of tactics that organizations use to respond to crises, and I have talked about the reasons for having theory-driven crisis response. In this chapter, I focus on the practicalities of how all of this comes together in the process of crisis planning, risk management, and issues management.

Crisis planning as a tailored campaign

What I lay out in this chapter should look familiar in form and function to anyone who is familiar with the campaign process: Crisis planning is simply a specialized type of campaign. Certainly, crisis response involves critical decision-making that works to balance the nature of the crisis, the organization, and stakeholders in order to create strategic messages that help an organization manage its crisis issues. Effective crisis response involves the identification of critical objectives for the crisis response (Austin, Liu, & Jin, 2014), targeted stakeholders (Wertz & Kim, 2010), identification of key messages (Claeys & Cauberghe, 2015), as well as the platforms to communicate (Canhoto et al., 2015) (see Figure 16.1). Most of what we do in crisis communication follows the same form and function that any other strategic communication effort does – it is just that it is driven by a different set of objectives. However, these objectives still need to demonstrate return on investment (ROI) and be connected to an organization's key performance indicators (KPIs), as I discussed in the previous chapter.

Given the number of tactics that an organization has and the factors that can influence them, it is not surprising that there could be a lot of ways to approach crisis response and many different ways to adapt the messaging. However, consistency and clarity is important. For example, in my analysis of BP's response to the 2010 disaster in the Gulf of Mexico, the team analyzed BP's crisis response across its press releases, Twitter, and Facebook posts from April to October 2010 and found that the core elements of the company's crisis response across its owned platforms emerged in press releases with Twitter and Facebook posts, but the core strategy was applied differently on each of the different platforms (Diers & Donohue, 2013).

As I mentioned in Chapter 1, research on crisis planning has not been a dominant theme in crisis communication research for a number of years because the literature generally agrees on what crisis planning is and should do. **Crisis planning** is a multidisciplinary, cross-department, strategic management function whose goal is to try to manage the challenges and problems that emerge in order to serve the

Figure 16.1 The crisis planning process

both stakeholder and organizational interests (Dilenschneider & Hyde, 1985; Gainey, 2009; Heath, 2004; Henderson, 1999; Sturges, Carrell, Newsom, & Barrera, 1991; Valackiene, 2010).

Internal obstacles to good crisis planning

Crisis planning is often not that easy – if it were, organizations would all commit meaningful resources to crisis planning, and that is just not the case. Even among the Fortune 500 companies, there are deep divides between what organizations 'ought' to be doing and what corporate leadership deems as necessary and sufficient (Pang, Cropp, & Cameron, 2006). Pang et al.'s (2006) research found five key schisms between what research and practice suggest organizations should be doing to plan for crises, and what Fortune 500 countries often do in practice.

- **While companies acknowledge value in creating crisis plans, recommended strategies are often just paid lip service.** Pang et al., found that companies will often agree, in practical terms, that they need to have a crisis plan. They will commission one to be created, but then fail to make the changes that would actually mitigate risk or improve the company's social obligations to its stakeholders. There may be a lot of reasons for this, including a lack of organizational capacity building to ensure the organization can implement the changes, internal politics, and simply a lack of urgency.

- **Communications functions still remain undervalued in many organizations.** While this is changing, and many organizations, have realized the vital business function that communications serves to helping an organization achieve its KPIs and strategic objectives, its value is often still underestimated. In part, this is about an organization's culture but in part this is about communications professionals being better advocates for ourselves – beyond just marketing and advertising and delivering evidence of ROI.

- **Power struggles over the ownership or crisis-related decision-making limit crisis planning.** Pang et al., point out that in some large multinational or even multiregional organizations, the question of whether crisis planning is a central or regional function remains a turf battle.

- **Schisms of style and communication preference limit crisis planning.** There are a lot of potential style conflicts and even conflicting recommendations. For example, some communications directors may focus on direct and open communication (because this is largely what stakeholders expect), but corporate leaders may view this as risky, legal recommendations often focus on concerns of liability, and there is limited agreement about the communication approach ahead of time.

257

- **There must be top-to-bottom and bottom-to-top understanding and support for crisis planning and response strategy.** Beyond the power struggles that may exist at different levels of the organization, it is vital that members from different levels of the organization are involved in, understand, and can enact crisis response strategies. Pang et al. (2006) make the point that if line managers do not understand the crisis plan and have not developed a rapport with the crisis responders within the organization, then there will be difficulties. This is, in part, why Heath (1998, 2004) focuses on the complete crisis involving relevant members of an organization.

Have confidence that crisis planning works

Despite the challenges that we may face – both in terms of the work and the resources that it requires – creating effective crisis plans pays off. Throughout the last 30 years, we have high-visibility evidence that crisis planning not only saves lives but also saves organizational reputations as well. Unfortunately, we also have a lot of evidence to show that failure to plan for crises, keep updated crisis plans, and devote resources to crisis planning can also carry great costs.

Let us start with the negative. During the US congressional hearings in 2010 on the oil and gas industry's poor crisis preparedness, what we learned was that even though every major energy company doing business in the Gulf of Mexico had a crisis plan, not a single one of them were up-to-date. In fact, most of them were pretty similar, identifying strategies for managing situations in arctic conditions, addressing the risks to species like walruses, and listing key contacts who had been dead for a number of years. Similarly. in 1967 NASA faced its first major crisis with the Apollo 1 mission when a fire killed three of its crew members. Unprepared for the situation, the agency responded poorly, failing to report the deaths, communicating inaccurate and incomplete information, and purposefully misleading Congress and the media – fundamentally damaging the organization's reputation and putting its mission at risk (Kauffman, 2000).

However, by 1970 NASA had learned from its crisis response failures when an explosion on the Apollo 13 mission threatened the lives of the astronauts. Instead of deceiving the public, NASA responded openly and quickly, not only securing political and public confidence in the organization but also ensuring that continuing support for space exploration would be possible (Kauffman, 2001). The same is true with hallmark cases in crisis response – like the 1982 Tylenol tampering case and a second tampering episode in 1986 when the company's proactive approach to managing the situation and crisis communication ensured that damage was minimized for both the company and its consumers (Benson, 1988).

When executed effectively, crisis planning can even help organizations use the issue management process to make material changes in their organization's practices and proactively communicate to demonstrate issue leadership within an industry. This has been demonstrated in a number of industries like the US cattle industry example discussed earlier in the book then the industry had not only planned for the risk of 'Mad Cow disease' but also an aggressive communication campaign to celebrate its success.

But the case that most clearly demonstrates how a company can use issue management to mitigate the impact of a crisis and build a strong communication strategy around that is Nike. In the 1980s the biggest athletic footwear companies were targeted for having poor labor conditions in Asia – functionally being accused of turning a blind eye to sweatshop labor conditions. Nike was not the largest footwear company. When the problem was identified, Nike was asked whether it was also guilty. It turned out that it was. Instead of trying to cover this up, in a 1998 speech Nike's founder Phil Knight announced new company initiatives in global manufacturing. He acknowledged that Nike had been a part of the problem, but it was making fundamental changes. In connecting action and an active campaign strategy, Nike was successful in building the argument that not only was Nike committed to being an ethical organization but also that violating international labor standards was unacceptable (Sellnow & Brand, 2001). This did not stop criticisms of the company, but it certainly mitigated the negative impact – and it also helped the company change its business model to ensure it could be ethical in action and advocacy.

Whether well-designed issue or crisis management campaigns are effective should not be the question asked. The better question is whether an organization's response is like Nike's, which focused on being a more socially responsible organization, or like the tobacco industry, which responded to years of challenges with lies and deception. As practitioners it can be difficult to see the forest for the trees; the question of ethics is not always an easy one to address, except in retrospect. For example, Robert Minton-Taylor, a public relations (PR) practitioner for 45 years, reflects on his work with the tobacco industry and the integrity of the work he did (see Box 16.1).

Box 16.1 Practitioner's perspective: The tobacco industry's big PR lie

By Robert Minton-Taylor

In my 45 years in PR there have been times when what I did and who I worked for was close to the wire – in terms of crossing that gray dividing line between what is right and what is wrong.

As the board director at Burson-Marsteller in charge of leisure, travel and tourism across Europe, I was brought in to advise Philip Morris on whether it could defend the continuation of smoking in designated areas on aircraft, in hotel lobbies, and in restaurants. This was when we still did not have evidence of the causal link between smoking and cancer.

Before I accepted work on the account I insisted on meeting some of Philip Morris's senior management. I told them that I was an asthmatic, didn't smoke, that I hated the smell of tobacco, and that I didn't like being in smoky rooms.

My get-out clause was an agreement to say that if I was asked whether smoking kills, I could emphatically say 'yes.' The Philip Morris executives smiled and agreed to this request. They said that my negatives about the tobacco industry were a positive reason for them wanting me to work on their account. They said I came across as being sincere. I had integrity, they said.

I spent three years working on the Philip Morris tobacco account. On reflection, I am not at all pleased nor am I happy with my work. Don't get me wrong, it produced tremendous results – full-page features in important media like the *International Herald Tribune*. But it is the way that I carried out that work that deeply troubles me.

Why am I so troubled?

The tobacco industry's tactics to persuade people it was all right to smoke in restaurants and hotels and on aircraft were clever, complex, and deceptive.

First, the industry appeared to engage, promising high-quality research into the issue. In my case it was convincing research to demonstrate that even if you banned smoking on aircraft the quality of the air inside the cabin would not be measurably be improved.

Why?

The public were assured that the best people were on the case – that is, well-intentioned 'independent' scientists whose research just happened to be sponsored by Philip Morris.

The thrust of the research was that in the modern passenger jet, air inside the cabin is recycled through filters rather than taken in fresh from outside the aircraft (where it would have to be re-heated from the minus 20 degrees C air temperature outside). This saved on heating and fuel. Peer-reviewed research showed that someone with flu boarding an aircraft in the Far East and landing in Alaska infected many people onboard the same flight – thus proving that air quality was not as good as it should be on board.

The second stage was to complicate the question and sow doubt: Lung cancer might have any number of causes, after all. Wasn't lung cancer, not cigarettes, what really mattered?

Stage three was to undermine serious research and expertise. Autopsy reports would be dismissed as anecdotal, epidemiological work as merely statistical, and animal studies as irrelevant.

We ran high-profile media tours across Europe to expose the so-called false science on aircraft cabin quality, which achieved great media coverage.

Finally came the normalisation: The industry would point out that the tobacco–cancer story was stale news. Couldn't journalists find something new and interesting to say?

Such tactics are now well documented – and researchers have carefully examined the psychological tendencies that they exploited. The gross misuse of PR can be seen in the current campaign waged by Philip Morris against the Uruguay government for increasing the size of the health warnings on cigarette packs. It is a cynical PR tactic that lacks integrity.

Creating an effective crisis plan

Now that we have situated crisis planning within the framework of good campaign development, identified some of the internal barriers that can stymie the process, and seen evidence of it working across industries and types of organizations, how do we create a good crisis plan? Not surprisingly, there is no single correct way to write a crisis plan. They need to be customized for the organizations and industries. That said, the rest of this chapter will present a generic model for approaching writing crisis plans to identify key elements that are common across most crisis plans.

Step 1: Risk summary

In Chapter 4 I introduced the issues management process and key components for identifying and evaluating the risks an organization faces (see Figure 16.2 for a refresher). I made the point in that chapter (and in Chapter 5) that issues management and stakeholder mapping are ongoing processes designed to give organizations action-able intelligence about its risks and its critical stakeholders.

What should emerge from the issues management and stakeholder mapping process are a continually evolving set of recommendations that:

- Identify and summarize issues
- Evaluate issue severity

Figure 16.2 Issues management process overview

- Identify recommended activities (both material actions and communication strategies) to mitigate risks
- Provide issue tracking and reporting over time

Unless these recommendations are reported in succinct and clear ways, then they are not likely to be acted upon. While there should be brief narratives to contextualize the issue summaries, much of the information should be digestible at a glance. The way this is communicated can certainly vary, but a simple table summary can be a good starting point. For example, a summary of the projected severity of issues can help in prioritizing how to manage the issues. This might look something like that shown in Table 16.1.

Similarly, planning and getting approval on the issue response involves coordinating both the material actions that need to be taken as well as the communication tactics to manage the issue. An example of a summary of the recommendations and issue response actions table might look something like that shown in Table 16.2.

Finally, a part of the issue tracking and reporting over time involves identifying specific people or at least departments responsible for executing the issue management strategies and the degree to which the material and communicative actions have been taken. When this part of the planning process is made as concrete as possible, with action points and action owners, and then signed off by decision-makers, then it can help to avoid some of the inertia and lip-service barriers identified in the previous section that can hamper good crisis planning.

Table 16.1 Issue severity summary

Issue	Impact type	Stakeholder(s) affected	Severity		
			High impact	Medium impact	Low impact

Table 16.2 Issue response (pre-crisis) recommendations

Issue	Activity	Material action	Communication tactic(s)	Platform		
				Social media	Media placement	In person

Step 2: Contingency planning for crisis

The purpose of beginning with issues management is to mitigate or avoid crises; of course, not all crises can be avoided. The second part of the process is contingency planning for crises. It is unrealistic for organizations to plan for every eventuality; however, they should plan across different types of crises, and more specifically for the ones to which they are most prone. At the very least, this means that organizations should have four active crisis contingency plans – one for each of the major types of crises:

- Transgressions
- Events
- Disasters
- Reputational attacks/risks

The reason for this is simple: As we have discussed, different types of crises require different types of material crisis response. They also directly and indirectly affect different types of stakeholders. In addition, blame attribution significantly influences crisis response. Finally, stakeholders have different expectations and communication needs based on the type of crisis. However, it is not realistic nor cost effective to plan for every type of crisis possible; rather, this is where the risk register and active issues management program will help to direct and focus the scope of discussion within each of the contingency plans. While each crisis will be unique, the development of this document should serve as the generalized structure, with core messages for each crisis type. These core messages should be adapted and developed as specific situations unfold and information becomes available.

For each of the four contingency plans, the following information should be captured, summarized, and routinely updated (see Parts 1–8). How often is a routine update required? Well, it depends (I know, a great politician's answers) on the changes in the environment, organization, current events, etc. But generally, an active issues management program will provide an evidence-based guideline for the need to update any of the contingency plans.

For the sake of clarity, I would suggest that each contingency plan be developed and summarized independently of one another (i.e., have a section for 'transgressions,' 'events,' 'disasters,' and 'reputational risks' separately). As such, an organization's crisis plan would have four separate contingency plans. Also, remember that this should be an active summary of the intelligence the organization has developed; it is not intended to be an excessively long document. Think bulleted lists with brief explanations. While there may need to be more detailed information kept in supporting documentation, the crisis plan should read like a playbook that can be enacted quickly. This also makes it easier to keep up-to-date.

Part 1: Understanding <insert crisis type name> crises

This summary should provide a brief (e.g., maximum 400–500 words) background on the type of crisis so that people who are not crisis experts can understand what is at stake. It should include the following types of information, all relative to the organization or industry:

- A clear definition of the crisis type
- Relevant recent or major examples of this crisis type
- Summary of the risk or threat posed by this kind of crisis
- Priority this kind of crisis should take
- Identifying the types of responsibilities the organization has in managing this type of crisis (e.g., material crisis response, internal stakeholder management, external stakeholder management types of responsibilities)

Part 2: Activating the crisis team

The purpose of this section is to identify the owners for the key crisis responsibilities that you identified in Part 1 and the people (by position or name preferably) who should be viewed as part of the 'first responders' team to this type of crisis for the organization. An example of the presentation of this information is presented in Table 16.3.

Part 3: Trigger points

Based on the intelligence developed as a part of the issues management process, the most likely triggers for each the types of the crisis type should be identified and briefly explained. The trigger points should indicate when the contingency plan for each crisis type should be activated.

Table 16.3 Key responsibilities table example

	Key responsibility	Responsibility owner (position)	Brief rationale for responsibility owner
1			
2			
3			
4			
5			
6			

Part 4: Situational assessment

As organizations address crises, they must understand the nature of the problem posed by the crisis in order to begin to build a position on the problem itself. Therefore, this section will highlight the most likely problems that the organization faces in this kind of a crisis and evidence of relevance to the organization and situation.

This section should identify key problems underlying the triggers for the crisis that is what is likely to have happened for the crisis to be triggered. Table 16.4 provides one way to summarize this information. To build the credibility of the situational assessment, including references for each of the problems, causes, and representative examples of this type of crisis in the organization or industry is generally recommended.

Part 5: Stakeholder assessment

Using the problems identified in previous parts, in Table 16.5 indicate stakeholders that are likely to be affected, matching critical problems and citing evidence of the relevance of the stakeholder group to the problem. Categorize stakeholders' relationship to the organization as well citing evidence of the relationship. Finally, rank the stakeholder's relevance to the problem, add stakeholder groups as appropriate.

This requires connecting the issues management process with the stakeholder mapping process, and any evidence the organization has about stakeholders' relationship to the issue or problem and the organization. Table 16.5 provides an example of one way to structure this brief summary.

Once the summary of the stakeholders involved in the situation is created, it is also important to identify how the stakeholders and their concerns must be prioritized in responding to the issue. The narrative should:

Table 16.4 Tangible problems underlying the triggers, causes, and examples

	Problem	Cause	Representative example
1			
2			
3			
4			
5			
6			

Table 16.5 Key stakeholders, relationship to the issue, and relationship to organization

Rank	Stakeholder	Identification of relevant problem(s) to stakeholder	Nature of relationship to organization
	Employees, families, retirees		
	Community where organization operates		
	Customers: past, present, future		
	Industrial (e.g., suppliers, competitors, partners)		
	Government (any level)		
	Media (professional media)		
	Investment/financial (e.g., shareholders, bankers)		
	Special interest groups		
	Others 1		
	Others 2		
	Others 3		

- Rank stakeholders based on the most important stake in the crisis
- Briefly explain stakeholder key concerns (e.g., directly related to the problem, but including factors like health, culture, identity, etc.). It is important this is evidence-driven.

Part 6: Action recommendations

Once the team, problems, and stakeholders are identified, the organization must identify and prioritize the actions taken at the onset of the crisis. Provide an overview of the best types of actions the organization can/should take and provide support. Remember, actions can include material actions as well as communication actions.

Part of this process is about **defining roles and assumptions** about the importance of those roles as a crisis emerges. Examples of the types of roles that could be adopted are listed here. This is not an exhaustive list, but a summary one.

- Leading the material problem resolution (where relevant)
- Clarification of industry standards and organization's compliance

- Protector of the organization
- Activist for the organization (e.g., providing advice)
- Spokesperson(s)
- Gathering and analyzing situational Information
- Communicating with members of the organization
- Communicating with the media
- Communicating with different agencies
- Others

Compiling the recommendations from the risk register, and the roles that are needed with research on this type of crisis, create a concrete and tangible list of actions that should be taken, the urgency of each one, the role to support it, and resources required to take action. This can accomplished with a summary table like Table 16.6.

Part 7: Crisis response strategy

In order to successfully respond to the crisis, the organization should have an agile crisis response strategy ready to deploy. This should involve an initial crisis response as well as an overall set of response strategies and primary messages.

Remember that initial crisis response should be based on the following best practices:

- Provide an initial statement as soon as possible (within the first hour)
- Be accurate in reflecting facts related to the situation

Table 16.6 Action recommendations, urgency, roles, and resources

Urgency (high, medium, low)	Action	Role supported (from list in Part 6)	Resources required to support action

- Be consistent by keeping spokespeople informed of the crisis and key messages
- Make stakeholder welfare the top priority
- Use all available communication channels
- Communicate empathy, if people are affected
- Be ready to provide/direct stakeholders to stress and trauma response (where appropriate)

Identify and summarize the theory or theories that would be most relevant to helping the organization structure its initial talking points for this type of crisis. Providing a brief summary of each of the recommended theories, including:

- Naming the theory
- Key target factors (e.g., EPPM targets susceptibility, severity, efficacy in order to help develop messages to ensure people can enact danger control responses and avoid fear control responses)
- Measurable objectives in crisis response
    - Identify how crisis response will demonstrate ROI
    - Identify how crisis response is aligned with organization's KPIs
    - Identify how crisis response is aligned with organization's mission
- Crisis-related tactics
    - Self-enhancement
    - Routine
    - Framing the crisis
    - Framing the organization
    - Anti-social/defensive
    - Accommodative
    - Excellence/renewal
    - Invoking interorganizational relationships
- Necessary initial talking points to address the situation and for each talking point identify:
    - The talking point's relevance to the situational problem
    - Which stakeholders the talking point directly targets
    - Information needed to support the talking point
    - Appropriate platform(s) for communication/engagement

The objective of this part is to develop the organization's playbook to respond to the crisis. It should provide an adaptable set of options for organizations to enact. The following list provides guidance for developing the crisis playbook.

- **Should the playbook include multiple theories?** Yes – because as we discussed, different theories target different crisis response needs. But the playbook should focus on the most appropriate approaches based on the convergence of situation, stakeholders affected, and organization's position.

- **Should key talking points mix and match options from across different theories?** A cautious no. Crisis responses should be well-aligned across different stakeholders. Using a single theory to guide the core talking points ensures message alignment to different stakeholders tailored to the situation. However, situations change and it may be necessary as a crisis develops to change strategy.

Part 8: Message samples for each of the potential strategies

As I noted earlier, being able to respond quickly and strategically to a crisis improves the potential success of the crisis response strategy. Likewise, it can help ensure that the organization establish itself as a credible source of information throughout the crisis. Having samples of key messages prepared ahead of time for each of the potential response strategies identified gives the organization a decisive advantage in ensuring its initial crisis response is as successful as possible, aligned with the organization's objectives, and builds the organization's credibility.

These will have to be adapted to the particulars of the situation, but will make the initial response effort more efficient, aligned, and polished. Recommended message samples to have ready for each strategy would include:

- One- or two-minute statement about the situation
- Brief backgrounder on the organization's history with the issue/stakeholders
- Sample fact sheet
- Sample press release
- Sample social media posts (i.e., 1 customized for each outlet used by the organization)
- Relevant visual materials

In review . . .

This chapter has positioned good crisis planning to following the same process that any good strategic communication does: It begins by establishing the need, identifies measurable objectives, develops a theoretically grounded message strategy, and produces campaign samples. We have also discussed some of the most common barriers to good crisis planning and examples of why crisis planning is advantageous to organizations. Finally, I have laid out the two-step process for crisis planning and an eight-part crisis contingency plan with recommendations for content and customization.

Review your understanding

By the end of this chapter, you should be able to do the following.

- Explain why crisis planning is similar to a tailored campaign:
  - Identify common internal obstacles to good crisis planning
  - Explain why crisis planning works for organizations
- Be able to follow the guidance to create an effective crisis plan by:
  - Providing a good risk summary
  - Developing contingency planning for crisis:
    - Identifying what thorough contingency planning implies
    - Being able to develop an eight-part contingency plan

References

Austin, L. L., Liu, B. F., & Jin, Y. (2014). Examining signs of recovery: How senior crisis communicators define organizational crisis recovery. *Public Relations Review*, 40(5), 844–846. doi:10.1016/j.pubrev.2014.06.003

Benson, J. A. (1988). Crisis revisited: An analysis of strategies used by Tylenol in the second tampering episode. *Communication Studies*, 39(1), 49–66.

Canhoto, A. I., vom Lehn, D., Kerrigan, F., Yalkin, C., Braun, M., & Steinmetz, N. (2015). Fall and redemption: Monitoring and engaging in social media conversations during a crisis. *Cogent Business & Management*, 2(1), 1084978. doi:10.1080/23311975.2015.1084978

Claeys, A.-S., & Cauberghe, V. (2015). The role of a favorable pre-crisis reputation in protecting organizations during crises. *Public Relations Review*, 41(1), 64–71. doi:10.1016/j.pubrev.2014.10.013

Diers, A. R., & Donohue, J. (2013). Synchronizing crisis responses after a transgression: An analysis of BP's enacted crisis response to the Deepwater Horizon crisis in 2010. *Journal of Communication Management*, 17(3), 252–269.

Dilenschneider, R. L., & Hyde, R. C. (1985). Crisis communications: Planning for the unplanned. *Business Horizons*, 35–38.

Gainey, B. S. (2009). Crisis management's new role in educational settings. *The Clearing House*, 82(6), 267–274.

Heath, R. L. (1998). Dealing with the complete crisis – The crisis management shell structure. *Safety Science*, 30, 139–150.

Heath, R. L. (2004). Crisis preparation: Planning for the inevitable. In D. P. Millar & R. L. Heath (Eds.), *Responding to crisis: A rhetorical approach to crisis communication* (pp. 33–35). Mahwah, NJ: Lawrence Erlbaum Associates.

Henderson, J. C. (1999). Tourism management and the Southeast Asian economic and environmental crisis: A Singapore perspective. *Managing Leisure*, 4(2), 107–120.

Kauffman, J. (2000). Adding fuel to the fire: NASA's crisis communications regarding Apollo 1. *Public Relations Review*, 25(4), 421–432.

Kauffman, J. (2001). A successful failure: NASA's crisis communications regarding Apollo 13. *Public Relations*, 27(4), 437–449.

Pang, A., Cropp, F., & Cameron, G. T. (2006). Corporate crisis planning: Tensions, issues, and contradictions. *Journal of Communication Management*, 10(4), 371–389.

Sellnow, T. L., & Brand, J. D. (2001). Establishing the structure of reality for an industry: Model and anti-model arguments as advocacy in Nike's crisis communication. *Journal of Applied Communication Research*, 29(3), 278–296.

Sturges, D. L., Carrell, B. J., Newsom, D. A., & Barrera, M. (1991). Crisis communication management: The public opinion node and its relationship to environmental nimbus. *SAM Advanced Management Journal*, 56(3), 22–27.

Valackiene, A. (2010). The expression of effective crisis communication in today's corporation: Theoretical insights and practical application. *Transformation in Business & Economics*, 9.

Wertz, E. K., & Kim, S. (2010). Cultural issues in crisis communication: A comparative study of messages chosen by South Korean and US print media. *Journal of Communication Management*, 14(1), 81–94.

PART

6

Shaping crisis outcomes: What do crises mean for organizations?

By this point in the book, you should already have formed some of your own opinions about what crises mean for organizations as well as the factors that influence how much risk they pose or how much opportunity they represent. In this last section, I want to focus on connecting what we have already talked about with three final topics: Agenda setting, organizational change, and providing some measurement strategy and tools designed for some of the critical factors identified in this text.

Therefore, in Chapter 17, I will take a look at agenda setting and agenda building as the intersection of activism, organizational response, and media engagement during crises. Then in Chapter 18 I will identify some of the outcomes connected to crisis response and discuss post-crisis organizational change within the context of organizational learning. Finally in Chapter 19 I will discuss the importance of measurement and provide both qualitative and quantitative approaches for evaluating the relationships between stakeholders, organizations, and issues.

Agenda setting

The intersection of multi-actor environments and media engagement during crises

Learning objectives

By the end of this chapter, the reader should:

- Understand agenda setting theory and its relevance to crisis communication
- Use agenda setting to critically evaluate the media's role in crisis communication
- Be able to critically reflect on the importance of the organization's voice in the media in complex and competitive message environments

In Chapter 13 I explored the complexities of multi-actor and multi-platform environments. In particular, I looked at the ways that brand communities can help organizations facing issues or crises be able to respond to them effectively. I also looked at how counter branding efforts can potentially create or exacerbated crises for organizations. At the heart of this, of course, is the organization's response to the situation. In Chapter 9 I discussed the vital role that organizational leadership plays in helping an organization to be viewed as a credible source of information about crises. Throughout the book I have explored examples – like Malaysian Airlines' poor crisis response or Nike's excellence in issue mitigation – to demonstrate the role that good crisis response plays in an organization's success. However, we have not yet considered the vital role of the media directly. Yet, we know that crises are played out in the public eye, so the core purpose of this chapter is to provide basic background on agenda setting within the context of risk and crisis response.

The importance of information consumption and the media

Many people are generally familiar with **agenda setting** and its core purpose is to describe the powerful influence of the media. In the past, agenda setting was traditionally researched in the context of legacy media; however, with the proliferation and impact of social media – including professional blogs, influencers, and the power of the platforms themselves to deliver information to people in ways never available before – in a crisis context we must also consider 'media' in a cross-platform context.

Throughout the book, I have talked about social media's emergence as a critical tool for crisis communicators. However, to genuinely appreciate this change in media consumption, I would suggest that you read Hawaiian resident Tess Morimoto's experience with the January 2018 ICBM scare in Hawaii (see Box 17.1). To provide a bit of context, on Saturday, January 13, 2018 at about eight o'clock in the morning, the alert shown in Figure 17.1 was sent out across the Hawaiian Emergency Alert System as well as across the Commercial Mobile Alert system.

A second message was sent about 40 minutes later describing the first as a 'false alarm' – but in that two-thirds of an hour the state stood still. Morimoto's account of her day captures the basic need for information in these moments and the challenges of getting good real-time information.

When we talk about agenda setting, we should be talking about more than just legacy media; we should be talking about any platform that is getting significant stakeholder attention during crises (van der Meer & Verhoeven, 2013). This is why the crisis research we have been discussing is increasingly focusing on the importance of communicating across different platforms and engaging with different kinds of stakeholders (Sung & Hwang, 2014).

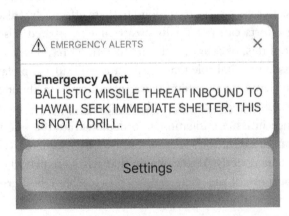

Figure 17.1 False missile alert sent across Hawaii's Emergency Alert and Commercial Mobile Alert System at 8:07 a.m. on January 13, 2018

Box 17.1 Citizen perspective: It just takes 40 minutes to decide to sign up for Twitter

By Tess Morimoto

You'll need to know that I live in Hawaii. On a Saturday morning in January, I was packing a picnic lunch when my brother came to me and said, "I don't know what this is on my phone. It says there's a ballistic missile coming?"

I immediately read the wireless emergency alert message aloud. The last words were: "THIS IS NOT A DRILL." We'd been watching months of coverage about the possibility of North Korea being able to launch an ICBM toward the United States, so this emergency alert system message warning of an actual attack was not entirely far-fetched. My oldest son – who follows the news more closely than I do – started crying. His young brothers, in sympathetic bewilderment, followed suit.

I rushed to my amateur radio to try to get news, between preparing our hallway for shelter and trying to calmly assure my children, "We're going to be okay, it's probably not true." There was nothing on my ham radio but a few people asking what was going on. My brother tuned into local broadcast radio stations (nothing but music) and checked Facebook (rumorville). My husband turned on the TV to see an emergency broadcast message scrolling alert under the Old Miss basketball game.

That was all. What was going on?

In the minutes immediately following the alert, there was zero information to be had. It would take almost 40 minutes for us to receive a second text message cancelling the original alert but, by then, we already knew that it could not have been a real attack because an ICBM would have already reached us.

News reporters were finally coming on air, piecing together how the mistake occurred, reporting on people's panicked reactions, and explaining what everyone should have done, had it been a real event.

The entire 38 minutes that it took for this debacle to resolve was jarring and confusing. The adults in my household were of the mind that it could not be real because there was nothing on media and the community-wide siren alert hadn't sounded (I prepared for the worst as we tried to get info because I insist on covering the bases). Partly because of our reliance on media to tell us what to think about and how to think about it, the lack of news coverage made us feel like there really was no threat.

I doubt this event had any effect nationally, except as a passing story to shake one's head over or laugh about. But it was very real for many people in

Hawaii and it upset me that it traumatized so many children. Locally, an investigation was launched, the employee responsible for the alert was fired, and procedures changed. But it showed our state and its citizens that we are ill-prepared at all levels for an attack. So perhaps some people have decided to better prepare for emergencies.

For me, it was the experience of a media vacuum that deeply bothered me. Twitter was the first platform on which correct information was reportedly issued, not radio or TV. In a small study of responses to the alarm by Deyoung, Sutton, Farmer, Neal, and Nichols (2019), almost 30% of respondents learned that the alert was false via social media, while less than 8% learned it via traditional radio and television. My family was part of the 18% that learned the truth from receiving a follow-up wireless alert on our cell phones.

We are repeatedly instructed by emergency management agencies to turn to traditional forms of media in emergencies, but my recent experience is teaching me otherwise. As technologies evolve, we have to reconsider how best to gather information that affects our lives.

I signed up for a Twitter account.

Brief introduction to agenda setting

Now that we are clear that media and media relations are evolving – especially during crisis contexts – we will take a step back to introduce agenda setting and its specific importance in planning responses to crises and anticipating crisis outcomes. Agenda setting theory tells us that the media has the ability to tell us what issues are important (Stromback & Kiousis, 2010) – but intense media attention increases the importance of certain topics, which means that media outlets ultimately decide what is important for the public to know about (Besova, 2006).

There are two levels of agenda setting commonly discussed across the literature. The first level is **influencing what people care about**. In this case, the media selects specific objects or issues to identify what journalists, influencers, or media organizations feel is important. For example, when the Ebola outbreak was initially reported in 2015, it was largely framed as an issue affecting a few countries such as Guinea, Sierra Leone, and Liberia. However, because of the extent of the coverage and impact of the outbreak, it became important to people.

The second level of agenda setting is that the media focuses on **what part of the subject is important**. This means that, drilling down from the broad issue, there is an effort to identify the part of the subject that will most resonate with viewers, readers, or followers – what is worth clicking on? One of the core assumptions for what is 'good news' is what is relevant to people. With the Ebola outbreak, this meant that while we still saw headlines like 'Ebola virus kills Liberian in Lagos' from *The Guardian*, we also began to see headlines like 'UK Ebola alert as infected medic to fly home' from *The Mail* or 'Outbreak of deadly Ebola virus could reach the UK' from *The Daily Telegraph*. This certainly was not unique to British coverage of the story; outlets everywhere that were reporting on the story were framing headlines to try to connect the news to their readers, viewers, and followers.

But why care about this? We will come back to the issues and crisis communication reasons shortly, but there are some broader 'responsible citizen' reasons we should care as well. Even if we do not open a newspaper (physically or online) or watch the evening news, the reality is that we all consume media of some kind and experience agenda setting. For example, we may never watch the news, but we do interact with people on social media. In fact, in a 2011 Pew Research poll to understand news consumption in the United States, a substantial number of Americans not only use social media regularly but also get a majority of their news and information about the world from social media sources (Hampton, Goulet, Rainie, & Purcell, 2011). Fast-forward to a 2018 Pew Research report and the findings remain consistent, identifying that two-thirds of American adults at least occasionally get their news online, despite concerns about whether the information is true (Masta & Shearer, 2018). When we get our news – from traditional media outlets or on social media – it is all filtered through what our sources consider to be important.

By the way, this is not a giant conspiracy that the media is trying to tell us what to think about. It is much more capitalistic in nature: It is about advertising revenue, influence development, and impact. People – no matter what platform – are creating content, putting their own perspectives on stories, and focusing on particular parts of stories because either they think that is going to get more people's attention or because it is genuinely what they care about. The point is that the media is shaping what everyone sees and how they see it.

The most susceptible to agenda setting effects

Even though we are all exposed to agenda setting, we can still get a relatively unfiltered view of the world. It just means we have to work a little harder to get well-rounded information. This means we have to ask the question: Who is more likely to be affected by agenda setting in a way that limits their understanding of the world and what is going on?

There are two attitudinal mind-sets that make people more susceptible to agenda setting, the first one being **people who believe the information is relevant**. Remember back to Chapters 3 and 10 when I focused on stakeholder attitudes and emotions, and the importance of the relationship between the issue and stakeholder was discussed. One of the factors in that relationship is how personally relevant an issue is – this is called the first-person effect (Duck, Hogg, & Terry, 1999; Reid, Byrne, Brundidge, Shoham, & Marlow, 2007). That is to say that if we believe an issue or piece of information could affect us, we are more likely to pay attention and seek more information; however, we are also more likely to believe the issue is really important simply because it is getting a lot of media coverage.

For example, each year at Christmas in the United States, Fox News launches its annual 'war on Christmas' storyline because it is a winner. It brings the story out at a time of year when the political news is often a bit slow – and it gets people stirred up and watching the news more. From a more reasonable perspective, is there a war on Christmas? Of course not, but the United States – like most Western democracies – is a pluralistic society where not everyone celebrates Christmas. Many people have alternative holidays, and so the ways that we experience the holiday in a public sense has changed over time. For those for whom Christmas is their holy season, the celebration is unimpeded. However, for those who are concerned about threats to 'Christian values' in the United States, this story is always going to make it seem like this is a very real risk – an outlet they likely know and trust talks about it, and when it talk about its each year, it seems more and more real over time.

The other key mind-set affecting peoples' susceptibility to agenda setting effects is held by **those who feel a strong degree of uncertainty** – that is, anyone who is already anxious in regard to particular issues, social or political situations, etc. The greater the feeling of uncertainty or fear, the more that people are more readily going to share information as a way of socially confirming the information is true (Sung & Hwang, 2014).

Good examples of these types of stories are those about about online scams. Most of us who are digital natives – or at least are very comfortable with online shopping – have a high level of both self and response efficacy regarding online shopping. We know how to do it and that it will lead to a positive result (at least most of the time). However, for those with lower levels of efficacy about shopping online, these kinds of stories cause a great deal of worry and thus garner a lot of attention.

Like many social theories, there are arguments about whether it happens and the degree to which it happens, but I would argue that the evidence suggests it is real and very connected to issues and crisis management. Think about it this way: Media saturation is inescapable on large issues. In the last couple of years it is been nearly impossible to avoid hearing about migrants in Europe, President Trump, or Brexit. In all three of these cases, there is a high degree of uncertainty surrounding the issues (or people) themselves and a growing number of people who believe these big issues could affect them personally.

Research also suggests that **negative coverage has greater agenda setting power** because of the greater share of media attention it receives (Kleinnijenhuis, Schultz,

Utz, & Oegema, 2013). In the case of BP, Kleinnijenhuis et al. (2013) found that coverage of BP affected not only the company's reputation but also its finances, such as its share price. This should not be surprising: When a disaster is visible from space, like the 2010 spill in the Gulf of Mexico was, it is going to get a lot of media coverage. Sung and Hwang (2014) found that during crises people seek information from any source initially – social media or legacy media. As time goes on, they are more likely to seek information from legacy news sources.

If we take the three conditions together that increase the likelihood that agenda setting will occur in the following contexts:

- Perceptions of relevance (susceptibility)
- Perceptions of uncertainty
- Negative coverage

It is pretty easy to see that crises make people particularly susceptible to agenda setting. This means that organizations that have effectively planned and are able to guide and manage the crisis narrative are not just 'victims' of agenda setting, but can be active participants in agenda building. In part, this is a leadership function, as I discussed in Chapter 9. This is also in part a function of communicating early and often: One of the implications of people being high information-seekers from any source (online, in person, across social media, and in legacy media) at the onset of a crisis suggests that organizations demonstrating strong crisis planning and effective early crisis information sharing and engagement can emerge as trusted and important sources of information for many different types of stakeholder (Sung & Hwang, 2014). Of course, this is assuming that an organization establishes itself as a reliable and transparent source of information at the onset of the crisis.

However, in the void of an organization providing information as an issue or crisis emerges into the public view, people are still going to fill in the gaps. Some of those people will be members of an organization's brand community, some of those people will be journalists and citizen journalists, and some will be adversaries of the organization taking the opportunity to counter brand. Where there are information voids, people will try to fill in the gaps because they are trying to make themselves feel more certain about the situation. It is seldom going to be in the organization's interests to be silent or late to the conversation.

In review . . .

In the end, because of the propensity for negative stories to spread quickly, of growing access to information across multiple platforms, and the nature of susceptibility to agenda setting, then from an issues, risk, and crisis perspective, organizations must get to the front of issues and crises and stay ahead of them as much as possible.

Review your understanding

By the end of this chapter, you should be able to do the following.

- Explain the importance of information consumption and the media in a multi-platform environment
- Define agenda setting:
  - Describe and discuss the two levels of agenda setting
  - Identify the types of people who would be most susceptible to agenda setting
- Discuss the implications of agenda setting on crisis response

References

Besova, A. A. (2006). *Foreign news and public opinion: Attribute agenda-setting theory revisited* (Master's). Louisiana State University, Baton Rouge, LA.

DeYoung, S. E., Sutton, J. N., Farmer, A. K., Neal, D., & Nichols, K. A. (2019). "Death was not in the agenda for the day": Emotions, behavioral reactions, and perceptions in response to the 2018 Hawaii Wireless Emergency Alert. *International Journal of Disaster Risk Reduction, 36.* doi:10.1016/j.ijdrr.2019.101078

Duck, J. M., Hogg, M. A., & Terry, D. J. (1999). Social identity and perceptions of media persuasion: Are we always less influenced than others? *Journal of Applied Social Psychology, 29*(9), 1879–1899.

Hampton, K. N., Goulet, L. S., Rainie, L., & Purcell, K. (2011). *Social networking sites and our lives: How people's trust, personal relationships, and civic and political involvement are connected to their use of social networking sites and other technologies.* Washington, DC. Retrieved from http://pewinternet.org/Reports/2011/Technology-and-social-networks.aspx

Kleinnijenhuis, J., Schultz, F., Utz, S., & Oegema, D. (2013). The mediating role of the news in the BP oil spill crisis 2010: How US news is influenced by public relations and in turn influences public awareness, foreign news, and the share price. *Communication Research,* 408–428. doi:10.1177/0093650213510940

Masta, K. E., & Shearer, E. (2018, 21/4/2019). News use across social media platforms 2018. *Pew Research Center.* Retrieved from www.journalism.org/2018/09/10/news-useacross-social-media-platforms-2018/. Accessed July 16, 2019.

Reid, S. A., Byrne, S., Brundidge, J. S., Shoham, M. D., & Marlow, M. L. (2007). A critical test of self-enhancement, exposure, and self-categorization explanations for first- and third-person perceptions. *Human Communication Research, 33*(2), 143–162.

Stromback, J., & Kiousis, S. (2010). A new look at agenda-setting effects: Comparing the predictive power of overall political news consumption and specific news media consumption across different media channels and media types. *Journal of Communication, 60,* 271–292. doi:10.1111/j.1460-2466.2010.01482.x

Sung, M., & Hwang, J.-S. (2014). Who drives a crisis? The diffusion of an issue through social networks. *Computers in Human Behavior, 36,* 246–257. doi:10.1016/j.chb.2014.03.063

van der Meer, T. G., & Verhoeven, P. (2013). Public framing organizational crisis situations: Social media versus news media. *Public Relations Review, 39*(3), 229–231.

Learning their lessons?

18 Crisis outcomes and crisis-driven organizational change

Learning objectives

By the end of this chapter, the reader should:

- Identify and discuss outcomes of crises for organizations
- Evaluate the factors that influence post-crisis learning in organizations
- Discuss planned change in response to crises

One of the assumptions that I have made throughout the textbook is that in order to effectively respond to issues, risks, and crises, organizations must be agile and able to adapt. Organizational learning is an inherent part of this process. As I indicated in Chapter 1, crises themselves can represent meaningful opportunities for organizations to learn and reflect on their practices. Therefore, this chapter will explore the nature of crisis outcomes for organizations and the process of organizational learning and crisis-driven change.

An overview of crisis outcomes

When crises happen, we know that they can affect stakeholder's attitudes about issues and organizations, but the question is: What happens as a result of changed stakeholder attitudes? Throughout the text I have argued that the extent to which an organization is successful in its crisis response may be a result of its success in managing stakeholder relationships (Bendheim, Waddock, & Graves, 1998; Brown & White, 2010; Diers-Lawson, 2017; Sellnow & Brand, 2001). Moreover, the relationships among external stakeholders can represent a measure of that organization's strengths and weaknesses as they are linked to the relationships between an organization's social, ethical, and financial performances – known as the triple bottom line (Barnett, 2019; Graafland & Smid, 2019; Jensen, 2002; Sirgy, 2002).

Additionally, the link between stakeholder evaluations of organizations and strategic decision-making by organizations has been discussed in three ways. First, the extent to which organizations are able to manage stakeholder 'activism' on issues that matter to stakeholders reflects an acknowledgement that economics is socially embedded (Jin & Drozdenko, 2010; Shepard, Betz, & O'Connell, 1997). Therefore, organizations that are likely to be successful consider the reactions of their stakeholders in making strategic decisions. For example, in a lumber company's decision to stop clear cutting, the company was successful because it recognized that the decision itself was important, but not as important as also effectively communicating that decision and managing its relationship with important stakeholders (Winn, 2001).

Second, a study by Waddock and Graves (1997) demonstrated that an organization's management success was linked to its performance in managing perceptions of the quality of its innovations or actions with critical stakeholders – specifically in this case the owners, employees, customers, and surrounding community. Similarly, Wright, Palmer, and Kavanaugh (1995) found that the 'promise' of educational innovation did not matter if the stakeholders – in this case the school board – did not support the change.

Third, an organization's success is also contingent upon its ability to build trust with its stakeholders and act ethically (Nielsen & Bartunek, 1996; Valentini, 2015). Thus, one of the reasons to manage stakeholder relationships is so that organizations can be perceived as engaging their social responsibilities (Bendheim et al., 1998).

Possible crisis consequences

The outcomes of organizational crises and their management can range from issues associated with basic organizational survival (Stacks, 2004) to organizational learning where changes in routines and practices are made because of the crises (Roux-Dufort, 2000). However, most assessments of crisis outcomes can be grouped into four categories: economic; image or legitimacy; organizational scrutiny; and interorganizational relationships.

- **Economic:** No matter the type, crises can significantly affect an organization's economic outlook. For example, in their study of crisis response in the tourism industry, Gonzales-Herrero and Pratt's (1998) critical outcome emphasized the relationship between the viability of tourism in a region following crises and consumer perceptions of risk. In recent years, we have seen airlines like Monarch Airlines going bust after terrorist attacks in places like Tunisia and Egypt decimated their business. Any sector can be financially affected by crises. Economic outcomes associated with crises often include stock losses, losses in sales and production, fines or punitive damages, and less reinvestment in innovation (Arpan, 2002; Baucus & Baucus, 1997).

- **Image or legitimacy:** By their very nature, crises are likely to affect stakeholder perceptions of the organization's image, viability, credibility, or legitimacy (Pearson & Clair, 1998). Of course, organizations often target organizational renewal as one way to rebuild the organization's image, like rebranding to focus on a more trustworthy image (Elsbach & Elofson, 2000). The Nike case that we discussed earlier in the text are great example of this: In the face of a crisis, the organizations announce changes to their offerings, their look, and their practices.

- **Increased organizational scrutiny:** Because of the media coverage that accompanies most crises, it is important to recognize that organizations going through or that have recently gone through crises are going to face more scrutiny. For example, Enron's accounting scandal in the late 1990s brought greater scrutiny and regulation over accounting practices in all organizations, leading to the Sarbanes-Oxley Act of 2002. The changes in accounting across industries are consistent with findings that crises can increase government scrutiny of both the industry and the organization facing the crisis (Arpan, 2002; Heath, 1998). Increased scrutiny is not, however, limited to government agencies; in fact, the media itself and other pressure groups (e.g., activist organizations, stakeholder groups affected by the crisis, etc.) can also become active in seeking information, regulation, participation with, and even taking action against organizations facing crises. This suggests that organizations should be prepared for more counter branding and activism and may even feel less support from their brand community.

- **Strategic alliance withdrawal:** Crises can affect organization's business-to-business (B2B) and other strategic alliances as well (Das & Teng, 1998; Jennings, Artz, Gillin, & Christodouloy, 2000). During organizational crises, the environment for an organization can be defined as unstable. Trice and Beyer (1993) argue that organizations seek interorganizational connections to stabilize their experiences in their environment; however, because of the instability that often surrounds an organization in crisis, at the time that the organization may be reaching out for support from its strategic alliances, those partners may be withdrawing from the relationships in order to mitigate their own risk (Heath & Millar, 2004; Mohamed, Gardner, & Paolillo, 1999).

It is not uncommon for organizations to experience some or all of these kinds of effects from crises. One good example of this is Cheng Zeng's case study of the impact that a student's death had on Chinese search engine Baidu (see Box 18.1).

Box 18.1 Case study: When an online search leads you to the devil: The role of Chinese search engine Baidu in Wei's death

By Cheng Zeng, Ph.D.

In 2014, Wei Zexi, a Chinese college student, was diagnosed with a rare form of cancer, synovial sarcoma. Like many other patients, Wei sought information about his disease and treatment online. Through a promoted result on Baidu, the Chinese Internet search giant (the Chinese version of Google), Wei discovered an immunotherapy treatment offered by the Second Hospital of the Beijing Armed Police Corps that promised an 80–90% success rate of curing Wei's cancer. Under its deceptive name, the hospital is a part of a private hospital union that is notoriously known for providing inadequate treatments and charging exorbitant prices. Immunotherapy treatment was widely considered to be in the experimental stage and its use had not been legalized in China. Nevertheless, Wei was sold the treatment; he died in April 2016 after spending up to 200,000 yuan ($30,000 USD). Wei's death spurred public outrage demanding to put Baidu under scrutiny for its role in promoting dubious medical treatments. Baidu quickly released a response in which it expressed their 'deepest condolences' and promised to cooperate in the investigation of Wei's death. Further investigation showed that Baidu's search results did not label promoted content and heavily favored advertisers. In fact, for many private hospitals, up to 70–80% of the marketing budget had been spent on advertisements on Baidu. The damage from Wei's case to the company's reputation for social responsibility was grave. Baidu shares plunged by 14% as a result of the reputation crisis. Facing harsh public criticism, Baidu pledged to change its 'pay for ranking' system, differentiate promoted ads from the other content, and toughen the screening process of misleading content.

Today people increasingly turn to the Internet for health information. Wei's case has received extensive attention from the public because people feel emotionally involved in the crisis as they could easily fall victim to false health information online. While the private hospital that lured desperate patients in with false promises was inexcusable, Baidu, the platform that led Wei to the vicious hospital, had been criticized for prioritizing profit over human lives. As it has a monopoly on search engines in China, Baidu's lack of social responsibility was appalling and has severely damaged its corporate reputation. Stakeholders quickly become disheartened when the organization's social responsibility is questioned. Despite Baidu's corrective actions in rectifying its ranking algorithms and limiting advertisement for the medical industry, distrust in Baidu largely persists in today's China.

Crises: Driving or inhibiting the conditions for change?

We have all probably heard a couple of clichés sayings like, "necessity is the mother of invention" or "insanity is doing the same thing over and over again and expecting different outcomes." Yet, risk and crisis response remain two of the critical drivers for organizational change (Barnett & Pratt, 2000). Barnett and Pratt's (2000) work even found evidence that organizations use risk management or crisis response as pre-emptive strategies to future crises in order to build support for change within an organization and push new agendas and new initiatives through.

But beyond drivers for management, one of the outcomes of crises is that managers and members of organizations often question their existing knowledge, assumptions, and behaviors, and that the dialogue that results not only primes organizations for change but also often drives it as well (Blackman & Ritchie, 2008; Huzey, Betts, & Vicari, 2014; Veil, 2011). Veil (2011) suggests that learning should be considered as one of the stages of crisis management – a critical reflection on what worked and what did not in the crisis lifecycle as a way to improve the organization and crisis response for future situations.

Yet, as Roux-Dufort (2000) points out, organizations do not always learn from past crises. While there are learning opportunities from crises, there are inhibitors as well. In fact, he argues that crises are paradoxical in that they reveal information critical for the organization to improve its performance and relationships with stakeholders while simultaneously making people resistant to change because of the uncertainty that accompanies them. Roux-Doufort's analysis suggests that the work to help organizations and stakeholders successfully negotiate the crisis results in **normalization process** that often inhibits organizational learning. This process includes three tactics:

- **Cognitive normalization** builds a simplified version of the crisis to make it more understandable. It focuses on quick explanations of the crisis instead of addressing root causes and confuses crisis management with problem solving. In so doing, once the 'fire' of the crisis is put out, the problem is viewed as solved and the status quo can be re-instated thus inhibiting learning.

- **Psychological and affective normalization** emphasizes reducing the emotional impact of the crisis. Throughout the textbook I defined crises as emotional events for internal and external stakeholders. In Chapter 9 I identified one of a leader's critical roles as psychological or emotional, in Chapter 10 I focused on the impact of crises on stakeholder emotion and attitude, and in Chapter 15 I highlight the importance of efficacy and danger control processes in our exploration of theories. But the paradox of managing emotion is that it can focus crisis manage on the human side instead of addressing the technical issues that might have triggered the crisis. In Roux-Dufort's analysis, removing the emotional charge from crises also reduces the motivation to change.

● **Sociopolitical normalization** makes the crisis itself socially, politically, or symbolically acceptable. As organizations take actions to address the immediate and material problems, public outrage often quiets, and the organization is unlikely to address deeper issues causing the problems. Certainly, this can be balanced against the increased scrutiny, but given how many organizations and industries have similar crises over and over, it should not be surprising that underlying problems are not meaningfully addressed.

Learning in crisis and organizational change

In our discussion of building crisis capacity from the inside out in Chapter 8, I discussed the concept of organizational culture and the culture of social responsibility as ways that organizations can build crisis capacity. Crisis capacity can also be fuelled in the context of learning from crises as well. Weick and Ashford (2001) focus on organizational learning as inextricably tied to an organization's culture. In the context of risk and crisis, how an organization interprets the meaning of risk and crisis depends on the ideologies and forms that exist within the organization. When organizations accommodate many different stakeholder interests, making changes to their organizational structure to address shortcomings, this communicates a 'trustworthy' culture (Hurley, Gillespie, Ferrin, & Dietz, 2013). As such, the first step in creating an organization that can learn from crises is improving its crisis capacity, as I discussed in Chapter 8.

Beyond that, Antonacopoulou and Sheaffer (2014) proposed a mode of learning – **learning in crisis (LiC)** – that provides an interesting model for organizations to adopt. Instead of the problem-solving approach that Roux-Dufort (2000) also problematized, the LiC approach highlights a flexible and emergent approach to learning. Antonacopoulou and Sheaffer suggest that as crises emerge, revealing known and unknown problems, successful organizations are agile in their reaction to them. This is something that we have also discussed throughout the textbook. However, they also argue that capturing critical judgements about crises, strategic responses (and their outcomes), and constant critical reflexivity not only improves crisis response but also helps organizations to capture lessons learned throughout the crisis experience. Figure 18.1 summarizes their discussion of LiC to reveal how the process might work.

The LiC perspective offers some important practical implications about how organizational change can and does occur within the risk and crisis context.

1   **Initiating and institutionalizing change through crisis:** Organizations will routinely make adaptations in their response, policies, procedures, and even structures as

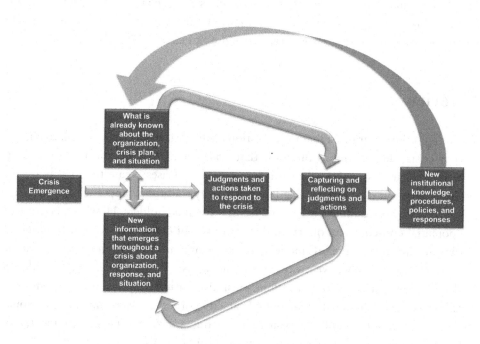

Figure 18.1 Summary of Antonacopoulou and Sheaffer's (2014) learning in crisis model

they manage and respond to situations (Antonacopoulou & Sheaffer, 2014; Carroll & Hatakenaka, 2001). However, in order for an organization to learn from reactions to its response, policies, and practices made during the crisis, these must all be captured and then the changes institutionalized after the crisis (Barnett & Pratt, 2000; Blackman & Ritchie, 2008).

2   **Best practices and lessons learned:** When organizations build new sets of best practices through their risk and crisis experiences, we can say that learning has taken place. However, that is not enough to ensure the organization has meaningfully mitigated the problems. Huzey et al. (2014) suggest that a 'post-crisis post mortem' is also necessary and suggest focusing on accurate attribution of causes, ensuring resources are devoted to making improvements in the organization, and seeking input from those outside the organization to help ensure that new institutional knowledge is refined and improved.

3   **Rehearsal of new approaches to engrain them:** A growing body of literature suggests that if organizations are going to improve their crisis capacity and ensure that any changes are applied, then organizations must rehearse them as a part of vicarious learning within the organization in order for the new processes to be learned (Lewis, 2011). A growing body of literature and practice emphasizes the importance of

using simulations to ensure that organizations are prepared for a crisis, as I discussed in Chapter 8. However, simulations are also useful as changes are brought into organizations, to improve crisis response ('t Hart, 1997; Helsloot, 2005).

In review . . .

We cannot take for granted that organizations will learn from crises or seek to change after a crisis, despite the assumption that crises create the conditions for organizational change. As we have learned, in as much as crises create the possibility for change, the paradox of crisis is that it can also reify traditional approaches, processes, and responses to re-establish a sense of security for stakeholders. However, because of the potential consequences of crises, they can prompt change. Instead of thinking of change in a linear way, the LiC model encourages organizations to think about change as a future-oriented reflective process for reducing risk. I have argued that in addition to the reflective activities, organizations must also ensure that best practices and lessons learned are evaluated, tested, and rehearsed in order to ensure any organizational changes are successful – and that instead of creating a zero-learning environment, risk and crisis response creates learning that fuels future organizational capacity.

Review your understanding

By the end of this chapter, you should be able to do the following:

- Identify and discuss the four possible crisis consequences:
  - Economic
  - Image or legitimacy
  - Increased organizational scrutiny
  - Strategic alliance withdrawal
- Reflect on crises as both change driving and inhibiting events:
  - Understand how normalization creates a paradox for crises, learning, and change
- Demonstrate understanding of learning in change:
  - Summarize the LiC model
  - Summarize the three implications for how organizational change occurs within a risk and crisis context

References

Antonacopoulou, E. P., & Sheaffer, Z. (2014). Learning in crisis rethinking the relationship between organizational learning and crisis management. *Journal of Management Inquiry*, 23(1), 5–21. doi:10.1177/1056492612472730

Arpan, L. M. (2002). When in Rome? The effects of spokesperson ethnicity on audience evaluation of crisis communication. *Journal of Business Communication*, 39(3), 314–339.

Barnett, C. K., & Pratt, M. G. (2000). From threat-rigidity to flexibility – Toward a learning model of autogenic crisis in organizations. *Journal of Organizational Change Management*, 13(1), 74–88.

Barnett, M. L. (2019). The business case for corporate social responsibility: A critique and an indirect path forward. *Business & Society*, 58(1), 167–190.

Baucus, M. S., & Baucus, D. A. (1997). Paying the piper: An empirical examination of longer-term financial consequences of illegal corporate behavior. *Academy of Management Journal*, 40(1), 129–152.

Bendheim, C. L., Waddock, S. A., & Graves, S. B. (1998). Determining best practice in corporate-stakeholder relations using data envelopment analysis: An industry-level study. *Business and Society*, 37(3), 306–339.

Blackman, D., & Ritchie, B. W. (2008). Tourism crisis management and organizational learning: The role of reflection in developing effective DMO crisis strategies. *Journal of Travel & Tourism Marketing*, 23(2–4), 45–57.

Brown, K. A., & White, C. L. (2010). Organization–public relationships and crisis response strategies: Impact on attribution of responsibility. *Journal of Public Relations Research*, 23(1), 75–92.

Carroll, J. S., & Hatakenaka, S. (2001). Driving organizational change in the midst of crisis. *Mt. Sloan Management Review* (Spring), 70–79.

Das, T. K., & Teng, B.-S. (1998). Between trust and control: Developing confidence in partner cooperation in alliances. *Academy of Management Review*, 23(3), 491–513.

Diers-Lawson, A. (2017). Will they like us when they're angry? Antecedents and indicators of strong emotional reactions to crises among stakeholders. In S. M. Croucher, B. Lewandowska-Tomaszczyk, & P. Wilson (Eds.), *Conflict, mediated message, and group dynamics* (pp. 81–136). Lanham, MD: Lexington Books.

Elsbach, K. D., & Elofson, G. (2000). How the packaging of decision explanations affects perceptions of trustworthiness. *Academy of Management Journal*, 43(1), 80–89.

Gonzales-Herrero, A., & Pratt, C. B. (1998). Marketing crises in tourism: Communication strategies in the United States and Spain. *Public Relations Review*, 24(1), 83–97.

Graafland, J., & Smid, H. (2019). Decoupling among CSR policies, programs, and impacts: An empirical study. *Business & Society*, 58(2), 231–267.

Heath, R. L. (1998). Working under pressure: Crisis management, pressure groups and the media. *Safety Science*, 209–221.

Heath, R. L., & Millar, D. P. (2004). A rhetorical approach to crisis communication: Management, communication processes, and strategic responses. In D. P. Millar & R. L. Heath (Eds.), *Responding to crisis: A rhetorical approach to crisis communication* (pp. 1–18). Mahwah, NJ: Lawrence Erlbaum Associates.

Helsloot, I. (2005). Bordering on reality: Findings on the bonfire crisis management simulation. *Journal of Contingencies and Crisis Management, 13*(4), 159–169.

Hurley, R. F., Gillespie, N., Ferrin, D. L., & Dietz, G. (2013). Designing trustworthy organizations. *MIT Sloan Management Review, 54*(4), 75.

Huzey, D., Betts, S. C., & Vicari, V. (2014). Learning the hard way vs. vicarious learning: Post crisis learning for small business. *Journal of Management and Marketing Research, 15*, 1.

Jennings, D. F., Artz, K., Gillin, L. M., & Christodouloy, C. (2000). Determinants of trust in global strategic alliances: Amrad and the Australian biomedial industry. *Competitiveness Review, 10*(1), 25–44.

Jensen, M. C. (2002). Value maximization, stakeholder theory, and the corporate objective function. *Business Ethics Quarterly, 12*(2), 235–257.

Jin, K. G., & Drozdenko, R. G. (2010). Relationships among perceived organizational core values, corporate social responsibility, ethics, and organizational performance outcomes: An empirical study of information technology professionals. *Journal of Business Ethics, 92*, 341–359.

Lewis, L. K. (2011). *Organizational change: Creating change through strategy communication.* London: Wiley-Blackwell.

Mohamed, A. A., Gardner, W. L., & Paolillo, J. G. P. (1999). A taxonomy of organizational impression management tactics. *Advances in Competitiveness Research, 7*(1), 108–128.

Nielsen, R. P., & Bartunek, J. M. (1996). Opening narrow, routinized schemata to ethical stakeholder consciousness and action. *Business and Society, 35*(4), 483–520.

Pearson, C. M., & Clair, J. A. (1998). Reframing crisis management. *Academy of Management Review, 23*(1), 58–76.

Roux-Dufort, C. (2000). Why organizations don't learn from crises: The perverse power of normalization. *Review of Business*, 25–30.

Sellnow, T. L., & Brand, J. D. (2001). Establishing the structure of reality for an industry: Model and anti-model arguments as advocacy in Nike's crisis communication. *Journal of Applied Communication Research, 29*(3), 278–296.

Shepard, J. M., Betz, M., & O'Connell, L. (1997). The proactive corporation: Its nature and causes. *Journal of Business Ethics, 16*(10), 1001–1011.

Sirgy, M. J. (2002). Measuring corporate performance by building on the stakeholders model of business ethics. *Journal of Business Ethics, 35*(3), 143–163.

Stacks, D. W. (2004). Crisis management: Toward a multidimension model of public relations. In D. P. Millar & R. L. Heath (Eds.), *Responding to crisis: A rhetorical approach to crisis communication* (pp. 37–49). Mahwah, NJ: Lawrence Erlbaum Associates.

't Hart, P. (1997). Preparing policy makers for crisis management: The role of simulations. *Journal of Contingencies and Crisis Management, 5*(4), 207–215.

Trice, H. M., & Beyer, J. M. (1993). *The cultures of work organizations.* Upper Saddle River, NJ: Prentice Hall.

Valentini, C. (2015). Is using social media "good" for the public relations profession? A critical reflection. *Public Relations Review, 41*(2), 170–177. doi:10.1016/j.pubrev.2014.11.009

Veil, S. R. (2011). Mindful learning in crisis management. *Journal of Business Communication, 48*(2), 116–147. doi:10.1177/0021943610382294

Waddock, S. A., & Graves, S. B. (1997). Quality of management and quality of stakeholder relations: Are they synonymous? *Business and Society, 36*(3), 250–280.

Weick, K. E., & Ashford, S. J. (2001). Learning in organizations. In F. M. Jablin & L. L. Putnam (Eds.), *The new handbook of organizational communication: Advances in theory, research, and methods* (pp. 704–731). Thousand Oaks, CA: Sage Publications.

Winn, M. I. (2001). Building stakeholder theory with a decision modeling methodology. *Business and Society, 40*(2), 133–167.

Wright, R. E., Palmar, J. C., & Kavanaugh, D. C. (1995). The importance of promoting stakeholder acceptance of educational innovations. *Education, 115*(4), 628–633.

19 Measuring behavioral outcomes to crises

Learning objectives

By the end of this chapter, the reader should:

- Identify the practical importance of research in managing relationships with stakeholders
- Consider behavioral indicators of changes in stakeholder attitudes towards organizations in crisis
- The types of measures and approaches organizations can use to develop strategy and apply theory

Throughout the textbook, I have positioned theory and practice as two sides of the same coin in risk and crisis response. What ensures they remain joined is research. Making data-based decisions is also something that I have emphasized improves organizational outcomes throughout the textbook, from the issues management and stakeholder mapping processes and tools presented in Chapters 4 and 5 to the discussions of the factors we need to understand the relationships between stakeholders, issues, and organizations. Throughout, I have positioned good issues and crisis management as process, research, and theory driven. Therefore, in this chapter, I will discuss some of the methods used to measured and explore these relationships.

Yes, research is practical and necessary

For the last 15–20 years I have heard countless students – both at the undergraduate and master's levels – say, "But I'm going into public relations, I don't need to understand research methods." To begin, let us just dispel with that myth. The broad field of integrated marketing communications – including PR, marketing, and advertising – is research-driven, especially in today's data-rich climate. Take a look at some of the annual reports from organizations like Hootsuite or the Pew Research Center that are industry standards for data on social media, news, and information consumption – all driving organizational choices. Agencies are also using research to drive their value proposition. For example, the global firm Edelman has developed research as one of its core offerings, with the annual production of its trust barometer or its earned brand studies to name just a couple.

The fact of the matter is that decision-makers want data to help them make decisions and need theory to optimize crisis response, no matter whether the return on investment (ROI) is about financial security for an organization, or saving lives as Ben Duncan describes in his experience in working with the World Health Organization (see Box 19.1).

Box 19.1 Practitioner perspective: How do we know what works?

By Ben Duncan

It's a scenario certain to deflate – and somewhat irritate – even the best of us. You are at an emergency management meeting. You have been asked to sketch out a crisis communication strategy to steer your organization through the heat of an emergency. You have just delivered what any reasonable observer would say is a *tour de force*: Insightful analysis of the crisis topped by best-practice recommendations for actions. You see the chief executive officer or director-general take in your wisdom and nod in agreement. Then some pointy-headed techie says: *"How can you be sure that's going to work?"*

The most annoying thing about this question is we can never be 100% sure – at least, not in the sense of having a pile of data showing that if we use strategy X then there is a 99.9% likelihood of outcome Y. As both private and public sector organizations become ever more data driven, this lack of 'hard data' on our impact is becoming a problem. It has long been a problem in the disease control sector.

The cornerstone of disease control is epidemiology: The study of epidemics. Public health doctors and mathematicians have been collecting and analyzing data about various diseases since the mid-19th century. Epidemiologists have been data driven since pretty much forever. And it's epidemiologists, generally, who lead the crisis teams that respond to epidemics. "Where's your data?" or

"Where's your evidence for that?" are the type of questions they instinctively ask. Or, if they want to be really nasty, "How do you know that your risk communication had its intended impact on your target audience?" In an epidemic, the key objective of communication is to encourage people who are at risk to adopt behaviors that prevent them from getting infected. For example, go and get vaccinated. Ideally, then, we need data showing not just an increase in people getting vaccinated after our communication, but also that it was the communication that motivated them to get the jab.

There are practical and as well as ethical barriers to surveying people about their thoughts and motivation who are under threat in an emergency. For example, deploying researchers to a crisis zone can put them in harm's danger – and maybe traumatised populations don't want to answer surveys. But, while we can convincingly argue that generating perfect evidence during a crisis is impractical, it would be good to have some sort of metrics to show.

Crisis and risk communicators in the health sector have been grappling with the issue of evidence for decades. They have had some success. In 2017, the World Health Organization completed an evidence review that validated some key cannons of best practice for risk communication during outbreaks (World Health Organization, 2018). But data generated during emergencies to show the impact or effectiveness of risk communication actions remain in short supply. Social media, Big Data and advances in automated text analysis hold out the promise of – maybe – being able to run real time analyses of risk communication's impact during a live emergency. But, for the moment, the technologies still need to be refined and methods validated.

When we go back to the playbook analogy from Chapter 15, what Duncan is suggesting is that having better playbooks can save lives in the context of health crises – but this also improves the confidence in the commitment of resources necessary to tackle any problem that an organization may face. Our responsibility as communications professionals is to be able to connect the recommendations we make with expected ROI and key performance indicators (KPIs).

Developing research methods knowledge

Of course, there are a lot of different job functions within the field of PR; and even within the context of issue management, risk, and crisis communication there are a number of job functions. So, my students have been somewhat right in their protests about research methods – they may not be researchers. However, all integrated marketing communications professionals should be familiar with the process and results of research if they are going to make judgements about the information produced and build strategic recommendations based on that research. Just as Robert Minton-Taylor's experience (see Box 16.2) indicates, one of the reasons the tobacco industry was able to mislead the public – including well-intentioned practitioners – was the misreporting of research. Developing a strong working knowledge of different research methods, their limitations, and their possibilities will improve practitioners' ability to strategize based on available research – no matter whether they collected the data or not.

For that reason, in the online student resources for this textbook, I have included a series of podcasts to introduce students to different research methods, including a seven-part series on quantitative data analysis.

What should we measure or evaluate?

In Chapter 18 I discussed economic, image, scrutiny, and alliance problems all as possible crisis consequences. The question is, if all of these represent potential effects an organization might experience, then what are the indicators that an organization might be headed towards damaging effects and how can organizations in crisis avoid them? If an organization focuses on stakeholders' behavioral outcomes as indicators of changing stakeholder attitudes and relationship with the organization, then the organization can better predict and manage its relationships.

We will begin with the stakeholder relationship model (SRM). As we have discussed, previous findings establish that stakeholder characteristics, public pressure from interested stakeholders, and engagement are all likely to influence stakeholder evaluations and behavioral intentions towards organizations. This means the model is aligned with previous research establishing that consumer attitudes (Claes, Rust, & Dekimpe, 2010), public pressure from interested stakeholders in the face of crises (Piotrowski & Guyette, 2010), and engagement with stakeholders (Hong, Yang, & Rim, 2010) are all likely to influence consumer evaluations and behavioral intentions towards organizations. Previous applications of the model to analyze stakeholder attitudes have demonstrated its effectiveness in identifying factors influencing consumer evaluations of the firm, such as an organization's reputation, consumer knowledge of the organization, perceptions of the organization's concern regarding the crisis, and consumers' interest regarding the crisis (Diers-Lawson, 2017; Diers, 2012).

Additionally, previous beliefs about a company are the strongest predictor of stakeholder reactions to the company when it is in crisis (Kim, 2013). As such, measuring an individual's prior attitudes about the company and/or an industry should also be predictive of stakeholder reactions. These kinds of prior experiences and even emotional reactions to crises can also potentially create a 'negative communication dynamic,' suggesting that two of the critical indicators of stakeholder reaction could be negative word-of-mouth (nWOM) (Coombs & Holladay, 2007; Kim, 2014; McDonald, Sparks, & Glendon, 2010) as well as reduced behavioral intention to make purchases after a crisis (Coombs & Holladay, 2007; Ping, Ishaq, & Li, 2015; Sellnow et al., 2015; Yum & Jeong, 2014).

So, where does all of this leave us? I would argue with a final understanding of the SRM that looks something like this the diagram in Figure 19.1.

In Table 19.1, I provide a starting point for a stakeholder relationship measurement tool. Of course, such a tool must be customized to suit the organization and situation. However, having used these tools across a number of different studies, I have found that these types of measures have been valid and reliable. Together, they provide a tool for measuring some of the vital relationships discussed throughout the book. Some of these are my own, and some have been developed from other sources.

While these measures are meant to provide a starting point for questionnaire-based research – whether simple surveys before, during or after crises – this is just a starting point. All methods can provide insight. Examples of different types of methods appropriate for measuring risk, crisis response messages, and stakeholder needs would include:

- Questionnaire-based experimental design to test message effects as part of the crisis planning process
- Big data analytics on social media for live evaluation of situations
- Rhetorical and content analyses of existing messaging (any platform) as well as analyzing social media engagement – part of issues management, crisis planning, or post crisis evaluation

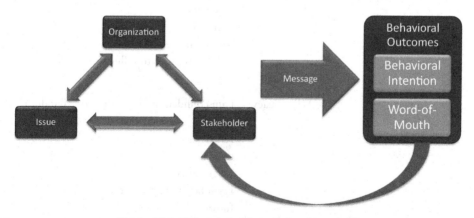

Figure 19.1 Full stakeholder relationship model

Table 19.1 Stakeholder relationship model measurement tool

Relationship tested	Theme	Variable	Questions	Key author(s)
Stakeholder to issue	Prior behaviors	Organization-related behavior	Ever _____ before _____ w/in last year Plan _____ w/in next 6 mo.	N/A
	Attitudes about issue	Personal risk perception	I often worry about _____. I believe _____ is something that affects me more than most people. I often worry that (specific bad outcome). I often worry that (organizations w/in industry are not protecting stakeholders). I often worry that I will be affected by _____.	Ajzen (2005)
		Personal issue importance	_____ is very important to me. I feel personally connected to the issue ____. I know _____ is relevant to my life.	N/A
		Low behavior anxiety	I am completely comfortable (performing behavior X) – never have anxiety.	
	Efficacy	Negative response efficacy	I feel as though there's nothing I can do to (identify desirable outcome). Even if I _____ effectively, it will not make a difference. There is no way to influence _____.	Bandura (1982)
		Self-efficacy	I am confident in my ability to _____. I have successfully _____ in the past. By getting practice at _____, I will be successful in the future.	Bandura (1982)

(Continued)

Relationship tested	Theme	Variable	Questions	Key author(s)
Organization to issue	Perception of responsibility	Competing blame attribution	Which is most responsible for ____ – government = 7, organization = 1	N/A
	Blame	Blame attribution	I believe the ___ is mostly at fault for ___. I blame _____ for ____. The ____ should be held responsible. If we are looking for someone to blame, I think _____ is most responsible.	Kim (2013)
		Issue competence	___demonstrates competent record of __. ___ intends to be ____(competent). I associate ____ with ___ in its industry. ___ demonstrates genuine concern for ___. ___ clearly shows a commitment to ___.	Hargis and Watt (2010), Jaques (2009)
Organization to stakeholder		Perceived knowledge	I have extensive overall knowledge of ___. I could accurately describe ___ overall ideology. I have extensive knowledge of range of ___ available when (insert org purpose).	Diers (2012)
		Trustworthiness	___ gives me a trustworthy impression. ___ gives me a feeling of trust. I feel I can trust ___. ___ seems trustworthy to me.	Morgan and Hunt (1994)
	Reputation	Social responsibility	___'s objectives are socially responsible. ___ cares about the environment. ___ cares about the people affected by its work. ___ cares about society.	

(Continued)

Table 19.1 (Continued)

Relationship tested	Theme	Variable	Questions	Key author(s)
		Reputation	___ sets a good example for industry. ___'s actions demonstrate dedication to being ethical. I would be willing to work for ___. ___ demonstrates a commitment to its own community. ___ is highly reputable. Overall, I am satisfied with ___.	Diers (2012); Walsh and Beatty (2007)
Behavioral intention		Purchase intention	I would be willing to purchase __ from ___. I would actively seek out ___ for ___. I would consider ___ to be my first choice on future ___. I would pay a higher price for __ than competitor ___.	Ajzen (2005)
		Listen to the organization's account	The information in __ 's response is likely to influence my attitudes about it. The information in ___'s response is likely to influence friends/family attitudes. The information in ___'s response is likely to influence people in my community. The information in ___'s response is likely to influence people in my country. The information in ___'s response is likely to influence people in other countries.	Jensen and Hurley (2005)

(Continued)

Relationship tested	Theme	Variable	Questions	Key author(s)
Word-of-mouth		Positive WOM	I would recommend ___ to friends/relatives who asked for my advice. I would recommend ___ to people looking for a good ___. If I were going to talk about ___, I would probably say positive things.	Maxham and Netemeyer (2002)
		Negative WOM	I would encourage my friends/ relatives NOT to purchase any ___ from ___. I would say negative things about ___ and its ___ to my friends, relatives. If I were going to talk about ___, I would probably be critical.	Coombs and Holladay (2008)

- Observational or ethnographic methods to better understand stakeholder reactions and needs across any domain in which the organization interacts to humanize the stakeholder experience with crises

- Interviewing and focus group discussions to get a focused and detailed understanding of the needs of organizations and stakeholders

The bottom line is that while research is necessary, it can be structured in any manner as long as the data is systematically captured and framed for managers in terms of ROI and KPIs. Oftentimes, we fail to remember that in order for our experiences, our observations, or any kind of data to be useful, it has to be framed in a way that decision-makers can understand; it has to be aligned with the organization's objectives; and it has to be interpreted authentically to help make strategic recommendations about what organizations should do in order to manage risks and respond effectively to crises.

In review . . .

As a practitioner, especially in today's business, geo-political, and data-driven environment, being familiar with research methods and more importantly how to translate different types of data into actionable recommendations to make realistic projections about the outcomes of risk and crisis communication is simply part of the job. My recommendation is to be as familiar with different research methods as possible because this allows practitioners to ask more intelligent questions; creatively identify ways to get actionable intelligence; and improve the decision-making, issues management, crisis planning, and crisis response.

Review your understanding

By the end of this chapter, you should be able to:

● Explain why research is practical and necessary in the context of issues and crisis management

● Use the SRM to identify what an organization should measure or evaluate in order to make strategic recommendations for action

● Be able to consider adaptations of research methods across platforms and objectives.

References

Claes, F., Rust, R. T., & Dekimpe, M. G. (2010). The effect of consumer satisfaction on consumer spending growth. *Journal of Marketing Research, 47*(1), 28–35. doi:10.1509/jmkr.47.1.28

Coombs, W. T., & Holladay, S. (2007). The negative communication dynamic: Exploring the impact of stakeholder affect on behavioral intentions. *Journal of Communication Management, 11*(4), 300–312.

Diers, A. R. (2012). Reconstructing stakeholder relationships using 'corporate social responsibility' as a response strategy to cases of corporate irresponsibility: The case of the 2010 BP spill in the Gulf of Mexico. In R. Tench, W. Sun, & B. Jones (Eds.), *Corporate social irresponsibility: A challenging concept* (Vol. 4, pp. 177–206). Bingley, UK: Emerald.

Diers-Lawson, A. (2017). Will they like us when they're angry? Antecedents and indicators of strong emotional reactions to crises among stakeholders. In S. M. Croucher, B. Lewandowska-Tomaszczyk, & P. Wilson (Eds.), *Conflict, mediated message, and group dynamics* (pp. 81–136). Lanham, MD: Lexington Books.

Hong, S., Yang, S., & Rim, H. (2010). The influence of corporate social responsibility and customer–company identification on publics' dialogic communication intentions. *Public Relations Review, 36*(2), 196–198. doi:10.1016/j.pubrev.2009.10.005

Kim, S. (2013). Corporate ability or virtue? Relative effectiveness of prior corporate associations in times of crisis. *International Journal of Strategic Communication, 7*(4), 241–256. doi:10.1080/1553118X.2013.824886

Kim, S. (2014). The role of prior expectancies and relational satisfaction in crisis. *Journalism & Mass Communication Quarterly, 91*(1), 139–158. doi:10.1177/1077699013514413

McDonald, L. M., Sparks, B., & Glendon, A. I. (2010). Stakeholder reactions to company crisis communication and causes. *Public Relations Review, 36*(3), 263–271.

Ping, Q., Ishaq, M., & Li, C. (2015). Product harm crisis, attribution of blame and decision making: An insight from the past. *Journal of Applied Environmental and Biological Sciences, 5*(5), 35–44.

Piotrowski, C., & Guyette, R. W. (2010). Toyota recall crisis: Public attitudes on leadership and ethics. *Organizational Development Journal, 28*(2), 89–97.

Sellnow, D. D., Lane, D., Littlefield, R. S., Sellnow, T. L., Wilson, B., Beauchamp, K., & Venette, S. (2015). A receiver-based approach to effective instructional crisis communication. *Journal of Contingencies and Crisis Management, 23*(3), 149–158. doi:10.1111/1468-5973.12066

Walsh, G., & Beatty, S. E. (2007). Customer-based corporate reputation of a service firm: Scale development and validation. *Journal of the Academy of Marketing Science, 35*(1), 127–143.

World Health Organization. (2018). *Guidelines: Communicating risk in public health emergencies*. Retrieved from www.who.int/risk-communication/guidance/en/.

Yum, J.-Y., & Jeong, S.-H. (2014). Examining the public's responses to crisis communication from the perspective of three models of attribution. *Journal of Business and Technical Communication, 29*(2), 159–183. doi:10.1177/1050651914560570

SRM measurement tool references

Ajzen, I. (2005). *Explaining intentions and behavior: Attitudes, personality, and behavior* (Vol. 2). Berkshire, England: McGraw-Hill Education.

Bandura, A. (1982). Self-efficacy mechanism in human agency. *American Psychologist, 37*(2), 122–147.

Coombs, W., & Holladay, S. J. (2008). Comparing apology to equivalent crisis response strategies: Clarifying apology's role and value in crisis communication. *Public Relations Review, 34*(3), 252–257. doi:10.1016/j.pubrev.2008.04.001

Diers, A. R. (2012). Reconstructing stakeholder relationships using 'corporate social responsibility' as a response strategy to cases of corporate irresponsibility: The case of the 2010 BP spill in the Gulf of Mexico. In R. Tench, W. Sun, & B. Jones (Eds.), *Corporate social irresponsibility: A challenging concept* (Vol. 4, pp. 177–206). Bingley, UK: Emerald.

Hargis, M., & Watt, J. D. (2010). Organizational perception management: A framework to overcome crisis events. *Organizational Development Journal, 28*(1), 73–87.

Jaques, T. (2009). Issue management as a post-crisis discipline: Identifying and responding to issue impacts beyond the crisis. *Journal of Public Affairs, 9*(1), 35–44.

Jensen, J. D., & Hurley, R. J. (2005). Third-person effects and the environment: Social distance, social desirability, and presumed behavior. *Journal of Communication, 55*(2), 242–256.

Kim, S. (2013). Corporate ability or virtue? Relative effectiveness of prior corporate associations in times of crisis. *International Journal of Strategic Communication, 7*(4), 241–256. doi:10.1080/1553118X.2013.824886

Maxham, J. G., & Netemeyer, R. G. (2002). Modeling customer perceptions of complaint handling over time: The effects of perceived justice on satisfaction and intent. *Journal of Retailing, 78*(4), 239–252.

Morgan, R. M., & Hunt, S. D. (1994). The commitment-trust theory of relationship marketing. *Journal of Marketing, 58*(3), 20–38. doi:10.2307/1252308

Index

Note: Page numbers in *italics* indicate figures and those in **bold** indicate tables.

accommodative crisis response tactics 227–228, 230
accommodative strategies, as crises response tactic 230
activism, counter branding and 215–216
Adidas 209–210
adversarial stakeholder relationships: counter branding and 212–217; Nike example 212–213
age, emotional reactions to crises and 172
agenda building 158
agenda setting 275–282; attitudinal mind-sets 279–280; effects, most susceptible to 279–281; information consumption and the media, importance of 276; introduction to 278–281; levels of 278–279; negative coverage and, power of 280–281
Ajzen, I. 167–168
Al-Hyari, K. 174

Allianz 98
Allison, D. 153
Alpaslan, C. 122
American Legacy Foundation 214
American Red Cross tainted-blood scandal 4
Amway 104
Anagondahalli, D. 48
anger, stakeholders and 184–185
anticipatory strategic management 20
anti-social/defensive crisis response tactics 226–227, 230
Antonacopoulou, E. P. 290–291, *291*
apologetic ethics framework 232
apologies, crisis response 231–234, *233*; apologetic ethics framework 232; atonement theory and 232; ethics of care and 231–232; lessons learned about 232–233

Apple 103
applied industry perspectives 17, *18*
Arthur Anderson 97
Ashford, S. J. 290
Ashwell, D. 133–134
atonement theory 232
attitudes: defined 167; emotional reactions to crises and 172; issue-specific 48; mind-sets 279–280; *see also* stakeholders' issue-related attitudes; stakeholders' organization-related attitudes
attribution theory 47
Austin, L. 48

Baidu 288
Bandura, A. 139–140, 185
Barcelona Football Club 82–83
Bauman, D. C. 231
Bayer 197–198
behavioral aspects of crisis leadership 152–154; honest and consistent communication 152–153;

leaders as inspiring 153–154; prompt and considered action 152; stakeholder emotional needs, connecting with 153

behavioral instability, crisis management and 35

behavioral outcomes to crisis, measuring 297–306; methods of 301; practitioner perspective 298–299; research and, necessity of 297–300; research methods knowledge, developing 299–300; stakeholder relationship model (SRM) and 300–305, *301*, 302–305

Ben David, A. 183

Ben & Jerry's Ice Cream 44–45

Benoit, W. L. 5, 21, 22, 224, 249

best practices and lessons learned, in LiC approach 291

Beyer, J. M. 130–131, *131*, 287

blame attribution 47, 182–183; crisis severity and 94; crisis types and 95; disasters and 104–107, *105*; events and 98–101, *99*; reputational crises and 102–104, *103*; transgressions and 95, 96–97, *97*–98

Borden, S. L. 232

BP 210, 281

brand communities 208–209

branding 213

brand loyalty 208

Brataas, K. 106–107, 210–212

Brexit 103, 280

Bridges, J. A. 66

Brown, K. A. 48

Burgoon, J. K. 60

Bush, G. 152

business-to-business (B2B) alliances 287

Cacioppo, J. T. 168–169

Cameron, G. 5

Cameron, G. T. 156

Cevik, T. 150

challenge 103

change, in LiC approach 290–291

Charlie Hebdo 107

Chen, C. P. 216–217

Chen, N. 120

Chernobyl disaster 97

Choi, Y. 185

Churchill, W. 151

classifying stakeholders 87–90, *88*, *88*

clear association 47, 184

Clinton, B. 151

Coca-Cola 89, 104

coercive power 155

cognitive normalization 289

Cokley, J. 172

collective response, mobilization of *30*, 31

collectivism 174

Comfort, L. K. 28

Commercial Mobile Alert system 276, 276–278

commitment 183–184

communication: crisis management and 34, 120–122; language and, crisis communication in 17, *18*; strategy development/implementation 5

communication theories 246–248, *247*; media theories *247*, 248;

persuasion theories *247*, 247–248; rhetorical theories *247*, 248; technology-related communication theories *247*, 248; traditional public relations (PR) and 246, 247, *247*

communities: co-creation of crisis response and 208–212; of consumption 209; psychological sense of 209

competence 47, 183, 195

complementary fields of study, theories from 248–249

conceptual knowledge 136

concern 183–184

conflict, crises and 34–35

Coombs, T. 5, 133, 196

Coombs, W. T. 22, 95, 104, 182, 185, 224, 249

Cooper, C. D. 196

cooperative relationship 208

corporate social responsibility (CSR) programs 132–134, *135*

counter branding: activism and 215–216; adversarial stakeholder relationships and 212–217; to change stakeholder/organization relationships 214–215; risks 213–214; whistleblowing and 216–217

Covello, V. T. 28

credibility 28, 29, 30, 124, 154, 184, 230, 233, 246, 247, 266, 270, 287

crisis, emergency, and risk communication model (CERC) 244, 245 crisis capacity: building, from inside out 129–130; defined 122–123; employees as internal stakeholders and 135–142; hard/soft skills needed to build 136–137, *138–139*; learning from crises and 290; organizational culture and 130–132, *131*; simulation's role in building 137, 139–142, 140; social responsibility and 132–134, *135*; theory to building 249–251, *250*

crisis communication: in applied industry perspectives 17, *18*; change in field of, over time 12–14; in communication and language 17, *18*; crisis response factors in 21–22; disciplines, reading across different 18–19; elements of 5; factors to understanding 19–22; field of study, growth and change within 5–7, 7; global aspects of 14; as interdisciplinary field of study *15–16*, 15–17; interests in 13–14; issues management and 20; key words/concepts studied in 6, 8–12; in management and business 16, *16*; in medicine and health 15, *15*; organizational factors of 20–21; outcome factors of 22; overview of 36, *37*; in public relations field 6–7; research, as data driven 13; research on 1; in science, engineering,

and technology 15, *16*; in social science and humanities 17, *17*; stakeholder factors of 21; stakeholder relationship management perspective of (*see* stakeholder relationships); for students and scholars 17–19

crisis contingency plan 263–270; Part 1: Understanding insert crisis type name crises 264–265; Part 2: Activating the crisis team 265, *265*; Part 3: Trigger points 265; Part 4: Situational assessment 266; Part 5: Stakeholder assessment 266–267, *266–267*; Part 6: Action recommendations 267–268, *268*; Part 7: Crisis response strategy 268–270; Part 8: Message samples for each of the potential strategies 270; for types of crisis 263–264

crisis/crises: characteristics of 4–5, 27; collective responsibility and 35; communication during 34; conflict and 34–35; critical outcomes of 22; defining 3–5; emotional reactions to, factors influencing 171–172; Heath and Millar's definition of 4; narrating 5; organizations and causes of 4; power struggles and 34; primary 95; as public in nature 4; response, parts to 5; and risk management (*see* risk); secondary 95;

stakeholder(s)/organization relationship and 4–5; types of 1, 3–4, *95*

crisis-driven organizational change 289–291

crisis leadership: functional role 154–157; *vs.* management 149–150, *150*; psychological/ emotional role 151–154; public relations role 157–158; to reduce fears/anxiety 151; roles 150–158

crisis management 34–36; behavioral instability and 35; challenges 34–35, 116; collective responsibility and 35; communication and 34, 120–122; conflict and 34–35; defined 34; diametric opportunities and 36; factors influencing 35–36; *vs.* leadership 149–150, *150*; Loosemore's theory of 20, 34–36, 116; objectives in 150; organizational decision-making and 122–123; organization type and 121; power struggles and 34; PR functions and 120; as public relations function 119–120; social adjustment and 35; social structures and 35–36; Stacks's model of PR and 20–21; targeted messaging and 121–122

crisis management theory *244*, 246

crisis outcomes 285–288; learning in crisis (LiC) 290–291, *291*; possible crisis consequences 286–288

crisis plan, creating effective 261–270; contingency planning for crisis 263–270; risk summary 261–263, 262, 263

crisis prone *versus* non-crisis prone industries 124

crisis resistant tourists 172

crisis response: brand communities and 208–209; communities and co-creation of 208–212; crisis communication and 21–22; organizational capacity for 120–124; organization type and 123–124; parts to 5; strategies 251–252; theories of (*see* theories of crisis response); virtual communities and co-creation of 209–212

crisis response messages, planning 255–271; confidence in plan 258–261; obstacles 257–258; practitioner's perspective 259–261; process 255–257, 256; *see also* crisis plan, creating effective

crisis response tactics: ethical apology in crisis response 231–234, 233; overview of 223–224; patterns of crisis response 230–231; taxonomy/summary of 224, 225–229, 229–230

crisis severity 94, 182

crisis theories 244, 246

critical outcomes of crises 22

CSR *see* corporate social responsibility (CSR) programs

cue to action 169

culture: components to 130; identities 172–173; stakeholder attitudes and 172–174

curvilinear relationship 155

danger control process 170

dangerous stakeholders 90

data-based decisions 297

Davis, J. H. 196

decision-making process, issues management 65, 68, 69–70, 71–73; components of 71–72; prioritization and 68, 71; strategic options and 71; taking action and 72–73

defensive strategies, as crises response tactic 230

demographics 169

desirable stakeholders 89

DeYoung, S. E. 278

diametric opportunities 36

Diers, A. R. 22

direct imposition of stakeholders will 82

Dirks, K. T. 196

disasters, blame attribution and 104–107, 105

Dukerich, J. M. 198

Duncan, B. 31–33, 298–299

Dutton, J. E. 198

Ebola crisis 105, 279

economic assessments of crisis outcomes 286–287

economic downturns 99

Edelman Intelligence 13, 298

efficacy 139–140

elaboration likelihood model (ELM) 168, 168–169

Elsbach, K. D. 124

emotion: involvement with issues 48; negative communication dynamic and 301; paradox of managing 289–290; stakeholder attitudes and 170–172

Enron accounting scandal 4, 287

environmental characteristics 60

ethical action, defined 231

ethical apology in crisis response 231–234; apologetic ethics framework 232; atonement theory and 232; ethics of care and 231–232; lessons learned about 232–233; model of 233

ethical ideology 174

ethics of care, apologies and 231–232

European Parliament 101

evaluation stage, issues management 65, 70, 73–74; evaluation scheme, identifying 74; failures/successes, capturing lessons learned from 74; objectives, clear and measurable 73

events, blame attribution and 98–101, 99

excellence/renewal crisis response tactics 228, 230

expectances 60

expectancy violation theory (EVT) 60, 196, 246, 247

experience, emotional reactions to crises and 172

expert power 156

extended parallel process model (EPPM) 170, *170*, 240, 246, *247*, 252
external violence 105
Exxon Valdez oil spill (1989) 3

failures/successes, capturing lessons learned from 74
Farmer, A. K. 278
fear control response 170
Fener, T. 150
Ferrin, D. L. 196
first-person effect 280
Fombrun, C. J. 42
Fox News 82, 280
Frandsen, F. 5, 216, 217
Freundberg, W. R. 30–31
Frisby, B. N. 137
frustration/anger, stakeholders and 184–185
Fukushima nuclear disaster 105
functional crisis leadership 154–157; ability to create/implement appropriate procedures 156; build long-term group relationships 157; develop participative culture 157; effectively manage relationships with people 156; legitimate authority to act 154; power sources 154–156

Gardner, W. L. 22, 224
gender, emotional reactions to crises and 172
Gilvary, B. 14, 135–136, 149
Giuliani, R. 157
Global Communications Report 13
Gonzales-Herrero, A. 286

Google 215
Green, S. E. 122
Greggs 215
Grenfell Tower 72–73
Griffin-Padgett, D. 153

Habibi, M. R. 209
Hackman, M. 196
Hajibaba, H. 172
Haley, E. 44–45
Halliday, S. 5
hard/soft skills for building crisis capacity 136–137, *138–139*
Harquail, C. V. 198
Harvard Business Review 139
Hawaiian Emergency Alert System 276, *276–278*
Hayward, T. 132
health belief model (HBM) 48, 169, *169*
Hearit, K. M. 232
Heath, R. 4, 5, 20, 28, 42–43, 45, 61, 68, 122
H&M 101
Holladay, S. 95, 133, 196
Holmes Report 13
Hookem, M. 101
Hootsuite 298
human breakdown accident/errors 96
Hurricane Katrina 28, 105, 121, 153, 157
Huzey, D. 291
Hwang, S. 156
Hyde, R. C. 28
hygiene-motivation theory 184

ICBM scare in Hawaii 276, *276–278*
IKEA 82

illegal corporate behavior 96
image of organization, crisis outcomes and 287
image-oriented responses, as crises response tactic 231
image repair theory (IRT) 21, 22, *244*, 245
income, emotional reactions to crises and 172
increased exposure to crisis 185
individualism 174
information consumption and the media, importance of 276
integrated crisis mapping model *244*, 246
intelligence, issues management and 64–65
interactant characteristics 60
interaction, history of 42
intercultural crisis communication (ICC) 173
internalization, distribution, explanation, and action (IDEA) model 243, *244*, 251
International Crisis and Risk Communication 13
Internet crisis potential *244*, 246
interorganizational relationships: crisis response tactics 228–229, 230; dimensions of 42
Iran-Contra Affair 3–4
issue response (pre-crisis) recommendations 262, *263*
issues: classifying risk as 60; described 60; expectance violations and 60–61; prior experience with and management of 48; resolution of 60

issue severity summary 262, 263
issues management:
assumptions about 64–65; complexity of, in changeable organizational environments 59–63; crisis communication and 20; decision-making process of 65, 68, 69–70, 71–73; described 20; emotional involvement and 48; evaluation stage of 65, 70, 73–74; intelligence and 64–65; issues described 60; Meng model of 62, 62–63; monitoring process of 65, 67–68, 69; prior experience with issues and 48; process, application of 64–74; risk register and 68, 69–70; in risk summary 261, 262; scanning process of 65, 65–67; social responsibility and 64; stewardship and 61–63; strategic business planning and 64; strong defense, smart offense and 65
issue-specific attitudes 48

Jacques, T. 72
James, E. H. 150
Jaques, T. 174
Jet2 case study 116–119
Jin, Y. 5, 34, 48, 171, 184
Jobs, S. 153
Johansen, W. 5, 216, 217
Jones, T. M. 193

Kaepernick, C. 212–213
key performance indicators (KPIs) 241, 243, 256, 257, 269, 299, 305

Ki, E.-J. 48
Kim, P. H. 196, 197
Kim, S. 185
Kleinnijenhuis, J. 158, 281
knowledge, levels of 136
KPMG 139
Kraft 215
Kramer, R. M. 197

Lai, C. T. 216–217
Lalonde, C. 136, 142
Lane, D. R. 137
Lariscy, R. W. 102, 183
Laroche, M. 209
leadership see crisis leadership
learning in crisis (LiC) 290–291, 291
legitimacy 42; mapping stakeholders and 83, 83–84; of organization, crisis outcomes and 287; stakeholder evaluations of organizations and 193–194
legitimate power 155
Lewicki, R. J. 197
Lin, C. A. 171
Lin, Y.-H. 185
Liu, B. F. 48
Liu, S.-M. 153
Lloyds Bank 100
Loosemore, M. 20, 34–36, 116
loyalty 49

Machiavellian view of power 155
Malaysian Airlines Flight MH370 97, 275
management and business, crisis communication in 16, 16

management vs. crisis leadership 149–150, 150
mapping stakeholders 79–91, 87; classifications of stakeholders 87–90, 88, 88; environments, complexity of 80, 80–81; legitimacy and 83, 83–84; overview of 79–80; power and 81–83, 82; relational valence and 85, 85–86; relationship history and 84, 84–85; urgency and 86–87, 87
Maresh, M. 185
masculinity 174
material crisis response 5
Mayer, R. C. 196
McCaffrey, S. 121–122
McDonald, L. M. 172
media: information consumption and 276; theories 247, 248
medicine and health, crisis communication in 15, 15
megadamage accidents 96
Meng, M. 62, 62–63
mergers/failed mergers 99
message-centered crisis theories 244, 245–246; image repair theory (IRT) 244, 245; situational crisis communication theory (SCCT) 244, 245; social-mediated crisis communication 244, 245–246
Millar, D. P. 4, 28
Minton-Taylor, R. 259–261, 300

misdeed with/with no injuries 97

Mitroff, I. 122

Mohamed, A. A. 22, 224

Moneyball (movie) 241

monitoring process, issues management 65, 67–68, 69; criteria for 68; risk register and 68

moral stakeholders 89–90

Morimoto, Tess 276, 277–278

Morreale, S. 196

Mou, Y. 171

Muniz, A. M. 208

Murphy, P. 158

Nagin, R. 157

Nando's 89

National Football League (NFL) 212–213

National Health Service (NHS) 100

natural disasters/epidemics 105

Neal, D. 278

negative communication dynamic 301

negative word-of-mouth (nWOM) 185, 301

Nelson, R. A. 66

Nichols, K. A. 278

Nike 212–213, 275, 287

9/11 terrorist attacks 4, 153, 157

normalization process 289–290

Noyce, R. 153–154

Obama, B. 151

objectives, setting clear and measurable 73

Oegema, D. 158

O'Guinn, T. C. 208

Oliveira, M. 158

online scams 280

online search 288

organizational culture: crisis capacity and 130–132; forms of 131, *131*

organizations: capacity for crisis response 120–124; change, learning in crisis and 290–291; competitive segment of 66; complexity within 42–44, *43*; crisis capacity and type of 123–124; crisis communication and 20–21; crisis management and type of 121; culture and 130–132, *131*; decision-making, crisis management and 122–123; economic segment of 66; events, blame and 98–101, *99*; issue and self, perception of 44–45; political/regulatory segment of 66; relationship between issues and 46–47; reputation 49, 195; social segment of 66; stakeholders relationship with 48–49

outcome or response efficacy 140

Oxford Research Encyclopedia of Intergroup Communication 95

Paolillo, J. G. P. 22, 224

paracrisis 103, 104

perceived control: behavioral 168; defined 184

perceived threat 169

persuasion, stakeholder attitudes and 165–170; elaboration likelihood model *168*, 168–169; extended parallel process model 170, *170*; health belief model 169, *169*; key predictors of 166–167; overview of 165–167; theory of planned behavior *167*, 167–168

persuasion theories *247*, 247–248

Peters, R. G. 28

Petty, R. E. 168–169

Pew Research Center 279, 298

Pitt, B. 241

political identities 174

positive intention, stakeholders and 47, 183–184

power 154; mapping stakeholders and 81–83, *82*; social, bases of 154–156; stakeholders and 42; struggles, during crises 34

power distance 174

PR *see* public relations (PR)

practical knowledge 136

practitioner perspective case studies: behavioral outcomes to crisis, measuring 298–299; crisis communication (Duncan) 31–34; crisis management and communication (Diers-Lawson) 116–119; crisis response messages, planning (Minton-Taylor) 259–261; CSR behaviors (Ashwell) 133–134;

disasters abroad, blame and (Bratass) 106–107; issues management (Diers-Lawson) 63–64; victim communities of support/advocacy (Brataas) 211–212

Pratt, C. B. 286

predictive expectancies 60

prescriptive expectancies 60

primary crisis 95

prioritization, decision-making process and 68, 71

Procter & Gamble 104

Promsri, C. 136, 137

psychological and affective normalization 289–290

psychological/emotional leadership role 151–154; behaviors to enact 152–154; to build trust 151; to generate optimism 151; reasoning for 151–152

psychological sense of community 209

public relations (PR): crisis communication as field of practice in 6–7; crisis leadership role 157–158; crisis management as 119–120; CSR programs and 132–133; see also stakeholder relationships

purchase intention 185

Reber, B. 5

referent power 155

reflective knowledge 136

rehearsal of new approaches, in LiC approach 291–292

relational valence: defined 42; mapping stakeholders and 85, 85–86

relationships: characteristics of 60; history of, mapping stakeholders and 84, 84–85; reputation and 194–196

religiosity 173–174

reputation, organization/stakeholder relationship and 194–196

reputational crises: blame attribution and 102–104; characteristics of 102; crisis outcomes and 288; types of 103

reputational threat 183

research: methods knowledge, developing 299–300; necessity of 297–300

responsibility: attribution 47; crises and collective 35

return on the investment (ROI) 13, 241, 243, 251, 256, 257, 269, 298, 299, 305

reward power 154

Rhee, H. T. 185

rhetorical theories 247, 248

Richard, M.-O. 209

risk: classifying, as issue 60; collective response and, mobilization of 30, 31; communication of 30, 30–31; concept of 28; detection 28, 30; evaluation of 28, 30, 30; perceptions of, factors influencing 28, 29–30

risk management 28–33, 30; challenges in process of 28; communication step of 30, 30–31; described 28; detection

step of 28, 30; evaluation step of 28, 30, 30; four-step process for 28, 30, 30–31; mobilization step of 30, 31

risk-oriented theories 243–245, 244; crisis, emergency, and risk communication model (CERC) 244, 245; internalization, distribution, explanation, and action (IDEA) model 243, 244; social amplification of risk framework 244, 245

risk register 68, 69–70

risk summary 261–263, 262, 263

routine communication crisis response tactics 224, 225, 230

Roux-Dufort, C. 136, 142, 289, 290

rumor 103

Sankaranarayanan, R. 209

scanning process of issues management 65, 65–67; environment segmentation for 66; recommendations for 67

Schoorman, F. D. 196

Schultz, F. 158

Schultz, M. S. 81

Schwartz, S. 183

Schwarz, A. 5

scrutiny of organization, crisis outcomes and 287

secondary crises 95

Second Hospital of the Beijing Armed Police Corps 288

Securities and Exchange Commission (SEC) 97

Seeger, M. 5, 240

self-efficacy 140–141

self-enhancement crisis response tactics 224, 225

Sellnow, D. 5, 137

Sellnow, T. 5, 137, 240

SEMATECH 154

7-Up 214

Sheaffer, Z. 290–291, 291

shifting political attitudes 103

Shockley-Zalabak, P. S. 196

Simola, S. 137, 231

simulation, crisis capacity building and 137, 139–142, 140

situational crisis communication theory (SCCT) 22, 182, 244, 245

social adjustment, crisis management and 35

social amplification of risk framework 244, 245

social cognitive theory 48, 185

social-mediated crisis communication 244, 245–246

social-mediated crisis communication model (SMCC) 48, 171

social media use, emotional reactions to crises and 172

social power, bases of 154–156; coercive 155; expert 156; legitimate 155; referent 155; reward 154

social responsibility: crisis capacity and 132–134, 135; issues management and 64; organization as 195

social science and humanities, crisis communication in 17, 17

social structures, crisis management in 35–36

sociopolitical normalization 290

soft skills for building crisis capacity 136–137, 138–139

Sohn, Y. 102, 183

Stacks, D. W. 20–21, 119, 120–121, 122

stakeholder attitudes: culture and 172–174; emotion and 170–172; issue-related 181–186; organization-related 191–200; persuasion and 165–170; see also individual headings

stakeholder classifications 87–90, 88, 88

stakeholder relationship model (SRM) 45, 45–49, 166, 191–192, 192, 240; behavioral outcomes to crisis measured by 300–305, 301, 302–305; crisis capacity and 130; issues, described 46; organization/issue relationship 46–47; organization/stakeholders relationship 48–49; overview of 45–46; stakeholder/issue relationship 47–48

stakeholder relationships: adversarial, counter branding and 212–217; characteristics of 42; as crisis communication element 5; interorganizational relationships and 42; organizational environments, complexity within 42–44, 43; stakeholder perceptions and 44–45

stakeholders: attitudes (see stakeholder attitudes); blame/responsibility attribution and 47; brand communities and 209; classifications of, in mapping process 87–90, 88, 88; clear association and 47; competence and 47; complexity 80; crisis communication and 21; dangerous 90; defined 4, 41; desirable 89; direct imposition of, will 82; issue relationship 47–48; mapping (see mapping stakeholders); moral 89–90; perceived knowledge of organization 49; perceptions, advocacy and 44–45; positive intention and 47; responsibility/blame attribution of 47; strategic 89; utilitarian or practical means of 82–83

stakeholders' issue-related attitudes: blame attribution 182–183; clear association 184; commitment 183–184; competence 183; concern 183–184; crisis severity 182; frustration/anger 184–185; perceived

control 184–185; positive attention 183–184; situational crisis communication theory 182
stakeholders' organization-related attitudes: building blocks for 194–199; identification and 198–199; legitimacy, stakeholder evaluations and 193–194; perceived knowledge and 198; reputation and 194–196; stakeholder evaluations of organizations in crisis 192–193; stakeholder relationship model as recursive process 191–192, 192; trustworthiness and 196–197; value congruence and 197
status updates, as crises response tactic 231
Steelman, T. A. 121–122
STEM fields (science, technology, engineering, and math) 15, 16, 119, 248
stewardship, issues management and 61–63
strategic alliance withdrawal, crisis outcomes and 287
strategic business planning, issues management and 64
strategic options, decision-making process and 71
strategic stakeholders 89
Strengths, Weaknesses, Opportunities, and Threats (SWOT) analysis 61
strikes 99

strong defense, smart offense 65
students and scholars, crisis communication for 17–19
subjective norm 167–168
Sutton, J. N. 278

taking action, decision-making process and 72–73
targeted messaging, crisis management and 121–122
technical breakdown accident 96
technical breakdown product recalls 96
technology-related communication theories 247, 248
terrorism 105
Thatcher, M. 100
theoretical knowledge 136
theoretical options in risk and crisis communication 243–249; communication theories 246–248, 247; risk and crisis theories 243–246, 244; theories from complementary fields of study 248–249
theories of crisis response: overview of 239–240; theoretical options in risk and crisis communication 243–249; theory, defined 241–243; theory-informed crisis response, developing 249–252; theory-informed practice, performance improved by 240–249
Theorizing Crisis Communication (Sellnow and Seeger) 240

theory, defined 241–243
theory-informed crisis response, developing 249–252; crisis capacity building 249–251, 250; crisis response strategies 251–252
theory-informed practice, performance improved by 240–249
theory of planned behavior (TPB) 167, 167–168
Tomaino, K. 22
traditional public relations (PR) and 246, 247, 247
transgressions: blame attribution and 95, 97–98; defined 95; examples of 96–97
Trice, H. M. 130–131, 131, 287
triple bottom line 286
Trump, D. 154, 213, 280
trustworthy organizations 49, 195, 196–197
Truth.com 214
TSB 100

uncertainty avoidance 174
uncertainty perceptions 166–167
UNICEF 82–83
Union Carbide explosion, Bhopal, India 98
United Kingdom Independence Party (UKIP) 101
urgency, stakeholders and 42, 86–87, 87
USC-Annenberg Center for Public Relations 13
Utz, S. 158

value congruence 197
value proposition 298
values 49, 195
Van Atteveldt, W. 158
Veil, S. R. 137, 215
virtual communities, crisis
  response and
  209–212
Volkswagen 98

war on Christmas 280
Weber Shandwick 13
Weick, K. E. 290
whistleblowing, counter
  branding and
  216–217
Williams, D. 185
Witte, K. 170
Wojtecki, J. G. 28

Woolfe, S. 101
Wooten, L. P. 150
workplace violence 99

Yang, S.-B. 185

Zeng, Cheng 287–288
Zexi, Wei 288
Zhao, Y. 173

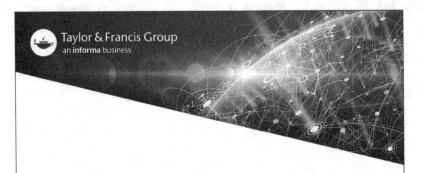